Anarchism in Korea

SUNY series in Global Modernity

Arif Dirlik, editor

Anarchism in Korea

*Independence, Transnationalism, and the
Question of National Development, 1919–1984*

Dongyoun Hwang

Published by State University of New York Press, Albany

© 2016 State University of New York

All rights reserved

Printed in the United States of America

No part of this book may be used or reproduced in any manner whatsoever without written permission. No part of this book may be stored in a retrieval system or transmitted in any form or by any means including electronic, electrostatic, magnetic tape, mechanical, photocopying, recording, or otherwise without the prior permission in writing of the publisher.

For information, contact State University of New York Press, Albany, NY
www.sunypress.edu

Production, Ryan Morris
Marketing, Michael Campochiaro

Library of Congress Cataloging-in-Publication Data

Names: Hwang, Dongyoun, author.
Title: Anarchism in Korea : independence, transnationalism, and the question of national development, 1919–1984 / Dongyoun Hwang.
Description: Albany : State University of New York Press, 2016. | Series: SUNY series in global modernity | Includes bibliographical references and index.
Identifiers: LCCN 2015036649 | ISBN 9781438461670 (hardcover : alk. paper) | ISBN 9781438461687 (pbk. : alk. paper) | ISBN 9781438461694 (e-book)
Subjects: LCSH: Anarchism—Korea—History—20th century. | Korean resistance movements, 1905–1945. | Nationalism and socialism—Korea—20th century.
Classification: LCC HX948.H83 2016 | DDC 335/.83095190904—dc23
LC record available at http://lccn.loc.gov/2015036649

10 9 8 7 6 5 4 3 2 1

Contents

Acknowledgments	vii
A Note on Romanization	xiii
Introduction	1
CHAPTER 1 Beyond Independence: The Dawn of Korean Anarchism in China	19
CHAPTER 2 The Wind of Anarchism in Japan	57
CHAPTER 3 Pushing the Limits in Colonial Korea	89
CHAPTER 4 Korean Anarchists in Wartime China and Japan	117
CHAPTER 5 Deradicalized Anarchism and the Question of National Development, 1945–1984	157
Conclusion	209
Notes	221
Bibliography	259
Index	281

Acknowledgments

By scholarly training I am a specialist in modern Chinese history. So, my journey to complete this study has been a pleasant deviation from my academic expertise and plan. I wrote a paper on Korean anarchism for Professor Arif Dirlik in my first semester as a doctoral student at Duke University. It was a very rough one, and I buried it in my document folder for more than a decade. In September 2003, I was developing it to present at a conference he was organizing at the University of Oregon. Since then, I have greatly enjoyed thinking and writing about anarchism in Korea, because I realized, somewhat belatedly, the significance of the subject after the conference. Needless to say, I am deeply indebted to Arif Dirlik, my former adviser at Duke, for not only teaching me with patience and affection about modern Chinese intellectual history but for guiding me to go beyond my specialty to understand a much broader history. Without his passionate encouragement and intellectual stimulation, this study would have never been made possible.

A number of my Korean colleagues deserve my gratitude for their assistance and support. Dr. Yi Horyong kindly responded to my call for help and introduced many materials to me, when I had just begun my research on this subject a decade ago. Dr. Oh Jang-Whan also helped me with several rare materials and shared information about Korean anarchism with me. Dr. Lee Hyun-Joo at the Ministry of Patriots and Veterans Affairs provided me with the Ministry's publications on Korean independence movement, and Professor Jo Sehyeon shared with me some Chinese and Japanese articles. Professor Baik Young-seo, former director of the Institute for Korean Studies at Yonsei University, offered me several opportunities to talk about my research on Korean anarchism at various occasions before many Korean specialists from whom I learned a lot and was encouraged with valuable comments, for which I thank him. Among others at Yonsei, Professors Yim Sung-Mo and Kim Sung-Bo showed their interest in my research and provided me with various supports whenever I visited Yonsei over past years. In particular, Professor Yim as a modern Japanese historian introduced me to some Japanese literature on Korean and/or Japanese anarchism. Professors Lee Sang-Euy, Jo Kyung Ran, and Sin Ju Back, all at Yonsei, offered me various comments. I particularly benefited from Professor Sin's comments as a discussant at my talk in March 2014, which made me rethink the structure of this book and my approach. During my stay at Yonsei in 2008 and 2014, I met several graduate students, who were very willing to offer their unconditional assistance and support to their "senior." I want to express my special thanks to Mr. Lee Han-Gyeol and the late Ms. Lee Hwa-jung for the materials and articles they introduced me to.

I would also like to thank Professors Ban Byung-yul at Hankuk University of Foreign Studies, Kim Kyeong-il at the Academy of Korean Studies, and Jeong Seon-tae at Kookmin University for their comments and interest. My thanks also go to Professors Bang Kwang Suk, Chung Moon Sang, Jeon In Gap, Choi Won-shik, Yim Hyung-taek, Lee Seong-Paik, Kim Seung Wook, Park Jin-su, Kwon Hee-ju, Choi Sung-sil, Kim Jang Hwan, Ha Se Bong, and Lee Hun Sang for their support and interest in my study on various occasions. Professor Emeritus Chong Key Ray gave me special support and encouragement. Professors Chung Byung Ho, Kim Gye-ja, Kim Hyo-soon, Yokoji Keiko, and Hibi Yoshitaka, all of whom I met in October 2013 at Korea University, encouraged me to pursue my regional perspective. I am also grateful to Roxann Prazniak, Rob Wilson, Bruce Cumings, Bryna Goodman, Tomoko Aoyama, Jesse Cohn, and Park Sunyoung for their interest, help, encouragement, or comments on various occasions. I would also like to thank two anonymous readers for the SUNY Press for their insightful comments and helpful suggestions.

In the years that were spent to write this book the most crucial help in terms of materials was provided by those at the Institute for the Study of National Culture (*Gungmin munhwa yeon-guso*). To name them: Mr. Lee Mun-Chang, the late Mr. Jo Gwanghae, Mr. Song Heon-jo, Mr. Um Dong-il, and Mr. Nam Yi-haeng, as well as Professors Oh Jang-Whan and Kim Myeongseop. Mr. Lee particularly spared his precious time with me to answer my questions and tell me about his experiences after 1945. I am also deeply grateful to Mr. Kim Young-Chun, Ms. Park Jeong-Hee, and Mr. Sin Nage, all at the Society to

Commemorate Yu Rim (*Yu Rim gi-nyeom sa-eophoe*). In particular, Mr. Kim not only provided his writings and materials on Yu Rim but spent long time with me on two different occasions to share his view on the history of Korean anarchism. He also traveled with me to the town of Anui where he arranged my meeting with Mr. Yi Dongwon and my visit to Anui Middle School and High School, respectively. I thank both of them for their enthusiastic support.

When I traveled to Tokyo in April 2014 to locate additional materials, I received warm welcome and help from Mr. Park Chan Jung and Mr. Cho Jung Bang, both of the Korea Sports Council in Japan, and President Oh Gong-Tae and Vice President Park An Soon of the Korean Residents Union in Japan. Ms. Lee Mi-Ae at the History Museum of Koreans in Japan gave me a guide to the museum, which helped me think Korean anarchists in Japan within a much broader context of the history of Koreans in Japan. My special thanks should go to Professor Sakai Hirobumi at Hitotsubashi University. I have never met him in person, but he generously responded to my inquiry and even agreed to share with me rare Chinese materials that were utilized in this study and will be further used later in a different project. When I was on my short trip to Quanzhou in June 2015 to visit Liming Vocational University and locate some additional materials there, he also introduced me to Professor Liang Yanli of Fudan University, who in turn introduced me to people at Liming. There I received warm welcome and crucial materials that I used in this study and plan on analyzing further in a different project, for which I thank Professors Wang Qiang, Su Yanming, and Lin Zhanghong, as well as Mr. Zhang Jianliang and Mr. Lin Yali. I also would like to thank my friend from Duke, Zhou Yongming at the University of Wisconsin at Madison, for introducing me to Professor Chen Shaofeng at Beida and Mr. Chen Zong, who helped me with my brief visit to the Quanzhou Library.

I have also received supports from my colleagues at Soka University of America. My special thanks go to Michael Hays (now retired) and Edward Feasel. Ed, in particular, as the dean of faculty, has supported my research activities in various ways. I also thank Osamu Ishiyama for his help with Japanese translation. And it has been a great joy to work with a group of wonderful undergraduate students at Soka. When I taught the Radicalism in Eastern Asia course per request from several students, I benefited a lot from classroom discussion. I particularly want to thank Yuka Kishida (now at

Bridgewater College) and Michael Bianco for their enthusiasm about the topic. The aid given by Momoca Nishimoto and Chitari Yamamoto as my research assistants in translating many articles in Japanese anarchist newspapers and journals must be noted here with gratitude. For the help with the Inter-Library Loan service at Soka, I would like to thank Lisa Polfer and Malgorzata (Gosha) Gomagala. For the years, I also visited several libraries in South Korea, Japan, and China, and I want to thank the librarians and staffs at the National Library of Korea in Seoul, the Yonsei University Library in Seoul, the National Diet Library in Tokyo, and the Quanzhou Library in Quanzhou.

During the decade I worked on this book, I had many opportunities to present portions of this book at a number of seminars and conferences: the conference on "From the Book to the Internet: Communication Technologies, Human Motions, and Cultural Formations in Eastern Asia," held at the University of Oregon (October 16–18, 2003); an annual seminar at the Institute of the Humanities, Yonsei University, South Korea (June 28, 2004); the International Conference on "Modern East Asian Intellectuals and Their Idea of 'Asia,'" held at Daedong Institute for Korean Studies of Sungkyunkwan University, Seoul, South Korea (January 20, 2005); the Conference on "Poetry, Pedagogy, and Alternative Internationalisms: From the Early Twentieth Century to the Present," held by Comparative and Interdisciplinary Research on Asia (CIRA), University of California at Los Angeles (June 10, 2005); the European Social Science History Conference (ESSHC), held from March 22 to 25, 2006, in Amsterdam; a monthly seminar held at the Institute of Modern Korea, the Academy of Korean Studies, Seongnam, South Korea (June 13, 2008); the conference on "Border-Crossers and the City: Mass Media, Migration and Globalization," organized by the Institute of Urban Humanities at the City University of Seoul, South Korea (June 21, 2010); the conference on "Japanese Magazines and Colonial Literature in East Asia," held by East Asia and Contemporary Japanese Literature Forum at the Center for Japanese Studies, Korea University (October 18–19, 2013); a seminar at the Institute of Korean Studies, Yonsei University (March 25, 2014); and the European Social Science History Conference (ESSHC) in Vienna (April 23–26, 2014). I thank the participants in these seminars and conferences for their comments and encouragement. At the latest ESSHC in 2014, I presented part of chapter 4 for a panel session on "Anarchists, Marxists, and Nationalists in the Colonial and Postcolonial World, 1870s–1940s: Antagonisms, Solidarities, and Syntheses," organized by Lucien van der Walt and Steve Hirsch. I would like to thank the two organizers, particularly Lucien, for his helpful comments. I also would like to thank Walter K. Lew for his invitation to participate in the conference at UCLA in 2005 and his enthusiastic support.

As a result of my participation in these seminars and conferences, parts of this book have been published earlier in "Beyond Independence: The Korean Anarchist Press in China and Japan in the 1920s and 1930s," *Asian Studies Review* 31 (March 2007): 3–23, and "Korean Anarchism before 1945: A Regional and Transnational Approach," in *Anarchism and Syndicalism in the Colonial and Postcolonial World, 1870–1940: The Praxis of National Liberation, Internationalism, and Social Revolution*, edited by Steven Hirsch and Lucien van der Walt, 95–129 (Leiden: Brill, 2010). I am grateful to the publishers, Taylor and Francis (www.tandfonline.com), and Brill, for giving me permission to reproduce them in this book.

I received a Short-Term Research Travel Grant in Korean Studies from the Northeast Asia Council (NEAC) of the Association for Asian Studies (AAS) in March 2004, which funded my first short trip to South Korea for collection of important materials and for my first publication on Korean anarchism in 2007. A Summer Research Grant in 2006 from the Pacific Basin Research Center at Soka University of America also helped me to take another short trip to South Korea in 2006 for this study. And the Faculty Research Fund from my home institution, Soka University of America, funded in part my short trips to Tokyo in April 2014, and to Quanzhou, Fujian in June 2015. Important parts of this study were funded and done from March to May in 2008, and in March 2014, when I received a Field Research Fellowship, respectively, from the Korea Foundation.

Last but not least, I would like to thank my family. I hope this book can reward my parents for their life dedicated to their children's education. I miss my deceased mother-in-law who always enjoyed supporting my research. My sisters have always provided me with timely emotional supports when I needed it. And I want to acknowledge the presence of my dear wife, Mihyun, in this book. It is not that she read the manuscript but that her love and dedication have been the main sources of support and inspiration to complete this project, for which I dedicate this book to her with love.

A Note on Romanization

In Romanizing Korean I follow the new Romanization of Korean adopted by the National Academy of Korean Language and the Ministry of Culture and Tourism of then South Korean Government in 2000, with some exceptions in the already known names and places such as Syngman Rhee and Pyongyang. I also respect and follow individually chosen Romanized names, if they are known to me through personal contact and public record, and so on, such as Oh Jang-Whan (not Oh Janghwan) and Lee Mun Chang (not Yi Munchang). If the Korean names and places such as Kim Koo (not Kim Gu) and Chosŏn Dynasty (not Joseon Dynasty) are more familiar in the West, I also add them in brackets on their first appearance. Korean names as well as Chinese and Japanese names are rendered in the text and notes in their own order, with the family name first and the personal name next. In the case of Korean names the personal names appear as one word or two words with or without a hyphen.

In Romanizing Japanese, I follow the Hepburn system for Japanese with the exceptions of Tokyo (not Tōkyō) and Osaka (not Ōsaka) in the text. In Romanizing Chinese, I follow the Pinyin system. However, where the Wade-Giles Romanization for Chinese names is known more commonly in the West, I follow it, as in the cases of Chiang Kai-shek (not Jiang Jieshi) and Sun Yat-sen (not Sun Zhongshan). If a Korean anarchist journal was published in Japanese or Chinese, I transliterate its title and articles into either Romanized Japanese or Chinese, with a few exceptions.

Introduction

Anarchism has been recently assessed by South Korean scholars as one of the ten thoughts (*sasang*) that moved Korea in the twentieth century.[1] This positive evaluation coincided with the overwhelming scholarly attention given to it unprecedentedly as the subject of study since the 1990s,[2] corresponding to the collapse of socialism in Soviet Russia and Eastern Europe in the early 1990s, when anarchism began to be labeled as a third ideology or way that could replace both capitalism and communism.[3] To the extent that anarchism has received scholarly attention and the positive assessment, it has been still treated somewhat unwisely within the framework of nationalism. In other words, it is understood mainly in the context of the victory of nationalism (i.e., independence movement) against Japanese colonialism in 1945, and thus as part of a nationalist ideology. In some cases it is even explained in the context of the rise of Korean communism and communist movement.[4]

This kind of mistreatment results from the fact that anarchism was indeed accepted by Koreans as a means and principle for independence after the March First Movement of 1919, a massive, nationwide popular protest against Japanese colonial rule in Korea since 1910.[5] Anarchism itself had already been known to Koreans much earlier at the turn of the twentieth century, but it was only after the 1919 mass movement that it increasingly gained popularity and influence among many Koreans, both at home and abroad, as a guiding principle for national liberation in both social and political senses. Korean students and expatriates in Japan and China first converted to it in the 1920s and then those who had returned from their study abroad mostly from Japan played a leading role in introducing it to and organizing Koreans in the Korean peninsula. This is why historian Horiuchi Minoru defines Korean anarchism as a "nationalistic anarchism" (*minzokudeki museifu shugi*),⁶ and many South Korean historians too understand the nature of Korean anarchism predominantly with reference to the nationalist impulse.⁷ Nationalism is thus often separated from anarchism, which is rather conjoined to the former's goal of independence, as if they were two entirely separate ideas in colonies like Korea. Of course, anarchism was initially accepted as a means and principle for Korea's independence, but that didn't determine the horizon of Korean anarchism. While nationalism was undeniably the main driving force in the rise of Korean anarchism, it is also true that Korean anarchists received anarchism, as I demonstrate in this study, as a guiding principle for social transformation of the Korean society and the world as well. Too much emphasis on nationalism in the study of Korean anarchism, in other words, has resulted in overlooking the complex colonial contexts in which nationalism arose with the rise and popularity of radicalism for social change. Needless to say, the rise of nationalism in colonies or semicolonies was closely tied with the emergence and subsequent popularity of radicalism, including anarchism, which connotes the complex relationship between an emerging, growing national consciousness against foreign colonialism and radical ideas that not only resisted imperialism and foreign domination but also criticized and challenged the existing state and social order/problems under capitalism.

In a Eurocentric understanding of anarchism, nationalism could often be separated from it, and Korean anarchism is thus viewed as one that lost "the basic principles in anarchism," "depart[ed] from anarchist principles," and finally "reduced 'anarchism' to a liberal concept" or nationalism.⁸ The waning fate of Korean anarchism in the 1960s was even attributed by a Korean anarchist in Japan to its origins in nationalism.⁹ Since its nationalist aspects are underlined more than the transnational, social revolutionary messages and goals of anarchism, Korean anarchists appear in the existing scholarship not as anarchists but rather as nationalists or, at best, as those whose anarchism was a "deviation" (*iltal*) from anarchism, abandoning the "real character" (*bollyeong*) of it in its European origins—especially as Korean anarchists supported in the 1930s and '40s the ideas of working with the Provisional Government of Korea in China and of supporting the establishment of a government of Korea after independence.¹⁰ This simplest, Eurocentric interpretation of Korean anarchism too accounts for the reason why its history has long been placed within the history of Korean independence movement, without enticing any serious scholarly challenge to the dominant line of its nationalist interpretation.

The recent political climate of South Korea for the past years under the conservative, rightist regimes has prevented South Korean historians from taking anarchism (in general, radicalism) seriously, placing the academics under the pressure of political risks in writing about and speaking in favor of radical or anarchist ideas. Under the situation, anarchism is still understood mainly as a nationalist ideology and scrutinized mostly in relation to and within the history of Korean independence movement, that is, national history, rather than within the history of radicalism or socialism in Korea or the region. Within the context of the rise of national consciousness in colonial situations, however, the relationship between anarchism and nationalism could be more complicated than it was in Europe. The complex, colonial context has been simply missing or put aside, albeit this is not to suggest that anarchism can be reduced to nationalism and vice versa.[11] In short, one of the tasks this book undertakes is to challenge the conventional understanding that the role of anarchism was to serve Korea's independence from Japan, which depicts it as part of a nationalist ideology without explaining its complex relationship with nationalism

Furthermore, many historians tend to identify the characteristics of Korean anarchism with its earlier emphasis on "terrorist actions" that were undoubtedly motivated by the goal of independence from Japanese colonialism and therefore recognized as justifiable due to the righteous cause of anticolonialism. As a result, rather than understood as a social revolutionary idea that served the goal of not only national liberation but a radical social transformation of Korean society, anarchism is still studied in the existing scholarship mainly as an idea that was adopted, for example, by "radical nationalists" who in the process of pursuing national independence used violence righteously and "utilized" anarchist ideas mainly to achieve their national goal of independence.[12] It is true that many Korean anarchists adopted and used in many cases "terrorism" as a means and even a concrete form of direct action to resist Japanese colonialism, but, as I demonstrate in this study, they nevertheless did so with the vision and programs to foster in the end the implementation of anarchist ideals. Social revolution was always their eventual destination, no matter how it was pursued and envisioned.

When nationalism evidently was an initial force to draw most Korean radicals and independence activists to anarchism, they all came to face a question of how to deal with the universal messages of anarchism while still pursuing their immediate national goal. This kind of question continued to arise as they came to realize the nature of their contemporary society and world at the time. For instance, the sufferings and maltreatment Chinese female workers received from the Western capitalist employers were to raise a question among Korean anarchists regarding the plight of the masses in capitalist system and help them realize the transnational issues of social justice and economic inequality in colonial and semicolonial societies including Korea, finally generating a sense of a shared fate among colonized peoples. This was exactly what occurred to Jeong Hwaam (1896–1981), one of the most active Korean anarchists in China before 1945, and an active participant in various anarchist and socialism-oriented political parties in South Korea after 1945.[13] Jeong recalls that between late 1924 and early 1925 he witnessed the maltreatment of Chinese female workers at a British-owned factory in Shanghai and began to have a "sense" that the goal for liberation of the oppressed peoples was the same as that of Korean independence movement. Removing such social and economic contradictions in a colony under capitalism as excessive work hours and unequal treatment of workers was, he came to conclude, a goal of anarchist movement. His realization of such social problems and ills in capitalist society subsequently prompted him to actively support the activities of Chinese and Taiwanese anarchists, let alone to participate in Korean independence activities in China.[14]

In the process of such a realization, Korean anarchists were to commonly confront a tension between a universal idea that promised as its ultimate goal, according to anarchist Yi Jeonggyu (1897–1984), a world of "great unity" (*daedong* in Korean or *datong* in Chinese), that is, a cosmopolitan world,[15] and nationalist aspirations to achieve an immediate goal of retaking independence from Japanese colonialism. Anarchist Sim Yongcheol (1914–?), one of Korean anarchists active in China but who became a Chinese citizen, describes the tension in the following terms:

> Korean anarchists, since they were slaves who lost their country, had to rely with affection on nationalism and patriotism and thus had difficulties in practice in discerning which was their main idea and which was their secondary

idea. The reason [for the difficulties] was due to that their enemy was the only one—Japanese imperialism. My life is one that has drifted along with this kind of contradiction inside.[16]

What we see here is a combination of the universal idea and the nationalist goal, with which Sim lived, which was indicative of the complex relationship (in Sim's word, the "contradiction") in colonial context between national consciousness and transnational concerns. Historian Henry Em, in his study of Shin Chaeho (1880–1936), a prominent Korean historian, journalist, writer, and anarchist, also indicates a possibility of the tension between Shin's earlier writings on the nation (*minjok*) and his later emphasis on the people (*minjung*), in which not only the Korean people but also the "have nots" of the world were included.[17]

Echoes to Sim's description of his complex life as both an anarchist and a nationalist can be found in Yi Jeonggyu's recall. Yi, a prominent anarchist active in various educational and rural movements before and after 1945, too poses his life as one with such a tension but, in his case, shifting further toward anarchism that offered him a vision of social revolution, rather than simply a nationalism-driven political revolution that aimed merely at national independence. Yi explains the shift that occurred in his life as follows:

The first half of my life had gone through a life for struggle for independence movement, and [then in the second half] turned for a movement for social revolution of an ideological idea [sic] that has been viewed in this world, without any good reason, as too extreme. [The second half has been] a life as one of the pioneers, who has been indulged in anarchism, that is, no-government movement [*mujeongbu juui undong*].[18]

Undoubtedly, the goal of Korean independence movement was to regain independence from Japanese colonialism, to which Yi had devoted himself with anarchism. However, he began to move gradually away from a simple, political nationalist independence movement, going beyond the question of independence and then stepping further toward the realization of anarchist ideals that inevitably embraced social dimensions of revolution. Yi's life after 1945 certainly demonstrates his endeavors to implement anarchist ideals mainly through the revival of rural villages, as I examine in chapter 5. This shift or tension in the cases of Sim, Shin, and Yi has long been disregarded as unimportant or missing in our understanding of anarchism in Korea. As Xioaqun Xu argues in his study of the *Chenbao fujuan* (*Morning News Supplement*), there was, among Chinese intellectuals in the 1920s, "the tension between cosmopolitanism as cultural longing and nationalism as political imperative,"[19] a tension that the Korean anarchists too had in the process of receiving anarchism and concretizing their ideals for their country and the world. The transnationality in Korean anarchism can be best described with the tension that sometimes allowed Korean anarchists to resist their national boundaries and even reject the existence of the state or "fatherland," but other times provided a space for reconfiguration of ideas and practices for their national goal in place-based setting with their confirmation of the significance of national goal and boundaries.

Emphasizing the colonial contexts of which Korean anarchism was a product, I argue that it had the ultimate transnational goal of social revolution bent on anarchist principles. Central to it was the vision of and the agreement on social revolution as the key for the liberation of Korea and its masses from Japanese colonialism, and, subsequently, for the liberation of the exploited, oppressed masses of the world from capitalism. Just like their Chinese counterparts,[20] Korean anarchists prioritized social revolution to political revolution or political movement, since the latter, in their minds, would end up only achieving independence (or at best reform under colonial condition) with all social problems and political/revolutionary questions unanswered and unsolved. In fact, as I demonstrate, Korean anarchists were drawn to anarchism through their contacts and associations with Chinese and Japanese anarchists or their readings of anarchist writings, either in original texts or translation in Chinese and/or Japanese, which evidences the role played by transnational elements from the inception in the rise of Korean anarchism.[21] As a colonized people, Korean radicals and/or students either were exiled to China to take political refuge or went to Japan for their study abroad, where they all contacted, were exposed, and accepted anarchism via their interactions, direct or indirect, with Asian counterparts. In short, Korean anarchists' interactions in the forms of introduction to, acceptance of, articulation of anarchism, as well as of joint activities, both organizational and publication, with their Asian counterparts in such locations as Tokyo and Shanghai, were, I argue, one of the decisive elements that disposed them to take seriously the transnational and cosmopolitan messages anarchist ideals offered and, in turn, to understand them in their national context.

Korean anarchists' idea on social revolution is of significance as evidence of their shared and transnational vision in anarchist principles, which in most cases drove them to take actions with their Asian counterparts. Achieving a social revolution had broader consequences than a political revolution. Korean anarchists before 1945 placed the former within a broader context of liberating the masses of people globally from their domination and exploitation under capitalism.[22] Their concrete, various methods to build a future world seemed to be shared with other Eastern Asian anarchists as exemplified in the following chapters in such joint activities and shared ideals in education and national development strategies that intended to combine mental and physical labors in education and building autonomous local communities through the combination of industry and agriculture for alternative development. Although they varied according to the time and space they were placed in, these ideas for an alternative education and national development seemed to be widely shared as crucial for an ideal society that Korean anarchists envisioned, and they even experimented often among anarchists in the region, which points to their anarchism as a product of regional anarchism. The post-1945 activities of Korean anarchists also demonstrate the deep ties in ideals and practices between Korean anarchists and other anarchists circulated in the region before 1945. I will explain the regional aspect of Korean anarchism in more detail below.

Serving the goal of social revolution, anarchism certainly played an important part in radical politics in Korea. However, little is known about it outside Korean-language circles, not to mention its regional and transnational aspects. As I emphasize the transnational character of anarchism in Korea, I would like to offer in this book a history of anarchism in Korea with particular attention to its East Asian regional context. Hence, my approach below employs a transnational and regional perspective with emphasis on the various interactions among anarchists across borders. In other words, I look into the ways that anarchist ideas were introduced, understood, and received by Korean anarchists, first in China and Japan, and then by examining the interactions in various forms between Korean anarchists and their counterparts in China and Japan before 1945. I also examine how the transnational and regional characters played out in various anarchist ventures and experiments in post-1945 South Korea. My transnational and regional approach here may tell us about the relationships between Eastern Asian anarchism and anarchism in its European origins, and, more importantly, about regional anarchism and Korean anarchism, both of which will account for the complexities in understanding and acceptance of anarchism in non-European societies. Korean anarchism, in other words, I argue, must be understood in a broader regional context, as Arif Dirlik notes, that underscores "interactions among radicals" that are "absent from or marginal to nationally based accounts."[23]

Locations are important in understanding the regional aspect of Korean anarchism. Koreans were introduced and converted to anarchism in various locations outside the Korean peninsula, such as Tokyo, Osaka, Beijing, and Shanghai, and took actions together there in most cases in league with their Asian counterparts. What is problematic in the existing scholarship, therefore, is the lack of considerations of how anarchism was first received by Korean radicals abroad and then practiced there accordingly by them who were scattered spatially here and there in the region (and even within the Korean peninsula as well).[24] Undeniable is that anarchism was first accepted by Korean exiles in China and radical study-abroad students in Japan.[25] The regional context has long been opted out in nationalist historiography.

There has already been growing scholarly attention to regional perspective. Recent works on the formation of radical politics in China, for instance, have revealed the usefulness of regional perspectives on, and the importance of transnational approaches to the history of modern East Asian history. Unlike earlier studies of regionalism in East Asia, which focused on the cultural arena, these underline the importance of direct and indirect interactions among radicals circulating in the region and, as a result, the role of transnationalism in the formation of national discourses. Arif Dirlik has pointed to the importance of a regional context in understanding the ups and downs of socialism in China.[26] Rebecca E. Karl's study of late Qing radicalism at the turn of the twentieth century likewise has revealed the importance of regional interactions in the formation of radical national discourses,[27] while Christopher E. Goscha has demonstrated the importance of a regional perspective in the study of the rise of Vietnamese communism.[28] Drawing on these works, I have also suggested that the rise and development of Korean anarchism since 1919 be understood as a product of regional radicalism, more specifically regional anarchism.[29] By regional anarchism I don't mean that there was a substantial existence that can be called regional or "East Asian anarchism," but want to indicate that the rise and development of Korean anarchism in the twentieth century were products of the direct and indirect interactions, both physical and intellectual, between Korean anarchists and other anarchists circulating in the region, particularly in those cities in China and Japan. In other words, Korean anarchists shared many common concerns, goals, and even solutions with other anarchists. As a result, the former embraced many of those transnational goals and ideas of the latter, and in some cases experimented with them together. As I demonstrate, Korean anarchists continuously materialized and experimented with the goals and ideals, even after 1945, in the process of concretizing and eventually Koreanizing their version of anarchist ideals. I do not suggest, however, that there was uniformity among all regional (and Korean) anarchists or no concern for their own distinctive national/local problems, to which I now turn.

In relation to my regional perspective, I take up, below, the question of place in the practice of anarchism among Korean anarchists. I argue that the history of Korean anarchism needs to be constructed as part of regional anarchism, with special attention to translocal connections among anarchists and place-based practices of anarchism by anarchists in various locations in the region. Arif Dirlik argues that "Anarchism in China is best grasped through a regional perspective that makes it possible to glimpse the many translocal ties within which anarchism flourished," "producing localized discourses on revolution."[30] So is anarchism in Korea, I argue. What distinguished Korean anarchism from Chinese anarchism was that the former was by and large a product of exiled radicals and their activities in China and the study-abroad students in Japan, whose common goal was the retaking of independence, but whose practice of anarchism went through a slightly different localized process of articulation and concretization, respectively, as I argue in this study. Anarchists in colonial Korea and Manchuria were no exception in this regard. Obvious in Korean anarchism were locally diverse discourses on and practices of anarchist ideals according to the locations of anarchists and the environment they faced there, which lead to an argument against the unity and uniformity in Korean anarchism.

The question of place in the rise of Korean anarchism has not received any attention from South Korean scholars. They have not been attentive to the importance of different locations where anarchists were concentrated and were exposed to various versions of anarchist ideals, subsequently bringing them into diverse practices. As a result, Korean anarchism has been unwisely described as the product of a coherent, unified principle or movement of Korean anarchists, no matter where they were placed and no matter how differently they practiced anarchism. They are thus often understood as a group in unity and conformity to both the national and anarchist goals and means, with almost the same understanding and practice of anarchism or, at best, with slight differences among them, which are usually negligible. However, as they were scattered in and constantly on the move to various places such as Beijing, Shanghai, Quanzhou, Tokyo, Osaka, Manchuria, and colonial Korea, they evidently encountered and dealt with different and diverse local-based issues and concerns. Their approaches to them differed, therefore. I posit that locations predisposed Korean anarchists to different local versions and practices of anarchism, pulling them frequently into the discussion of local-based issues and concerns with reference to universal problems. Even their strategies for their respective movement were different, as well as their sources for the understanding of anarchism, be they direct ones through their interactions with other anarchists or indirect through reading printed materials, chiefly books. What I think of as significant is, given the frequent movement of Korean anarchists from one to other locations, not only the importance of location but also interlocation or translocal connections in the rise of Korean anarchism, which requires a broad regional approach in the study of Korean anarchism. The case in question here is those anarchists who moved, for example, from Tokyo to Shanghai, from Tokyo and Manchuria to colonial Korea, and even from one to other cities within China, Japan, and the Korean peninsula.

Although Korean anarchists commonly designated national liberation and independence as their primary goal, for which they were united, they interpreted and then applied anarchism to the concrete environment of the location they were placed in, which helped them articulate its universal messages with the help of local language, issues, and concerns. Rather than constructing the history of Korean anarchist movement as the coherent story of a group of anarchists with unity and unanimity in theory and practice, regardless of the local, internal differences among them, I point to the internal divisions among Korean anarchists, if not conflicts, corresponding to their respective location and practice, over the question, for example, as to what issues and concerns deserved their priority, be they local, national, or universal in nature. And the divisions shifted according to changes in the situation in their locations. This, however, is not to deny that Korean anarchists, regardless of their different locations and practices, endeavored together with some kind of common consciousness to realize both national and anarchist goals; but to recognize localized versions of anarchism, which in many cases allowed them to identify their priorities with different, immediate issues they faced, and thus necessitated slightly different practices of anarchism.

In analyzing "the relation between social circumstances and a temporally associated form of ideology" during the periods of the Protestant Reformation, the Enlightenment, and the rise of European socialism, Robert Wuthnow uses the term "communities of discourse," where "a process of mutual influence, adjustment, accommodation" occurred and produced "culture as a form of behavior and as the tangible results of that behavior."[31] I posit that there was a similar process in such locations as Shanghai and Tokyo, of which Korean anarchism was a product; the process produced the transnational radical networks of discourse and practice.[32] My assumption is that Tokyo and Shanghai, among other places, served as the nodes of the transnational radical networks in early twentieth century. There, Eastern Asian anarchists (or radicals, broadly speaking) met each other either through printed materials or in person, got to know one another, discussed the issues of their own countries and of the world, shared much of them in common, and finally, in many cases, organized themselves and took actions together; after sharing the common discourse, vision, and activities, many of them moved back to their countries or other cities to begin their own various radical/anarchist projects/movements. From the turn of the twentieth century, Tokyo had been a popular and ultimate destination for study abroad and political refuge for many Eastern Asian students and radicals, and Shanghai had also become a gathering place of many radicals and political refugees from colonies and semicolonies. Tokyo and Shanghai, among other places, served as crucibles within which radicals with various backgrounds met each other, and consequently radical cultures and languages were forged and informed there as much by their immediate environments as they were by more distant goals of national independence. To many, anarchism was most suitable at once for the articulation of their own location within the radical networks of discourse and practice in their immediate environments.

It may be even possible to call the regional range of the Eastern Asian anarchists' interactions an "ecumene" where "intense and sustained cultural interactions" among Eastern Asian radicals took place.[33] Whatever we call it, the point here is the consistent intense interactions, direct and indirect, of radicals circulating in the region, that were the product of mutual influence and inspiration in such cities among radicals in the forms of discourse using radical languages and transnational concerns; and practices that often resulted in joint activities, either organizational or publication, both of which being the long-lasting source of their common radical culture.[34] These radical networks gave rise to transnational connections in the region in the 1920s, utilizing cities like Tokyo and Shanghai as their nodes, from which it is possible to argue that the history of Korean anarchism is part of the history of regional anarchism, and vice versa.[35]

Kim San's descriptions of Tokyo and Shanghai in 1919 tell us about how the radical networks of discourse and practice functioned. Kim San (1905–1938), whose real name was Jang Jirak, had begun his revolutionary career as an anarchist but soon converted to communism in China, participated in the Guangzhou Uprising of 1927 led by the Chinese Communist Party (CCP), and went to Yan'an, the CCP's revolutionary base from 1937 to 1947, where he as a CCP member raised and educated Korean revolutionaries but was charged and executed for being a spy of Japan in 1938. In his interview with Helen Foster in Yan'an, which developed later into a book titled *Song of Ariran*,[36] Kim recalls that Tokyo in 1919 was "the Mecca for students [from] all over the Far East and a refuge for revolutionaries of many kinds" and Shanghai, in the same year, was "the new center of the nationalist movement where the Korean provisional government was functioning." In the cities Kim, like many other Korean and Eastern Asian radicals, "met all kinds of people and was thrown into a maelstrom of conflicting political ideas and discussions."[37] While Tokyo offered many sources for their radicalization, such as both original and translated works on socialism, including anarchism, Shanghai as a colonial "contact zone" provided a favorable space for Korean anarchists to organize and take actions with other anarchists directly against Japanese imperialism for independence, which was one of the main reasons, as I demonstrate later, why many Korean anarchists in the late 1920s and early 1930s moved from Tokyo to Shanghai after being radicalized, particularly after having witnessed the tightened surveillance and oppression of Japanese police in colonial Korea and

Japan. In Shanghai they interacted with other Asian radicals and anarchists, as well as their compatriots, with all of whom they would come to share national and/or social goals, let alone begin various activities together.

The Korean anarchist discourse was to go far beyond independence and present problems pertinent both to their society and the world, which would result in the production of radical culture and language with their own meanings attached to them. Korean anarchists, of course, were not initial producers of the discourse and language. For example, a language of revolution was a contribution of the Paris Chinese anarchists, while the problem of modernity was what the Tokyo Chinese anarchists had wrestled with.[38] The resistance against centralized authority was the focus of the Japanese anarchists between the mid-1910s and 1923. And Ōsugi Sakae's (1885–1923) passionate commitment to "individual liberation" in his support of the aims and methods of anarcho-syndicalism[39] could have been deeply influenced how Bak Yeol (1902–1074) and his fellow Japan-based anarchists understood the importance of individuals in making an anarchist society, as I demonstrate in chapter 2.[40] The point here is the significance of the interaction itself, and the resulting mutual inspiration and influence among East Asian anarchists in the rise of anarchism in East Asia.

Kim San particularly notes the special influence of Japan in radical thinking among Koreans and the outcome of it as the following:

> From 1919 to 1923 Korean students were far in advance of Chinese in social thinking, partly because of our more pressing need for revolution and partly because of *our closer contacts with Japan, the fountainhead of the radical movement, both anarchist and Marxist, in the Far East at that time*. It was from Japanese translations of Marxism that both Koreans and Chinese first became acquainted with this theory.[41] (Emphasis added)

Reading such translated Japanese books that were available, Korean anarchists were first exposed to the languages of Japanese (and Chinese) anarchists, and used them to participate in the production (and reproduction) of a radical discourse on and activities for Korea's independence and social revolution. Such anarchist languages as "democracy" and, most importantly, "freedom" particularly had strong appeal to many Korean radicals abroad, according to Kim San.[42] In any case, Korean anarchists, to be sure, were active participants in the discourse and practice, using the languages of revolution so that they came to share many concerns and vision in common with other anarchists. And they finally were to "select" from the languages what they thought necessary and crucial for Korean independence and society and related them to the problems of the world. During the process of "selection," it is again noteworthy, Korean anarchists had probably to face a tension between their national goal and transnational concerns and vision, and attempted to reconcile the two seeming contradictory tasks.

In chapter 5, I examine how the pre-1945 anarchist discourse and language played out in post-1945 South Korea, and how Korean anarchists deradicalized them to cope with the unfavorable political climate under which they used to become an easy target of political suppression by the undemocratic and military regimes in South Korea since 1948. While the transnational linkages and regional elements continued to play a role in formulating the post-1945 direction and character of Korean anarchism, they removed its revolutionary agenda and vision and launched an experimental, but failed anarchist political party. Their focus of activities gradually shifted to social movements for the goal of national development on the basis of national autonomy in both political and economic senses. This deradicalization was caused under the political climate of South Korea that was unfavorable and even appeared as a threat to Korean anarchists, but had also its roots in the idea of the national front (*minjok jeonseon*) from the 1930s, which gave its priority to national liberation over transnational goal and, at the same time, to the national problem over social problem.

As I demonstrate in chapter 4, the national front idea was actively proposed and put into practice after Japan's all-out invasion of China in the 1930s, by many anarchists who saw the wartime situation in China and the world as a new opportunity for Korea's independence. Understanding that their anarchist goal could never be achieved without national liberation, Korean anarchists came up with a plan that stressed their national goal through the national front idea to put aside all the differences, social and ideological, among all Korean revolutionaries and independence activists. They were even willing to work and cooperate with, and even support the Korean Provisional Government under the leadership of conservative nationalists. An anarchist society could never be realized in Korea, they concluded, if Korea remained as Japan's colony, which required a prioritization of national unity to fight their common enemy. The world situation where various forms of united front, including the United Front in China and the People's Front in Spain, were formed as responses to Japan's invasion in China and fascism in Europe, respectively, prompted them to have their own national front. The idea of national front proposed and accepted by Korean anarchists in China turned out to be determinant in the direction of post-1945 Korean anarchism with its emphasis on national development.

Korean anarchists after 1945 never discarded anarchist principles and ideals, mostly Kropotkinite ones, such as mutual aid, spontaneity, the combination of mental and intellectual labor, and the combination of agriculture and industry in development. Indeed, Peter Kropotkin (1842–1921) left the deepest influence on Koreans' initial interest in and conversion to anarchism, no matter where they were, and was probably the most important anarchist theoretician to have widespread influence in East Asia.[43] In particular, Korean anarchists, just like their regional counterparts, must have found in his mutual aid idea a response to the social Darwinist explanation of human progress, and even saw its affinity to the cooperative principle Korean rural villagers had long practiced. They toiled strenuously, though, to maintain "national voice" in practicing the universal principle, as I demonstrate in chapter 5.

Korean anarchists after 1945 even began to identify themselves not just as anarchists but rather also as "believers in an autonomous government" (*jayul jeongbu juuija*) and "autonomous persons" (*jaju in*), and even renamed anarchism "democratic socialism" (*minju sahoe juui*), without much reference to its radical social revolutionary premises. And after failing in their experiments with political parties, anarchism was gradually translated into a more practical idea of social movement, which underscored the importance of rural villages in the course of national development and the preparedness of farmers to become responsible citizens whose role was deemed crucial to make Korea a modern, developed nation in its transition to modernity. The point was to maintain the balances between the rural and urban areas in development and between traditions and modern benefits. And the main focus of anarchist activities was on redirecting the state-led modernization to an alternative developmental trajectory that could reflect anarchist ideas, because the state-projected modernization would only end up sacrificing and thus ruining rural villages for the sake of the urban and the modern.

This idea, widely practiced in the 1960s and '70s, however, needs not be seen as a sign of deviation or deterioration from anarchism in European origins. It rather reflects, I argue, a process of localization of anarchism, more broadly a "Koreanization" to accommodate the atmosphere after 1945 under which anarchism was redefined to cope with the division of Korea and meet the new demands of the time for national liberation and development. Anarchists endeavored to avoid a false accusation of anarchism being a "cousin of communism"[44] and thus survive the suppression by dictatorial anticommunist South Korean regimes. When I call this a Koreanization of anarchism, I do not emphasize the roles of Korean culture and past in the Korean understanding of anarchism but point to a place-based modification of anarchism. This deradicalized and Koreanized anarchism by Yi Jeong-gyu and his fellow anarchists, as I demonstrate in chapter 5, obviously threw out its revolutionary agenda and vision; its main focus was placed until the 1980s on boosting national economy through the revival of rural villages, along with increased income for farmers.

To sum up, this study first underlines the role of nationalism in converting Koreans to anarchism but also, more importantly, points to various forms of interactions among anarchists themselves circulating in the region, to demonstrate, first, that transnationalism, too, played an important role in the acceptance and development of Korean anarchism; Korean anarchists accepted anarchism not only for independence but ultimately for a social revolution that was a shared goal with other anarchists in many locations in the region. The origins and development of Korean anarchism, therefore, I argue, need to be understood in the context of the rise and development of anarchism, more broadly of radical ideas and culture, in the region, with reference to its various localized means and goals for an anarchist ideal society. Korean anarchists as a product of the transnational radical networks of discourse and practice also developed, maintained, and displayed concerns for prevailing social and political problems under capitalism that were marked by anarchist inspiration. In response to the concerns and problems, they envisioned a future country and world through joint projects with their Asian counterparts, based on such fundamental anarchist principles and ideas as "spontaneous alliance," "mutual aid," and "individual freedom" of a radical bent. This was, I think, how a regional identity as "Asians" (versus the invader Westerners) or broadly a transnational identity as "oppressed peoples" arose among anarchists beyond their respective national identity and came to play a role in the transnational and translocal interactions and solidarity among them, including Koreans in China and Japan.[45] Many accounts of anarchism in the region miss the regional identity, the transnational aspects, and the movement of anarchists themselves and their ideas within the region. All of these were still visible in the post-1945 movement of Korean anarchists. What I will consider below are these Korean anarchists in motion in the region, pursuing their transnational as much as national goal through various place-based practices of anarchism,[46] in some cases with their Asian counterparts.

CHAPTER 1

Beyond Independence

The Dawn of Korean Anarchism in China

Anarchism had already been introduced to Koreans exiled in China before 1919.[1] But it was only after 1919 that anarchism was viewed as a suitable principle for the construction of a new Korean society, as well as for their country's independence. Needless to say, the Russian Revolution of 1917 first greatly impacted Koreans in China and elsewhere, as it generated their strong interest and desire in socialism, including anarchism. At the same time, anarchism was also considered by many Korean exiles in China in the wake of factional strife within the independence camp, especially those in the Korean Provisional Government in Shanghai, established as a direct outcome of the 1919 March First Movement; the ongoing internal conflicts within the government and among the independence activists nurtured an antipolitical aura among many Koreans in China, which laid the groundwork for them to distrust politics, and thus also for their interest in anarchism, because of its disdain of politics and political movement. They were in dire need of a guiding principle for their united activities for both independence and anticolonialism. Anarchist repudiation of the nation-state at the same time led to the foundation for a regional alliance and solidarity among anarchists, paving the way for their transnational joint activity for a cosmopolitan world. This regional and transnational aspects of anarchism, as well as the negation of the state, may explain why many Korean anarchists had a rupture with the Provisional Government, at least until the late 1930s and early 1940s when, as I demonstrate in chapter 4, some anarchists shifted their prime priority to national liberation and even decided to participate in the government to form a united national front against Japanese imperialism and render it a precondition to liberate Korea and then construct an anarchist society afterward.

The growing interest of China-based Korean independence activists in anarchism and their subsequent reception of it in the late 1910s and early 1920s resulted most importantly from their increased opportunities to have contacts with anarchist ideals and principles that were introduced to them through their encounters with Chinese anarchists and readings of anarchist writings available at the time in China, either in original Chinese text or in translation. In particular, their potential exposures to anarchist literature available in China in Chinese by 1920, which was, according to Arif Dirlik, "unmatched in scope and comprehensiveness by any other social and political philosophies of European origin,"[2] as well as their direct associations/ interactions with Chinese anarchists and their organizations, played a crucial role in their growing interest in and acceptance of anarchism. As Peter Zarrow adds, the years "from the New Culture Movement of the mid-1910s to about 1925" were "the heyday of Chinese anarchism," during which "a good deal of organizational activity, especially anarcho-syndicalism, as well as ideological refinement" were visible.[3] With the abundance and richness of anarchist literature and increased anarchist activities through organizations, Korean exiles were exposed and then converted to anarchism, finally joining and/or cofounding many anarchist organizations together with Chinese and other Asian counterparts, not to mention publishing many anarchist journals jointly or independently.

Becoming Anarchist in Beijing

Many sources demonstrate the increased contacts and interactions after the March First Movement of 1919 between Korean exiles/ radicals and Chinese anarchists, which marks the dawn of Korean anarchist movement in China.[4] While the Provisional Government of Korea was established in Shanghai, many Korean radical exiles seemed to concentrate in Beijing as well as Shanghai for their activities for independence movement. Some had even gone to south China, especially Guangzhou. One of the earlier such cases can be found in the publication of an anarchism-oriented journal titled *The Light*

(*Guangming* in Chinese and *Gwangmyeong* in Korean), first published in Guangzhou on December 1, 1921. *The Light* was the only journal published jointly in the early twentieth century with the collaboration of Koreans and Chinese, albeit most of the articles it carried were written by Chinese.[5] It was not a Korean anarchist journal per se, but nevertheless carried some anarchism-oriented articles, for example, in its inaugural issue. The author of an article in the issue titled "The Future of the Light Movement," propagated mutual aid with a prediction that "the future of the Light Movement lies within the world of freedom, equality, universal love, and mutual aid."[6] In another article titled "The Light Movement in China and Korea," the author of it asserted that the revolutions in China and Korea aimed at achieving a social revolution, for China, having gone only through a political revolution (i.e., the 1911 Revolution), still had to be under the rule of and pressure from the warlords.[7] It is safe to say that by the early 1920s, a fraternal alliance between Chinese and Koreans against Japanese aggression had become a commonly shared agenda of both Korean exiles in China and Chinese intellectuals. In the process of making an alliance, Korean radicals accepted anarchism in those Chinese cities with help from Chinese anarchists; Korean radicals' associations and interactions in various forms with Chinese anarchists and their organizations surely prompted the interest and ultimate reception of anarchism among them. However, not only through personal relationships with Chinese anarchists but also through readings on socialism and anarchism, Korean exiles/radicals in China were also increasingly drawn to anarchism, enticed initially to its principles like mutual aid and social transformation based on freedom and equality.

Among the first Korean anarchists in China was Shin Chaeho (1880–1936), a prominent Korean historian, journalist, and writer. Along with other Korean radicals in China, Shin had already published a journal in Shanghai called *New Greater Korea* (*Sin daehan*), basically an anarchism-oriented journal,[8] for about four months between October 1919 and January 1920, in which socialism and anarchism were introduced and discussed. Although it is not clear if he was physically in Shanghai around that time, Shin also published a monthly journal called *Heavenly Drum* (*Cheon-go*), also in Shanghai in classical Chinese, between January and July 1921. This monthly journal was, in its orientation and content, not anarchist but carried articles written both by Koreans and Chinese, on the issues of mutual aid, and also promoted the Korean-Chinese alliance. For example, in its third issue, published in February 1921, there was an article on Kropotkin's death in January of the same year, written by Shin himself with his pen name of Nammyeong, which introduced Kropotkin's idea of mutual aid and praised Kropotkin's personality.[9]

Shin had long had interest in anarchism, but became an anarchist only in the early 1920s, preferring "direct action" in the course of Korea's independence and revolution. Despite his long-held interest in anarchism, it seems Shin became an anarchist through his good relationship with some prominent Chinese anarchists like Li Shizeng (1881–1873), a Paris Chinese anarchist and one of the key members of the Guomindang (GMD, the Nationalist Party of China), and Cai Yuanpei (1868–1940), both at Beijing University. Li as a professor at Beijing University provided Shin in 1918 with a place to stay and an access to the Complete Library in Four Branches of Literature (Sigu quanshu), at the same university, to assist Shin's study of prehistoric Korean history. And according to a Korean source, around the time Shin was indulged and interested in reading the writings of Liu Sifu, commonly known as Shifu and called the "soul of Chinese anarchism,"[10] Shin was also deeply influenced by what Kropotkin stated in his *An Appeal to the Young*. Kōtoku Shūsui's (1871–1911) many writings, particularly *On the Obliteration of Christ* (*Kirisuto Massatsuron*),[11] must have impressed Shin as well. At his trial later in 1929, after being arrested by Japanese police, Shin even testified that he had understood that Kōtoku's anarchist works were the most "reasonable" ones for the understanding of anarchism.[12] Not only through personal relationships and associations with Chinese/Japanese anarchists, but also through the readings of their writings on anarchism, both original and in translation, Korean exiles in Beijing like Shin were increasingly drawn to anarchism and became acquainted with other Asian anarchists.

In addition, Shin's friendship with Yi Hoeyeong (1867–1932), often called "the pioneer of Korean anarchism,"[13] must have been a factor as well for his acceptance of anarchism. Yi had exiled to China in 1910 with his five brothers for independence movement and had been in Beijing with Shin as exiles, having a wide range of relationship with many Korean expatriates, including anarchists such as Yu Ja-myeong (1894–1985).[14] Yu, born in Northern Chungcheong Province in Korea, was known as "the best [anarchist] theoretician of the time."[15] After participating in the March First Movement of 1919 as teacher of a school in the city of Chungju, Yu moved to Shanghai and became a member of the Provisional Government of Korea in Shanghai. He seemed to be interested in socialism at the time but rejected communism because he believed that the most urgent task for Korean people was national liberation, not class struggle or class liberation.[16] His range of activities was wide: as an anarchist he participated in the Righteous Group (Uiyeoldan), a terror-oriented Korean anarchist-like group in China, and in the formation of the United Society of the Eastern Oppressed Peoples (Dongfang beiyapo minzu lianhehui) in Wuhan in 1927;[17] and as a teacher Yu taught briefly at Dawn Advanced Middle School (Liming gaoji zhongxue) and Lida College (Lida xueyuan) in 1930. In China in the 1930s, Yu would become a central figure in the formation of the national front.[18] Yu along with Kim Wonbong (1898–1958),[19] leader of the Righteous Group, requested Shin Chaeho to write the famous "Declaration of the Korean Revolution" ("Joseon [Chosŏn] hyeokmyeong seoneon"), which Shin penned in January 1923 and is now believed to be a sign of his conversion to anarchism.[20]

The case of Yu Rim (1894–1961) illuminates a constant move of Korean anarchists from and to Korea and even within China. Yu moved to Manchuria in 1919 for independence movement and became soon an anarchist, interacting with Shin Chaeho and others in Beijing but at the same time possibly with Sichuanese Chinese anarchists between 1922 and 1925, when he was a student at National Chengdu University in Sichuan Province. After participating in the Wuchang Uprising and the Guangzhou Uprising in 1927, Yu returned to Manchuria where he organized the United Society of All Korean People (Hanjok chong yeonhaphoe) with Yi Eulgyu (1894–1972) and Kim Jongjin (1900–1931) in 1929. In November of the same year, he sneaked into the Korean peninsula to help establish the Korean Anarcho-Communist Federation (KAF, Joseon gongsan mujeongbu juuija yeonmaeng) with his comrades in colonial Korea. After being prisoned for his anarchist activities in Korea, he returned to Manchuria and then moved to Chongqing where he joined the Provisional Government of Korea in the name of a united fight of all Koreans against the Japanese.[21] According to his loyal disciplines, Yu was the most important Korean anarchist in the history of Korean anarchist movement, since he not only endeavored unflinchingly to embark on the anarchist movement in colonial Korea before 1945 at the risk of his life when he crossed the border between Manchuria and Korea, but also because he consistently understood the importance of promoting a mass movement and educating of workers and peasants in realizing anarchism before and after 1945.[22]

Yi Jeonggyu (1897–1984), one of the most active Korean anarchists in 1920s China, just like other Korean exiles, began his career as an independence activist and converted later to anarchism. Unlike many Korean anarchists in China, he was first exposed to and become interested in socialism in Tokyo when he was a student at Keiō University in 1918.[23] When the 1919 March First Movement occurred, Yi returned to Korea at once and then left for Shanghai in April 1919, where he immediately participated in the Provisional Government of Korea there, representing the Province of Chungcheong, his home province. Until he was arrested and brought to colonial Korea for trial by Japanese police in October 1928, he had conducted his anarchist activities in China. According to his own recollection, Yi had been attracted by the news from Russia about the Russian Revolution and initially had a plan to go to Russia from China. Changing his plan, however, on his way to Russia at the end of 1921 to attend the Far East University in Chita, because of a rumor he heard about a potential danger of losing his life as a result of factional strife among Korean communists at the time, Yi decided to stay in Beijing. There he met Yu Ja-myeong and Chinese anarchists such as Li Shizeng and Cai Yuanpei, who gave him a chance to continue his education at Beijing University where he was enrolled as a sophomore in the Economics Department. The two years in Beijing from 1921 to 1923 were a "very important period" to Yi in formulating his ideas and personality, particularly in launching his life as an anarchist for the cause of independence and anarchist society.[24] Explaining how he had thrown himself to the divine cause of independence, Yi later stated that "living a life to fight for liberation of the fatherland was the one thing we the [Korean] youth only could do and felt proud of," when they had to stay and live in China as exiles.[25] Yi must have accepted anarchism in regard to his national goal for Korea's independence. In China he used to be called "the tip of a writing brush" (*pilbong*),[26] meaning that he had a sharp theoretical understanding of anarchism, while Yi Eulgyu, his elder brother who converted to anarchism in China as well, used to be nicknamed and known as "Korea's Kropotkin" at that time for his extensive knowledge of anarchist "theories" and his cogency.[27]

To many Korean anarchists in China like Yi Jeonggyu, establishing their own organizations was the first task, and they had two simultaneous goals in organizing themselves: independence and building a new society in Korea based on anarchist ideals and principles, for both of which they first looked for alliance with their Chinese counterparts and actively engaged in the latter's activities. One earliest such a case comes from Yi Jeonggyu's association with Chinese anarchists and Esperantists. According to a police report of the Beiyang warlord government in Beijing, dated June 5, 1922, the Association for the Study of World Language (i.e., Esperanto) in China (Shijieyu xuehui) had just held a meeting over tea, days before the report was composed. The purpose of the meeting was to welcome a Japanese "communist" (sic) and two Koreans, Yi Jeonggyu and Yi Byeonggyu (probably Yi Eulgyu). A Chinese representative of the Association delivered a welcoming address, in which he explained to the attendees the current situation of the "Chinese anarchist party" (Zhongguo wuzhengfu dang) in various locations in China.[28] This was followed by Yi Jeonggyu's response. Yi, thanking the Chinese present, stated that all Koreans wished to recover Korea's national sovereignty and land, and thus strove for national liberation without any fear of sacrificing themselves. Yi then briefly expressed his hope that youths in China, Japan, and Korea could be united to move forward. At the meeting it was decided, according to the report, that those present from the three countries would get permission from their respective comrades to look into the possibility of convening a conference for all, at one place.[29]

About a year after the meeting, Yi Jeonggyu collaborated with a Chinese man named Chen Kongshan to set up Beijing Special School for Esperanto (Beijing shijieyu zhuanmen xuexiao) and was appointed as a faculty member at Dawn Middle School (Liming zhongxue) attached to the Special School. Chen was allegedly an alumnus of Beijing University with Yi, who entered it in 1922.[30] In September of 1923, Yi also participated with Chen Weiqi (or Chen Weiguang) in a project proposed by a Chinese anarchist with surname of Zhou, which schemed to move about fifty Korean peasant families from Korea to Hanshui Xian in Hunan Province in China, to construct an ideal farming village together with Chinese peasants there. The project was intended to have them cultivate ginseng together to increase their income. Although it failed because the Zhou family was scattered around as a result of the internal warfare in Hunan, the proposed project is highly praised by Korean historians as "the first experiment that attempted to build an ideal society in farming villages in the history of Korean anarchism."[31] The failed project could be included in the history of Korean anarchism, mostly because the underlining goal of it, to build an ideal society in rural villages by increasing farmers' income, was to be revived again and again by Yi, among others, even after 1945.

Besides participating in the anarchist activities of Chinese comrades, Yi Jeonggyu also interacted in Beijing with many other radicals and anarchists such as Lu Xun (1881–1936), a pen name of Zhou Shuren, who was one of the most influential figures in Chinese literature; Zhou Zuoren (1885–1967), Lu Xun's brother and a well-known writer and essayist; and Taiwanese anarchist Fan Benliang (1897–1945). The latter deserves special attention. Just like Yi, Fan used to be a study-abroad student in Tokyo, where he had converted to anarchism. He had moved to Beijing where he organized the New Taiwanese Anarchist Society (Xin taiwan ansha), and launched its journal called *New Taiwan* (*Xin taiwan*) in Beijing in December 1924, which became a newspaper beginning with its third issue on March 1, 1925.[32] Fan's name appears quite often throughout the history of Korean anarchist movement in 1920s China as one of its main non-Korean comrades.

In addition to Fan, Vasilij Eroshenko (1889–1952) was one of the most important anarchists Yi had met and interacted with in Beijing. Eroshenko was a blind Russian poet and anarchist who visited China in the early 1920s, and delivered his cosmopolitanism to the Chinese audience and possibly Korean exiles and anarchists in China, as well.[33] In fact, what Eroshenko talked to Yi about the situation in Soviet Russia under Lenin's rule convinced Yi that anarchist principles, not those of the Soviet-style communism, must be used to achieve social revolution.[34] When he became aware of then–Russian situation from Eroshenko, Yi probably recalled what he had heard about the rift among Korean communists in the early 1920s over the funds given to them from Lenin and their bloody factional fight, which stopped him from taking a trip to Chita in Siberia. In fact, Eroshenko was instrumental in not only introducing anarchist ideas to Korean anarchists in China, particularly in Beijing, but also to giving Korean radicals the sense of what Leninist communism in the Soviet Union looked like. An example, in this regard, is the case of Jeong Hwaam who, just like others in China, heard from Eroshenko about the political realities of Soviet Russia after the Bolshevik Revolution of 1917, such as the purge of anarchists there. Jeong was one of the Korean exiles in China who converted to anarchism through his interactions with Eroshenko, among many others.[35] Yi and Jeong were the ones who were ultimately convinced of the value of anarchism through their interactions with other anarchists in Beijing, and accepted it as the principle most suitable for Korea's independence and social transformation.

In pursuing the above-mentioned project to build an ideal farming village in Hunan, Yi Jeonggyu widely solicited support from other Korean exiles in Beijing. One of them was Yi Hoeyeong, who had worked with many Korean exiles and anarchists, including Shin Chaeho, Yu Ja-myeong, Han Yeongbok, and Bak Seungbyeong, all of whom published with Yi an anarchism-inspired journal called *Heavenly Drum* in 1921. According to a Korea source, in December 1922, Yi Hoeyeong was in search of a principle that he thought could answer the question of independence and its related problems, for which he met with not only Koreans such as Yu Ja-myeong, Yi Eulgyu, and Yi Jeonggyu, but others as well, including Lu Xun, Eroshenko and Fan Benliang. His search for an answer to the question of independence must have stopped when he found anarchism, which is quite obvious from his statement about what had enticed him to it. Yi Hoeyeong allegedly explained later in 1925 that "I don't think I have consciously become or converted to be an anarchist. From a contemporary perspective of thoughts, my idea and plan for the realization of Korea's independence are coincident with those of anarchism."[36] Yi had met with a wide range of radicals and independence activists, including the ones listed above. In fact, it is believed that there were no Korean independence activists in Beijing who didn't drop by Yi Hoeyeong's residence in Beijing.[37] It seems that Yi Hoeyeong surely was impressed with Yi Jeonggyu's project and anarchist ideas with regard to the proposed ideal farming villages in Hunan. Indeed, it is said that Yi Jeonggyu's role was decisive in converting Yi Hoeyeong, who was persuaded by the former about the goal of anarchism and thus accepted it in later 1923.[38] Discussing with many kinds of independence activists and radicals, including Chinese and Taiwanese, Yi Hoeyeong finally chose anarchism for his own answer. The national goal, of course, was the key that drew him to anarchism.

Yi Hoeyeong was one of those who frequently proposed that Korean anarchists must participate in the movement of Chinese anarchists and vice versa; he saw making close connections between the two movements through reciprocal cooperation so crucial.[39] This proposed interactiveness between Korean and Chinese anarchists remained of importance until 1945, as we will see in chapter 4, and at the same time explains the existential conditions Koran anarchists faced in China. In other words, from the Korean anarchist perspective, their cooperation and alliance with Chinese comrades was simply necessary and even essential, first, for their survival as political refugee and, then, for the effectiveness of their independence activities, but, most importantly, for the implementation of their shared anarchist ideals in a foreign soil. Anarchism with its cosmopolitan messages and principles, to put it blatantly, allowed Korean anarchists to emphasize an alliance with other anarchists beyond their national boundaries, which in turn was imperative to seek safety in their activities in China. In this sense, to call Yi Hoeyeong "the pioneer of Korean anarchism" is an interesting indication of the coming trajectory and transnational character of Korean anarchism in China in the 1930s and '40s. Their deep, shared belief with other anarchists, especially Chinese, that without a social revolution no political changes in both Korea and the world could be made, was to play a crucial role in having them transcend their national and, even in some cases, regional boundaries for, first, an independent Korea and, then, a better world.

Next, Jeong Hwaam explains how he converted to anarchism in China, which vindicates the importance of national consciousness and the popularity of socialism in general as the most important two motives for Korean anarchists to accept anarchism in China. Jeong, one of the leading Korean anarchists in China before 1945,[40] recalls two elements that attracted the Korean exiles in China, including himself, to anarchism: their resistance to Japanese imperialism in order to secure independence, and their adoration for "communism," with the emphasis on the former. He was particularly attracted to anarchism because of his "instinctive nationalist impulse" to resist Japan, and became convinced that "the final goal of the anarchist movement" was "the overthrow of Japanese imperialism" and "independence through resistance against Japan [*hang-il*]."[41] Jeong also discussed with other anarchists such as the Yi brothers (Yi Eulgyu and Yi Jeonggyu) and Yu Ja-myeong, finding a "non-theoretical ideology" (*sic*) for the independence movement to clarify "the objectives of [Korean] nation-building."[42] It was at this moment, I think, that anarchism began to be read and understood by these theoretically equipped Korean anarchists, not just for the goal of independence but with reference to a new society after independence. Nevertheless, as Jeong recalls, to him anarchism "sounded good anyway at first," more emotionally than theoretically.[43] As their activities in the ensuing years demonstrate, however, he and others were not deaf at all to the universal messages with the theoretical implications anarchism delivered to them, such as freedom, equality, revolution, democracy, development, and so on. As I mentioned in the Introduction, Jeong was also drawn to anarchism as a result of his increased awareness of the universal problems under capitalism.

Indeed, with their growing interest in and acceptance of anarchism, Korean exiles and radicals in Beijing now began to organize themselves and engage in various activities, chief among them involving organizations and publications for the cause of both independence and anarchism. The Beijing Branch of the Black Youth Alliance (BBBYA, Heuksaek cheongnyeon dongmaeng or Heise qingnian tongmeng), presumably the first Korean anarchist organization in China, was allegedly organized in the early 1920s, but didn't publish its own journal. Not many facts are known about it and its membership, but it seemed that the BBBYA could have possibly been organized by Shin Chaeho.[44] And next, sponsored by Chinese anarchist Cai Yuanpei, Zhang Ji (1882–1947), Li Shizeng and Wu Zhihui (1865–1953), the Black Flag League (BFL, Heukgi yeonmaeng or Heiqi lianmeng) was organized at Beijing Minguo University in October 1924 by some Korean anarchist students like Yu Seo (or Yu Giseok, 1905–1980) and Sim Yonghae (Sim Yeochu, or Shen Ruqiu in Chinese, 1904–1930) with participation of Chinese such as Ba Jin (1904–2005) and Xiang Peiliang.[45] The BFL, a product of the like-minded Korean and Chinese anarchists and of their joint activities, had its own journal titled the *Eastern Miscellaneous* (*Dongfang zazhi*), published in Chinese. Some of the Korean anarchist students such as Yu Seo and Sim Yongcheol (Sim Geukchu, or Shen Keqiu in Chinese, 1914–?), Sim Yonghae's younger brother, organized a group for the study of Kropotkin later in September of 1926, and began to exchange their unknown journals with other anarchists groups.[46]

Here, Yu Seo's activities draw our special attention in terms of intense interactions between Korean and Chinese anarchists. Yu, born in the Province of Hwanghae in Korea, left for China in 1912 and became a Chinese citizen in 1916, after his family had moved in 1913 to the city of Yanji in Jilin Province of China. Believing that "the life of a person who has lost the country (*wangguo nu*) is more miserable than that of a dog in the house of death,"[47] he readily participated in both anarchist and Korean independence movements in China. In 1925 he promoted the establishment of the Society of the Masses (Minzhongshe) with Chinese anarchists. And probably due to his relationship with Lu Xun, whose short story titled "A Madman's Diary" (Kuangren riji) was translated by Yu in Korean, when there was a debate with Marxists led by the Young Chinese Anarchist Federation (Xiaonian Zhongguo wuzhengfu zhuyi lianmeng), later in 1928 Yu, in defense of anarchist literature against Marxist literature, participated in Shanghai in the publication of Chinese anarchist literary journals, *Contemporary Culture* (*Xiandai wenhua*), *Popular Culture* (*Minjian wenhua*), and *Cultural Front* (*Wenhua zhanxian*), contributing articles to them with other Chinese anarchists such as Mao Yipo (1901–1996) and Lu Jianbo (1904–1990), and advocating the "literature of the masses" (*minzhong wenxue*). According to Sim Yongcheol, Yu once plotted an assassination of Chiang Kai-shek with Chinese anarchist Wang Yachu (1897–1936) in January 1933, after the "Shanghai Incident."[48]

Evidence of the intimate interactions in China between Korean and Chinese and other Asian anarchists could be found further in the case of the Sim brothers. Sim Yonghae, a young Korean anarchist who was fluent both in Chinese and Esperanto, and was murdered by Japanese military in Manchuria in 1930, once worked as an editor for the *National Customs Daily* (*Guofeng ribao*), published by Chinese anarchists such as Jing Meijiu (1882–1959), as publisher, and Hua Lin (1889–1980), as editor-in-chief. Sim made the newspaper's editing office his workplace and home as well and shared it with Chinese anarchist Suofei and two Japanese anarchists whose surnames were Sano (probably Sano Ichirō) and Matsumoto, respectively. Sim and the Japanese anarchists shared the idea of "Great Unity" (*datong*), believing that "All under Heaven [*tianxia*] comprises one family and the whole world [*sihai*] is full of whole brothers." Not only did they share the cosmopolitan idea, but they worked together. For example, Sim translated Matsumoto's article titled "The so-called Rebellious Koreans" (*Suowei 'bucheng xianren'*) into Chinese, which was subsequently carried in *Sea of Learning* (*Xuehui*), a supplement of the *National Customs Daily*.[49] The Sea of Learning Society (Xuehuishe), which published *Sea of Learning* from October 1922 to 1924, was an important base for Chinese anarchists and had extensive connections with not only Chinese but also other anarchists, creating a relatively huge influence on the latter.[50] Sim and the Japanese anarchists must have been associated with the Society, given their consensus that the only enemy was Japanese imperialism.

Sim Yonghae also published *Korean Youth* (*Gaoli qingnian*) in the winter of 1924, to which prominent Chinese anarchist Ba Jin contributed his writings.⁵¹ Sim's younger brother, Sim Yongcheol, confirms the close relationship between his brother and Chinese anarchists. He recalls that his brother, in addition to Yu Seo, worked closely with Chinese anarchists such as Ba Jin, Shen Zhongjiu (1887–1968), Wei Huilin (1900–1992), and so forth to publish the biweekly magazine *The Masses* (*Minzhong*) in Shanghai in 1925.⁵² According to Yu Ja-myeong, Ba Jin also was befriended by Sim there, as well and later acquainted with Yu Seo through Sim.⁵³ Sim Yongcheol became friends with Fan Benliang and Lin Bingwen (1897–1945), Taiwanese anarchists who throughout their presence in China worked closely with Korean anarchists on many occasions. Sim Yongcheol also recalls that he had once studied and made friends in China with a Vietnamese student whose Chinese name was Yuan Xingguo, who, Sim later realized, was a younger brother of Ho Chih Minh.⁵⁴

After having some experience with small and sporadic organizations and publications, Korean anarchists in China, in an effort to organize themselves, finally gathered in Beijing to establish the Korean Anarchist League in China (KALC, Jae jungguk joseon mujeongbu juuija yeonmaeng) in April 1924. It included almost all Korean anarchists active in then-China as participants, such as Yi Hoeyeong, Yu Ja-myeong, the Yi brothers, Jeong Hwaam, and Baek Jeonggi (1896–1934), all of whom were expatriates also working for Korea's independence in China. Not much is known about the KALC's activity but many have testified that it published its organ *Justice Newspaper* (*Jeong-ui gongbo* in Korean or *Zhengyi gongbao* in Chinese),⁵⁵ supposedly the first Korean anarchist newspaper published in China. The newspaper has not survived and only fragmentary information about it is available today. Yi Hoeyeong was its editor-in-chief, and among the frequent contributors to it was Shin Chaeho who, for unknown reasons, didn't join the KALC itself but obviously partook in its newspaper works. The basic stance of the newspaper was to criticize the "wrong ideas" for Korea's independence, mainly led and employed by the Korean nationalist independence camp in China, represented by the Provisional Government of Korea in Shanghai, which had functioned as the legitimate exile government of Korea since 1919. The newspaper's criticism was also directed toward the factional strife within the nationalist camp and the Provisional Government itself. Bolshevism, of course, was another target of the newspaper's criticism. In addition, the newspaper insisted on the cooperation and coalition of various Korean independence groups in China, on the basis of the anarchist "spontaneous alliance" principle. Due to the shortage of funds, it is said, after publishing its ninth issue, the newspaper was discontinued.[56]

Although no issue of *Justice Newspaper* is available now for the current study, the comments of Yi Hoeyeong, its editor-in-chief, at about the time of its publication, regarding a future Korea after independence may help us to understand the newspaper's vision of a postindependence Korean society. In his conversation in 1926 with Kim Jongjin, a young Korean anarchist then active in Manchuria, but who was to be murdered there later in 1931 by Korean communists at the age of thirty-one, Yi is said to have stated that:

> It is expected that the internal political structure [of Korea] after independence should definitely avoid the concentration of power and that a local autonomous system, based upon the principle of decentralization of power, would be established and, at the same time, the central political structure, drawing upon the alliance of the local autonomous bodies, would be constructed.[57]

And the "economic system [of the postindependence Korean society] should be managed by the society," Yi added. "Since anarchism, unlike communism, does not require uniformity, anarchism, while maintaining its basic principles, can be accommodated to [Korea's] custom or tradition, and cultural or economic situation," Yi further contended.[58] In sum, the newspaper under his editorship probably propagated spontaneous alliance as the main principle to construct a new Korea and the unity of all independence movement organizations in China, not to mention anti-Bolshevism along with its critique of factionalism in the Korean nationalist camp in China.[59] What is most revealing is Yi's openness to an understanding of anarchism for its "Koreanized" practice. As it will become clear in this study, the general anarchist principles adopted earlier but subsequently Koreanized or localized were to be of importance in the practice of anarchism among Korean anarchists in China, even after 1945.

It might be possible to locate some other factors that might have had some "influence" on the KALC's activity and its newspaper's vision for a new Korea. According to some Korean sources, the members of KALC frequently met and maintained a relationship with a group of Chinese anarchists such as Li Shizeng, Wu Zhihui, and Cai

Yuanpei.⁶⁰ The former two were the well-known core members of the Paris Chinese anarchists who were "modernists," fetishized science, called for a cultural revolution, and favored "universal education,"⁶¹ while the latter was one who "shared some of the philosophical premises of anarchism and its vision of a cosmopolitan world."⁶² Given their long relationship with Korean anarchists that would in fact continue until the 1940s,⁶³ it is quite possible that their version of anarchism was shared and possibly considered by Korean anarchists in shaping their version of it, which was the case as I demonstrate in chapter 4. The KALC anarchists also frequently met and interacted with other anarchists such as Vasilij Eroshenko and Fan Benliang. Of importance were not just their encounters and meetings but their possible engagement in the discussions of anarchism and the vision of a future world, as well as of the problems of their respective nation and the world with their solutions. Eroshenko particularly has been known as the one who converted many Korean exiles in China to anarchism, and Fan, probably sharing many concerns and problems as a colonized people with Korean anarchists, consented with his Korean comrades and they took actions together. These Korean interactions with other anarchists and their possible influences on Korean anarchists' understanding of nationalism, anarchism, and the world problems, let alone their joint actions, cannot be treated lightly. There is no clear, direct evidence that shows that the influence from Chinese and other anarchists on Korean anarchists was decisive or formative in the latter's conversion to anarchism, but it is revealing that many Korean exiles accepted anarchism in Beijing in the early 1920s through their various interactions with other anarchists in the course of their quest for Korea's independence. More important was the nationalist direction of Korean anarchism they seemed to set at its inception, which had longer and more lasting impacts than they initially thought on the history of Korean anarchism.

Experimenting Anarchist Ideals Jointly in Shanghai

Since the turn of the twentieth century, Shanghai as a breeding place of Chinese revolutionaries and reformers had already made "the Tokyo-Shanghai connection," posing a threat to the Qing dynasty, while Tokyo was a base for their revolutionary/reform activities.⁶⁴ For example, in Shanghai radical literary figures from China and Japan frequently met at Uchiyama Bookstore (Uchiyama shōten), run by Uchiyama Kanzō (1885–1959), who had vague but "longstanding [sic] sympathy for the left," and there also was the Gongfei Coffee Shop, where "leftwing [sic] Chinese and Japanese writers and cultural types frequently congregated."[65] Shanghai in the 1910s was "readily becoming a breeding ground for subversive types from both" China and Japan.[66] This trend continued and was even strengthened after the Russian Revolution of 1917, and the arrival in Shanghai in 1920 of the representative of the Communist International (Comintern), George Voitinsky (1893–1953). With the formation of the alliance in 1924 between the GMD and the CCP under the sponsorship of the Comintern, Shanghai became a place where many kinds of radicals gathered from all over the world. By the early 1920s, Shanghai played a role as a node of the transnational network of radicals in Eastern Asia. Under the situation the "wind" of anarchism also blew in Shanghai to Korean radicals and exiles, as anarchist Yi Honggeun (1907–?) recalls.[67]

Huaguang Hospital (Huaguang yiyuan) in the French Concession of Shanghai, established and run by Chinese anarchist Deng Mengxian, served from the early 1920s to the 1930s as a place for communication and contact not only among Chinese anarchists such as Ba Jin, Mao Yipo, and Lu Jianbo, but also among all other East Asian anarchists, including Yu Ja-myeong who became acquainted there with Sano Ichirō, who used his Chinese name Tian Huamin,[68] as well as with Ba Jin, Mao, Lu, and Deng.[69] The encounter between Yu and Ba Jin, in particular, developed later into a short story about Yu, written by Ba Jin. As Olga Lang notes, Ba Jin's short story titled "A Story of Hair" (*Fa de gushi*), published later in 1936, "deals with Korean rebels (most probably anarchists), their struggle against the Japanese, and the relations between Chinese and Korean revolutionaries," and was primarily based on Yu and his activities.[70] Deng had established a good relationship with Japanese anarchists since his study abroad in Japan and had provided his private hospital as a place of contact and communication for anarchists. According to historian Kim Myeongseop, the hospital was to host the Eastern anarchist convention later on June 14, 1928, at which the representatives from six countries decided to establish the Eastern Anarchist Federation (EAF, Dongfang wuzhengfu zhuyizhe lianmeng).[71] Other than Yu, many other young Korean anarchists in Shanghai such as Kim Gwangju, Yi Gyeongson, Kim Myeongsu, and An Usaeng were among those who used to drop by Deng's hospital.[72] In the case of Jeong Hwaam, he had a chance to meet Japanese anarchist Shiroyama Hideo (1901–1982) there, with whose help Jeong was able to develop a plan with Yi Jeonggyu later to threaten the then-Japanese consul general and a consul in Shanghai, whose surnames were Yatabe and Shimizu, respectively, to expose their corruption and humiliate them. Japanese anarchist Akagawa Haruki (1906–1974), who deserted from the Japanese army, and Take Riyōji (1895–?) with whom Jeong became acquainted also at the hospital, took part in this plan, albeit it ultimately failed. Yi Jeonggyu, Akagawa, Shiroyama, and Take were all arrested by Japanese police, charged with the crimes of blackmailing and intimidation, and Yi was brought to colonial Korea for his trial.[73] In addition to Deng's hospital, it is said that there was a bookstore in Shanghai, run by Chen Guangguo, which also functioned as a place for book exchanges among anarchists and for contact and communication for all anarchists.[74]

In addition, Shanghai was where the Provisional Government of Korea was established in 1919, and served as the center of its activities until the Japanese invasion of the city in the 1930s. As Kim San stated, it was quite commonplace to see Korean exiles heading to Shanghai and working for and with the Provisional Government, sometimes turning to radical thinking and thus taking various anti-Japanese violent actions, independently or in tandem with the government or other radicals there.[75] The latter case was the Society of Taiwanese and Korean Comrades (*Taihan tongzhi hui*), organized in 1924 in the French Concession in Shanghai. There also was an anarchism-oriented journal published three times a month by the Equality Society (Pingshe), a radical society organized by Sichuanese anarchist Luo Hua (1899–?); Taiwanese radicals such as Peng Huaying, Lin Yaokun, and Zhang Xiuzhen; and Korean radicals such as Tak Mucho, Yeo Unhyeong, and Yun Jahyeong. Luo was the key figure who led the establishment of the society and the publication of its journal, *Equality* (*Pingping*), the goals of which were, among other things, the accomplishment of mutual aid of mankind and the opposition to proletarian dictatorship and the Russian Revolution. Carried in the journal, first published in April 1924, were the articles that contained its criticism of Japanese colonialism and its advocacy of Korean independence, and the writings of Chinese anarchists, for example, by Lu Jianbo. The significance of the publication of *Equality* is that, although not a Korean anarchist journal, it was the earlier product of the collaboration and joint publication activity in Shanghai of three East Asian radicals, including anarchists.[76]

By late 1924, Yi Jeonggyu had moved to Shanghai from Beijing and was hired there as an apprentice at a British-owned foundry, but soon was fired for his activities for a labor union and a labor school he helped to open. A year after he was reemployed by Shanghai Tramway Company, where he again attempted to organize a labor union. On May 30 of the year, Yi participated with his Taiwanese friends from Shanghai University, such as Wong Zesheng and Zhuang Hongshu, and Chinese anarchist Mao Yipo, in the general strike in the wake of the May 30th Movement in Shanghai. Possibly due to these activities, it seems Yi had to bear the hardships of life in Shanghai without a job or under Japanese surveillance. As a solution to the hardships in life and to get away from his extreme and dire situation, he began to translate many anarchist books and works for publication. It is unknown who the publisher was, but included in his translations for publication were, according to Yi, Kropotkin's *Law and Authority* and *Anarchist Morality*, and some pamphlets that contained the writings by Bakunin, Malatesta, and Elisée Reclus.[77]

One of the joint activities Shanghai-based Korean anarchists participated was the educational experiments of Chinese anarchists in Shanghai. It was unthinkable for them to do so without sharing their anarchist ideals with their Chinese counterparts. Lida College (Lida xueyuan) provides the first case in this regard. Lida College was established in Shanghai by Hunanese anarchist Kuang Husheng (1891–1933), and was operated for about ten years from the early 1920s until the Japanese attacked Shanghai in 1932.[78] As "the immediate precedent for Labor University in Shanghai" (see below), it became "an esteemed example for many of what an institution for alternative education could accomplish."[79] Its main offices were located at Jiangwan in Shanghai, where no anarchists were hired. However, the faculty at the Department of Rural Village Education (Nongcun jiaoyuke) of the senior middle school of Lida College were all anarchists. Wu Zhihui and Li Shizeng, two prominent GMD anarchists, had supported Lida College, because of which the funding for the college came also from the Department of Education in the GMD, and anarchists were hired to teach in the department. And it was since then that the department became a gathering place for all anarchists, because of which Yu Ja-myeong remembered Lida College as "a home [*bogeum jari*] for anarchists."[80]

Among Korean anarchists, Yu Ja-myeong was hired to teach agriculture and Japanese language in the department where students received an education that combined education and productive labor including poultry farming, beekeeping, and fruit growing.[81] Although similar to Shanghai Labor University in its educational goals and method, Lida College nevertheless was an independent and autonomous educational institution, free of the GMD influence. In fact it was quite the opposite to the Labor University in terms of its curricula; it was open to criticism of Sun Yat-sen's Three People's Principles (*Sanmin zhuyi*) and no worship of Sun was practiced among the faculty and students, therefore.[82] According to Korean sources, some Korean anarchists attended Lida College as a student. One of them was Yi Gyuchang (1913–2005), a son of Yi Hoeyeong and a member of the League of Korean Youth in South China (LKYSC, Namhwa hanin cheongnyeon yeonmaeng) in the 1930s, although he later recalled that he did not believe he learned much there.[83] Later, according to Jeong Hwaam, Lida College was to become a base of Korean anarchist activities in Shanghai, particularly the LKYSC (see chapter 4), at least until the Japanese occupation of Shanghai in 1937.[84]

Another educational experiment Korean anarchists joined was the opening and operation of Shanghai National Labor University (Shanghai guoli laodong daxue), although it is difficult to say to what extent they were involved in the establishment and operation of it. Shanghai Labor University was a national university funded by and under the control of the GMD. The university, often abbreviated as Laoda, was "a Chinese instance of socialist experiments with alternative education that have sought a means to the creation of socialism through the integration of labor and education."[85] Yi Jeonggyu, one of the Korean anarchists who participated as a "guest" in 1927, in Laoda's opening from the beginning, also recalls that the importance of Laoda needs to be understood in relation to the Movement for Self-Defensive Rural Communities in Quanzhou (hereafter Quanzhou Movement; see more on it below). According to Yi, Laoda as an educational institution was assigned its responsibility to teach students how to organize urban workers through theory and practice in order to raise them as new urban leaders, while the Quanzhou Movement was responsible for organizing and raising the ability of rural villagers in Quanzhou.[86]

Both Shen Zhongjiu (1887–1968), "one of the anarchists instrumental in founding"[87] Laoda, and Wu Kegang (1903–1999) invited the

Yi brothers to join them as guest members for the preparation of the opening of Laoda. Yi Jeonggyu accepted a faculty position there as lecturer but didn't have a chance to teach there, for he soon had to leave Laoda to join the Quanzhou Movement.[88] Among other Korean anarchists, Jeong Hwaam recalled that he also used to go to Laoda and studied "labor issues" there,[89] although it is unclear if he was enrolled as a student or just went there to study. Other than Korean anarchists, some Japanese anarchists also partook in Laoda. Iwasa Sakutarō (1879–1967) had arrived at Laoda in May 1927, and was opposed to the idea of establishing Laoda with the GMD funding, and so on, along with Chinese anarchist Lu Jianbo and Mao Yipo. Iwasa ultimately joined others, just like the Yi brothers and other Chinese anarchists, from the earlier stage of planning and founding Laoda.[90] According to Japanese anarchist Yamaga Taiji (1892–1970), Iwasa taught the French Revolution at Laoda, while Ishikawa Sanshirō (1876–1956) taught courses on socialism.[91] And Yamaga himself was in charge of teaching Esperanto, which was a requirement at Laoda.[92] Although it was a national university under the GMD's auspices, the faculty members there were international in terms of their origins and backgrounds; such important anarchists from Korea and Japan, let alone prominent Chinese anarchists, as well as some French anarchists were invited to join as its faculty. Yi Jeonggyu, a participant, remembers that Korean anarchists used Laoda as a place for communication among them and at the same time turned it into a base for their contact and communication with their Chinese comrades.[93] These functions and international aspects of Laoda apparently left an impression on a Korean anarchist that the "representative brains of Far Eastern anarchists" had gathered and taught at Laoda.[94]

With their increased interactions and growing relationships in Shanghai, the establishment of the Eastern Anarchist Federation (EAF) was planned. But the place and date of its establishment are still unclear, although, as I mentioned above, historian Kim Myeongseop contends that Huaguang Hospital was the venue of its inaugural meeting in 1928.[95] Neither is it clear if it was actually established and in operation. It is safe to say, nevertheless, that the establishment of the EAF with regional anarchists as its members had already long been discussed and even decided but possibly deferred until 1928, since the aforementioned tea meeting of anarchists in Beijing in 1922 at which the Yi brothers were present, due possibly to Ōsugi Sakae's murder in 1923 in the aftermath of the Kantō earthquake in Japan.[96]

The time of the EAF's formal establishment in 1928 coincided with the Laoda's opening and the Quanzhou movement, when Chinese anarchists maintained quite good relations with the GMD and received various supports as well from it, let alone that there were many Asian anarchists present in China, particularly in Shanghai. Unfortunately, very limited information about its inaugural meeting and no materials about the EAF are available for the current study.

From some fragmentary information we now know that Shin Chaeho represented Korean anarchists at the inaugural meeting of the EAF, per the request from Taiwanese anarchist Lin Bingwen.[97] Decided at the meeting were that the EAF's headquarters would be placed in Shanghai and that it would build a network of anarchist organizations by establishing connections with their counterparts in other countries in the region. Among other Korean anarchists, Yi Hoeyeong, unable to attend but congratulating the establishment of the EAF, sent in his writing titled "Korea's Independence Movement and the Movement of Anarchism," in which he explained that the genuine liberation movement in Korea was that of anarchism, and Koreans' anarchist movement itself was a genuine national liberation movement. And he proposed that all anarchist comrades present at the inaugural meeting support the Korean liberation movement actively. It is said that his writing was adopted as a resolution at this meeting. The EAF seemed to propagate the transnational idea that described its struggles as an effort "to establish an ideal society" that "does not remain partially or within a specific location." In other words, its struggles "must not be stopped by nationalist sentiment [*kokka deki kanjō*] and the idea of national borders [*kokkyō no seishin*] but rather transcend the national borders."[98]

The EAF published its journal *The East* (*Dongbang* in Korean, *Tōhō* in Japanese, and *Dongfang* in Chinese), and its first issue seemed to come out on August 20, 1928. In addition, *The East* was presumably published in three East Asian languages (Korean, Chinese, and Japanese),[99] although it is not clear if there were three different editions of the journal using each language respectively or if their languages were used in one edition of it. In celebration of its publication, Yi Jeonggyu also sent his painting in Chinese ink (*mukhwa*) to be carried in the journal's inaugural issue.[100] Although no issue of it is available today, it is said that Yi Jeonggyu also contributed to the first issue an article titled "To Inform Eastern Asian Anarchists" (*Dongbang mujeongbu juuija ege gohanda*), in which he called for solidarity and a rally of "Eastern Anarchists," as well as for the revolution in Korea. At the meeting Yi was also appointed in absentee to serve along with Akagawa, Mao Yipo, and Wang Shuren as secretaries of the EAF. After the conclusion of the meeting, Shin Chaeho returned to Beijing and conspired with Lin Bingwen, who was working at the time at Foreign Exchange Section of Beijing Postal Management Department, to raise funds for the EAF by printing 200 counterfeit foreign notes. Their plan was foiled, and they were arrested in Taiwan by Japanese police and died in prison.[101]

While collaborating with other anarchists for various joint activities, including the EAF and Laoda, Korean anarchists in Shanghai organized the Korean Anarchist Federation in China (KAFC, Jae jungguk mujeongbu gongsan juuija yeonmaeng) in 1928, and expanded their publication activities. First, the discontinued *Justice Newspaper* was revived as a journal and renamed the *Conquest* (*Talhwan*), named after Kropotkin's *The Conquest of Bread*, with its first issue published in Shanghai in June 1928.[102] The revived journal allegedly continued to publish its issue until 1930, when it stopped publishing after its seventh issue. Its first issue and a supplementary to it are available today. It is not clear why the latter was called supplementary to the former rather than its second issue. And the KAFC's Korean name could be translated as the Korean Anarcho-Communist Federation in China, but somehow in its official English name, which appeared on the first page of the journal's first issue, the word *Communist* was dropped. It could be because of the conflict and mutual rejection between anarchists and communists at the time, in addition to the GMD's anticommunist stance. According to a Korean source, although difficult to confirm its reliability, the renamed journal of the KAFC might have been published in three languages—Korean, Chinese, and Japanese. The same contemporary source also claimed that its issues used to be delivered to many in different places in the region to reach out to its readers in Korea, Japan, Taiwan, Manchuria, as well as to other places within China.[103]

Named after Kropotkin's book though, the title in Korean of the journalof the KAFC explains that the main goal of the KAFC and its publication was to "retake" (*talhwan*) Korea's independence that had been lost to the Japanese and give back their lost country, Korea, to "the oppressed class of the Korean masses." What it actually advocated, however, was, according to its first editorial in the first issue, not just the retaking of Korea's independence from Japan but also the retaking of "the civilization of a capitalist class and, then, return[ing] it to the whole masses" of the world. "By doing so," the editorial continues, "the capitalist society will be replaced with a new society founded upon the principles of freedom and equality that guarantee the autonomy of the producers." This was, in addition, "in order to retake the masses and their possession now under the control of a compulsory power, to restore the true life of human beings, and to provoke a spontaneous surge of the masses," for all of which the journal rejected the existence of government, including the "soviet government," capitalism and capitalist class, private property, and "power, no matter what rules and forms it has."[104] The character of the *Conquest* was revolutionary and radical in its nature and vision. Besides the goal, the first issue of the *Conquest*, published on June 1, 1928, placed two slogans on its cover page that read "Throw a Bomb to God" and "Eradicate All Kinds of Capitalism," and carried an article by Heuk-no (pseudonym, literally black slave) on the situation and hardships of Korean peasants in the Maritime Province of Siberia. Two Korean translations were included in it; one was of Kropotkin's *An Appeal to the Young*, and the other of anarcho-syndicalism. On the final page of its first issue, it introduced in English some Korean anarchist activities in both Korea and China.[105] Critiques of capitalism and the socioeconomic situation it had created were evident throughout the supplementary issue. According to the anonymous author of an article that appeared in the supplementary issue, titled "The Principles of Revolution and Retaking," the majority of the people in the contemporary society were not able to live a satisfactory and free life under the social conditions of the time. Pain and hardship had been rather added to their life and, at the same time, the state of oppressions and lack of freedom had increased, rendering "Revolution" a slogan for the twentieth century. Accordingly, revolution appeared as a hope for those who stood up against oppression and suppression, but it had "degenerated," "stagnated," and "corrupted" due to the lack of any concrete methods for the masses to realize the hope. This, the author of the article claimed, necessitated a righteous organization and strategies based on a principle, that is, spontaneous alliance, to "retake" freedom and the fettered rights and economic conditions from the capitalists and the rulers in whose hands power had been concentrated.[106]

The basic premise of the *Conquest*, that is, "direct revolution of the masses," was in accordance with the aforementioned Shin Chae-ho's 1923 "Declaration of the Korean Revolution." Yi Jeonggyu, using his pseudonym Ugwan and contributing his article to the supplementary issue, titled "The First Voice of '*The Conquest*,'" unequivocally explained that what the masses needed to retake was not only their fatherland but the conditions for their own survival and living, such as land, house, and freedom. For the substantial and conditional losses Yi encouraged the masses to retake what had been lost to both the Korean rulers and to Japanese. After a successful "retaking," the masses would become the owners of the country, which, according to Yi, was a condition for a new Korea that would turn out to be an anarchist-communist society.[107] Yi was making it clear that an anarchist revolution, to which he and other Korean anarchists had been devoted as of 1928, was embracing its social goal as well as the national goal of independence. Historian Oh Jang-Whan correctly argues that the general focus of the supplementary issue was not only on the retaking of political liberation of Korea but also on a "biological" liberation (i.e., physical survival) of human beings from social institutions such as regulations and order, and from the socioeconomic contradictions ubiquitous in the Korea society under capitalism.[108]

With two slogans on its front page, "Let's retake all the deprived freedom" and "Let every person become the owner of freedom we retake," the supplementary issue to the first issue also included an article, translated in Korean, by a seeming Russian anarchist named Pasarov. It is impossible to identify who this Russian-named anarchist was, for there is no further information available about the person. This alleged Russian anarchist asserted in the article that, since "a genuine communism does not come from the state" and "happiness does not come from exploitation," an ideal society be organized from the bottom up, drawing on the spontaneous alliance principle, and that the society maximize its guarantee of welfare for its all constituencies. Pasarov, therefore, came to conclude that the "nation-building movement" exemplified by the Soviet Union had been "nothing but a fulfillment of their [the communist vanguard's] capitalism that makes the state [their] puppet." Consequently, the Russian anarchist, argued, the social revolution led by a party of the few (i.e., the vanguards) in Soviet Russia ignored people's will and thus wouldn't be beneficial to the people.[109]

The Conquest is a good example that demonstrates Korean anarchists as of 1928 underscored a social revolution bent on anarchist principles and made it their ultimate goal, rather than just independence. It also indicates the transnational aspect of Korean anarchism in its understanding of Korea's colonial conditions not just as a national issue but rather as part of the world problem under capitalism. It is also transnational in term of its universal messages as well as the wide range of news and information it carried, in addition to its authorship. Besides *The Conquest*, according to historian Yi Horyong, there had been a Korean anarchist journal, published already in early 1920s Shanghai, called *News on Struggles* (*Tubo*), which carried the slogan on its cover page, "It is a sin to be submissive to compulsory power." It advocated the accomplishment of social revolution via direct action of the masses, Yi notes.[110]

The above-mentioned examples, among others, help us see a certain range of mutual inspirations and influences and measure the breadth and depth of Korean anarchists' writings and ideas, as well as interactions and relationships with Chinese and other anarchists in Shanghai. They also tell us about the transnational character of Korean anarchism in China, which began to form in the 1920s. It is, however, unlikely that the Chinese or other anarchists influence was decisive to the character of Korean anarchism in 1920s China or afterward. What historian Jo Sehyun posits is suggestive, though: the political positions of Chinese anarchists like Li Shizeng and Wu Zhihui had probably direct impact on the activities and ideas of Korean anarchists in China.[111] In other words, as in the cases of Yu Ja-myeong and Yu Rim,[112] their associations later with the Provisional Government of Korea in Shanghai seem to coincide with the idea of Wu and Li, who saw the revolution as an endless process and, as a result, saw the establishment of the republic in China as a progressive process.[113] It is revealing that Yu Rim, when he returned to Korea after Japan's surrender in August 1945, began to identify him as "one who favors an autonomous government" (*jayul jeongbu juuija*).[114] In this regard, it is noteworthy that, while China-based Korean anarchists were by and large affiliated later with the Provisional Government of Korea, their counterparts in Japan, as far as I know, did not develop any visible relationship with the government itself and rather severely criticized it at least until 1945 (see below), although the geographical distance between Japan and Shanghai, among others, must be taken into consideration for the absence of the relationship.

Korean anarchists in Shanghai seemed to expand and enhance their activities with other anarchists by establishing, either independently or jointly, various organizations and publishing journals, through which they experimented with anarchist ideals and fostered

Korea's independence. Their various activities in Shanghai with support and participation of the Chinese anarchists didn't last long, though, because of the GMD's anticommunist purge from which they too took refuge and Japan's invasion of Manchuria and north China at the arrival of a new decade.

Empowering Rural Villages through Education in Quanzhou

In addition to the above-mentioned Lida College and Laoda in Shanghai, Chinese anarchists also undertook some additional educational experiments in Quanzhou in Fujian Province to test a new kind of educational institution and theory, in which Korean anarchists, as well as Japanese anarchists, took part. They were Dawn Advanced Middle School (*Liming gaoji zhongxue*), established in 1929, and its sister school, Common People's Middle School (*Pingmin zhongxue*), established a year later in 1930, both of which were introduced in Quanzhou after the failure of the Quanzhou Movement, which intended to organize and raise the ability of rural villagers to enable them to defend their rural communities from local bandits and the communists. According to Yi Jeonggyu, the goal of the Quanzhou Movement for Self-Defensive Rural Communities was inseparable from that of Laoda, as the directions and goals of the two were all discussed together by the participating anarchist comrades at Laoda.[115]

Indeed, one of the most significant joint activities carried in the late 1920s together by Chinese, Korean, and Japanese anarchists was the Quanzhou Movement in the Province of Fujian, which was, just like Laoda, conducted under the banner of the GMD. Quanzhou had been called "a heaven of peace" (*shiwai taoyuan*: literally the Land of Peach Blossoms, meaning a utopia) for the Chinese anarchists from Sichuan, Hunan, and Guangdong Provinces, who took refuge there from the 1927 "party purification" (*qingdang*) movement of the GMD. In April 1927, the GMD under Chiang Kai-shek launched the movement after his April 12 military coup in Shanghai to brutally suppress and kill communists and their sympathizers in and outside the party, which concluded the GMD-CCP Alliance that had lasted since 1924. In the wake of the hunt for communists many anarchists had been arrested and accused of being communists or their sympathizers so that many of them had moved to Quanzhou to escape any possible arrest and execution by the GMD. In Quanzhou Chinese anarchist Qin Wangshan (1891–1970) in collaboration with Xu Zhuoran (1855–1930), who had sympathy with anarchist ideals, held a firm control of the area under the banner of the GMD, because of which anarchist refugees usually gathered and felt safe there.[116] Indeed Quanzhou and its vicinity were to remain as the largest, most active center of Chinese anarchist movement between the winter of 1926 and the spring of 1934.[117]

Qin Wangshan was the leading figure in the Quanzhou Movement, who had a favorable reputation in the area around Quanzhou and promised to gain the funding from overseas Chinese in the "south sea" (*nanyang*) to support the movement.[118] He also was the one who invited Korean and Japanese anarchists to join it. Yi Jeonggyu recalls that Liang Longguang (1907–?), on behalf of Qin, came to Shanghai in 1927 to invite Yi, who was at Laoda at that time to assist the opening of it as a "guest," as mentioned earlier. Liang had participated with Yi in the Shanghai General Strike in March 1927, and, since then, had become Yi's close comrade. Among Korean anarchists, Yi Jeonggyu, Yi Eulgyu, Yu Seo, and Yi Gihwan joined, and, among the Japanese, Iwasa Sakutarō, and Akagawa Haruki were invited to take part in the Quanzhou Movement. When invited to join it, at first Yi seemed reluctant to leave Laoda, but followed the decision to leave for Quanzhou, made by the "Five-Person Meeting" held in Iwasa Sakutarō's room at Lida College. Attendants at this meeting were Wu Kegang, Iwasa, Liang, and the Yi brothers, all of whom decided collectively that Yi and Liang would take responsibility in the proposed movement in Quanzhou to educate and organize rural youth there. Shortly thereafter, in June 1927, Yi with Liang left for Quanzhou in Fujian.[119]

The Quanzhou Movement's goal was to train and help the youth in rural villages in order for them to raise their ability to defend their own communities from local bandits (*tufei*) and the communists. Raising young anarchist leaders to realize anarchist ideals as a more distant goal and organizing self-defensive rural people's militia (*mintuan*) as an immediate concern, were, in other words, its two main goals.[120] The latter goal had its origins in the ideas of the Chinese Paris anarchists such as Li Shizeng and Wu Zhihui, who preferred a "people's militia" over a regular army on the ground that the latter would end up only serving the interests of those in power.[121] It was possible that the movement organizers received various supports from the GMD and used the GMD banner because of those GMD anarchists and their support. At the same time, the Korean anarchists themselves had had their own experience in an "autonomous village movement" in September 1923, when, as mentioned earlier, Yi Jeonggyu and Jeong Hwaam with Chen Weiguang, together attempted, but failed, to build an ideal rural village in Hunan.[122]

Hence, it was no wonder that Yi Jeonggyu took a leading position among the participants as an organizer of the Quanzhou Movement. At the same time he took a job as a faculty member of the Center for Training Propaganda Personnel at Jinjiang County (*Jinjiang xian xuanzhuan yuan yangchengsuo*) in Quanzhou, where rural youth were to be trained and educated to become "cadres" in the rural communities. Due mainly to Yi's and other Korean anarchists' active participations in the movement and the Center, a Korean anarchist remembers the experimental Quanzhou Movement basically as a Chinese-Korean joint project,[123] although also participated were some Japanese anarchists and there was the GMD behind it. Two other Korean anarchists, Yu Seo and Yi Gihwan, were also invited to join there to take responsibilities of training and teaching Chinese youth, respectively, in addition to Yi Jeonggyu who had already taught there from July 1927. Courses Yi Jeonggyu taught at the Center were on the history of social movement in the West, critiques of Communism, new politics, and organizing rural societies, while Yu taught courses on new economics, sociology, feudal society, and the analysis of capitalist society.[124]

The formal outcome of the Quanzhou Movement was the creation of the Agency for the Organizing and Training People's Militias in Quanzhou and Yongchun Counties (*Quanyong ershu mintuan pianlianchu*) under the GMD's auspices. Qin Wangshan directed the Agency. Yi Jeonggyu was appointed as its secretary, Yi Eulgyu as one of two heads of General Affairs Section, Yu Seo as a member of Propaganda and Education Section, and, finally, Yi Gihwan and Yu Jicheong as members of Training and Guidance Section. The objectives of the Agency reveal anarchists principles embedded in it: to achieve (1) a free and autonomous life, (2) a cooperative laboring life, and (3) a cooperative defensive life.[125] The Quanzhou Movement as an anarchist project ultimately failed in less than a year, due mainly to the lack of funds and the instable political situation in the Quanzhou area, as well as the GMD's order to dissolve it.[126]

Notable here is Iwasa Sakutarō's activities during his stay in Quanzhou for the Quanzhou Movement and educational experiment.

Apart from translating a book on the French Revolution into Japanese,[127] he also planned to establish a "Greater Alliance of East Asian Anarchists" (*Dongya wuzhengfu zhuyizhe datongmeng*) in Quanzhou, which he believed could form a revolutionary base for joint East Asian anarchist struggle against imperialism.[128] It is not clear how he planned to realize his scheme, but the idea itself was not novel, as it had already been suggested by Korean anarchist Yi Jeonggyu and Yu Seo. There is no further evidence if Yi, other than the EAF, had directly involved in any more regional organization with other anarchists, but in the case of Yu, there was consistency in his idea for the regional solidarity. In an article in the Chinese anarchist journal *Minzhong* (*People's Tocsin*), on December 15, 1926, Yu had called for the establishment in China of a Greater Alliance of East Asian Anarchists.[129] It is quite possible that Iwasa and Yu (and Yi), while in Quanzhou, discussed the possibility of establishing the alliance together.

In the same article, Yu presented a concrete reasoning to form the alliance of anarchists. Arguing that the first step toward anarchist revolution was to launch a movement to liberate colonies, Yu warned that there was a "mad wave" of patriotism among Korean, Indian, Filipino, Vietnamese, and Taiwanese anarchists. The anarchist movement "must not draw any distinctions among peoples (*minzu*)," so the "mad wave" posed a potential danger to it: it might end up a narrow nationalist movement whose aim was simply political independence. East Asian anarchists thus had a responsibility to "extinguish the mad wave of patriotism" sweeping the region. He advised that it was crucial for anarchists to unite, otherwise their righteous activities and efforts could be seriously undermined. However, Yu also maintained that Koreans still needed to overthrow Japanese imperialism (i.e., independence) prior to the achievement of a social revolution that transcended national boundaries.[130] As indicated, the EAF was formally established in 1928, possibly in response to Yu's above proposal in 1926 and Iwasa's effort in 1927 to realize it in China, after having been long delayed, probably since Ōsugi's murder in 1923.

The two schools in Quanzhou, Dawn Advanced Middle School and Common People's Middle School, were supervised by the same board of trustees, of which Qin Wangshan was chairperson.[131] The schools shared their teachers as well as their facilities and even their educational objectives, that is, to cultivate persons of ability through a "living education" (*shenghuo jiaoyu*), who were to be "revolutionary, scientific, socializing, laboring, and artistic." Introduced and then implemented for the objective was a "commune system" (*gongshezhi*) at Common People's Middle School, which integrated the faculty, students, and laborers (i.e., staff) into one unit; for example, the faculty and students resided, had meals, and even worked together. Just like at Laoda, the faculties at both schools too were international in their backgrounds. In addition to Chinese anarchists, there were Korean counterparts among the faculty, including Yu Ja-myeong, Yu Seo, Heo Yeolchu, Jang Sumin, and Kim Gyuseon, all of whom taught at either both or one of the schools. Yu Ja-myeong, for example, taught botany at Dawn Senior Middle School for a semester in 1929, in place of Chen Fanyu (1901–1941), who used to teach "social problems" and biology there. Yu soon left the school next January to teach at Lida College in Shanghai. Yu Seo and Heo also taught at Dawn Advanced Middle School.[132] Among other Korean anarchists, Sim Yongcheol is a graduate of Dawn Advanced Middle School and/or Common People's Middle School.[133] Besides Korean anarchists there were two Taiwanese faculty members at Dawn Advanced Middle School, Cai Xiaoqian and Zheng Yingbai, albeit it is not known what they taught and/or did at the school. Esperanto was an elective foreign language at Common People's Middle School and was taught by Japanese anarchist Yatabe Yūji , who used his Chinese name, Wu Shimin, there. Up to the early 1930s, the two schools were to serve as the centers of social movements in Quanzhou and as the important bases for anarchist projects in the area.[134] The two schools were closed after January 1934, when the "Fujian Incident" led by the Nineteenth Route Army under Chen Mingshu finally failed and subsequently the rule and control of the GMD under Chiang Kai-shek was consolidated in Fujian Province.[135]

Experimenting Place-Based Anarchism in Manchuria

Korean anarchists were not as active and organized in Manchuria as in north and south China. In addition to the harsh natural setting, Manchuria had long been notorious for the lack of political stability and social order and for the presence of antisocialist warlord, Zhang Zuolin (1873–1928) from 1916 to 1928, whose pro-Japanese and antisocialist stance never allowed any socialist activities and organizations. In many occasions Zhang indeed cooperated with the Japanese "in stamping out Korean resistance activities" in Manchuria.[136] In fact, the Japanese had long been interested in Manchuria to consolidate and perpetuate their interest there, because of which they were looking for an opportunity to intervene and send their troops, which they finally did in 1931 ("the Manchurian Incident" or "the September 18th Incident"). Despite these unfavorable and even dangerous environments, Manchuria had been one of the main destinations of Koreans who decided to leave their homes in Korea, especially after 1910, under the Japanese colonial rule. Hence, Korean anarchists in Manchuria needed to deal with this unique situation if they were to have any hold there. Many hardships and difficulties, both natural and man-made, that they encountered in Manchuria usually made their activities short-lived but somewhat unique.

Yi Hoeyeong was one of those who moved to Manchuria in 1910, and made Manchuria his first destination to escape the Japanese colonial rule in Korea. Yi came to Manchuria with his family and soon organized the Society for Cultivation and Study (*Gyeonghaksa*) and even set up a military school called the Newly Burgeoning School (*Sinheung hakgyo*) to make a preparation for independence activities. It was, of course, much before his conversion to anarchism in the early 1920s. After converting to anarchism later, Yi seemed to cherish his early experiences and efforts in Manchuria in the 1910s; he was arrested by Japanese police on his way back to Manchuria from Tianjin in November 1932, when he had become aware that all the anarchist activities had suffered suppression and thus collapsed in Manchuria with the murder of young anarchist Kim Jongjin in 1931. The leadership of Kim, who, it seems, had converted to anarchism as a result of Yi's role and influence, had been of paramount importance, as I will explain below, in organizing and leading the first anarchist organization in Manchuria, the League of Korean Anarchists in Manchuria (LKAM, *Jaeman joseon mujeongbu juuija yeonmaeng*), in the city of Hailin in northern Manchuria in July 21, 1929.[137]

Manchuria had been ceded without military conflicts to the GMD government under Chiang Kai-shek in 1928 by Zhang Xueliang (1898–2001), who had succeeded his father, Zhang Zuolin, as the new ruler and believed that the Japanese Kantō (or Guandong) Army had been responsible for his father's death in 1928. Zhang Xueliang maintained his anti-Japanese stance throughout the 1930s to 1940s. Anarchist activities in Manchuria had been minimal and sporadic under his father's reign but after his rule began in 1928, Korean anarchists became more active with the LKAM's establishment in 1929, possibly utilizing the anti-Japanese aura in Manchuria under the new militarist. Of significance was the outcome of the political change in Manchuria under which anarchists were provided with much space and psychological assistance for their activities, which was quite revealing in implications particularly because Korean anarchists, as well as independence activists, were not turned over often and easily to the Japanese police in Manchuria anymore. They must have felt relatively safer there, although the safety didn't last long.

The LKAM had a small group of anarchists as its members, including Kim Jongjin, Yu Rim, and Yi Eulgyu, who, per the request from Kim, came from south China, as leading figures who were joined later by Yi Dal (1910–1942), Eom Hyeongsun, Kim Yabong, Yi Ganghun (1903–2003), and so on. Not much information is available about the LKAM other than from a biography of Kim Jongjin written later by Yi Eulgyu, in which Yi details the origins, background, programs of the LKAM and how it was incorporated later into a much larger united-front-like organization, the United Society of All Korean People (USAKP, *Hanjok chong yeonhaphoe*),[138] which I will return to later. According to the biography, the LKAM was a unique anarchist organization in the sense that it was basically formed not to propagate anarchism or fight against Japanese colonialism for Korean independence, but primarily to deal with the economic issues pertinent to the survival of Korean migrant farmers in Manchuria; it was, in other words, a "cooperative [*hyeopryeok*] organization on the basis of economic communities," the eventual goal of which was to establish an autonomous rural organization in which the farmers as members were mutually aiding one another for their survival in the harsh natural environment of Manchuria. It was thus "a practical [*silcheonjeok*] organization" to deal with the livelihood of the Koreans in Manchuria, who numbered about two million at the time of its establishment in 1929. However practical it was, the LKAM's platform nevertheless reveals that it was indeed an anarchist organization with anarchist principles and goals. In the platform its defined goal was to realize a society of "no rule," in which human dignity and individual freedom were all completely ensured. In such a society, all individuals were expected to be socially equal and freely strive for their individual development through their own free will and free alliance based on the mutual aid idea. And finally all the individuals would strive to establish an economic order under which they could offer their labor for production according to their ability and then consume according to their needs.[139] While maintaining certain anarchist principles and ideals, the LKAM members accommodated the local needs for economic survival, which probably was a concern of theirs as well.

The LKAM was soon resolved and integrated into a new, larger organization in August 1929, just a month after its establishment in July. The new organization was the USAKP, a united, amalgamated organization between the LKAM and part of the nationalists in the New People's Government (*Sinminbu*) in northern Manchuria, led by General Kim Jwajin (1889–1930). The New People's Government was one of the three self-ruling Korean authorities in Manchuria, all of which as of 1929 functioned as sort of an autonomous administrative and military polity in their own respective jurisdiction in Manchuria. The other two were the "General Staff Headquarters" (*Cham-uibu*) near the region of mid-Yalu River on the Chinese side and the "Righteous Government" (*Jeong-uibu*) in Jilin and Fengtian Provinces. The amalgamation of the LKAM into the USAKP was made possible, according to a South Korean historian, due to the immediate threat of the communists in the jurisdiction of the New People's Government who thus was in need of anarchist principles to cope with the expanding influence of communism there.[140] The USAKP, however, didn't last long either, since the key figure of it, Kim Jwajin, who was elected as its chairperson in August 1929, was murdered in January 20, 1930 by Korean communists, which was followed by the murder of Kim Jongjin in July of the next year.

The USAKP has been highly evaluated by Korean anarchists as the embodiment of anarchist principles, because it seemed to have its own seeming territorial jurisdiction. As shown in its two goals to improve the economic and political status of Koreans in Manchuria and to concentrate their capacity on completing saving the nation through resisting Japan, strictly speaking, it was not an anarchist organization. It rather defined itself in its platform as "an autonomous, self-ruling, cooperative organization" that had its own distinctive jurisdiction, similar to its predecessor, the LKAM. In particular, the USAKP's plans for agricultural development, education, and military training within its jurisdiction, as well as for its representative system along with its administrative body, have all been praised as a reflection of the anarchist ideal of "a government without [compulsory] government" that assured the principles of no-rule, no-naked power, and no-exploitation.[141] It is unclear, though, whether the USAKP had a substantial chance to implement these or related principles, programs, or polices during the short span of its existence or just had them only planned on paper. Likewise, the USAKP immediately suffered financial difficulties after the loss of its chairperson, Kim Jwajin, and had another huge setback when Yi Eulgyu, one of the leading anarchists in it, was arrested in September 1930 by Japanese police and was subsequently sent back to Korea for his trial. No matter how we assess the USAKP and its programs that were obviously put forward by anarchists, it is undoubtedly clear that it gave an opportunity for the Korean anarchists to materialize their anarchist principles through the programs of the polity with its own jurisdiction, which they created with the anticommunist nationalists like General Kim.[142]

What is revealing is that the Korean anarchists in the LKAM and its successor, the USAKP, were organized in response to and in consideration of the general environment surrounding the life of Koreans in Manchuria, besides the communist factor. Their programs demonstrate, although possibly only on paper, a place-based approach to meet the demands and needs of the Korean migrants and their hardships in their settlement and life there. Going beyond both the national and anarchist goals, anarchists in Manchuria took up the issue of economic survival as their priority in the harsh land. The immediate outcome of it was their corresponding place-based programs and plans, rather than a grand plan and program for independence struggle or a future-oriented anarchist society. What was more important than announcing the distant goal of retaking Korea's independence or realizing an anarchist society after independence, in other words, was, I suspect, meeting the immediate needs of migrant Koreans there, who usually first experienced hardships and difficulties in settling down in Manchuria and then suffered economic exploitations by both Chinese landlords and other Korean authorities who collected taxes and even confiscated their annual agricultural yields, and so forth in the name of supporting their independence activity. For the protection of the Korean migrants, the USAKP, for example, introduced programs to assist their smooth transition to settlement and their cultivation of land, which included collectivization of production and collective sale of their produce. Also, a Safety Unit (*Chiandae*) as well as an Anti-Japanese Guerilla Unit were planned to be organized for their further protection from both the local bandits and the Japanese.[143]

These place-based programs, whether implemented or just planned, point to the diverse approaches Korean anarchists adopted in their movement in Manchuria, where they had to deal with many unexpected and unfavorable environments for their activities and ideals, not to mention for their survival. And the USAKP was a product of their first cooperation with nationalists in implementing their anarchist ideals and thus serves as a predecessor of the national front they would form in the late 1930s, with nationalists in the name of national liberation during China's War of Resistance against Japan. The major difference between the 1938 national front and the one in Manchuria in 1929 was that the latter was formed at once to save the life of Korean migrant workers, not the nation itself. Due to the lack of further information about the Manchurian activities of Korean anarchists, it is extremely difficult to come to a concrete conclusion that their programs were of cardinal significance in terms of their implications to the later activities and characteristics of Korean anarchism. It is still possible to say, nevertheless, that their short-lived activities and programs in Manchuria were evidence of the role played by their location in practicing their anarchist ideals through their place-based accommodation. In short, they didn't seem to have any strong and fixed ideological attachments but rather were flexible in handling local needs and conditions, out of which the collaboration with the nationalists was realized. In Manchuria, Korean anarchists were willing to work together with nationalists as long as the latter considered and adopted anarchist principles in their response to the demands and needs of Korean migrants there. In doing so Korean anarchists must have prioritized economic survival and postponed their activities for independence and an anarchist society to the near future, probably after independence, in order to tackle the immanent daily life-and-death situation of the Koreans in Manchuria, eventually expecting the latter's forthcoming support of their anarchist ideals.

Many Korean anarchists considered and accepted anarchism first in Beijing in the early 1920s for their struggle to regain independence with the help and support from many Chinese anarchists there, influential among whom were the Chinese Paris (later GMD) anarchists like Li Shizeng, Wu Zhihui, and Cai Yuanpei, as well as Eroshenko and other Asian anarchists they encountered in the capital city of China. If they accepted anarchism via other anarchists in Beijing and solicited support from them for their independence activities, Korean anarchists began their activities, both organizational and publication-related, more actively in Shanghai where they enjoyed relative freedom to do so, in particular when the National Revolution of China under the First United Front between the GMD and the

CCP was successful through the military campaign from Guangzhou beginning in 1926, and sweeping south and central China in 1926–27. Korean anarchists in China seemed to have a brief heyday in 1927 and 1928 when they participated in Laoda in Shanghai and the Quanzhou Movement and established their new anarchist organization, KAF, with its auxiliary journal, *The Conquest*. During that period they continued to strengthen their close relationship with many Chinese and Japanese anarchists for educational and rural village projects. The favorable condition and political climate under the victorious National Revolution of China paved the way for the Korean anarchists to revive their organization and their activities, although short-lived, and they had to prove no connections with communists to survive the GMD's "party purification."

Korean anarchists in China took active part in the transnational anarchist organization, the EAF, which was a culmination of their transnational relationship with regional anarchists in the 1920s, although it is unclear what kind of concrete activities or projects it pursued, in particular across the national boundaries. After the general political environment in China was reversed, as the GMD declined to support further and sponsor various anarchist projects, among which Laoda and the Quanzhou Movement were of most significance, Korean anarchists as exiles in China had to endure difficult years ahead without their major sponsors, Chinese anarchists. As a result, their activities after 1928 became sporadic and were mainly concentrated in Quanzhou, where many Chinese and other anarchists still took refuge away from the GMD's internal political cleavages. There they focused on the educational projects such as the two schools in Quanzhou to breed rural leaders of the next generation. The political environment of China was fundamentally shaken later by the Japanese invasion of Manchuria and later north/central China, beginning on September 18, 1931. Until then Korean anarchists were to remain silent, inactive, or, it seems, wander around, considering a new deadlock-breaking direction of their activities for both national and transnational goals. During the difficult years, Manchuria could have served them as a location where they expected and enjoyed a brief implementation of their anarchist principles through a polity with substantial authorities over Korean migrant farmers and their lands, as exemplified in the programs of the USAKP.

In sum, it is possible to say that the activities and projects Korean anarchists in China took part in and/or initiated in the 1920s were basically part of much broader regional anarchist movements and/ or regional history, of which they themselves were a product. At the same time there were some signs of a Koreanized practice of anarchism during the 1920s. Korean anarchists in China seemed to be forward-looking in their attitude and never believed that Korea's independence was doomed to never come to fruition, no matter what happened to them.

CHAPTER 2

The Wind of Anarchism in Japan

Becoming Anarchist in Tokyo

As early as the 1890s, in the eyes of the Westerners Japan was "a shining beacon of enlightenment," and "for other Asians" "a mecca of progress"[1] toward modernity. Since then Tokyo had served Asian students and radicals as "a mecca of progress" not only as "an exciting place" as the seat of Japanese government, "but also [as] the center of the economic, cultural, and intellectual life of Japan," which was "seeth[ing] with liberal and radical ideas."[2] There, Japanese readers of various radical publications and presses were usually able to "obtain the news and documents of world socialism only weeks, sometimes days, after the events,"[3] and so were all Asian students/radicals in Tokyo, including Koreans. Naturally, Tokyo emerged as a breeding place for many kinds of radicals. Even in the 1930s, Tokyo was still called "the Library on Marxism in the East" (*makesi zhuyi dongfang tushuguan*) because of the availability of the news and information about various types of socialisms.[4]

Japanese radicals, often based on racial unity as Asians, also supported the anti-Western struggles of other Asians who were usually marked by radical and nationalist ideas.[5] It was no wonder that "Tokyo in 1908" was "a haven" even for Muslim activists from West Asia, who were "seeking collaboration with Japan against Western powers."[6] To many Asians, Tokyo was a symbol of both Asian racial unity against the West and their progress for modernity, both physical and intellectual. On the other hand, in Tokyo many Asians found Japan's expansionist Asianism unacceptable, and thus realized the necessity to promote universal humanism through "alliance and cooperation over knowledge" among Asians in regard to Japan's version of Asianism.[7]

Since the turn of the twentieth century, Korean students had chosen Japan, more specifically Tokyo, as their study abroad place for three primary reasons. First, Tokyo had already been known to Korean students as a location where they could satisfy their intellectual curiosity and learn the most up-to-date new, modern knowledge, due to Japan's emergence as a power and the availability of higher education there. To many Korean students in the early twentieth century, Tokyo indeed served as "the source in the East [*dongyang*] of importing the Western culture," taking the leadership role in assisting the development of the "poor" Korean academic and intellectual circles.[8] An example of this kind of observation can be further found in the words of An Jaehong (1891–1965), one of the leaders of the New Branch Society (*Sin-ganhoe*), a united-front organization between the socialists and the nationalists in the late 1920s in colonial Korea, and an influential political leader immediately after 1945 in South Korea. An recalled in 1935 that "Tokyo was a heaven in our daydream" in the 1910s, whereas "Seoul was a hell in reality."[9]

Second, just like Chinese students,[10] Korean students understood the obvious advantages of studying abroad in Japan, such as the geographical proximity and cultural affinities between Korea and Japan. Study-abroad in Japan would allow them to save on travel and living expenses and to settle down in Japan almost immediately without much culture shock. The latter was particularly the case in the 1910s to '20s, because Korea had become a Japanese colony in 1910. What Kim San explained in the 1930s is revealing in this regard. According to him, Korean students had gone to Tokyo in the 1910s and '20s, where schools were "liberal" and offered "intellectual excitement," especially after the end of World War I, which was not available in colonial Korea because "no colleges existed at home."[11]

In other words, third, Korean students since 1910, as a colonized people, didn't have the option to choose where to study abroad, but had to go to Tokyo, for it was the only place that was allowed; further, no higher education was available in colonial Korea at least until 1924, when Keijō Imperial University finally opened in Keijō (Seoul). As a result, the number of Korean students in Japan reached about 500 or 600 in 1918.[12]

The political climate of 1910s Japan affected Korean students studying abroad in Tokyo. Radicalism in Japan had been in a state of "winter hibernation," since Kōtoku Shūsui's execution in 1911, and in the 1910s, students were usually exposed to and therefore possessed liberal ideas of "the Western bourgeois class" rather than "radical ideas"; thus, they saw the role of the state as "decisive in solving social problems"[13] prevalent in then-Japan. When the "winter period" of Japanese socialism ended in 1918,[14] which corresponded to the increasing number of Korean students in Japan, they were to contact radical ideas more often and easily than before. In addition, Korean students studying abroad in 1910s Japan came mostly from wealthy families, while those from the late 1910s and 1920s were basically "poor work-study" (*gohak*) students, which may also explain why there were more radicalized Korean students in 1920s Tokyo.

It was under the political and intellectual environments of Tokyo that a Korean reception of anarchism was made there, almost in the same way that was the case of their Chinese counterparts who also came to Tokyo as study-abroad students since the 1900s and were radicalized.[15] It is well known that the Chinese Tokyo anarchists became anarchist through exposure to and associations/interactions with early Japanese socialists and anarchists, including reading their books on socialism and anarchism that were readily and abundantly available in Tokyo at the time, both in original text and/or in Japanese translation.[16] And in Tokyo, many of the Korean students too developed interest in socialism and were radicalized accordingly. For example, Yi Jeonggyu was studying abroad in Tokyo in the 1910s, as a student in the Economics Department at Keiō University, where he was exposed to socialist ideas in the wake of developing his national consciousness between 1918 and 1919, similar to the experience of many Korean other students in Tokyo around that time.[17]

As historian Park Chan Seung posits, the United States and Japan are two major countries that have played a significant role even until today in breeding modern Korean intellectuals and their "modern ideas," including radicalism. Study abroad in the two countries, in other words, Park notes, has played the most significant role in the formation of modern Korean intellectuals and their academic circles,[18] as well as, I may add, that of radicals and their radicalism, particularly in the case of Japan. Suffice to say that, as historian Im Kyeongseok notes, early Korean socialists were born out of the "wind" blowing from two places, one "from the East [i.e., Japan], the other the north [i.e., Eastern Siberia, including Vladivostok]."[19] Many Korean radical students certainly responded to the blowing anarchist wind in Japan, especially Tokyo.

It must be noted here that Korean students, unlike Chinese students, often had different experiences and a radicalizing process in Tokyo, when they arrived there as work-study students in the 1920s. The difference in experiences and process attests to the fact that Koreans were a colonized people of Japan. It was a sense or realization of their being in the colonizer's country, which was commonly experienced and shared by Koreans based on the treatments they usually received from their Japanese colonizers once they arrived in Japan. Not only was Japanese national discrimination, but also social discrimination they witnessed and even encountered everyday against them, because they were mostly "poor work-study students" (*gohaksaeng*). The social discrimination didn't just come from the Japanese, but also from their wealthy compatriots as well, according to anarchist Yang Sanggi, who remembers the mistreatment of Koreans by the members of the Mutual Love Society (Sang-ae hoe), an organization run in the 1920s by a group of Koreans who worked in Tokyo for the Japanese. The society was notorious for its exploitation and "bullying" of other Korean workers who were sent by it to work for Japanese companies and factories in Japan, but as it turned out, they ended up often being wounded, disabled, and even dead without being fully paid for their work.[20] What awaited Koreans in Japan, in short, were two kinds of discriminations, national and social. As a matter of fact, their experiences as work-study students helped them gradually develop their social consciousness as a poor and exploited class under capitalism worldwide in addition to national consciousness as a colonized people.

Hence, the students were frequently introduced to Japanese labor activists or Korean organizations by those who had come from their hometown in Korea and had already formed place-based networks in Tokyo. Students were often grouped according to their native province, hometown, and/or even schools in Korea. Their placed-based networks and/or alma mater usually played an important role in their selection of an organization or in enticing them to a particular radical group. The number of "poor work-study students" continued to increase in the 1920s, particularly as the decade approached its end. Unlike those Korean students in Japan in the 1910s, they had to earn an education and a living at the same time, earning money during the daytime and attending school at night. Almost a half of the Korean students in Tokyo in 1925 were allegedly the "poor work-study students," who increasingly relied on labor for their school tuition and even living, such as newspaper delivery and/or peddling. No wonder, therefore, that, while working, they frequently got in touch with Japanese labor activists and organizations, let alone socialists, including anarchists. Sometimes they swiftly organized themselves and began their own labor movement. An example was the Society of Like-Minded Work-Study Students in Tokyo (Tōkyō kugaksei dōyūkai), organized in 1921 by work-study students who had been radicalized and interacted with and attended the gatherings of Japanese socialists.[21] Among the Japanese radical groups and societies, including anarchist and communist ones, in the 1910s to early 1920s, with which Koreans were associated or affiliated, were the New Comers Society (Shinjinkai), the Awakened People Society (Gyōminkai), the Free People's Federation (Jiyūjin renmei), the Socialist Alliance (Shakaishūgi dōmei), and the Cosmo Club (Kosumo gurabu).

The combination of national and class consciousness was a visible complex, ubiquitous phenomenon among Korean students in 1920s Tokyo, which was the main force that gave rise to Korean anarchist movement in Japan. Two kinds of discrimination they received drew them to Japanese radicals and socialists for assistance and consultation at first, and then for the common cause of social justice, although their nationalist aspirations for Korea's independence from Japan never got debilitated. This explains why the Japanese authorities initially labeled and categorized Korean anarchists and their activities in Japan broadly as "nationalistic,"[22] rather than just as radical or socialist. The Japanese police report on Koreans in Japan, dated December 1926, still reconfirmed their initial evaluation of Korean radicals as being nationalistic, explaining the increasing tendency among Koreans to add socialism to their nationalism.[23] The sense of social justice as well as anticolonialism (i.e., national consciousness) Korean anarchists deeply felt was shared with Japanese anarchists, and by the 1930s convinced the former that the key to "our liberation is anarchism."[24]

Evidence tells us that anarchist ideas had already been known to many Korean radicals and students studying abroad in Japan, since the beginning of the twentieth century, although their actual reception of anarchism was also prompted mainly around the time during and after World War I, especially after the March First Movement in colonial Korea. For example, the *Light of Learning* (*Hak ji gwang*), a journal of the Fraternal Society of Korean Students in Tokyo, Japan (Zai nihon tōkyō chōsen ryugaksei gakuyu kai), published in Korean beginning on April 2, 1914, carried articles written by Korean study-abroad students in Tokyo, which advocated direct actions of tenant peasants as a way for their survival from poverty and hardships. Also included in the journal were such anarchism-oriented or -inspired articles as "On Mutual Aid" ("Sangjo ron") by Choe Seungman and "A Transformation of 'Self'" ("Jagi ui gaejo"), both of which introduced and contained anarchist ideas.[25] It is quite obvious that anarchism was broadly discussed by Korean students in 1910s Tokyo, but was not yet elevated to a leading idea and guiding principle for their struggle and movement against Japanese colonialism for the retaking of Korea's independence. In the 1910s, their interest in anarchism was more or less a product of their intellectual curiosity, in particular in relation to Kropotkin's mutual aid, when they seemed to be disappointed with the mainstream ideas of Western civilization, such as competition and the survival of the fittest, particularly after World War I. However, it must be noted here that various Korean students' fraternal organizations in Japan were burgeoning in the 1910s, not just for the promotion of their fraternal relationship and student life but gradually also for equipping and preparing themselves for anti-Japanese national consciousness.[26] According to a Korean historian, as early as 1913 Na Gyeongseok (1890–1959) and Jeong Taesin converted to anarchism and accepted syndicalism as well after interacting with Ōsugi Sakae, Yokota Shōjirō, and Hasegawa Ichimatsu.[27]

Many kinds of publications on radicalism were also readily available in Tokyo for Korean students and radicals. Once they arrived in Tokyo, Korean students were to get intellectually excited by the abundance of information about various modern, radical ideas and the opportunities they had for interactions with Japanese radicals. Books on socialism were abundant and classes at school were taught on the subject of radical ideas, sometimes by radical scholars. They could acquire books and newspapers on anarchism at school, bookstores, and even newsstands on the street. Their intellectual thirst for the origins of social and national discriminations was therefore usually quenched immediately and, as a result, they ended up accepting socialism and becoming radicals in Tokyo, which was commonplace among almost all Korean youth in early 1920s Tokyo. This intellectual phenomenon was even described as catching naturally the common "measles" for the students in Tokyo.[28] Jo Bong-am (1895–1959), enrolled in the Department of Political Economy at Chūo University in Tokyo, came to realize in 1921 that he was "indulged in the books" he had come by in Tokyo. And he realized that they were in quality "good books" he had never known of before, and, as a result, for the first time in his life he read many of them thoroughly, as if, he thought, he would not be able to do so again. Through the readings, he became first aware of "the robber-like invasion of Japanese imperialism" on Korea, and then realized how Japan had possibly exploited the national resources of Korea. In addition, he was also able to understand why Korea had been under the oppression of Japanese imperialism, and had undergone many other difficulties such as the problem of poverty. After reading those books available in Tokyo, Jo was gradually and ultimately transformed into a socialist who was determined to strive for Korea's independence, but at the same time dedicate himself to transforming Korea into a country good enough to have all people live well and freely. In other words, he found himself drawn into the maelstrom of radical thoughts through the readings that were taking place at the time in the Japanese circle of thoughts. Jo was thus specifically introduced to anarchism, syndicalism, social democracy, nihilism, and Marxism. While in the vortex, Jo eventually made a decision to "study socialism, become a socialist, and join socialist movement."[29]

It is revealing that Jo in fact was initially drawn to anarchism, which was most popular in Tokyo at the time, and in November 1921 joined Bak Yeol, Kim Yaksu, and Kim Saguk in organizing the Black Wave Society (Heukdo hoe or Kokutō kai), the first anarchism-oriented Korean organization in 1920s Tokyo; he initially accepted anarchism to make "Resisting Japan" (*hang-il*) his lifetime goal. Key to his conversion to anarchism were the books on social issues, which geared him toward launching a social revolution of his own, not just political independence of Korea. And no Korean students in Tokyo, he recalls, were able to keep distance from the maelstrom of radical thoughts that was sweeping through Japan at the time.[30] Many Korean students like Jo might have been attracted to going to Tokyo for an opportunity for higher education, but what Tokyo offered them was a "broadly defined free [intellectual] space" that often radicalized them. Such space was hardly imaginable at the time for them in their own country.[31] Tokyo certainly was a place where many Korean students felt jolted intellectually.

The next case further demonstrates the particular intellectual milieu Korean study-abroad/work-study students encountered in Tokyo. Choe Gapryong (1904–2003) came to Tokyo via Shimonoseki in December 1921,[32] and was joined in Tokyo later by two other work-study students, Yi Honggeun (1907–?) and Han Won-yeol. The three students rented a room together and soon organized a book-reading society of their own, while selling the Japanese food *nattō* or delivering milk to earn money for their education and living. In the meantime Choe realized that reading books on socialism in the book-reading society was awakening him to take the first step toward "social movement" (sic). Among the books on socialism he read with the society, Choe found Ōsugi Sakae's *A Heart Seeking Justice* (*Seigi o motomeru kokoro*), of most interest and was impressed especially by a phrase in it that read "the liberation of workers is the responsibility of workers themselves."[33] Choe was to return to Korea later and became a leader of anarchist movement in colonial Korea, particularly in industrializing northern Korea under Japanese colonial government. Yi Honggeun, one of Choe's roommates, came to Tokyo in 1924, but had already been exposed in Korea to books on socialism in Japanese, and so had a "good understanding" of anarchist theories;[34] Yi had already read the same and some other books by Ōsugi, in addition to some translated works of Kropotkin, for example, on mutual aid. In other words, he had already been attracted to Ōsugi's "exciting" and "to-the-point" writings, as he recalls. Therefore, once he arrived in Tokyo, Yi immediately looked for Japanese anarchists and their activities, and soon decided to join their anarchist movement.[35] Yi Honggeun was to be active both in Tokyo and colonial Korea, as he would become a member or organizer of many Korean anarchist organizations such as the Black Friends Society (Kokutomo kai) and the Union of Korean Free Labor (Chōsen jiyū rōdō kumiai), established on February 3, 1927 in Tokyo, and in colonial Korea the Gwanseo Black Friends Society (Gwanseo heuk-u hoe) in 1927, the Federation of Korean Communist-Anarchists (Joseon gongsan mujeongbu juuija yeonmaeng) in 1929, and the Wonsan General Labor Union (Wonsan ilban nodong johap).

Just like Choe and Yi, who converted to anarchism through their readings of Ōsugi Sakae's works, Won Simchang (1906–1971) also became an anarchist in Tokyo after reading Ōsugi's works as well as Kropotkin's *The Conquest of Bread* probably in Japanese translation. The latter's idea on mutual aid was of particular interest to him. In the case of Baek Jeonggi (1896–1943), he read Kōtoku Shūsui's *Modern Anarchists* (*Gindai museifu shugisha*) and Ōsugi's works, as well as Kropotkin's works on mutual aid and his *The Conquest of Bread*.[36] Won and Baek had converted to anarchism in Japan but later in the 1930s became active in China in such anarchist groups as the Black Terror Party (BTP) and the League of Korean Youth in South China (LKYSC). In addition, Choe Jungheon, a former member of the Dongheung (Tōko) Korean Labor League (Tōko chōsen rōdō renmei), a Korean anarchist-led labor union, established in September 1926,[37] recalls that he was indulged in reading Ōsugi's works, which, according to him, paved the way for him to be an anarchist. Yi Yongjun (1905–?), who was a member of two anarchist organizations later in early 1930s China, the LKYSC and the Alliance to Save the Nation through Anti-Japan (Hang-il guguk yeonmaeng), offers another good example. Yi was drawn to anarchism through his readings of Ōsugi Sakae's translations of Kropotkin's works, among which *An Appeal to the Young* particularly impressed him in regard to anarchism.[38]

As Thomas A. Stanley suggests, Ōsugi, for sure, had "great impact on a wider audience,"[39] and Korean anarchists certainly were in the audience in the 1920s. Besides his "impact," there was a practical reason for Ōsugi's popularity among Koran anarchists because of his anti-Japanese government and anticolonial stance. For example, Ōsugi gave a special talk at a gathering in Kanda District of Tokyo before the audience from China, Taiwan, Russia, and Korea to criticize the colonial policies of the Government-General in colonial Korea.[40] He even supported Korea's independence as he hurrahed (*banzai*) three times for Korea's independence at a reception held to welcome Yeo Unhyeong (1888–1947), who came to Japan as an official representative of the Korean Provisional Government in Shanghai at the invitation of the Japanese authorities.[41] Besides the works by Ōsugi and Kropotkin, Japanese anarchist newspapers and magazines such as *Labor Movement* (*Rōdō undō*), *Spontaneous Alliance* (*Jiyū rengō*), *Tenant Farmers* (*Kōsakunin*), and *Black Youth* (*Kokushoku seinen*) were all easily and mostly available and accessible at the bookstores in the area called Jimbocho in Tokyo. Anarchist books were available at the night market on Jimbocho as well, where Choe Gapryong bought another Ōsugi's book titled *The Philosophy of Labor Movement* (*Rōdō undo no tetsugaku*), which, according to him, changed his view of life for good.[42]

In some cases Korean students were aware of the national question of Korea being a colony of Japan even before their arrival in Tokyo. On his way to Tokyo for study abroad, for example, Bak Giseong (1907–1991) already decided to "save my country with my strength." It was before his arrival in Tokyo. What happened was that on his way to Tokyo Bak heard from a Korean student of his age, who was returning to a school in Tokyo, about the indescribable pressure and treatment Korean students in Tokyo had been receiving from the Japanese, which made Bak become more nationalistic. What made Bak more so was his own experience in Tokyo after arrival, when he himself received discriminatory treatments from Japanese. He increasingly believed that the retaking of his country from the Japanese was more urgent than his study in Tokyo, thus deciding not to go to a college in Tokyo and rather to join a Korean anarchist group.[43] In his conversion to anarchism in Tokyo, what seemed to be decisive, besides his realization of such discrimination, was not his direct interaction with Japanese anarchists but rather his association with Korean anarchists who had already been in Tokyo. When Bak arrived in Tokyo, he stayed at a place called the Korea Residence (Gyerim jang) in the Nagano District, where Korean students were provided things and information necessary for their self-reliant life in Tokyo. It was there that he met and interacted with some Korean anarchists like Song Jiha, Yi Jihwal, Jeong Chanjin, and Na Wolhwan (1912–1942).[44] Bak subsequently organized the League of Free Youth (Jiyū seinen renmei) in Tokyo with Jeong and Hong Yeong-u. Bak was one of the Korean anarchists who converted to anarchism in Tokyo in the 1920s, but moved to Shanghai in the early 1930s, where he joined the LKYSC and later in the late 1930s organized with Na Wolhwan the Warfront Operation Unit of Korean Youth (see chapter 4). Finally, the case of Im Bongsun (1897–1966) tells us that Bak's experience in becoming an anarchist was quite commonplace among Korean students in Tokyo. Im had attended many meetings of Koreans in Tokyo, including religious worship services at YMCA, which were held for Koreans in Japan in Kanda District in Tokyo. There, he recalls, he was able to meet with many Korean radicals and gradually became sympathetic with socialist ideas.[45]

To sum up, Korean students in search of higher education had to come to Tokyo where they usually were radicalized and accepted anarchism through their realization of both national and social discriminations, which they experienced by themselves as both a colonized people and "poor work-study students." Their radicalization and conversion to anarchism took place in many cases through their readings of the works by Japanese anarchists. Most influential on them was Ōsugi Sakae and his works, as well as Kropotkin's. Of course, some Korean anarchists turned to anarchism through their associations with their radical compatriots in Tokyo. Their radicalization in Tokyo was not surprising because Tokyo had already played an important role as "a mecca of progress" since the turn of the twentieth century in breeding and connecting Asian radicals, and thus by the early 1920s had become a node of the network of radicals in the region as well as a center of radical activities of Japanese radicals, albeit they always suffered from the Japanese police surveillance and continuous suppression. Tokyo was an unlikely center of Korean anarchist movement. Korean anarchists now were ready to organize themselves and propagate anarchism for the cause of both national and social liberation. To do so, however, the support and sponsorship from their Japanese counterparts were of crucial necessity, as their activities, both organizational and publication, were under the much tighter Japanese surveillance and were therefore limited and vulnerable in Tokyo.[46] If not only for their survival, of utmost necessity to them were their close and intimate relationships and interactions with Japanese anarchists, to which now I turn below.

Propagating Anarchism in Tokyo

It was from the early 1920s that the first Korean anarchist organization and its journal appeared in Tokyo. The Black Wave Society (Heukdo hoe or Kokutō kai) was organized in Tokyo in November 1921. The society has been usually regarded as the first Korean anarchist organization in Japan; but it was not an anarchist society per se, as it had diverse Korean radicals in their ideological orientation, most of whom were study-abroad students including work-study students and workers. Its total members numbered about thirty to thirty-five.[47] It was established under the sponsorship of Japanese anarchists such as Ōsugi Sakae, Iwasa Sakutarō, Sakai Toshihiko (1870–1933), and Takatsu Seido (1893–1974).[48] Bak Yeol (1902–1974) was a central figure in this society and was the editor-in-chief and publisher of its journal *Black Wave* (*Kokutō*), published in Japanese from July 10, 1922. Bak was a prominent Korean anarchist in Japan, active in the early 1920s, and was later arrested by Japanese police along with his Japanese lover and comrade, Kaneko Fumiko (1903–1926), in the wake of the Greater

Kantō Earthquake in 1923, for their "plot" to assassinate the Japanese emperor, which was fabricated by the Japanese police.

Bak Yeol came to Tokyo in October 1919, and was also a poor work-study student who delivered newspaper at the dawn. He had been in and out of many organizations: he had joined the Society of Like-Minded Korean Poor Work Study Students (Chōsen kugaksei dōyūkai),[49] and organized with other students the Righteous Deed Group (Gikyo dan), which was renamed the Iron Righteous Group (Tekkan dan) and again the Bloody Righteous Group (Kekken dan). Bak also used to visit Mochizuki Katsura (1887–1975) at his home where he met Ōsugi and Yamagawa Hitoshi (1880–1958). In particular, Bak seemed to convert to anarchism through his relations with Ōsugi, which leaves an impression that in many aspects such as personality and behavior, Bak was almost a replica of Ōsugi; every bit as audacious as the latter.[50] In fact, Ōsugi's works deeply convinced Bak at first that the path to socialism lay in labor movement.[51] Given Bak's prison writings, however, what made Bak different from Ōsugi was his nationalist aspiration, which made him underline the threat and oppression of Japan over Koreans as much more serious and immanent than imperialism of the white race.[52] Bak's anarchism is usually characterized as his nationalist, individualist understanding of it and a nihilist attitude toward the self, as well as his negation of the state as a "major exploitive company" that exploited human bodies, lives, properties, and even freedom as an organized gangster group. To him, the military and police were equal to the state itself, the latter being unable to exist without the former two. He obviously was opposed to the Japanese emperorship. In addition, he was a believer in direct action, as he thought it was the necessary source for the masses to grasp the power and at the same time for social revolution.[53] Other than Ōsugi, Bak's various meetings with Iwasa Sakutarō,[54] a "pure anarchist" in the history of Japanese anarchism,[55] seemed to have also been decisive for him to become an anarchist. Bak indeed organized the Black Wave Society at Iwasa's home in 1921, albeit only a month later the Society was ordered to be dissolved by the Japanese authorities.

Since the Black Wave Society consisted of both anarchists and communists, it was resolved and broken up in December 1922 into two different societies: the Black Labor Society (Heungno hoe or Kokuro kai), led by anarchists, and the North Star Society (Bukseong hoe or Hoksei kai), led by communists. A year later the Black Labor Society was renamed and reorganized into the Black Friends Society (Heuk-u hoe or Kokutomo kai) and began to publish its journal, *Recalcitrant Koreans* (*Hutoi senjin*), which later was renamed *The Contemporary Society* (*Hyeon sahoe* or *Gen shakai*). The *Black Wave*, in its first issue on July 10, 1922, carried a short inaugural editorial in which the journal's main goal was stated: to introduce the actual situation and conditions of Koreans as "the weak" in Japan to those Japanese who had "warmhearted humanity." The ultimate goal in publishing it, however, was, through the stated introduction, the realization of the "amalgamation of Japan and Korea" (*nitsen yūgō*) by removing the "barriers" such as national prejudice and hatred, which stood in the way of realizing the journal's ultimate goal. The two peoples' amalgamation would eventually develop into the foundation for an "amalgamated world" (*sekai yūgō*), where national prejudice and hatred were nonexistent, the editorial predicted. And when the amalgamated world came true in the future, it would be "our days," the editorial added. Toward a realization of the envisioned cosmopolitan world, its readers were asked sincerely to offer their spiritual and material supports for the society's cause, concluded the editorial, which was probably written by Bak Yeol or at least with a collective agreement of the Society's members.[56] The cosmopolitan idea the Black Wave Society promoted was, I suspect, possibly a factor for Kaneko Fumiko to join with Bak in the Korean-led anarchist society.[57]

Of interest here is the journal's propagation of the amalgamation of Japan and Korea, a kind of pan-Asian idea on the basis of transnational solidarity of the masses. At first hearing, it may sound strange and even incomprehensible that the journal projected an amalgamation of Korea and Japan and made it as the foundation for a future amalgamated, cosmopolitan world, if we consider that Korea had been a colony of Japan since 1910. The journal, the society, and its editor and members could easily be branded as "traitors" to their country and compatriots and "running dogs" or "tools" of Japanese colonialism and expansionist version of Asianism for this kind of idea and advocacy. Their idea of the amalgamation, of course, was far from being identical or similar to that of Japanese pan-Asian expansionists as it was based on transnational ideas rather than cultural and racial solidarity, which would become evident, as I demonstrate below.

The declaration of the Black Wave Society carried in the inaugural issue of its journal further clarified its two main goals for the cosmopolitan world: social revolution and cultural transformation of "self" (*ja-a* or *jiga*) into the one who understood mutual aid and liberated oneself from any compulsory forces hindering self-development. Valuing a self through the mutual aid principle was the society's point of departure for the realization of a social revolution it advocated and ultimately of the amalgamated cosmopolitan world. Both a forced, man-made (as opposed to natural) unity of individuals and "any fixed ism" were not preconditions for such a cultural transformation.[58] Historian Oh Jang-Whan suggests that we understand this declaration, in particular its emphasis on self, in the context of Max Stirner's individualist anarchism, and also argues that Korean anarchists in Japan were much more attached to theoretical issues in anarchism than their counterparts in China.[59] I rather think the declaration expressed the importance of individual transformation as a point of departure for social revolution (and thus for national liberation). Given the intense interactions with many Japanese anarchists in the process of receiving anarchism, it probably was true that Korean anarchists were engrossed in some theoretical problems more frequently than their counterparts in China or colonial Korea. They nevertheless must have taken into consideration national problems as well as place-based demands in applying theory, as I demonstrate below.

Yi Gangha, who in February 1923 had organized the first anarchist organization in Seoul, the Black Labor Society (Heungno hoe), not the one with the same name in Tokyo that was renamed the Black Friends Society, contributed his writing to the same inaugural issue of *Black Wave*, in which he expressed his transnational concerns about capitalist society and its "propertyless class." In the article titled "Our Outcries," he pointed to the evils of capitalism that had forced people to work all day without gaining a piece of bread, a suit of clothes, and a place to call home, starving and freezing them to death as if they were wild dogs. This situation made Yi lament how "unnatural" and "unreasonable" the human society at the time was and that "propertyless class," breaking down the "unnaturalness" and "unreasonableness," was making "righteous outcries" for freedom and equality. Yi, therefore, concluded that there would be no peace without a struggle against his contemporary society under such rampant exploitation and that there couldn't be a construction without destruction of it.[60] The same issue of the journal also carried Bak Yeol's "An Example of Direct Action" in which Bak showed his belief that direct action was the only assured method to debilitate the power of laws, the moral, and customs.[61]

The Black Friends Society, renamed in February 1923 from the Black Labor Society, was formed initially with ten members but later grew in its membership to list twenty to thirty members on its roster, including Japanese female anarchist/nihilist Kaneko Fumiko, but most importantly Korean work-study students along with some workers. In 1923, the society published two issues of its journal titled *Recalcitrant Koreans* (*Hutoi senjin*), but was soon ordered not to use the title by the Japanese authorities due to its alleged provocativeness.[62] The first issue of *Recalcitrant Koreans*, although some parts of it were deleted due to the Japanese censorship, carried its short inaugural editorial containing the journal's two goals. According to the editorial, one goal was to determine whether the "rebellious Koreans" (*hutei senjin*) in Japan were human beings who were living with a burning wish for freedom or were they just secretly plotting assassinations, destruction, and other conspiracies, and to inform many Japanese workers who were in a similar situation as the Koreans in Japan of the Korean workers' situation.[63] The other goal was deleted by the Japanese censorship, but it could possibly have been about Korea's independence. As is clear in the editorial, the journal attempted to juxtapose the Koreans in Japan with Japanese workers, by which the meaning and implication of "rebellious Koreans" began to transcend national distinctions and boundaries. It is quite arguable, therefore, that the journal's main goal was social. The second issue of *Recalcitrant Koreans* carried Bak Yeol's critical article on Asianism propagated by the Japanese government at the time. In it Bak rejected the Japanese version of Asianism, since, he contended, it was wrong to have Koreans united forcefully with Japanese as Asians, when there was an unmovable fact that Korea had been invaded and colonized by Japan. Korea could not be united with Japan just because they belonged to the same "Asian race," Bak maintained.[64] Here we can see again that the idea of the "amalgamation of Korea and Japan" advocated by the journal's predecessor, the *Black Wave* journal with which Bak had been affiliated, was profoundly different from that of Japanese expansionists.[65]

The Black Friends Society also published another journal titled *Mass Movement* (*Minshū undō*), in order to study workers and their thought.[66] In addition, it held various lectures for which it received support and sponsorship from their Japanese comrades, and the lectures were given by Japanese anarchists such as Iwasa Sakutarō, Kondo Kenji (1895–1969), Hatta Shūzō (1886–1934), and Mochizuki

Katsura (1887–1975). The society also gained support from the Black Youth League (*Kokushoku seinen renmei*), one of the two nationwide federations of Japanese anarchists formed in 1926, which was usually abbreviated in Japanese as *Kokuren* and swiftly expanded its organization to include even anarchists in Japanese colonies, Korea and Taiwan.[67] The Black Youth League was known for its support and sponsorship of Korean anarchists and their national goal. For example, it once sponsored a meeting of 500 attendees to support the demand for a solution of the "Korea question" (*chōsen mondai*) on March 29, 1926. At the meeting Iwasa and Kondo delivered a speech, respectively. Also present at the meeting were Hatta, Mukumoto Unyū, Hirano Shōken (1891–1940), Mochizuki Katsura, and Take Riyōji (1895–1976?).[68] Among these Japanese, Mukumoto is known for keeping Kaneko Fumiko's ashes after her death in 1926, and his role played later in the attempted assassination with Korean anarchists of Ariyoshi Akira, Japanese consul general in 1930s Shanghai.

Some members of the Black Friends Society, like Bak Yeol, Kaneko Fumiko, Hong Jin-yu, Yuk Hongpyo, Han Hyeonsang (1900–?), and Choe Gyujong (1895–?) also organized a separate society, called the Rebellious Society (Futeisha), with the participation of Japanese anarchists like Kurihara Kazuo (1903–1981), Niiyama Hatsuyo (1902–1923), and Noguchi Shinaji (1899–1973). This society, unlike its sister organization, the Black Friends Society, was basically formed by both Korean and Japanese anarchists to study and propagate anarchism together without any visible direct action, because of which most of its members were not even arraigned by Japanese prosecutors when Bak and Kaneko along with Kim Junghan were arrested, tried, and sentenced at their trials for their alleged plot to kill the Japanese emperor.[69]

The Black Friends Society's journal was renamed later *The Contemporary Society*, and its first issue was published in July 1923, with the circulation of about 300 copies of an issue per month.[70] Bak Yeol contributed to its fourth issue an article titled "The Masses and Political Movement in Korea—Rejecting the Swindling Power-Minded Maniacs," in which he problematized the relationship between politics and power. Drawing on the situation of the workers in Soviet Russia at the time, he specifically accused the Bolsheviks of having become a "new privileged class," exploiting and ruling the masses, and, therefore, of simply replacing bourgeoisie. Bak, after explaining further the situation of the workers of the world, insisted the usefulness of direct action as the most efficient means against communism and capitalism, in order to prevent the problem of creating a new privileged class from happening in Korea. "Crushing capitalism by a means of general strike," however, was excluded in his definition of direct action.[71] Given that his initial conversion to anarchism was affected by a syndicalist version of anarchism, this was a bit of surprise. Yuk Honggeun's writing in the same issue also maintained the same tone and position regarding the critiques of the communists and their reliance not on labor union but on the majority or the masses; to Yuk, the communists simply made use of the term the *masses* to grasp power and satisfy their ambition.[72]

The fact that Bak still preferred direct action but rejected union-led activities (i.e., general strike) could be a sign of his (and possibly other Tokyo-based Korean anarchists') departure from anarcho-syndicalism, which had been dominant until the early 1920s in the Japanese anarchist movement since the "high treason" incident in 1910. It is premature, though, to judge whether this one article by Bak could be seen as a sign of his (and therefore, the Tokyo-based Korean anarchists') turning to "pure anarchism" that came to the forefront of Japanese anarchist movement after Ōsugi's murder in 1923,[73] or to "nihilism" as he stated later in his trial.[74] It seems, however, that his statement was at least a clear reflection of the split between Korean anarchists and communists in Japan after the long polemics between the two in the 1920s,[75] which began when the Black Wave Society was split into two. In the same issue of *The Contemporary Society*, an article by Han Hyeonsang, who joined the Black Friends Society in March of 1923,[76] delineated the meaning of social movement led by anarchists as an expression of rebellion and righteous indignation against the contradictions in his contemporary society. Criticizing communists for their power-mindedness and disrespect for individuals, Han asserted that spontaneous will of individuals be the most crucial factor in the consideration of struggle for an individual's life.[77]

Later in May 1926, the *Black Friends* (*Heuk-u* or *Kokutomo*) journal was allegedly planning to be launched by a Korean anarchist organization, the Black Movement Society (Heuksaek undongsa or Kokushoku undōsha) led by Choe Gyujong, Yi Honggeun, Jang Sangjung (1901–1961), and Won Simchang. It is not known, though, if it was actually published and, if so, how long it continued. At least it seems that the Black Movement Society too had a close relationship with Japanese anarchists, as it regularly held several study meetings or seminars among its members with their invited Japanese anarchist lecturers, including Iwasa Sakutarō, Ishikawa Sanshirō (1876–1956), Mochizuki Kei (1886–1975), and Hatta Shūzō, the latter in particular being the primary lecturer of those meetings probably because he was a renowned "anarchism polemicist" (*anakizumu ronkaku*).[78] Later, possibly in 1927, the society renamed their Korean-language journal *Black Friends* as *Free Society* (*Jiyū shakai*), published in Japanese. The Black Movement Society was a registered member of *Kokuren*. Some of Korean anarchists worked for Japanese anarchist press; for example, Yi Honggeun was involved in 1929 in the publication of *International Information* (*Kokusai joho*), which was renamed later *International Workers* (*Kokusai rōdōsha*), and Hong Yeong-u in 1929 participated in the publication of *Free Youth* (*Jiyū seinen*).[79]

According to Yi Honggeun's recollection in 1984, he and other members of the Black Movement Society subscribed to Japanese anarchist journals such as *Black Youth* (*Kokushoku seinen*), *Tenant Farming* (*Kōsaku*), and *Labor Movement* (*Rōdō undō*) to study their respective theories. Yi also recalls that they were also able to construct a "communication network" (*tongsin mang*) with those anarchists in Korea, China, and Manchuria.[80] It is unclear, though, to what extent the transnational "communication network" was actually able to work and function to connect the dispersed anarchists in different locations in the region and, thus, generate mutual inspiration and influence as well as to share their transnational commitments. What Yi recalls nevertheless is indicative of the interactions across the borders among Asian anarchists, in general, and Korean anarchists in different locations, in particular. Tokyo, to be sure, functioned as a node of the network of radicals, confirming its earlier role as "a mecca of progress."

Korean Anarchists and Labor Issues in Osaka

During the first two decades of the twentieth century, Osaka emerged as one of the "growing industrial centers" in Japan, along with Tokyo, Kobe, and Yokohama. And with the development of "an energetic working-class movement"[81] it would become the most active city, only second to Tokyo, in terms of Korean anarchist activities.[82] In fact, Osaka in the 1910s and 1920s was enjoying economic prosperity as the center of various industries, such as the textile industry (especially cotton textiles) and the machine industry, as well as of commerce and finance. Emerging as the biggest industrial city in Asia at the time,

Osaka was transforming itself into a significant industrial zone, probably because of which the city had earned its nickname, an "Amsterdam in the Orient." In addition, Osaka outnumbered Tokyo in terms of the concentration of people in it, who were probably from both inside and outside Japan, and presented itself as a different kind of concentrated location of various people. Among the people arriving in the city were Korean workers who were mostly from the southern rural areas of the Korean peninsula, deprived of their land after Japan's colonization in 1910, because of the new land investigation and subsequent policy that were enforced on them by the Japanese colonial government. These Koreans who left their hometown now provided Osaka with its much needed cheap labor forces, which in turn upheld from the bottom the prosperity of the city during the Taishō period (1912–1926).[83] Unlike Tokyo, Osaka was known to Koreans at the time mainly as a place of opportunity to earn money as cheap labor workers, certainly not as a place in which to receive higher education.

Indeed, those who came to Osaka from the peninsula were largely workers in search of jobs available there, but there too were some students in Osaka. And the first Korean anarchism-oriented organization in Osaka was the Fraternal Society of Koreans in Osaka (Ōsaka chōsenjin shinbokkai), organized on September 1, 1914, by Korean radical students in Osaka, such as Jeong Taesin, Bu Namhui, and Sin Taegyun. It was not an anarchist organization but the radical students, it seemed, had already been associated with Japanese anarchists in Osaka such as Hasegawa Ichimatsu (1883–1917) and Yokota Shōjirō (1883–1936). Jeong, in particular, gradually accepted anarchism through his interactions with Yokota and Hasegawa.[84] Just like in Tokyo, the role of individual Japanese anarchists must have been of paramount importance in the initial reception and activities of Korean anarchists in Osaka.

In the 1920s Osaka remained as an industrializing city in need of workers, and Koreans were to fill the need. The number of Korean workers who came from Busan to Shimonoseki by ferry between the late 1920s and early 1930s numbered from about 100 thousand or 160 thousand annually, many of whom came to Osaka. Those who came from Jeju Island to Osaka directly by ferry were approximately between fifteen and twenty thousand annually. Osaka was the destination of people particularly from Jeju Island,[85] because most of them were desperately in search of a job. And it seemed that once they came to Osaka they had a tendency to continue to stay and settle in the city, rather than to move to other cities in Japan.[86] This explains why there used to be many Korean anarchists from Jeju Island in Osaka. Go Sunheum (1890–1975) was one of them. Go came from Jeju island to Osaka in March 1924, but had already been inspired by Kropotkin's mutual aid idea[87] and involved in a labor organization in Seoul, having played a key role in penning the platform and charter of the Association for Labor and Mutual Relief in Korea (Joseon nodong gongje hoe), established in April 1920 as the first labor association in colonial Korea. Go was arrested in August 1922 in Korea for his activities for the Association. After released from prison in 1924, he crossed the Korea Strait to come to Osaka in the same year, where he immediately became engaged in the activities of the Namheung Dawn Society (Nagyo reimei kai) led by Choe Seonmyeong, and also organized the Alliance of the Societies of Korean Propertyless People (ASKPP, Chōsen muchansha shakai dōmei) with Choe and Kim Taeyeop in June of 1924. Although the Alliance had just a handful of members, it often was empowered by collaborations with other radicals and radical organizations in Osaka. The Alliance defined its mission "to definitely escape from the current [colonized] status [of Korea] by Koreans' own strength and construct a new culture."[88] Later Go returned to his native province of Jeju Island, where he participated in a mutual relief/financing native organization called Our Mutual Loan Club (Uri gye) which, according to his memoir, attempted to realize an ideal society in the island by adopting to his anarchist ideas Laozi's idea of "Three Treasures" (sambo) in human life, that is, diligence (geun), frugality (geom), and modesty (yang).[89]

The ASKPP held a mass gathering in June and July (or August) of 1924, respectively, in protest against the Japanese oppression of Koreans' freedom of speech and gathering, in collaboration with the Society for Korean Labor Alliance in Osaka (Ōsaka chōsen rōdō dōmei kai), the March First Korean Youth Society in Kansai (Kansai chōsenjin sanpin seinen kai), the Osaka Korean Study-Abroad Students' Fraternal Society (Ōsaka chōsen ryūgaksei gakuyū kai), and the Namheung Dawn Society, with which Go had been affiliated closely since his arrival in Osaka. At the gathering Go gave a speech along with Choe Seonmyeong and Kim Taeyeop. In addition, in an effort to protect Korean women workers' rights in Osaka, Go also organized the Society to Protect Korean Women Workers (Chōsen jokō hogo kai) on January 6, 1926, partly because most of the female workers in Osaka were from Jeju Island, of which he also was a native. The Society, the first and unique Korean anarchist organization that exclusively worked or advocated for Korean female workers and their rights, had fifty members and continued to be active until 1929. Go also subsequently organized the League of Free Korean Workers in Sakai (Sakai chōsen jiyū rōdōsha renmei) and the League of Free Workers in Osaka (Ōsaka jiyū rōdōsha renmei). Thanks to Go's efforts and activities in Osaka and later in colonial Korea, Jeju Island became known at that time as a center of Korean anarchist movement, breeding many young anarchists. More importantly, with his activities in Osaka, Korean workers' movement in Osaka enjoyed its golden years until the mid-1927, when their movement began to be undermined by Korean communists and their activities there. Go would become a central figure in Korean anarchist movement in Osaka, along with Kim Taeyeop and Choe Seonmyeong.[90]

Besides Go, one of the frequently mentioned Korean anarchists in Osaka was Choe Seonmyeong, but little is known about Choe. What is known today is that Choe was a graduate of Tōyō University and had organized the Namheung Dawn Society in Osaka with Kim Taeyeop, before Go Sunheum's arrival in Osaka in 1924. Choe is believed to have gone to Soviet Russia sometime after Go's arrival in Osaka, but seemed to disappear after being arrested by Japanese police on the way back to northern Korea from Soviet Russia. Also unclear are when Choe traveled to Soviet Russia, when Choe's arrest took place, and the whereabouts of Choe afterward. Choe seemed to have been close to Kim Taeyeop, who remembers and describes Choe in his memoir as a nationalist, without reference to Choe's gender, who fought against the proletarian dictatorship of the Communists.[91]

In addition to Choe and Go, Kim Taeyeop (1902–1985) played an important role in Korean anarchist movement in Osaka. Kim came to Osaka along with many other Korean workers in 1915 as a child labor worker. Until he was deported to Korea in September 1935, after having spent four years in Japanese prison, Kim had been known for his involvement in many labor movements in the Kansai area of Japan.[92] He began to work as a child laborer in Osaka at a shipbuilding yard, where he realized that, somewhat prematurely, "we workers just work to death and are only exploited" and that "we Koreans" suffered from the harsh oppression from Japanese.[93] Gradually developing class consciousness as a worker as well as national consciousness, he attended a "labor night school" (*rōdō yagaku*) in Osaka, at which he learned that workers could liberate themselves from poverty only by uniting themselves and resisting unjust oppression and exploitations by all enterprisers.[94] Kim's case is revealing in that he developed his interest in labor issues because they were his own; and he then was increasingly inclined to anarchism. Unlike most Korean anarchists in Tokyo, who in general encountered both national and social discriminations and almost simultaneously contacted anarchism through reading anarchist works and/or becoming acquainted with Japanese/Korean anarchists, subsequently converting to anarchism, Kim first faced hardships and pains in labor as a child laborer and gradually came to realize this as a social issue. He then found an answer to it in anarchism, or at least found anarchist principles as a way to tackle the problem.[95]

Kim's anarchism was most likely based on syndicalist labor movement but without any leading theory that guided his labor activities. In his memoir he recalls that in the labor movements he was involved in Osaka and other places he needed no theoretical explanations for Korean workers there to organize and mobilize them, because the main effective principle to mobilize and organize them was to provoke their national consciousness by indicating that they were colonized people who lost their country, rather than offering them any meaningless labor theory.[96] In Osaka, just like Tokyo, national consciousness too must have been utilized to raise social consciousness among the workers. Unlike in Tokyo, however, it seems Korean anarchists like Kim prioritized and dealt first with the labor-related issues prevalent in Osaka, which directly affected their lives and labor conditions, rather than heavily relied on such unappealing issues as the fate and status of their nation or the broader issues pertinent to the question of freedom and equality. There certainly were some peculiar aspects to the Osaka-based Korean anarchist/labor movement in the 1920s, which were different from those in Tokyo. Kim probably knew this and thus recalls that he combined two different categories, the nation (*minjok*) and the "working masses" (*geullo daejung*), and rendered them the main guiding ideas for his labor movement activities in the ensuing years.[97]

After spending many years in Osaka, Kim, just like all other Koreans of 1910s to 1920s Japan, left for Tokyo from Osaka in 1920, in search of his education at Nihon (Japan) University as a work-study student. When he traveled to and stayed in Tokyo for a while in 1920, Kim interacted and associated himself with many Japanese and

Korean anarchists and even communists there. Obviously Kim was open to various ideologies and also willing to become acquainted with many kinds of socialists. He soon participated in the establishment of the Society for Korean Labor Alliance in Japan (Zainichi chōsen rōdō dōmei kai) in November of that year. While living in Tokyo, he continued to meet many Korean anarchists such as Jeong Taeseong (1901–?), and Bak Yeol. His perspective was accordingly transformed in Tokyo, Kim recalls. It was at this moment that he began to focus more on labor issues and socialist theories and that, according to him, he was inclined toward Fabianism.[98] His stay in Tokyo didn't last long. In the wake of the Greater Kantō Earthquake in 1923, he was detained and tortured by the Japanese police like many Koreans, and, once released, thus decided to return to Osaka in December of that year. Back in Osaka he actively organized and led a meeting to criticize the Japanese massacre of Koreans in Tokyo after the earthquake. Also organized by him was the ASKPP in June 1924, in league with Choe Seonmyeong and Go Sunheum, two major figures in Osaka-based Korean anarchist movement.

The next year Kim Taeyeop opened a Korean Labor School (Chōsen rōdō gakkō) with Kim Suhyeon. The former also organized the New Advance Society (Shinshin kai) with Yi Chunsik in January 1926, and subsequently the Voice of Self Society (Jigasei sha) also with Yi as chair of the Society, which published its journal, *The Voice of Self* (*Chigasei* [sic]). While involved in the above-mentioned several anarchist organizations, Kim Taeyeop was in charge of publishing and editing the journal of the Voice of Self Society, the first Korean anarchist publication published in Osaka. It is notable that the journal could have been endorsed by Bak Yeol, who had been arrested and in prison at the time of its publication in 1926, for his alleged plot with Kaneko Fumiko to assassinate the Japanese emperor. Kim could have possibly developed friendship or comradeship with Bak when he was in Tokyo between 1920 and 1923, since Bak contributed a short piece of writing from prison to the inaugural issue of *The Voice of Self*, titled "The Declaration of the Strong," albeit most parts of Bak's contribution were deleted and thus not readable due to Japanese censorship.[99]

In fact, the first issue of *The Voice of Self*, published on March 20, 1926, was banned just two days after it had come out, albeit the issue has survived and was available for the current study. The "Declaration" of *The Voice of Self*, written by Yi Chunsik, chair (*daihyō*) of the Society, carried in its first issue, also had some parts deleted.

Nevertheless, from the part readable, it is clear that the Society maintained its harsh criticism against Korean independence movement activists, socialists, and "labor union activists" (i.e., communists). First, Yi in the Declaration labeled Korean independence activists "our enemy" because they were those who, "entrapping us," utilized "our unity" for independence and national liberation for the sake of their ambition and power-mindedness. Both socialists and "labor union activists" too were avaricious for power, Yi continued, so that they also "force us to be united" under a certain type of theory in order to sacrifice "us" to meet their "avarice." All of them, independence activists, socialists, and "labor union activists," eventually were in fact acting on behalf of capitalists, adding oppression and tyranny to "us," Yi insisted in the Declaration. According to Yi, therefore, it would turn out that digging the graves of the capitalists must be a work "we" had to do in "our" lives.[100] Here, Yi separated "us"—those who were anarchists (and possibly the masses)—from both other socialists, including communists and syndicalists, as well as the nationalists working for independence.

A similar criticism of nationalists was made by Kim Taeyeop in the same issue. Kim, using his nickname *Toppa* in Japanese or *Dolpa* in Korean, meaning "breaking through," which he had earned after his audacious actions against Japanese, wrote in the inaugural issue an article on "The Movement in Korea," in which he placed Korea's liberation movement in the context of global movement for "the liberation of propertyless class." According to him, the liberation of "weak and small nations" in the world had two meanings, that is, independence and national liberation, for "the powerful nations" had exploited them economically and enslaved their people as well. Political movements such as the March First Movement of 1919 in those "weak and small nations," therefore, could have no essential effect on liberation, Kim contended. The nature of their liberation rather must be economic and social in consequence, although the March First Movement as a political movement paved the way to the coming socialist as well as labor union movements in Korea, Kim added. For the Koreans without jobs and food under capitalist exploitations, their "savior" was a "socialist new thinking" (*shakaishugi deki sin shisō*) with the "self-awareness of the masses." The "savior" called for a liberation movement generated by the power of the unity of the proletarian masses, Kim asserted. In his analysis, the new liberation movement appeared as a response to the call from the "savior," which had exhibited its genuine power to the movements by labor unions, tenant unions, and so on. throughout Korea. He, of course, observed that there had been terrible oppressions and tyranny by the authorities and police in colonial Korea that had suppressed the new movement. However, "we must not be saddened and depressed," because the more oppressive and tyrannical the suppression became, the more powerful and intensified became "our movement," which based itself on the "awareness of humanity" and the "social truth," Kim concluded. To him, the target of anarchism was not only imperialism or colonialism but also capitalism that had economically exploited and enslaved people, in addition to the privileged ruling class called *yangban* of the Korean society.[101]

The "powerless people" were not just limited to those colonized in Korea. Yi Chunsik in the next issue of *The Voice of Self* called for the establishment of the right for human beings to live, not based on the competition for existence between the strong and the weak but rather based on Kropotkin's mutual aid idea.[102] Here we find the transnational concerns and cosmopolitan outlook of the journal. It is quite arguable here, once again, that, just like Yi Hayu and Shin Chaeho in his new conceptualization of *minjung*, Yi Chunsik and Kim Taeyeop along with the members of the Voice of Self Society opened up a way to expand the meaning of "people" to transcend the national boundaries of Korea and encompass the exploited and oppressed in the other parts of the world. The contemporary liberation of the "powerless people" (or "propertyless class") would not spring from an old-fashioned political independence movement, with which the Society seemed to agree; rather, it would stem from the liberation movement for all human beings that was demanded by contemporary socialism.[103] Transnational concerns and goals were to be put forward by the Korean anarchists in the Society, which in turn required them to prioritize and discuss the social rather than the national questions. And the transnational meaning of "powerless people" could possibly have been dissipated to the region quite effectively, as Choe Gapryong recalls that *The Voice of Self* was sent out as far as to northern Manchuria, so as to eventually convert radicals like Bak Seokhong there to anarchism.[104]

Drawing on Kropotkin's mutual aid idea, Yi Chunsik continued to express his rejection of the "formula" that "the powerful wins over the weak" and pointed out that one truth was that all the living things possessed the right to live. Yi contended that "we the Korean proletariat," although they had been "loyal slaves" and "silent," now had only one path of life under hardships, starvation, oppressions, and so forth, which after all was "to be rebellious." Only this way, Yi posited, they were able to grasp their own freedom and happiness by their own hands.[105] Here, the meaning of freedom, probably shared by the Society members, was undoubtedly anarchist. An anonymous author of a short article carried also in the inaugural issue of *The Voice of Self* defined "genuine freedom" as "the freedom of will,"[106] close to what many Korean anarchists upheld at the time, that is, absolute freedom of individuals. The shared understanding of freedom as "the freedom of will" of individuals developed into a much more refined understanding of a self, as Kim Taeyeop in his writing went further to say that without understanding a self it was impossible to understand the masses; likewise, without transforming a self, it was impossible to transform the masses; and without perfecting and comprehending a self, no one could return to a self. Therefore, Kim simply raised two related questions: "how can you claim that you understand the masses when you don't have any understanding of yourself at all?" and "Are there such things as a class separated from a self?" According to Kim, the motive to pursue a national proletarian movement sprang from the concept that a self was an incomplete product (of the society). In other words, if a self is comprehended as hypocritical and feeble-minded, that would have the self endeavor to perfect the self and ultimately launch a movement to set up a genuine society full of natural humanness.[107] Corresponding to the Society's name, the Voice of Self, its members seemed to stress individuals and their self-reflections as a way to deal with their contemporary society and its problems under capitalism.

Another influential anarchism-oriented organization established in Osaka was the New Advance Society, although just fragment pieces of information about it are available now. It was established on January 16, 1926, with Yi Chunsik as its chairperson and 500 members, including Kim Taeyeop. The Society passed its platform on the same day of its establishment, which included the following: (1) we anticipate absolute liberation through united actions and mutual aid spirit of the compatriots; (2) we, from a particular national position, endeavor to break down the unreasonable environment and gain economic freedom; and (3) we, from a civilizational position, make a rush to create a new culture.[108] The Society's main activities included one that cherished the memory of Sunjong, the last emperor of the Joseon (Chosŏn) dynasty of Korea, as well as the participation with other Korean and Japanese organizations in a much larger Osaka-based organization named the Central Council for Koreans (Chōsenjin chūo kyōgi kai). The core members of the Council included Korean anarchist organizations in Osaka such as the New Advance Society and the Voice of Self Society, although it was not to develop at all as an anarchist organization. The Council dealt with the standing issues regarding Korean workers in the Kansai area, including Osaka.

The New Advance Society shared its main office with the Voice of Self Society Yi and Kim had already established. It is not clear why Yi and Kim established an additional anarchist society, but it seems the New Advance Society, as its platform and activities demonstrate, was probably concerned with some standing national issues that required the Society's attention as much as its anarchist goal, which was not disclosed transparently in the platform. Anyhow, the New Advance Society published the first issue of its organ newsletter on March 20, 1926, with the same title as its name,[109] albeit not much is known about it. Other than the New Advance Society, there were the ASKPP, the Union of Free Korean Workers in Sakai (Chōsen sakai jiyū rōdōsha kumiai), established in 1925, and the Osaka Free Workers Federation (Ōsaka jiyū rōdōsha renmei), also established in the same year. Korean anarchists in Osaka continued to work with their Japanese counterparts well into the early 1930s.[110]

As historian Jeong Hyegyeong correctly suggests, Korea anarchist movement in Osaka needs to be approached and understood from a comparative perspective. It had its own salient traits quite different from that in Tokyo, in terms of its focus of activities and tactics, not to mention the nature of the issues in need of its attention. According to Jeong, there were several conspicuous differences in the Korean anarchist movement in the two cities of Japan. The Korean anarchist organizations in Osaka were quite small in their size, particularly in terms of their membership. And it seems to me there were overall far fewer anarchist organizations in Osaka than in Tokyo in the 1920s. In addition, many anarchist or anarchism-oriented organizations in Osaka stated and included anarchist principles in their platform and goals but not just for the purposes of propagating anarchism and realizing an outright ideal anarchist society. And, as the case of the New Advance Society's activity to commemorate the last Korean emperor reveals, their activities were sometimes undiscernible from those of other nationalist or socialist organizations, as Jeong points out. Other than the languages of freedom, individual, liberation, mutual aid, and so on, the Osaka-based Korean anarchist organizations, sometimes with no pithiness in theory, did not go further in their respective platform and goals to propagate their radical anarchist ideals, such as revolution. According to Jeong, this explains, in part, why there were fewer conflicts and tensions between the Korean anarchist and other socialist organizations in Osaka, at least around the time when the above-mentioned anarchist societies were organized and active simultaneously.[111] Maybe it was a necessity for them to cooperate closely with other organizations for the maximum effective result of their movement or to cope with and survive the Japanese police surveillance and oppression in the city. It is also possible that they didn't or didn't want to distinguish any theoretical differences among various branches of socialisms from anarchism, as in the case with Kim Taeyeop.

The differences between the Korean anarchist movement in Tokyo and Osaka, I argue, need to be approached additionally with the understanding of different local practice of anarchism. As Jeong criticizes historian Horiuchi's general assessment of all Korean anarchist movements in Japan as a "thought movement" (shisō undō) and "nationalistic," Horiuchi's assessment is mainly tenable to the anarchist organizations in Tokyo. This does not mean that the Osaka-based anarchist organizations were not nationalistic. It seems the Korean anarchist organizations in Osaka mainly had their activities more focused on the standing issues of Korean workers in Osaka, such as the improvement of their treatment as workers and the protection of their rights at the workplace. This prioritization of labor issues stemmed from two facts—that many Korean anarchists themselves were workers and that Osaka was an industrializing city full of Korean workers as cheap labor forces. The Osaka-based Korean anarchist emphasized individuals, as opposed to the society, and their transformation, which was as a point of departure for the projected coming cultural transformation toward an anarchist society in the future. This vision was exemplified in *The Voice of Self*. To be sure, they projected a social transformation in the city with their particular local-based vision, which in turn helped them escape any outright suppression of their activities by the Japanese police. Indeed, the Japanese police were less attentive to these anarchist organizations in Osaka than those in Tokyo.

The above-mentioned two facts might have been of importance to the anarchists in Osaka and thus may be able to explain the differences in their practice of anarchism and focus of activities from their counterparts in Tokyo. As long as their focus was, at least on surface, not placed on national liberation and independence of Korea but on the livelihood and well-being of Korean workers, their movement could be viewed as part of a much broad social, labor movement in Japan, led by Japanese anarchist and socialist organizations. On the contrary, the Korean anarchist movements in Tokyo not only were inspired by nationalist aspirations that usually resulted from national discrimination against Korean study-abroad students in the metropolitan city, but also in many cases were involved in radical revolutionary movements, potentially making them a threat to the Japanese state and its rule in Korea.[112] Comparatively speaking, the number and size of anarchists and their organizations in Tokyo seemed to far surpass those in Osaka, which obviously was one of the reasons why Korean anarchists seemed to have relatively more breathing room in Osaka without much tighter Japanese police surveillance.

We are reminded here that Kim Taeyeop decided to move back to Osaka from Tokyo after the 1923 Greater Kantō Earthquake, and was able to continue his labor activities there without being arrested and put in prison until he was finally deported to Korea in 1935.[113] It is also notable here that Kim's labor activities must have been known to the Chinese through some kind of information network. Kim, whose activities were mainly limited to Osaka and its vicinity in the mid-1920s, was, to his surprise, formally invited to the congress of the All-China Federation of Trade Unions (Zhonghua minguo zonggonhui), which took place in Shanghai on May Day 1925. There Kim met many labor activists from across the world, including CCP leaders like Liu Shaoqi (1898–1969).[114] It seems that there was a kind of network that did connect and work effectively among radicals in the regional labor movement.

As one of the important anarchist labor movement organizers and activists in Osaka and non-Tokyo area, Kim corroborates regarding the difference between Tokyo and Osaka in his memoir by calling himself more of a nationalist, not an anarchist like those in Tokyo. He nevertheless admits that his success in forming a labor organization in Osaka came basically from how effectively he was able to utilize the national sentiments among Korean workers and relate them to their hardship in daily life. In his view, the workers at the time in Osaka were not able to understand any difficult theories and ideas about labor movement, and so on.[115] I think the key could be the hard life of Korean workers who generally received much lower wages than Japanese workers, as well as various kinds of discrimination experienced; of course, they often must have been victims of national discriminations in the process of employment and in terms of salary, but I think the focus of the Kim-led movements must have been placed on workers' "hard life" as foreigners in Osaka.[116] Therefore, if I may add to Jeong's observation, the differences in the Korean anarchist movement between Tokyo and Osaka had something to do with the place of their activities and the composition of Korean population in the two cities, which must have resulted in the different way Korean anarchists in Osaka practiced anarchism. Tokyo certainly was a metropolitan city with abundant opportunities for higher education, the best place for Korean study-abroad students and intellectuals, while Osaka was an industrializing city where Koreans came to earn money as cheap labor forces, and thus had fewer students and intellectuals.

Korean anarchists in Tokyo in the 1920s were generally following the polemics in the Japanese anarchist movement, regarding ideological and theoretical issues, which could have ushered in the vitality of their own movement. Korean anarchists in the second city of Japan, keeping their distance from the polemics, must have seen "life-related issues" corresponding to Korean workers' living and working conditions as more important. And this difference, in addition to all the others mentioned above, must have contributed to the different deployment of anarchist movements by Koreans in the two cities. Above all, Korean labor/anarchist society organizers in Osaka were in many cases workers themselves in the city and were working for their own families/relatives and those from their hometown, as Go Sunheum's case demonstrates. Theories that didn't meet the reality in Osaka could have received less attention from Korean anarchists there. A different practice of anarchism was therefore an obvious and logical outcome of the environment and conditions surrounding Korean anarchists in Osaka.

Korean students and radicals in Japan received and considered anarchism, just like their counterparts in China, as a means and principle for both independence and social transformation. The conversion of Korean students and radicals in Japan to anarchism was a product of their interactions—both direct and indirect—with their Japanese counterparts. And due mainly to their intimate associations with the Japanese anarchists, their particular focus, somewhat different from that of Korean anarchists in China, was more on the social, including the labor issues, and on organizing and educating Korean workers who experienced both national and social discriminations. As a result, comparatively speaking, they often had a sophisticated understanding of anarchist principles, union activities, and so forth, for which Korean anarchists in Japan were all often called "theoreticians,"[117] which can be confirmed by what Kim San says about the general level of Korean anarchists' theoretical understanding of anarchism by the early 1920s.[118] Among all others, Ōsugi Sakae's works were most widely read and thus he was considered the most influential of Korean anarchists in Japan, even posthumously. Iwasa Sakutarō, also influential and supportive of Korean anarchists, seemed to develop and maintain his personal relationship with many Korean anarchists by teaching Esperanto at his house or sponsoring and supporting many of their organizations and activities.[119] Indeed, the connectedness of Korean anarchism to Japanese anarchism was inevitable also for the survival of Korean anarchists.

The experiences and activities of Korean anarchists in Japan were to be of great importance in nourishing Korean anarchists and their movements in colonial Korea, as I examine in the next chapter. This does not mean that Korean anarchist movement in Japan was in unity in terms of its activities and visions. The major activities of Tokyo-based Korean anarchists were focused mainly on propagating anarchist ideals and principles for social revolution, as well as national liberation, through their organizations and their publications, jointly with their Japanese comrades. On the contrary, Osaka-based anarchists were eager to protect Korean workers and promote their rights at their workplace. Korean anarchist movement in Japan, mainly organized and conducted in Tokyo and Osaka, sometimes with their Japanese comrades, can be characterized by its general trend toward pure anarchism, an obvious sign of their overall ties with Japanese anarchist movement.

However, there too was a trend toward labor movement in Tokyo and Osaka. A large number of Korean workers in Osaka, who provided cheap labor for the Japanese industrial development, were the object of Korean anarchist movement in Osaka, but they were not necessarily anarcho-syndicalists. What Korean students in 1910s Japan received was mainly anarcho-syndicalism, because it was a leading trend among Japanese anarchists at the time. This influence was to culminate in helping Korean workers organize themselves into various labor organizations after 1922, when Korean workers were murdered at the Nakatsuka dam construction site in Nagata Prefecture, which in turn resulted later in the culmination of labor movements in the late 1920s. There must have been close relationships between Korean anarcho-syndicalists and their Japanese counterparts.

The split in Japanese anarchist movement between pure anarchists, represented by Hatta Shūzō,[120] and anarcho-syndicalists, represented by Ishikawa Sanshirō, also had an impact on Korean anarchists in Japan, who replicated the split.[121] However, it didn't develop into conflicts among them, according to Yang Sanggi, a former member of Tōkō Labor Alliance of Koreans. Yang recalls that Korean workers in Japan, compared to their Japanese counterparts, experienced double or triple oppressions in daily life because of which Korean pure anarchists too had to organize labor unions, albeit to them it was theoretically contradictory when, as he states, it was anarcho-syndicalists who organized unions and conducted union activities. There was, therefore, he continues, no tensions and conflicts in the League between (pure) anarchists and anarcho-syndicalists, although it was a different story in the Japanese anarchist movement.[122] Yang's explanation vindicates that, unlike the Japanese anarchists, there were no major clashes or conflicts among Korean anarchists regarding the difference between pure anarchists and syndicalists, when it came to the issue of labor unions and their roles in anarchist movement. Rather, Korean anarchists were generally involved in union activities between the mid-1920s and -30s, covering their other goal for Korea's independence. What I suggest above does not mean, however, that anarcho-syndicalism disappeared in the Japan-based Korean anarchist movement; rather, unionization activities of Korean workers in Japan by Korean anarchists continued until the 1930s.[123]

CHAPTER 3

Pushing the Limits in Colonial Korea

It is not an exaggeration to say that the anarchist movement in colonial Korea was launched largely by the returned Korean students from study-abroad in Japan. In the mid-1920s, they made many attempts within colonial Korea to form anarchist organizations and disseminate anarchist ideas. Their anarchist movements and activities within the Korean peninsula before 1945 were quite closely tied to those of Korean anarchists based in Japan. Their attempts, however, always met prompt and brutal suppression at their inception from the Japanese colonial police. As a result, while many anarchist or anarchism-oriented organizations, small and large, were established throughout colonial Korea in the 1920s and afterward, all were short-lived or, in some cases, existed only on paper.

The situation became even harsher and worse once Japan invaded China in the early 1930s, because of Japan's much tightened control and suppression of so-called dangerous ideas and rebellious Koreans. In dealing with the situation, anarchists in colonial Korea generally had limited options, and chose to go underground, remain silent, or be arrested for their audacity under Japan's wartime repression. Attempts to publish anarchist press and materials continued even under the Japanese brutal suppression into the 1930s, but, if arrested and tried, it is said, no anarchist would be able to walk on his or her own two legs or even remain alive after having spent time in prison, due to brutal and repeated torture, malnutrition, and an unspeakable environment.[1]

Anarchists in colonial Korea maintained their relationship and contacts with Korean and Japanese anarchists in Japan, whose activities and understanding of and writings on anarchism had been exposed to and/or inspired them. As I examined in chapter 2, it is undeniable that the Japanese works on and understanding of anarchism had been widely influential, and thus the major source for Korean anarchists' understanding of it and the social/labor problems of the world under capitalism. Although this does not mean that the Korean version of anarchism was a replica of Japanese anarchism, it is still arguable nevertheless that the role and part Japanese anarchism played in the rise of anarchism in colonial Korea were of significance in introducing to Koreans anarchist principles, languages, and ideals, and thus in helping them interpret and then apply to them Korea's colonial condition and situation. In his book on cultural nationalism in colonial Korea in the 1920s, historian Michael Robinson notes that Korean radicals who returned to colonial Korea from abroad were a product of broad regional radical movements in China and Japan after 1919, as following shows:

> "Radicals" describes loosely a group of nationalist intellectuals that came to prominence after 1919. The political universe of this group was shaped by the widespread fascination with social revolutionary thought after the Russian revolution. Nurtured in the political hothouses of Tokyo, Peking, and Shanghai, Korean students abroad had thrown themselves into the intellectual ferment of contending doctrines. Like their Chinese and Japanese counterparts in the post–World War I era, Korean students searched amidst the whirl of ideas-political democracy, bolshevism, social democracy, syndicalism, guild socialism, anarchism, Fabianism, and national socialism—for a solution to the Korean national problem. . . . offering . . . more radical solutions for the dual problem of Japanese imperialism and Korean independence.[2]

Various activities, either publication or organization, by Korean anarchists in colonial Korea from the 1920s were by and large a product of this process of receiving, understanding, and applying "social revolutionary thought," including anarchism, to colonial Korea. In other words, the intimate ties between Korean and Japanese anarchism, as well as Chinese anarchism, were quite obvious and conspicuous, although their relationship must not be understood in the context of one-way influence to Korean anarchists. There are ample evidence and examples, as I have demonstrated in the previous chapters, that show that Japanese anarchists too learned or became increasingly aware of the colonial conditions and situations and often some other related issues from Korean and Taiwanese comrades.

In addition, as noted above, there was a strong intellectual aura in colonial Korea that pointed to a tendency among intellectuals and radicals toward socialism, including anarchism, mainly due to anticolonial sentiments growing in Korea since the Russian Revolution of 1917, which had become much stronger especially after the nationwide mass movement on March 1, 1919. These served as an intellectual foundation in the 1920s for the reception and spread of anarchism in the peninsula when it was brought in and introduced directly by the Japanese works in flux on anarchism in Japanese texts or translation, but most importantly, by former Korean study-abroad students. Just like Sun Yat-sen (1866–1925) described the Chinese radials who had returned to China after finishing their education in Japan in early twentieth century, as the carriers of "the spark of revolution" (*geming de huozhong*),[3] many Korean students and radicals must have also returned to Korea from Japan after accepting anarchism with their own "spark" bent on anarchist ideals. In the case of Korea, the "spark" readily ignited the fire of anarchism because of the Japanese works that had already been widely known and available to Korean readers in colonial Korea; since 1910, many Korean students and radicals in colonial Korea had been able to obtain books on socialism and newspapers published in Japan by anarchists easily at the bookstores run by either Korean or Japanese owners. For example, Yi Hyeok (1907—?), who had been involved in various anarchist activities in Southern Hamgyeong Province, opened Twentieth Century Bookstore (Isipsegi seobang) in downtown Seoul, where he not only sold books on anarchism but distributed copies of the Japanese anarchist newspaper *Free Alliance Newspaper* (*Jiyū rengō shimbun*) and ran his own institute called Modern Thoughts Research Institute (Geundae sasang yeon-guso), to teach Esperanto to Koreans. Another role of his bookstore was to function as a communication place among Korean anarchists.[4] The "wind" of anarchism was blowing strongly in colonial Korea to set the fire of anarchism with the help of the "spark" the returning students had brought. And the fire certainly shook the peninsula intellectually and shaped the direction and character of anarchist movement in colonial Korea continuously, if not exclusively.

In a colony like Korea, however, it was almost impossible to witness a nationwide development of the anarchist movement largely due to the pressure of Japanese colonial police and their tight surveillance and suppression of radicals and radicalism, especially if it initially arose with nationalist aspirations. But, as described above, anarchist movement and organizations in colonial Korea were somewhat able to survive and continue to do so, if not grow, and, in fact, were quite "resilient" and remain relatively "active," as historian Horiuchi Minoru assesses, particularly about anarchist activities in the northern part of Korea around the cities of Wonsan and Pyongyang.[5] Nevertheless, Korean anarchist movements usually went underground and their organizations sometimes existed briefly and/or only on paper. Of interest is that the anarchist organizations in colonial Korea, as I demonstrate below, didn't take any terrorist or terror-oriented actions against Japanese colonial institutions and figures, nor did they strive for independence, at least on surface. They rather in general turned them into a kind of social movement to educate and organize peasants and workers, and so on regarding the protection of their rights, probably because of the Japanese police suppression and at the same time the influence from the Japanese anarchist movement via Korean anarchists returned from Japan.[6] In other words, under the colonial conditions the Korean anarchist movement was mainly conducted to make changes in society with collective awareness and actions of workers and peasants, but without any physical revolutionary actions that usually accompanied larger revolutionary organizations and massive physical protests. Many anarchist organizations and their activities were thus often sporadic, small-scale, and even disguised, in some cases, as a "legally acceptable" social and/or enlightenment movement. Given all constrains under the colonial condition, it may be possible to say that the anarchist organizations in colonial Korea were not able to exist long enough to launch and pursue any meaningful revolutionary actions against Japanese colonial rule.

Korean anarchists in colonial Korea generally left information and materials on their anarchist movements much less often or even not at all, due to the confidential nature of their underground activities plus the Japanese police confiscation. Materials on their activities are scarce and hard to come by, therefore. Compared to Korean anarchists in China and Japan, whose activities have been known from various, if fragmentary, pieces of information historians can still find from various sources, it has been extremely difficult to excavate materials on their activities in colonial Korea. Extreme scarcity of materials and information about Korean anarchists and their activities in colonial Korea prevents the construction of the whole picture of their movement and a vision of a society they endeavored to build. Japanese police reports that describe Korean anarchists and their activities through interrogation and investigation are not always trustworthy because of their frequent exaggerations and distortions of what Korean anarchists had done and envisioned. Regardless of the limits in constructing a story of their movements in colonial Korea, it is still quite possible to draw the general picture of them, thanks to some secondary sources and memoirs.

It is safe to say that serious attempts to form anarchist organizations with their subsequent activities in colonial Korea began around in 1925, a little later than their comrades in China and Japan did, and Korean anarchist movement in the Korean peninsula under Japanese colonialism was and continued to be, not surprisingly, much weaker than those in China and Japan, as the Japanese police reports also confirmed it.[7] Nevertheless, it was no doubt true that the general intellectual aura of colonial Korea was placed under the strong influence of socialist thoughts, including anarchism, affected by the "spark" the returning students brought in and the "wind" blowing from Japan from the 1910s to throughout the 1920s.

Japan, Anarchism, and Colonial Korea

The influence of various socialist thoughts including anarchism had already been conspicuous in the Korean peninsula through the introduction of various Japanese printed media, especially books on anarchism in Japanese original text or Japanese translation. For example, Yu Ja-myeong recalls that Japanese socialist newspapers and magazines such as *Transformation* (*Kaijō*), *Liberation* (*Kaihō*), and *Criticism* (*Hihyō*) were easily purchasable at Japanese bookstores in Manchuria, Shanghai, and Seoul around the time when the March First Movement occurred in 1919. He and other Korean radicals in China and Korea had been able to purchase them without any major obstacles and consequently studied socialism together.[8] In Yu's case, he became particularly interested in anarchism after he heard about Japanese Professor Morito Tatsuo (1888–1984), who had been dismissed from Tokyo Imperial University in 1919 and subsequently arrested in 1920 for his writing on Kropotkin.⁹ Indeed, anarchism was among the socialist thoughts flowing into the peninsula and was in fact the most popular socialist idea among Korean radicals in the late 1910s and early 1920s. Kim Seongsuk (1898–1969) spoke of popularity of anarchism in the early 1920s among Korean radicals as follows:

> At that time [in early 1920s Korea], the books on socialism were almost all translations by Japanese socialists. I read the books by Sakai Toshihiko and Yamakawa Hitoshi. A book among others that still remains in my memory is Yamakawa's *The Apparatus of Capitalism* published in 1923. . . . On the other hand, anarchism was the most popular one among all the isms. I think, all of the leftist ideas were infused in it [anarchism]. For anarchism, I read Kropotkin's *Confession* [i.e., *Memoirs of a Revolutionist*]. This was a very good book for [the understanding of] socialism.¹⁰

Obviously confused at that time with socialism in general, Kim, a Marxist and independence activist, nevertheless testifies here to the popularity of anarchism among Koreans in the early 1920s, and the source of socialism: Japanese socialists who had provided their translated and/or original works on socialism. Indeed, upon his release from a colonial jail in Korea in April 1921, he found that Korean society was "filled with socialist ideas," which he believed was due to the influence of Japanese books and translation.¹¹

Jo Bong-am (1899–1959), then a study-abroad student in Tokyo and later a leader of the Progressive Party (*Jinbo dang*) in 1950s Korea, also witnessed the influence of socialism in the summer of 1922, in colonial Korea. When he returned in July of the year to Korea as a member of Korean students studying abroad in Japan, he traveled around Korea with an organized lecture group. And what he saw in Korea was of surprise: "socialist ideas" were "widely dispersed in the Korean society beyond what had been imagined in Tokyo, and numerous [socialist] societies and circles of youth had already been formed everywhere"¹² in the peninsula. Consequently, what was to emerge in colonial Korea by May 1927 was an intellectual environment in which socialism had become the subject of daily conversations among all Korean youth; if socialism were not spoken of among them, they themselves would feel anachronistic.¹³

In some cases the rise of national consciousness corresponded to the rapid development into social consciousness and the willingness of Korean youth to accept socialism, in particular anarchist ideas and principles. Some Korean youths, even in a small town like Anui in southern Korea, were easily introduced to anarchism and readily accepted it, since Kropotkin and his writings had already been popular and circulated even among them.[14] Additional evidence of the ongoing popularity of anarchism among Korean youth in the 1920s can also be found in the case of Lee Chong-Ha (1913–2007), a former member of the Korean Esperanto Association. He testifies that when he was a high school student in late 1920s in the city of Daegu, he found in a bookstore in the city books in Japanese on Esperanto, titled *Lectures on Proletarian Esperanto* (*Puroretaria esperanto kōza*) and *A Shortcut to Esperanto* (*Esperanto shōkei*). Instilled in the books were anarchist ideas, he realized. He then subsequently became aware later that there were many students in the area who had already learned Esperanto, and believed that anarchists used Esperanto to realize anarchism, for all the Esperantists he met at the time were theoretically equipped with anarchism.[15]

What we can see here are the influence of Japanese translations/works of socialism and the popularity of anarchism, and the works of Peter Kropotkin were the ones most translated in Korea (and East Asia too).[16] Shin Chaeho, while in China, wrote his "A Miscellaneous Writing of a Man of Nonsense and Emptiness on the Occasion of a New Year" article in celebration of the arrival of a new year and sent it to *East Asia Daily* (*Dong-a Ilbo*) in Korea, which carried it on its January 2, 1925 issue. In the article Shin suggested that Korean youth in colonial Korea "become baptized by Kropotkin's '*An Appeal to the Young*,'" which he insisted was "the right prescription for a disease" then-Korean youth suffered from.[17] Shin's suggestion must have been well received, effective, and worked well among Korean youth in colonial Korea.

The strong influence of socialism, including anarchism in colonial Korea by the early 1920s and the ongoing popularity of anarchism throughout the 1920s, did not mean that Koreans were ready to have their own anarchist organizations to advocate an anarchist revolution. It was the opposite; no major anarchist organizations were established easily on the peninsula, mainly because of the presence of Japanese colonial police. Korean anarchists in colonial Korea were in constant fear of being arrested and tortured, and would never have a chance any time soon to develop a nationally unified, active anarchist organization there. Even their local and small organizations usually were short-lived. Their movements and activities were thus normally sporadic, small scale in size, camouflaged as those of study circles, and/or conducted underground activities throughout the colonial period. Of course, one can never put aside the general trend of anarchists that they were not fond of having an organization with centralized and concentrated power or unity. It was in 1929 that the first and last attempt was finally undertaken by anarchists to organize a unified nationwide entity within Korea during the colonial period, as I explain below.

In general, anarchism was always the target of the Japanese suppression just because it was believed to be associated with terrorism and violence against the colonial government, although anarchist movements in colonial Korea were not terrorism-oriented in most cases. Their activities rather were labeled as "a thought movement" (*sasang undong*), rather than either an independence movement or a revolutionary movement, without any major involvements in labor movement or major violent protests against the colonial government.[18] To put it differently, anarchist movement in colonial Korea didn't (or were not able to) openly propagate nationalism and/or violent anti-colonial struggle, albeit it remained basically in line with the anarchist principle of direct action. Considering the constraints and limits in colonial Korea, Korean anarchists in colonial Korea, as I demonstrate below, largely adopted modest and local-based means and actions probably for the survival of themselves and for the continuation of their activities.[19] Despite the popularity of anarchism in colonial Korea and the continuous attempts to organize Korean anarchists under the anarchist wind from Japan, there seemed to be an internal division among them in terms of their strategy for their movements and activity, according to their location of activity. Their sources of anarchism might have been almost the same, but their application and practice seemed to vary and be very much place-based, as I turn below to the anarchist movements in colonial Korea in two different areas, northern and southern Korea.

Anarchists in Southern Korea

Before any organization that was anarchist in its character and vision was established in colonial Korea, there had been at least one anarchism-oriented organization in colonial Korea. It was the Association for Labor and Mutual Relief in Korea (Joseon nodong gongjehoe), established in April 1920 as the first labor association in Korea, in which Go Sunheum, a soon-to-be anarchist in Osaka in 1924, played a key role in penning its platform and charter. It is a moot question if we can call it an anarchist organization, but I think it is safe to say that it was a good example that demonstrates the popularity of anarchist ideas in colonial Korea, especially that of the mutual aid idea of Peter Kropotkin. The Association's journal, *Mutual Relief* (*Gongje*), carried more articles on anarchism as a solution to then-labor issues in colonial Korea than on any other branches of socialism.[20] Another journal that often published articles on socialism, including anarchism, was *New Life* (*Sin saenghwal*), which carried many anarchism-related articles and possibly laid out an intellectual foundation for the flourishing of anarchist organizations in the ensuing years.[21]

Organizations we can identify as anarchist in character and vision began to appear in colonial Korea first in 1923, mostly in the southern part of Korea, albeit the first anarchist organization in colonial Korea was formed in the same year in Seoul. It was the Black Labor Society (Heungno hoe), which was organized in Seoul by Kim Junghan, Yi Yunhi, Yi Gangha, and Sin Gichang in early January of 1923, but was soon dissolved possibly by the order of Japanese colonial police. The Society was allegedly planned to be established when Tokyo-based anarchist Bak Yeol was paying his visit to Keijō (present-day Seoul) in September 1922, to give a report to Koreans on the massacre of Korean workers in Niigata Prefecture in the same year. During the visit, Bak could have discussed a possibility to organize an anarchist group in Korea with the above-mentioned radicals. Bak could have also wanted to get involved in organizing the Society while at the same time looking for a chance to obtain some bombs for his planned activity in Japan during his stay in Korea,[22] because of which he was to be arrested in 1923. It is at least likely that the Black Labor Society was established in 1923 as a result of Bak's trip to Korea from Tokyo in 1922, even though it seemed to exist only on paper and soon disappeared.[23]

The failed Black Labor Society was replaced with the Black Flag League (Heukgi yeonmaeng) in 1925, which was ventured by Korean youth in Seoul and Chungju, including Sin Yeong-u, Seo Sanggyeong, and Hong Jin-u. Their plan was to establish the Black Flag League as "the successor to the Black Wave Society of Tokyo,"[24] but it was discovered prior to its inauguration on May 3, 1925 by the Japanese police. Among the founding members, Seo and Hong used to be members of the Rebellious Society (Futeisha) in Tokyo, when Bak Yeol, along with his Japanese lover and comrade Kaneko Fumiko, were arrested for their alleged conspiracy to kill the Japanese emperor in 1923. Seo and Hong were among those who had returned to Korea soon after being radicalized and accepted anarchism in Tokyo. All the listed members of the Black Flag League were arrested, tried, found guilty, and sentenced to one year in prison, respectively.[25] According to what the Black Flag League's members testified at their trials, its mission was "the fundamental destruction of all absurd institutions that trample everybody's happiness and undermine individual progress [*ja-a hwakchung*], and the thorough rejection of power-minded organizations."[26] The Black Flag League proved to be another failed undertaking attempted by returned Korean students from Japan. One tragic thing about its members was that almost all of them died in prison, possibly from illness, or killed themselves after their release from prison after suffering from either physical or mental illness, as a result of tortures and/or malnutrition in prison. They all were still in their twenties, and their deaths must have been a strong message from Japanese police to other emerging anarchists in colonial Korea.

Nonetheless, a new attempt to set up an anarchist organization continued and was successfully processed several months later in the city of Daegu in September 1925. The new anarchist organization was named the True Friends League (Jin-u yeonmaeng), again led by those returned students from Japan. At least it existed and survived for about one year. Of interest is that the True Friends League avoided using the word *black* in its name, possibly in order to escape Japanese suppression due to the connotation of the word for anarchists, which could have been one of the reasons for its exceptional existence for a year. The leading figures of the League like Seo Dongseong (1895–1941), Bang Hansang (1900–1970), and Kim Jeonggeun (1909–1927) all used to be students in Tokyo. The League was to be suppressed and dissolved with Seo's arrest a year later. In fact, Seo had been already arrested once in Tokyo in complicity of Bak Yeol's "treason incident" in 1923 but had been released and returned to Korea. In the case of Bang, he traveled back to Japan in November of 1925, after the establishment of the League and met with many Korean and Japanese comrades in Tokyo, Osaka, and Nagoya, including Bak Yeol and Kaneko Fumiko in Ichigaya Prison.[27] Those involved in establishing this League were, again, all arrested by the Japanese police a year later for the charge of organizing a "violent group." In the case of Kim

Jeonggeun, he used to be a student at the Political Science Department at Waseda University in Tokyo and a member of the Black Friends Society also in Tokyo, who had believed that his liberation could be realized only through anarchism. Before gaining his individual liberation, unfortunately, however, he was arrested and prematurely died of pneumonia contracted after a hunger strike in prison.[28]

What draws our attention is Bak Yeol's obvious involvement, either direct or indirect, in the establishment of the above-mentioned two anarchist leagues in colonial Korea, the Black Flag League and the True Friends League. The members of the anarchist groups in colonial Korea who had attempted to join or get involved in these two organizations, had been associated with the Bak Yeol's "treason incident" and for the very reason had been categorized by Japanese police as "persons who must be under the most intensive observation" (*koshu yōshisatsu jin*)[29] for their allegedly "dangerous" thoughts as anarchists. This accounts for the place of Bak Yeol and the impact of his "treason incident" in the early Korean anarchist movement in Tokyo and colonial Korea. To put it bluntly, the two Leagues exemplify the close ties early anarchist movements in colonial Korea had with their counterparts in Japan, in particular those in Tokyo under Bak Yeol's leadership.

In addition to Bak Yeol's involvement in it, the True Friends League was of greater interest and significance because of the visible collaboration for the first time between Japanese and Korean anarchists in colonial Korea. When the Japanese police raided the League's office in Daegu and arrested its members, they captured two unidentified Japanese anarchists there as well, who were then detained for longer than usual for unknown reasons. Given their presence in its office, the True Friends League could have possibly been a collaborative, transnational anarchist organization formed by Korean and Japanese anarchists in colonial Korea, possibly for the first time, albeit the details are unknown due to the lack of materials, in particular with regard to their activities and programs. Some evidence suggests, though, that the League was more committed to social or labor issues than Korea's independence. At his trial Sin Jaemo, one of the League's members, testified that "what we want is only a revolution in Korea," which does not necessarily mean its abandonment of the national goal of Korea's independence but, as the League probably attempted to penetrate into a labor organization in Daegu, it must have been focusing on organizing workers and envisioning a social revolution in the future.³⁰ The League's members were all arrested, tried, and sentenced to two to five years in prison for their goal to build a new society bent on anarchism, albeit without clear evidence.³¹

In addition to Sin's testimony, what was also noteworthy during the trials was the appointment of Japanese lawyer Fuse Tatsuji (1880–1953) as defending attorney for some of the arrested True Friends League members, possibly also for the unknown arrested Japanese anarchists, although he was not able to attend their trail in Daegu. Fuse, who was called "our lawyer" by Koreans at the time and a "socialist lawyer" in Japan for his role in many trials of Japanese and Korean anarchists in Japan, was obviously in sympathy with Korean independence and anarchist movements. Before his appointment for this trial case he had already been in Korea in July and August 1923, with a group of Korean radicals, mostly communists, from the North Star Society, which was organized separately out of the Black Wave Society in Tokyo. While in Korea, Fuse gave talks in many cities for about ten times along with other Japanese socialists like Kitahara Tatsuo (1892–?), then-editor of *Advancing* (*Susume*). Fuse stayed in the peninsula until August 12. Due to his personal popularity among Korean radicals in colonial Korea, he was given a special chance during his stay to deliver his own talk, titled "The Spirit of Propertyless Class" (*Musan gyeguep ui jeongsin*), all by himself in the city of Masan in August 1923, which anarchist Kim Hyeong-yun (1903–1973) from the city, attended and found to be a "great talk."³² Fuse's talk must have had an immense impact on many in the city of Masan and its vicinity, as Masan became one of the centers of Korean anarchist activities in southern Korea.

Kim Hyeong-yun belonged to an anarchist group based in the cities of Masan and Changwon, both near Busan. Kim seemed to have spent some years in Tokyo and Osaka around in 1923 or 1924, where he supposedly met many anarchists and probably himself became one. He was known for his audacious anti-Japanese action in 1925, in the city of Miryang near Masan; he allegedly took out the eyeballs of a Japanese person during his fight, which in turn earned him the nickname of Mokbal (literally meaning "eyeballs taken out"). Later in the 1930s, Kim planned to establish with Jo Jungbok and Yi Jeonggyu, one of the Yi brothers in China, a publishing company named Freedom (*jayu*), named after the Freedom Press in England, but was unable to do so.³³ Another notable anarchist in the Masan and Changwon anarchist group was Kim San (1898–?, not to be confused with Kim

San in *SOA*), who exiled to Shanghai in 1922 and studied theology at Jinling University (today's Nanjing University) in Nanjing. During his stay in Nanjing, Kim became acquainted with Korean anarchists, including Yi Jeonggyu and Yi Eulgyu, and was convinced that the Bible contained an anarchist spirit. When he returned to Masan from China, he opened his own church, possibly to spread anarchist ideals as well as the God's messages. It is believed that Kim received a request from Yi Jeonggyu in 1928 to send a representative of Korean anarchists in the city of Masan to attend the scheduled meeting of Eastern anarchists in Nanjing, to establish the Eastern Anarchist Federation in 1928. In response, Kim seemed to work with Kim Hyeongyun and Kim Yongchan to select Yi Seokgyu, who was dispatched to Nanjing to attend the anarchist meeting as a representative of Korean anarchists in colonial Korea. Later in the 1930s, Kim San schemed to set up an ideal rural village in northern Korea, for which he was in and out of Japanese prison, since his activities involved some student movement and the Rural Village Society (Nongchon sa).[34]

Although Japanese colonial prosecutors at the trials of those Korean anarchists from the cities accounted for the Korean anarchist activities and organizations in Masan and Changwon as a "systematic" organizational movement, given the frequently attempted fabrications about those organizations by the Japanese police and prosecutors, the organizations in question were without visible activities and were in fact more like study groups for anarchist books of young people in the small cities,[35] rather than any systematically organized anarchist organization with any concrete program, and so forth. Until the return of Choe Gapryong and Yi Honggeun from Tokyo to colonial Korea in October 1927, there were no major visible, lasting, and active nationwide anarchist movement/organization in colonial Korea, as all the attempts I have described thus far were, as explained above, immediately suppressed and resolved, in most cases with fabricated or at least exaggerated stories about them as dangerous violent anarchist groups. Note that no above-mentioned anarchist groups put forward any terrorism-oriented agenda/goals or carried out terror-oriented actions.

On the other hand, it is also true that some anarchism-inspired youth audaciously continued to disperse anarchist ideals, also often propagating violence but only in vain. For example, Yu Uyeol and others, it is said, published and sent out the Declaration of the Nihilist Party (*Heo-mu dang seoneon*) in January 1926 to their compatriots in the peninsula. Yu, the leading person in writing and dissipating the declaration by regular mail, used to be in Tokyo for study, and had been associated with other Korean anarchists since 1923, in Seoul and Daegu. He was obviously inspired by Russian nihilists and the Declaration of Korean Revolution written by Shin Chaeho in 1923 for the Righteous Group in China. The declaration Yi sent out in 1926 emphasized a revolution that would inevitably take place in Korea, for the Korean masses through their direct action, including violent destruction, and the fundamental destruction of all institutions that bore power involving such things as politics and law. Propagating violence and destruction, Yu's declaration was driven by nationalist aspiration in nature but nevertheless pointed to its social dimensions of the revolution in vision and direction.[36]

Anarchists in Industrializing Northern Korea

While almost all anarchists' attempts to have their own organizations in southern Korea had failed as of 1925, the popularity of anarchism seemed to survive and continue to spread throughout colonial Korea. And the center of anarchist activities gradually moved northward from 1927. In fact, similar to the situation in southern Korea, several attempts to establish anarchism-oriented or anarchist organizations in northeastern Korea could have already been made after 1919, but their existence only became visible after 1927, with some substantial and visible activities there. On August 8, 1927, a secret society called the Icheon Free Society (Icheon jayuhoe) was allegedly planning to form in Icheon County (*Gun*) in the northern part of Gangwon Province. It is unknown if it was finally organized. The planned society's goal was to build an anarcho-communist society by rejecting the state and private property. It seems that those working in rural villages were the society's leading figures who in its inception wanted to promote rural culture and help rural youth receive education.[37]

Farther northeast, in the city of Wonsan in Southern Hamgyeong Province, a society called the League of the Men of Instincts (Bonneung-a yeonmaeng) was established on April 1, 1927, by Yi Hyang and Jo Siwon. The former's career and concept he invented deserve our special attention. Yi was an anarchist literary figure and has been known for his role in the debate between anarchist and Bolshevik literary figures in the 1920s, but most importantly for his own concept of "destitute and humble [*bincheon*] class," in place of the proletarian class.³⁸ He coined the term *destitute and humble class* after his reflections on the Korean situation. Simply speaking, he wanted to avoid using the term *proletariat* (*musan gyegeup*, literally propertyless class), since he thought that the proletarian class meant for him only the wage workers who sold their labor without actual production means. The concept of the proletarian class, however, he believed, could not include and embrace many Koreans who had been deprived of all production means whatsoever for their survival, and, therefore, they were the ones to be liberated from domination and oppression.³⁹ His concept of "destitute and humble class" meant to be a much broader term, to include the majority in Korea who, in his thinking, were not wage workers necessarily at the time. In his literary understanding, Yi also emphasized "the national reality" (*minjokjeok hyeonsil*), "the present" (*hyeonjae*), and "place-based-ness" (*hyeonjang*).⁴⁰ His concept seemed to have more appealing power to many and thus was widely accepted, gaining its popularity in northern Korea among anarchists, as it was used by many other anarchists in the north, which I demonstrate below. The League of the Men of Instincts Yi co-organized conducted its secret activities through a much larger organization called the Wonsan Youth Society (Wonsan cheongnyeon hoe), possibly an anarchism-oriented society, also formed in 1927 in the city of Wonsan, with its basic mission to cope with the communist activities in the area.⁴¹

Also established in the same year in northeastern Korea were the League of Free Workers in Wonsan (Wonsan jayu nodongja yeonmaeng), organized on September 8, 1927, and the Hamheung Society of the Youth Moving Forward (Hamheung jeongjin cheongnyeon hoe), organized on November 13, 1927, both of which were targeting workers and youths in the two cities, Wonsan and Hamheung in Northern Hamgyeong Province. In addition, a year later, in 1928, the Free Youth Society in Hamheung (Hamheung jayu so-nyeon hoe) was also established. Unfortunately, not much information is available about these organizations. Other than those in the cities of Wonsan and Hamheung, there was the Black Friends Society in Dancheon (Dancheon heuk-u hoe), organized on April 22, 1929 or in May 1929, in the city of Dancheon in Southern Hamgyeong Province. It is said that, the Black Friends Society in Dancheon, collaborating with various youth, workers, and tenant farmers' organizations in the area, adopted and used the term *destitute and humble class* that Yi Hyang from Wonsan conceptualized, in order to realize its goal to "promote a liberation movement of the destitute and humble class, based upon the spirit of spontaneous alliance."[42]

Following the activities in the northeastern part of colonial Korea Korean anarchists in the northwestern part of the Korean peninsula also began to organize themselves but only sporadically. At the time when Choe Gapryong and Yi Honggeun returned to Korea from Tokyo around in 1927, Korean anarchists in colonial Korea had been, as demonstrated above, quite active in the cities like Wonsan and Hamheung, possibly because many Korean anarchists in Japan had already been rushing back to Korea since July 1926.[43] It is not clear why many Japan-based anarchists were returning en masse to Korea suddenly from mid-1926. It is quite possible, though, that their homecoming from 1926 had something to do with the arrest and trial of Bak Yeol and his Japanese comrade and lover Kaneko Fumiko, in particular the latter's death in prison in Utsunomiya in Tochigi Prefecture on July 23 1926. Their return to Korea might have had something to do with their fear of arrest and torture in Japan after witnessing Bak's trial and Kaneko's death in prison. Or they could have schemed Kaneko's revenge in colonial Korea by reviving Korean anarchist activities in the Korean peninsula, particularly in northern Korea, after 1927, a year after Kaneko's death in prison.

In addition, it is also plausible that those returned anarchists could have wanted to rebuild their movement after most attempts to build anarchist organizations in southern Korea, particularly in the cities of Daegu, Masan, and Changwon, let alone Seoul, had all been discovered in advance and crushed by Japanese police, resulting in the arrest and loss of many involved anarchists. These obvious failures in the south by 1925, too, could have prompted the return of Korean anarchists in Japan to colonial Korea, in order to renew their anarchist activities by expanding or building new anarchist organizations in the north, if not again in the south. Finally, the increased activities of the communists in colonial Korea by the mid-1920s could have been another factor for this rush of Korean anarchists in Japan back to Korea. Industrializing northern Korea must have appeared to them, just like to the communists, as a place with much more favorable conditions for their movement, in particular, with the presence of an increasing number of workers.

It was in this context that one of the biggest anarchist organizations in colonial Korea was established in northwestern Korea, in the city of Pyongyang. It was the Black Friends Society in Gwanseo Region (Gwanseo Heuk-u hoe), organized again by those who had returned to Korea since 1926, such as Yi Honggeun and Choe Gapryong. Yi and Choe were two leading figures in this new anarchist venture attempted on December 22, 1927, at Cheondogyo Hall in the city of Pyongyang. It is believed that the Society was first named the Like-Minded Friends Society in Gwanseo Region (Gwanseo dong-u hoe), possibly in an attempt to camouflage it as an apolitical ordinary fraternity organization to escape Japanese surveillance. Soon after, however, for unknown reasons, it was renamed the Black Friends Society in Gwanseo Region, disclosing its main anarchist identity, goals, and principles with the use of the word *black*. The Society placed its goals on the total liberation of labor class and the repudiation of "professional activists" (i.e., communists) and their "naked power-ism" (*ganggwon juui*), as well as the propagation of the spontaneous alliance principle. In other words, its main struggle took aim at liberating workers and peasants through spontaneous organizations and fighting the communists. The Society also opened and ran a branch office of another anarchist organization, the Black Front Society (Heuksaek jeonseon sa), at Choe's home, possibly in the city of Pyongyang, to dissipate anarchist ideas in Korea, while continuing to launch other popular organizations, in particular labor unions in the area. The Black Friends Society in Gwanseo Region maintained its contacts with many other anarchists both at home and abroad through the branch office of the Black Front Society. Besides organizing workers into labor unions together, the relationship between the two societies is unknown. The Black Friends Society in Gwanseo Region was to host the first national convention of Korean anarchists in 1929, possibly utilizing the various contacts or the network it had maintained through its suborganization. The Black Front Society also opened later a Labor Night School (*Nodong yahak*) to promote the spirit of work-study and social consciousness among workers.[44]

The platform of the Black Friends Society in Gwanseo Region delineates its goals in great detail. In it the Society first mandated that its members (1) repudiate the idea of centralization (*jung-ang jipgwon*) and naked power-ism (*ganggwon juui*) and emphasize the idea of spontaneous alliance (*jayu yeonhap*), (2) pledge the complete liberation of the "destitute and humble class," and finally (3) repudiate all kinds of idol worships. According to some South Korean scholars, the Society, "for the first time in colonial Korea," intended to work "systematically" for the improvement of the rights of Korean peasants and workers, in particular, the latter's working conditions.[45] In addition, of special interest is the Society's seeming avoidance of mentioning independence, just like most anarchist organizations in colonial Korea in the 1920s; there was no mention of Korea's independence or national liberation in the Society's platform and/or declaration, albeit nationalism clearly was one of its moving forces in their activities.[46] The Society's reference to the "destitute and humble class" in its platform, as historian Horiuchi Minoru posits, also indicates the popularity and influence of Yi Hyang's concept, even in the northwestern area, which possibly suggests that its immediate goal was set with consideration of the local conditions where the liberation of the "destitute and humble class" from their hardship was of immediate importance. It also denotes that, given that Yi Hyang had mostly been active in the northeastern area and the city of Wonsan and its vicinity, and had stayed in the city of Pyongyang in northwestern area at the time only for about four months, Yi's concept of the "destitute and humble class" must have been spread widely and received well by Korean anarchists throughout the northern part of Korea,[47] even by those who had returned from Japan, such as Yi Honggeun and Choe Gapryong. The concept must have been new to many anarchists returned from Japan, but their adoption and use of it clearly demonstrate their openness and willingness to meet the local conditions and use the local language in launching their movement.

As explained above, the term *destitute and humble class* seemed to be accepted and used widely to define and include those of the ruled and exploited in both urban and rural areas of northern Korea, who had no survival and production means whatsoever, unlike the proletariat who were, by definition, basically wage workers.[48] As mentioned, the popularity and acceptance of Yi's concept can be explained in terms of the ongoing industrialization in northern Korea by Japanese colonial government. In comparison with agricultural southern Korea at the time, the immediate issue anarchists faced and wanted to tackle in the northern part of the peninsula, in other words, could have been some rural problems and labor-related issues at hand as a result of rapid industrialization and its consequences in the 1920s, rather than any seemingly distant national or transnational goal. Another possibility is the influence of Japan-based Korean anarchists whose understanding of anarchism had been influenced by Japanese anarchism; their goal in activity had possibly been placed more on social issues in league with the various trends of Japanese anarchist movement of the time, which made them more willing to consider such a placed-based term. Whatever the reason, the application of Yi Hyang's concept to anarchist movements in northern Korea points to the emphasis Korean anarchists in the area put in their practice of anarchism on the social problems in the place they were, unlike most anarchists in southern Korea. In fact, local accommodations could have been a useful tactic for Korean anarchists to avoid temporarily or postpone their mentioning of independence, primarily in order to escape the intelligence network of and outright suppression by the Japanese police. Above all, however, Korean anarchists in colonial Korea seemed to be willing to meet the diverse demands and needs of the people, which usually sprang from different local conditions and situations, and practiced anarchism accordingly.

Always facing outright suppression, small anarchist groups nevertheless continued to emerge in northern Korea, albeit all short-lived without any good visible trace. In Anju of Southern Pyeong-an Province, An Bong-yeon, Kim Hansu, Yi Sunchang, Kim Yongho, and so on organized the Anju Black Friends Society (Anju heuk-u hoe) in April 1929, and were later joined by Yi Hyeok and An Yeonggeun, both of whom had been in Tokyo for study and had been involved in Korean anarchist activities there. Among its members, An Bong-yeon would die in the notorious West Gate (Seodaemun) Prison in Seoul after being arrested later in the same year for his participation in the Korean Anarcho-Communist Federation (see below). Years later in 1930, a secret society–like anarchist group, called the Cheolsan Black Friends Society (Cheolsan Huek-u hoe), was also organized in the county of Cheolsan in Northern Pyeong-an Province by a group of youths, led by Jeong Cheol, who had been interested in social issues from his high school years. Its members soon numbered about one hundred, but were all arrested. The Society, therefore, was soon dissolved.[49]

The last major attempt by Korean anarchists in the northern part of colonial Korea to organize themselves was the foiled undertaking to establish the Korean Anarcho-Communist Federation (KAF, Joseon gongsan mujeongbu juuija yeonmaeng) secretly on November 10, 1929, after the Japanese suppression of the aborted Convention of All Korea Black Movement Activists (Jeon joseon heuksaek sahoe undongja daehoe), originally scheduled to be held in Pyongyang from November 10 to 11, 1929. The central figures in these two undertakings were Yi Honggeun and Choe Gapryong, and the convener of the Convention was the Black Friends Society in Gwanseo Region of which both Yi and Choe were members. Choe presided over the preliminary meeting for the Convention on August 5 of the same year. The decision made at the meeting with attendance of some anarchists was regarding their plan to hold the first-ever national convention of all Korean anarchists from both colonial Korea and abroad. The audacious plan went smoothly only until the scheduled Convention drew attention from Japanese police. When the plan was finally discovered, those who had already arrived in the area on time for the Convention had to hide to escape any possible arrest, and those who were on their way to the area to attend it had to abort their trip. The Convention itself was therefore aborted. But many anarchists were already in custody of Japanese police in the name of so-called in-advance detention, or had been deported.

According to the plan made for the Convention at its preliminary meeting, anarchists from Japan and Manchuria in addition to those in colonial Korea were expected to be present at it. Yu Rim was among those who at the risk of potential arrest and even his life had come from Manchuria to attend the Convention. Yu had been active mostly in Manchuria but was not well known to the Japanese police at the time of it in 1929, so at first he escaped any police attention and arrest. Although eventually arrested, he was released and then deported to Manchuria, due to the lack of evidence for Japanese police to hold and prosecute him. Anarchists from Japan who were included on the list of attendants were deported to Japan as well. For example, when Yu Hyeontae arrived at Pyongyang Train Station to attend the first national convention of anarchists as a representative of the Tōko Labor Union in Tokyo, he was arrested at site and sent back to Japan. Almost all anarchists who came for the Convention were detained, arrested, deported, or fled and hid from the Japanese police.[50]

The idea to hold a national convention of all Korean anarchists both at home and abroad was probably bold but not realistic in the late 1920s. The holding of the first national convention of Korean anarchists would have to wait until 1946, as I demonstrate in chapter 5. The schedule for the ambitious national convention of Korean anarchists in 1929 evidently didn't go as smoothly as planned, but it was the first attempt by Korean anarchists in and outside Korea to establish their own nationwide organization within colonial Korea, not in a foreign soil. It was a somewhat audacious but reckless attempt, given the unfavorable political climate of colonial Korea and the tightened

Japanese police surveillance. As some scholars suggest, it could rather have been planned not only to organize all Korean anarchists but also to cope with the growing influence of the communists and their activities in colonial Korea at the time,[51] although it can't be confirmed.

Even though failed, the Convention entailed as its fruit an extended effort to organize all Korean anarchists. Those anarchists who were in the area near Pyongyang for the convention but were not immediately caught, arrested, or detained by the Japanese police were able to secretly meet and establish the Korean Anarcho-Communist Federation (KAF) on the scheduled date of the convention. The KAF was a product of an extended, secret effort to set up an organization of all Korean anarchists, led mainly by five anarchists, including Choe Gapryong and Yu Rim. It is said that before their arrest they managed to have a chance to meet together and were able to announce formally the establishment of the KAF. Although the KAF was the outcome of the attempt to have a nationwide organization led by anarchists themselves in colonial Korea, it is quite doubtful, given the arrest or deportation of the leading anarchist like Choe and Yu, whether the KAF actually was able to function as such and exercise its role and responsibility to oversee or take the leadership role for all anarchist activities in Korea and possibly abroad as well.

It must be noted here that the KAF's platform didn't seem to include any concrete word about Korea's independence or national liberation, either. This was not unusual for anarchist organizations at the time in colonial Korea, as I have demonstrated. Included in its platform rather were radical and revolutionary programs that aimed at a social revolution and thus were transnational in nature. For a new Korea, the platform stated, the KAF would strive for "the abolition of the existing state system and the transformation of it into a social organization that is founded on free alliance and commune as its principle unit"; "the abolition of the existing private property system and reform [national economic unit] into a decentralized industrial organization"; and "the abolition of the existing class and national discriminations and the attempt to construct a society for all mankind of freedom, equality, and fraternity." The mention of abolishing "national discrimination" in the platform could possibly be geared toward the KAF's both national and transnational goals to gain independence and to construct a genuine human society for all mankind.[52] Another interesting thing about the KAF is that it had its concrete, strict code of conduct for its members in their movement. The code prohibited its members from becoming engaged in a confrontational struggle with communists, possibly to avoid any wasteful, meaningless, unnecessary conflicts with communists. While encouraged to endeavor to advance the movement for peasantry, the code did not allow its members to join any other nationalist group, which is understandable if we consider anarchists' critiques of nationalist movements at the time, especially those by the Japan-based anarchists, as narrowly focused political movements for incomplete liberation.[53]

The KAF could exist for a while but probably only in name without any major activities; it continued to be in hibernation until the Japanese police accidently found out about its existence in 1931. Besides arrest and continuous tight surveillance by Japanese police of its members, which were the very reasons why the KAF could have no chance to emerge as a nationwide organization with some notable activities, there were additional reasons for its long hibernation. Since its establishment in 1929, the family of its members in Korea seemed to suffer immensely as well from the hardships of life with economic distress and other problems, part of which was due to the Japanese police's intended harsh and brutal treatment of them. In hindsight, it seems it was inevitable for many Korean anarchists, particularly those in colonial Korea, to give up their faith in anarchism or move away from their anarchist activities and remain silent, not only due to their personal hardships and, if arrested, potential torture, but due as well to the sufferings and hardships of their families deliberately caused by the Japanese police, which they had to painfully witness and probably found unendurable.[54]

With the discovery by the Japanese colonial police in 1931 of the existence (if not activities) of the KAF, the anarchist movement and activities in colonial Korea began to rapidly wane, or more precisely disappear,[55] and it never recovered even after 1945, at least not as a revolutionary movement for social transformation. However, as historian Oh Jang-Whan explains, various small-scale anarchist activities seemed to manage to survive and somehow continue until 1945, without any major intellectual or political impacts in colonial Korea. In other words, activities to disseminate anarchist ideas with the formation of circles and the publications on anarchism never ceased, although it is doubtful how influential they were. The anarchist publications obviously were still available in colonial Korea, at least, at Twentieth Century Bookstore, which as mentioned, opened in Seoul and was run by Yi Hyeok. Yi seemed to be involved also in the publication of a couple of other anarchist journals—*New East Magazine* (*Sin dongbangji*) and *Black Whirlwind* (*Heuk seonpung*). As examined earlier, Kim Hyeong-yun with Jo Jungbok and Yi Jeonggyu attempted together in September 1932 to open a Korean version of the Freedom Press of England, in order to publish anarchism-related books, which too were restricted by Japanese police. Some anarchists like Yi Jeonggyu, who was brought into Korea from China after his arrest in October 1928 in Shanghai, turned their eyes to the failed venture to organize a customer's cooperative association (*sobi johap undong*) in 1934, which, according to historian Oh Jang-Whan, was an attempt to lay out a foundation for an anarchist society in the farming villages of colonial Korea. Some other anarchists formed the Pioneer Society for Reading Books (Seon-gu dokseo hoe) in 1938.[56] However we evaluate these endeavors after 1931, it is certain that, given all these accounts, anarchists like Yi in colonial Korea seemed to turn anarchism into a principle for social movement, not as a revolutionary movement, from the 1930s until 1945, if only to facilitate their survival under Japanese surveillance and suppression. To be sure, Korean anarchists in colonial Korea never discontinued their anarchist activities in the 1930s and '40s but at the same time never wanted or were willing to get any attention from the Japanese colonial police. They had to endure during the long "combat period" in the history of Korean anarchism from the 1930s until 1945, without any actual ability and organization to fight Japan.[57]

Pushing the Limits

Despite that Korea was a colony of Japan, the anarchist movement in colonial Korea readily began to develop in the mid-1920s, albeit it only lasted for a half decade as a visible movement. At its outset, there were some favorable conditions in colonial Korea for acceptance and development of anarchism, which ironically came from the colonial conditions. The availability of Japanese anarchist publications and press contributed to the popularity and reception of anarchism, which was a by-product of Korea being a colony of Japan and in geographical proximity to it. Korean anarchists who organized themselves and started their activities in the mid-1920s in colonial Korea were either former study-abroad students to Japan or those who had been in contact with anarchist works, in particular by Ōsugi Sakae and/or Peter

Kropotkin, although anarchism had already been known to Koreans. Koreans under Japanese colonialism indeed had no other choice but to go to Japan for study abroad or for jobs. Their colonizer somehow provided Korean students with important nutrition for their radicalization, both at home and in Japan, and also offered abundant chances to work with Japanese anarchists with whom they often associated and took actions together. In many cases, the Japanese anarchists were not just their teachers of anarchism but comrades in activity as well. It was at the time that anarchism worldwide also began to retreat and wane in the wake of the rise of Bolshevism from the early 1920s, and colonial Korea was not an exception in this regard. To make things worse, any attempt to organize or disseminate anarchist groups or ideas suffered from outright, brutal suppression by Japanese police who reacted to anarchists out of their fear of terrorism and violence.

Those who began anarchist movements in colonial Korea were former Korean "poor work-study students," who were constantly on the move to and from Japan. And they were mostly affiliated with Bak Yeol's anarchist organizations in Tokyo and led the anarchist movement in southern Korea. And their various movements were characterized by their promotion of anarchist ideals, with little reference to Korea's independence. In both Northern and Southern Gyeongsang Provinces of southern Korea in the 1920s, anarchists enjoyed their geographical proximity to Japan to bring in the "spark of revolution" directly from Japan through the returning students and to sow the seeds of anarchist movements, riding "the wind blowing from the East." The general social trend in the two southern provinces, Northern and Southern Gyeongsang Provinces, were indeed "under the great influence of [the socialist trend in] Japan,"[58] and they were to become a home of Korean anarchists even after 1945, with a series of anarchist conventions held there, about which I will explain in chapter 5.

Unlike in southern Korea, where the anarchist movement began and flourished as a "thought movement" to propagate anarchism, the industrializing areas of Hamgyeong and Pyeong-an Provinces in northern Korea provided different grounds for Korean anarchists with abundant labor forces. Reflecting the composition and situation of the population in northern Korea, many anarchists willingly employed Yi Hyang's new concept of "poor and humble class" in place of the proletarian class to describe the existential conditions and social relations there, where peasants as well as workers together faced the hardships and pains under the industrialization pursued by the Japanese colonial government. In addition, many Korean anarchist organizations in northern Korea in their labor-related activities began to use the term *black* again in the name of their organizations, while involved in various activities, as if they were no longer afraid of Japanese attention. In short, in northern Korea, anarchists were oriented and geared more toward the social and labor issues, which was a product of industrialization there, and their placed-based approach.

While the Korean anarchist movement in 1920s colonial Korea was generally driven by "pure anarchism,"[59] the labor union–related activities, including those for peasants, in northern Korea, in particular by Choe Gapryong, reveal evidence of the practice of anarcho-syndicalist ideas among Korean anarchists since Choe's return to Korea in 1926. This is not to suggest that those anarchist activities in northern Korea were more advanced in theory or organized better systematically, but to indicate the differences in their understanding and practice of anarchism even within colonial Korea, which usually resulted from different local environments surrounding their reception and application of it. Simply put, anarchism was accepted, understood, and practiced diversely in correspondence with local demands and situation in colonial Korea. Usually crucial in defining the goal and determining the means and methods to achieve it in the Korean anarchist movement in colonial Korea were, I argue, the local differences. The differences were due to the fact that northern Korea was developed into an industrial area and its southern part remained largely agrarian under the Japanese colonial policy.

In addition, as the Choe Gapryong's case demonstrates, it is quite obvious that early anarchist movements in colonial Korea had close ties with its counterparts abroad, in particular in Japan, through anarchists themselves in motion mainly between two places, Tokyo and the Korean peninsula.[60] Heavily dependent on "the wind from the East," Korean anarchists in colonial Korea, however, were not insulated, even from their counterparts in China, including Manchuria. Yu Rim's case in the late 1920s at the failed convention of Korean anarchists, among others, clearly demonstrates the existence of some kind of a network among them, which made them remain connected with many Koreans around the region. In addition, Yi Jeonggyu's call from China for a representative from colonial Korea to attend the meeting of the Eastern anarchists in Nanjing in 1928 also demonstratesthe existence of a different kind of network among them. While extremely impossible to detail the existence and operation of the network of Korean anarchists, due mainly to its confidential nature and lack of evidence and supporting information, many sources and memoirs available today unanimously indicate a close relationship maintained throughout the 1920s to 1940s between many anarchists and their organizations in Korea and abroad. The relationship seemed to be built and then maintained in the forms of direct and/or secret personal contacts and sending and receiving their journals and other forms of printed materials including letters, and so forth.[61] No matter where they were, Korean anarchists continued to communicate with each other, not to mention that anarchists were always on the move from one to other places. The underlying issues in their communication must have been national liberation, sometimes explicitly and in other times implicitly, as well as social revolution.

Although imbued with nationalist aspiration for independence just like all Korean anarchists abroad, those in colonial Korea did not, were not able to, or even were not willing to put forward directly and openly the question of independence in their organizational and publication activities. The reasons for this seeming passivity in propagating anarchism for the cause of national liberation were possibly twofold. The first probable reason was to avoid the attention of Japanese police as much as possible by avoiding referring to their national aspiration. Once they attempted to propagate independence, they met with outright Japanese suppression, and thus witnessed the ultimate limits in their movement under colonialism. The increasing suppression and tightened control by Japanese colonial police must have deepened their frustration and sometimes despair. Accordingly, the question of independence must have been avoided as much as possible, albeit temporarily. Second, given the major roles played by those from Tokyo, it is quite possible that they were focusing on revolution than just on political independence itself, affected by the general trend in Japanese anarchism of the 1920s, which had no roots in national longing for independence. In short, they deliberately avoided referring to the question of independence for their own survival or strategy, and at the same time were predisposed to the cause of social revolution by their orientation.

It is true that Korean anarchists in colonial Korea had to deal with very limited, restricted ranges of activities. However, they left a long-lasting impression that their movement generally was for a "livelihood struggle" (as opposed to "ideological struggle") against economic distress and hardships Koreans in the peninsula frequently underwent under the exploitive, discriminatory colonial rule. Without presenting an idea and vision to break down the hardships of life in colony, especially to the "destitute and humble class," they might have thought it would be meaningless to propagate anarchism and would even undermine their noble goal for an ideal society, which was the case particularly in northern Korea. In reality, Korean anarchists faced other serious issues pertinent to the political and economic hardships their families, as well as they themselves, had to endure directly under the colonial control and suppression, which in many cases rendered some Korean anarchists unfaithful in the end to their anarchist belief and even caused some to give it up later in the 1930s. Some of them could have possibly have supported the Japanese colonial rule and the Japanese pan-Asian vision of the region during the Pacific War.[62]

Given the extremely fragmented and biased materials available on the Korean anarchist movement, it is almost impossible to create a comprehensive picture of it in colonial Korea. However, to place it in the broader context of Korean anarchist movement before 1945, I think a general picture can be made without risking distortion or overgeneralization. Korean anarchist activities in colonial Korea were generally sporadic and small in size, rather than organized and systematic. No single organization or group lasted a few years. Very weak and secret organizations, most anarchist organizations sometimes experienced outright dissolution even before they were established. As for the issue of independence, they seemed to be future-oriented by postponing it to the near future. Anarchist activities in colonial Korea were not commanded uniformly by a nationwide organization. They were locally concentrated and autonomous in their goals and direction, mainly because of the Japanese suppression but at the same time possibly because of their distaste for power concentration and their belief in spontaneity.[63]

Korean anarchists in colonial Korea posed no major threat to the colonial rule as part of a leading anticolonial/independence movement. Although they seemed to get involved in various activities, including labor union activities in northern Korea, they didn't seem to be divided or in conflict over theoretical issues; rather in the end they attempted to set up a united organization in 1929. Historian Horiuchi even argues that there were no theoretical differences between Korean pure anarchists and syndicalists.[64] Indeed, the theoretical differences between pure anarchism and anarcho-syndicalism were quite commonplace and conspicuous among the Japanese anarchists in the 1920s. But the differences, if there were any, it seems, were not seriously taken among Korean anarchists and thus didn't bother them throughout the colonial period, as long as they could work on their two goals: social revolution through "livelihood struggle" and national liberation. Or they might have no ideological attachments, just like their Japanese counterparts. As Crump suggests with regard to Japanese anarchists, Korean anarchists in colonial Korea had "little time" or even were not willing to consider theoretical differences, given their harsh environment and brutal suppression of their families as well as themselves under the direct colonial rule.[65] Neither were Korean anarchists in colonial Korea willing to nor able to consider some theoretical issues in anarchism. This doesn't mean that there was no theoretical consideration at all by Korean anarchists in Korea. Indeed, they were more interested in accommodating their unfavorable environment and conditions in applying and practicing anarchism, as exemplified by the invention and popularity of the term *destitute and humble class* Yi Hyang coined. In fact, they might have not wanted to consider vexing theoretical considerations in their anarchist movement in colonial Korea, but they nevertheless willingly and flexibly localized anarchism in response to the demands and needs of the location they were situated in, if not just for their strategy and goals.

CHAPTER 4

Korean Anarchists in Wartime China and Japan

The 1930s witnessed the overall decline of Korean anarchist movement in both China and Japan, not to mention in colonial Korea, due mainly to Japan's invasion of China beginning in 1931, and, as a result, increased tight control and suppression of "dangerous thoughts" in Japan, its colonies, and occupied areas in China such as Shanghai. Both Chinese and Japanese anarchist movements too were on the wane during the same period.[1] In fact, since the introduction of the notorious Peace Preservation Law in 1925, the anarchist movement in Japan had been further suppressed in the 1930s and so had been in colonial Korea. In China, too, since the April 12th Coup of 1927 in Shanghai by Chiang Kai-shek and the failure of the Canton Commune in Guangzhou in December of the same year, radical movements in general had lost their strength and vigor. Anarchists had not been an immediate target of the suppression in China, but their activities were not as active as usual since the closure of Laoda and the failure of the Quanzhou Movement in the late 1920s.

In most scholarship on the history of anarchism in Eastern Asia the 1930s and '40s remain generally untouched and/or in need of further research, either due to the lack of information and sources or the silence and secrecy on the part of anarchists themselves in their various activities, reflecting the general decline of the anarchist movement in the region. Although Japan-based Korean anarchists as well as those in colonial Korea gradually either disappeared or went underground in the 1930s to '40s, unseen on the stage and leaving almost no trace of their activities in many cases, Korean anarchists in China were able to continue to undertake their various activities in league with anti-Japanese forces in China. In fact, Japan's invasion of China beginning in 1931, and, as a consequence, its military occupation of Manchuria and north China by the mid-1930s were perceived by many Korean anarchists in China as "a new revolutionary situation."[2] Unlike their comrades in Japan and colonial Korea, Korean anarchists in China, utilizing Japan's aggression in China, turned the 1930s to early 1940s into "the Combat Period" or "the Wartime Struggle Period"[3] against Japan in the history of Korean anarchism. It was during this period that they began to propose a united front idea and even arm themselves to engage in warfare, somewhat unconventionally. Japan's all-out invasion of China and tight thought control in the occupied areas could not stop Korean anarchists in China from fighting back for the cause of national liberation. The help and support from other Asian anarchists, as well as the National Government of China and even the CCP in Yan'an, were all readily available for them to continue their activities, this time mainly terror-oriented or armed struggle. My focus in this chapter is, first, how Japan-based anarchists coped with the unfavorable situation in 1930s Japan, with emphasis on their propaganda activities with the *Black Newspaper* (*Heuksaek sinmun*), a kind of propaganda warfare in Japan by Korean "militant" anarchists. And second, I will examine how China-based Korean anarchists responded to Japan's invasion of China by focusing on their terror-oriented activities and then on the national front idea that was put forward by them to utilize the "new revolutionary situation" they faced in a foreign soil.

Black Newspaper (*Heuksaek sinmun*) and "Militant Anarchism" in Japan

During the 1930s, Korean anarchists in Japan managed to continue to publish their own journals and newspapers, working still closely with their Japanese counterparts. The alliance with the letter was still much needed for Korean anarchists for their activities and survival. Under the tightened control and suppression of radicalism and radical movement in 1930s Japan, their activity was usually confined to the continuation of publications to propagate anarchism and criticize what was happening in colonial Korea under the colonial government. Any activities that might involve anti-Japanese colonialism could have brought immediate attention from the Japanese police.

From the late 1920s to early 1930s, a number of Korean anarchist publications continued to come out in Japan. Yi Jeonggyu (not to be confused with one of the Yi brothers in China) and others worked together in 1929 to publish *Liberation Movement* (*Haebang undong*) in Korean, while Hong Yeong-u and others, representing the Federation of Free Youth (Jiyū seinen renmei), were able to publish *Free Youth* (*Jiyū seinen*) in January 1929. Another anarchist journal called *Movement for Mutual Aid* (*Gojo undō*) could have possibly been published in January 1928 by Won Simchang, Jang Sangjung, and Oh Chiseop, but it is unclear if it actually came out.[4] The Free Commune Society (Jiyū komyūn shakai) was established under the leadership of Han Hayeon (1903–1960) and Hong Hyeong-ui (1911–1968) with its journal titled *Free Commune* (*Jiyū komyūn*) that began to be published in 1932 under Hong's editorship but soon discontinued in December 1933, after publishing its number one of the second volume, due to financial problems.

In addition to these publication activities, Korean anarchists in Japan continued their collaboration in publication with their Japanese comrades. While Yi Yunhi (1906–1951) took part in the publication of *Free Alliance-ism* (*Jiyū rengōshugi*), published in Osaka in 1930 by the Black Youth Free Alliance (Kokushoku seinen jiyū rengō), Jang Sangjung served with Irie Ichirō as the publishers of *Debate on Freedom* (*Jiyū ronsen*), possibly in 1932.[5] In 1933, the *Natives* (*Domin*), a literary journal of the Natives Society (Dominsha), came out and continued until the publication of its seventh issue. The establishment of the Natives Society and publication of its journal by Korean anarchists were supposedly "influenced" by the establishment and activities of the Society of the Youth in Farming Villages (Nōson seinensha) of Japanese anarchists, which was organized in February 1932 in Tokyo. This Japanese anarchist society emphasized a movement of the youth in farming villages, inspired by a slogan "Let's appeal to the peasantry."[6] Drawing on self-reliance and economic direct action, the movement had its strong commitment to "creative activities" of the masses[7] and placed its emphasis on the activities "from within the peasantry."[8] The movement also had its attachment to the ideas of decentralization and, somewhat interestingly, "a crucial role" anarchists had to play "as an organised fraction which guides the people's rebellion in an anarchist direction."[9]

After Japan's invasion of Manchuria in 1931, Japan-based Korean anarchists did not seem to rest on propagating anarchist principles and ideals; their movement entered its audacious "combat period"[10] against Japan's aggression in China and suppression at home, as well as against Korean nationalist movement. At the forefront in this "combat" against Japan was *Black Newspaper* (*Heuksaek sinmun*), the most important Korean anarchist newspaper in 1930s Japan, which represented all Korean anarchist groups in Japan and published its inaugural issue on August 1 (or July 22), 1930.[11] Unlike many Korean anarchist publications in Japan, it survived and continued to publish its issues for about five years. *Black Newspaper* was funded by Korean anarchist organizations and Korean labor unions in Japan, and used Korean for its language, albeit its publication was well received with a warm welcome and support from the Japanese anarchist newspaper *Spontaneous Alliance Newspaper* (*Jiyū rengō shimbun*).[12] The publisher of *Black Newspaper* was initially the Tōko Labor Alliance (Tōko rōdō domei), a union organization of Korean workers in Japan under the leadership of Korean anarchists. Later, the Federation of Black Friends and Free Youth (Kokutomo jiyū seinen renmei) became its publisher.[13] Each issue of it seems to be published with only two pages, but in the limited space it carried widely local, national. and global news, more than any of its predecessors, not to mention news about colonial Korea and their comrades in China. Due mainly to the notorious Japanese censorship, *Black Newspaper*, until its formal discontinuation due to financial difficulties after its thirty-seventh issue in May 1935,[14] was repeatedly banned and in many cases its issues were confiscated by Japanese police. And the editors were in and out of prison continuously.[15] Its issues, however, were allegedly sent out and delivered continuously in a sealed envelope to the readers, presumably Korean anarchists in Japan, China, and colonial Korea.[16]

From its slogan of "Rush with revolutionary actions at the irrational contemporary society," which appeared on the cover page of its inaugural issue, we can see that the newspaper's primary concern was about the social rather than the national, at least in the beginning of its publication. But it is also clear that its other goals were the liberation of Korea from Japanese colonialism and the opposition to Japanese imperialism. For example, the newspaper's special issue (18) on August 29, 1932, on the topic of Japan's annexation of Korea in 1910, proposed a joint struggle of Korean and Chinese peoples against Japanese imperialism.[17] In fact, the newspaper, according to an article carried in it later in 1935, was launched with an expectation to "take actions" by delivering its issues to the masses and letting them understand what it advocated, for which Korean anarchist comrades were encouraged to allow it to speak for them and function as an organizer to help integrate all the different opinions of them.[18] In short, *Black Newspaper* led a kind of verbal warfare against Japanese imperialism as well as propagated the anarchist idea of social revolution.

The *Black Newspaper* interspersed with diverse news, quite a broad range of local, regional, and global news and information, covering updates on the revolutionary movements/activities and events in the countries in Europe (Spain, Greece, France, Soviet Russia, Bulgaria, and Yugoslavia), Latin America (Mexico and Colombia), North America (the U.S. and Canada), and Asia (Korea, Japan, and China), as well as reactionary movements in Germany and Soviet Russia. It also carried many pieces of writing that discussed anarchist theories by Korean anarchists, both in China and Japan, and many translations of Kropotkin's writings. The diversity of news of the world and analyses it offered about them indicate the newspaper's transnational dimension in selecting and carrying news, although it is unclear exactly how it received the news and what its sources of information were. One possible clue is Japanese anarchist newspapers like *Spontaneous Alliance* (*Jiyū rengō*) and *Spontaneous Alliance Newspaper*, both of which seemed to share many articles and reports with *Black Newspaper*, albeit they were mostly carried in the Japanese first and then many of them were reproduced in *Black Newspaper* in Korean translation. Of interest is that Japanese anarchist presses such as the ones mentioned above not only carried news about the activities of Korean anarchists in Japan, China, and Korea, but also often called Korean anarchists "Korean brothers" (*Chōsen kyōdai*).[19] In addition, *Spontaneous Alliance* carried many writings by Korean anarchists and reports on colonial Korea and/or Korean anarchists and their activities in China and Korea. All this tells us about the close relationship and even possible partnership in publication between them.

The *Black Newspaper* was transnational in its character, and its transnational idea of the state and negation of patriotism seemed to be shared and accepted by Korean anarchists who contributed to it.[20] In fact, nationalist movement in colonies already had been under critical scrutiny and nationalism had been identified as not being a path toward social revolution by a Korean anarchist in 1929. Yi Honggeun contributed to *Spontaneous Alliance Newspaper* an article titled "Liberation Movement and National Movement," in which he stated that since the masses in colonies had received the dual oppressions, class and national, a liberation movement in colonies couldn't be achieved only by nationalism. Yi explained that there was a process in the revolutionary movement of a colony, which deepened the initial national discontent and consciousness and then intensified them into national struggle relentlessly, finally developing into the consciousness of and struggle for social revolution. Labor and peasant movements in a colony, therefore, took their shape as a liberation movement of colony, and the struggle for liberation of a colony had to shoulder the duty for national liberation and social liberation movements simultaneously. To make genuine national liberation and have independent countries, in short, Yi asserted that all nations (*minzoku*) bring everything to equal ground by transcending racial and national discrimination. In addition, to solve other problems in colonies, the overthrow of capitalism must be presupposed, Yi added.[21]

Many articles and reports carried in the *Black Newspaper* supported and maintained Yi's stance, especially his criticism of the nationalist and/or patriotic movements by Korean exiles, the goal of which, according to the newspaper, was limited to gaining only political independence and the class interest of national capitalists. An article titled "Fallacies in the National Movement," carried in its twenty-sixth issue on February 28, 1934, included its harsh criticism against the "fundamentally innate contradictions" in the Korean nationalist movement at the time. Its anonymous author argued that both theory and fact had vindicated that the liberation of a colony or a weak people could never be accomplished by a patriotic national movement. On the contrary, the patriotic national movement organized in the name of building a nation and an independent state, the author contended, had hamstrung the righteous movement of the masses to reclaim their justice and freedom and, therefore, the nationalist revolution had faced the objection and denunciation of the masses. Hence, revolutionary movements in such colonies as Korea, Taiwan, and India, where sufferings from both class and national oppression were present, the author added, had thoroughly abandoned their "nationalist tones" (*minjok gijo*). In addition, according to the author, from a standpoint of political righteousness, the nationalists might have dreamed of having one independent movement that would embrace people of all social standings and classes, who had demanded political liberation through their nation's independence, but the capitalist class in the nation compromised easily with imperialists in order to accumulate their influence and capital. The Korean capitalists, for example, when they were asked for the funds to support Korea's independence movement, called for a protection from Japanese police. And in the case of China, the National Government of China, although its goal was China's national liberation, had become nothing but a puppet of imperialists, the author maintained. However pure its motive had been, the author concluded, nationalist movements had only been movements for autonomy under a society of compulsory power and had been, therefore, nothing but a movement for social reforms. The author was not convinced by a claim that achieving a national revolution could serve as a transitional period to open up a road to eventual social revolution. Rather, in the view of the author of the article, only after the time when a social revolution was accomplished, would the genuine realization of independence of a colony be accomplished. In the author's eyes the KAFC, established in 1928, was the one that moved toward that direction with a new thought and a new catchphrase.[22]

The "realities" of patriotic movements were further examined in an article carried in *Black Newspaper* on December 28, 1934. Its anonymous contributor from China began an analysis of "patriotic movements" with the remarks on the tides of "reactions" (*bandong*) and "patriotism" that the author believed had swept the world at the time. Suggesting a struggle against the tide of patriotism and patriotic movement, the author called into question the meanings of *state* (*gukka*) and *fatherland* (*joguk*). To the author, *state* meant capitalist states and *fatherland* meant nothing but "capitalist militarist countries." The life of the masses had nothing to do with both "state" and "fatherland," therefore.[23] The author continued,

> What the masses must love is their own life [*saenghwal*] and native place [*hyangto*]. Why would [they] love [their] fatherland that serves the capitalist militarists' domination and exploitation? They [militarists] posit a different position from ours on this regard and, therefore, exist as our absolute enemy in the struggle . . . Since all states maintain their existence by depriving the masses of their blood and flesh, today's states cannot exist, once the masses reject their domination and exploitation. The projects [*sa-eop*] currently being conducted in the name of state are nothing but the ones in service of the exploitation by the rule, and there is nothing else . . . To protect the state's projects is called patriotism [*aeguk*] and, at the same time, protecting the

state [*hoguk*]. Therefore, those who launch out into what they [i.e., the rule] call the movements for patriotism and fatherland, will become their slaves . . . Let's thoroughly destroy their patriotism and consciousness about fatherland . . . [W]hat was contrived for the maintenance of the existence [of capitalism] is the patriotic movement, for which they cry out. Therefore, a national crisis [*gungnan*] they fuss about is a crisis of their domination and exploitation! The so-called [national] emergency in Japan means a crisis of the Japanese capitalists' domination and exploitation.[24]

The author challenged the meaning of *state* by negating patriotism as something that served only the rule and the capitalists and thus had nothing to do with the interest and life of the masses. The national projects such as education and national industry were also denied by the author, since they only protected the position and status of the rule and the capitalists.[25] This author rather propagated a place-based approach for the masses in identifying their self-consciousness. This author's negation of the state and patriotism was not novel. A Korean anarchist with pseudonym of Gwang had already insisted in 1929 in *Liberation Movement* that the anarchists in East Asia destroy the border signs on the borderlines between the countries, since the fatherland of anarchists was the universe and the earth, not their own respective country.[26]

The *Black Newspaper* played a role as a medium that connected Korean anarchists in China and Japan. Those anarchists in China contributed their writings to it. And there were many articles, in addition to the ones mentioned above, dealing with news on the Korean anarchists in China and their activities. In its twenty-ninth issue, for example, was the "An Outline of the Korean Anarchist Movement in China" article, and in the thirty-sixth issue "Second Anniversary of the Shanghai Black Terrorist Group and the Three Major Incidents" appeared. Carried in the ensuing issues of the newspaper were many follow-up articles on the Korean anarchists in China, and the terrorist group Black Terrorist Party (BTP) and its members. Its thirty-first issue, published on June 27, 1934, carried an article by a Korean anarchist in Shanghai, in which it was argued that social revolution was what had been agreed on by anarchists and, more important, what made anarchism realizable. And in this short article, the anarchist contributor from Shanghai engaged in a discussion of whether anarchism had "practical-ness" (*hyeonsil seong*) or just encompassed unrealistic utopian ideas. The answer offered by the author was that, since in a society founded on human instincts there had been no compulsory power and no domination, having no compulsory power and no domination in society were both an ideal and a reality. The crises and misfortunes of humankind, the author explained, arose from the fact that the absolute freedom of individual human beings had been rejected and, therefore, the goal of anarchist movement was to break through the crises and get rid of the misfortunes. To do so it was imperative to "destroy all that rejects freedom and equality" and to "retake each one's freedom and equality." Although the goal of social revolution was in this sense to retake the human life that had been lost, "social revolution does not spring from the rash acts of those who always use compulsory power [*ganggwon juui ja*]"; rather it arose only from independent/autonomous actions (*jaju haengdong*) of the masses, which were shaped from their own position. The author finally concluded the short article with a confirmation of "practical-ness" of anarchism, stating that "the ideal is not of the other world but is a fruit that is borne in reality."[27]

Anarchism's "practical-ness," along with its "strong attraction" as an idea, appeared again in an article in the thirty-third issue of the *Black Newspaper* published on October 24, 1934, written by Yi Dal (1910–1942), who was then in Shanghai and used the pseudonym Geumwol.[28] What he argued in it was the importance of "human desires" and "unnecessariness of a leading principle" in the course of constructing a new society with freedom and happiness after the destruction of his contemporary society. Since it was from their human, righteous desire for life that the masses longed for liberation, he believed that there was no need to have any "social science theories," such as Karl Marx's analysis of capital and the Communist Party's theories some intellectuals and artists had advocated. To him, anarchism was in no need of theorization, because it originated in and was a natural reflection and outcome of human desires.[29]

In some cases, *Black Newspaper* strongly asked Korean anarchists for their contributions to it by sending in their reports, suggestions, and/or opinions. To its editors lack of communication with the newspaper was a sign of passive and coward actions of anarchists during the "combat period." What they also wanted was to receive updates on the situation and activities of anarchists not only in Tokyo but in many other places outside Japan.[30] Probably because of these urges for further communication and contribution, interconnectedness among Korean anarchists themselves increased and was quite visible, as they were continuously informed by the newspaper of each other's activities in different places. Yi Hayu (1909–1950) and Won Simchang (1906–1971), in particular, either wanted by Japanese police or on probation for their anarchist and independence activities in Japan, moved to China in the beginning of the 1930s and joined Korean anarchist organizations there. In addition to Yi Dal, they probably were the ones who introduced the activities of Korean anarchists in China to their former comrades in Japan and vice versa, when the newspaper requested better communications with its anarchist comrades in other parts of East Asia during the "combat period."

Thanks to the presence of the two Yi's and Won in China, among all the others, the geographical as well as political barriers, at least between Korean anarchists in China and Japan, seemed to be to some extent overcome, as they remained connected with and informed each other of Korea's independence and the realization of a new anarchist society through the newspaper, which turned out to be the best way for them to achieve their goals. Although Jeong Hwaam recalls that there were no relations between the Korean anarchists in China and Japan,[31] the two articles mentioned above quite conversely vindicate that there was considerable communication between them. In addition, the physical movement of Korean anarchists from Japan to China also tells us about their extended connections and relations. With Korean anarchists on the move, a cosmopolitan sentiment seemed to be shared by them, when one of their comrades was arrested and imprisoned in a Japanese prison. In an obituary in the thirtieth issue, published on July 31, 1934, Baek Jeonggi was remembered and praised by the newspaper as "a rebel who stood on the front line of the human liberation" and a "fervent Tolstoyan."[32] Baek had been initially active in Japan but later went to China and was arrested there with Yi Ganghun and Won Simchang for the famous "Six Three Arbor Restaurant Incident" of March 1933, a failed assassination of Japanese consular Ariyoshi Akira by the so-called Black Terrorist Party (BTP), a terror-oriented Korean anarchist group in Shanghai,[33] As a sequel to this obituary, the newspaper carried a personal recollection by an anarchist in China, named Yang Jachu, of Yi Ganghun (1903–2003) who had also been arrested for the same incident.[34]

Baek, Yi, and Won were all arrested, tried, and sentenced to lifetime in prison. And their plot has been called in the South Korean historiography "a heroic deed at Six-Three Pavilion [Restaurant]" by the three Korean anarchists. Won Simchang had been a student in the Department of Sociology of Japan (Nihon) University in Tokyo since 1924, and had been a member of various Korean anarchist organizations in Tokyo. Won decided to move to Shanghai in 1930, after he was released from prison, and finally arrived in Shanghai in 1931 to conduct more active activities against Japan. Since then he had been a core member of the League of Korean Youth in South China (LKYSC) in Shanghai.[35] Baek Jeonggi (1896–1934) was inspired by *Labor Newspaper* (*Rōdō shimbun*) and became a socialist, while he indulged in reading books on socialism and laboring for living as a work-study student in Tokyo from 1921 to 1924. He moved to Beijing and then to Shanghai in 1924, where he joined other Korean anarchists.[36] Yi Ganghun came to China in 1920, but moved to Manchuria in 1925, where he took part in various independence movement activities. Yi escaped to Shanghai from the Japanese arrest in 1932, and became a member of the LKYSC in Shanghai.[37]

In an editorial notice in the thirtieth issue, the editor of *Black Newspaper*, indicating the lack of revolutionary forces in the world, which the editor believed to be the main reason why the revolution in Spain and the general strike in Chicago failed to ignite the fire of and generate a world revolution, contended that the revolutionary forces in the Far East were in need of systematic and organized activities. The failure, according to the editor, was due to, first, the theoretical and methodological incompleteness among the revolutionary forces and, second, the lack of mutual contacts and cooperation among the comrades in different countries. The notice further asked for increased interactions among them and suggested that the revolutionary task not be placed on the shoulders of one person in one region but on the shoulders of all human beings living in the world. The editor, therefore, insisted that the exploited propertyless masses of the world make all the efforts to "respond to each other in the East and the West."[38]

The *Black Newspaper* demonstrates the resilience of Korean anarchists in Japan in their struggle during the period of the most tightened surveillance and brutal suppression of radicals by Japanese police. At the same time it points to some militant characteristics of Korean anarchist movement in 1930s Japan; it was quite audacious to advocate the overthrow of Japanese imperialism in the capital city. Not as theoretical in character as its Japanese counterpart, it nevertheless was fervently against the nationalist movement, disclosing its transnational direction as exemplified by its emphasis on social revolution. *Black Newspaper* must have utilized a kind of anarchist network in the region that cut across the geographical as well as national boundaries. As the articles it carried demonstrate, Japan-based Korean anarchists, unlike their counterparts in China, were more concerned with the social and world problems than with the national goal, even during the "combat period" against their national enemy. This makes a clear difference from the activities and direction of China-based Korean anarchists who, as I examine below, were more inclined toward the formation of national unity or national front during "the combat period."

Finally, some Korean anarchists in Japan, such as Yi Dongsun, Han Gukdong, and Yi Suyong, participated in the short-lived Anarchist Communist Party (*Museifu kyōsantō*), established by Japanese anarchists in January 30, 1934, only to be crushed by the Japanese police in November 1935. According to John Crump, the Japanese anarchist party was established with "Bolshevik organizational methods for anarchist purposes"[39] with an aim of "preserving the anarchist movement in the face of a state that was determined to crush it." Joining it could have served Korean anarchists a precedent for their post-1945 experiment with two political parties. The brief participation in the Japanese anarchist party seemed to be the last visible activity of Korean anarchists in Japan before 1945.

Terrorism in Service of the Nation and Social Revolution

During the first half of the 1930s Korean anarchists' activities in China were at first in jeopardy because of Japan's invasion of Manchuria and north China. Unlike in Japan or colonial Korea, Korean anarchists in China had enjoyed relative freedom of organizing themselves and propagating anarchism with various supports from Chinese anarchists and at times even from the National Government of China, which enabled them to fight in China against Japanese colonialism.[40] However, the National Government of China under Chiang Kai-shek's leadership had continued to retreat since Japan's invasion of Manchuria in 1931, without resisting it, ultimately losing Manchuria and consequently part of north China by the mid-1930s. As a result, some Korean anarchists too had to move by the mid-1930s from north China and Manchuria to central China, particularly to Shanghai where they faced increased tensions between China and Japan as well as increased Japanese police activities. To Korean anarchists both at home and abroad, nothing now seemed to go athwart their plan for various movements and activities. The outbreak of the Sino-Japanese War on July 7, 1937 further exacerbated the unfavorable situation in China for their activities. Under the belligerent conditions between China and Japan that many Korean anarchists had to deal with, they were often more concerned with their daily survival than their anarchist ideals and goals or their country's liberation from the shackles of Japanese colonialism. Kim Gwangju (1910–1973) recalls this kind of complex situation and state of mind many Korean youth possessed and/or had to go through in 1930s Shanghai. Kim ended his life as a journalist and novelist in South Korea, but had been a member of the League of Korean Youth in South China (LKYSC), a terror-oriented anarchist group organized and based in 1930s Shanghai. I will return to this organization below. According to Kim, the lives of Korean youths in the first half of the 1930s in Shanghai could be described with such words as *despair, extreme pessimism, self-abandonment, wandering*, and *longing*, all of which were the signs of declined, low-key spirit for revolutionaries. They, including Kim himself, even began to wonder if there actually existed a country they could call their fatherland (*joguk*), and finally called into question the very existence and meaning of fatherland, which in their minds had only given to them a difficult, harsh time and had been unable to do anything for them under the sword-reliant rule of the Japanese and their police. To the Korean youths, therefore, Kim recalls, *fatherland* appeared as neither an attractive word nor a substantial existence. They also began to view commonly used terms like *patriots* and *revolutionaries* as equivalent in meaning to *hypocrisy* (*wiseon*) and *self-righteousness* (*dokseon*). Consequently, Kim came to conclude at the time that this kind of a life, including the one he was living, could be described like those of the Gypsies or bohemians.[41]

As a matter of fact, some Korean anarchists in China from the early to mid-1930s, who seemed to have no stable life or reliable organizations for their survival and activities, turned their eyes increasingly to extreme, violent means, such as terror-oriented actions against Japanese invaders, sometimes in tandem with Chinese or other Asian anarchists. Their terror-focused activities included the assassination of Japanese high officials and military commanders as well as so-called Korean traitors residing mostly in Shanghai. Such actions were initiated and conducted first by the LKYSC, which was organized to some extent as a reaction to the "September 18th Incident" (or the "Manchurian Incident"), which occurred in 1931—a spark of the fifteen-year-long military conflict between China and Japan. Because of its well-known activities, historian Horiuchi Minoru even posits that Korean anarchist movement in 1930s China was mainly led and conducted by the LKYSC.[42] Indeed the LKYSC functioned in the first half of the 1930s, almost as the headquarters of Korean anarchists gathered and concentrated in Shanghai from various places like the Korean peninsula, Japan, Manchuria, and China.[43] Its membership included Yu Seo, Yu Ja-myeong, Jeong Haeri, Jang Dosin, An Gonggeun, Sin Hyeonsang, Choe Seokyeong, and Won Simchang.[44] The latter three, in particular, had become anarchists in Japan and then moved to China at the turn of the 1930s to continue their activities, finally joining the LKYSC. Among the three Won is revered and remembered now as an anarchist who usually took actions first, rather than one who had theoretical considerations beforehand: he was simply "an anti-Japanese revolutionary."[45] The LKYSC was joined later by additional members in China like Jeong Hwaam and Yi Dal.

The LKYSC justified its terrorism-oriented activities against the Japanese, since the Korean anarchists believed that there was no other means for them but terrorism to resist Japan's military invasion of China. At the same time, according to Kim Seongsuk (1898–1969), a prominent Marxist independence activist who worked closely with Korean anarchists before 1945, they in general possessed a sense of self-justifying conviction that terrorism against the oppressive foreign force always carried the spirit of "the utmost humanity," as well as the meaning of "liberation" and "freeing ourselves" from the foreign aggressor. In short, as Kim recalls, Korean anarchists knew that their terrorism might entail some negative connotations to their activities but, as long as it did not just mean violence and destruction with no reason against unidentified objects, they believed that their actions would lay out the true meaning of terrorism, if understood from the point of their "constructive" intention.[46]

To be sure, regardless of its terrorist actions and often verbal threats to the Japanese officials and military commanders for their lives, the LKYSC can never be portrayed as a terrorist group, at least not for its platform. Some of the languages associated with revolutionary changes in Korean society were maintained in its platform. What is revealing in it (and its declaration), in other words, as I examine below, are its concerns with the social and also its direction toward a social revolution. It must have inherited, continued, and even preserved the social goal and direction of the Korean anarchist movement from the previous decade. This social dimension of the LKYSC can be found in its platform, regulations, and declaration. First, in its platform, the LKYSC's members expressed their denial and rejection of all kinds of political or syndicalist movements as well as the family system and religion, all of which they believed were simply covered nominally with morality. They also announced in their declaration their reliance on the principle of spontaneous alliance in organizing themselves, and denied the private property system under capitalism. The LKYSC members pledged themselves to build a new utopian society of absolute freedom and equality after independence. This could be realized only with the total destruction of social ills like private property and the nation-state, including the "pseudo-morality" of the latter. The new society would be based on absolutely spontaneous alliances among individuals, who would work according to their abilities, and receive in accordance with their needs. In such a society, the declaration explained, cities would have the appearance of farming villages, while villages would have the conveniences. Farming villages and cities alike would be characterized by a scientific combination of agriculture and industry in order to ensure the most effective production. Finally, the declaration argued that such an "artistic" society would have no need for money, as it would be "a society chosen from each individual's free will, and individuals can work freely there." Ultimately, "there will be no distinction between intellectual labor [ji-neung nodong] and physical labor [geun-yuk nodong]," so "no one would come to dislike working."[47]

The LKYSC's goals, reflected in the above declaration, reveal the ideal anarchist society it wanted to construct by social revolution. Of cardinal significance in the declaration are ideas like combining agriculture and industry and combining mental and manual labor, with individual transformation as the point of departure in the project of social change. These ideas had already been widely propagated and professed by the Paris Chinese anarchists.[48] These ideas were also the ideals of the Shanghai National Labour University and of the educational experiments of Chinese (and East Asian) anarchists. These ideals and languages were seemingly still alive here, employed by Korean anarchists in 1930s China. There is no concrete evidence explaining why and how the ideas were revived by the Alliance at the time it started armed, terror-oriented struggles against Japan. It is nevertheless revealing that many Koreans in the Alliance had worked with Chinese and Japanese anarchists in such joint anarchist projects like Lida College, the Labor University, and the Quanzhou Movement. It is also revealing that one of the post-1945 Korean anarchist projects promoted (in the 1960s) "domestic industry" in rural villages, as I demonstrate in chapter 5, and the LKYSC members identified themselves as "persons with free will and for no-government" (*mujeongbu jayu juuija*).[49] The definition was going to be readopted after 1945 with modifications.

Likewise, given the participation of those who had studied abroad in Japan, it is not baseless to say that the LKYSC endeavored to realize a worldwide social revolution and pursued almost the same ideal society Japanese pure anarchists such as Hatta Shūzō sought to achieve in the 1930s,[50] not to mention the one Chinese anarchists attempted at the Laoda and in Quanzhou with other East Asian anarchists. The idea of such an ideal society achieved by a social revolution bent on anarchist principles evidently reveals the transnational linkages of Korean anarchism. Although terror-oriented in action, the LKYSC certainly projected "a genuine social revolution" in the future. Its members pledged in the declaration to build a new Korean society after Korea's independence, which they assumed would be realized only after a total destruction of social ills under capitalism, such as private property and the institutions and pseudo-morality of the nation-state.[51] They also believed that "the Korea problem" could never be separated from the world problems and that a social revolution in Korea would be "a unit" of the world's social revolution.[52]

Also notable in their declaration is that the LKYSC's members saw the importance and necessity of arming the Korean masses, especially those in rural villages, in defense of "rural community villages" (*gongdong nongchon*) of freedom and equality against any military forces that might approach and destroy them, albeit they admitted that armament itself was unnecessary in principle. As I will explain below, the idea of the necessity and importance of having armed forces were to be reintroduced and subsequently reconfirmed later in the idea of the national front many Korean anarchists in the LKYSC actively proposed after 1936. What is interesting here is that Chinese anarchists too "wrote about using armed forces" in the process of revolution, during their debate with communists in mid-1920s,[53] another sign of the transnational linkages between Korean and Chinese anarchists.

The LKYSC published its journal, *South China Correspondence* (*Namhwa tongsin*), from January 1936 and possibly continued to do so until the end of 1937. And it is not surprising that it was published at Lida College in Shanghai.[54] Lida College didn't function just as its printing place, however; its members used the college to have their own gatherings to conspire and set their plan to execute "Korean traitors" (*han-gan*) in Shanghai, who they believed had handed the information about Korean independence movement and activists including anarchists over to the Japanese police in Shanghai. The fact that Lida College played its role as a gathering place for Korean anarchists and their activities is revealing, because it is another example that points to a close relationship and intimate collaboration between Korean and Chinese anarchists over their common enemy, Japan, and probably their common anarchist goal. And Yu Ja-myeong was the one who made all these possible. Yu had been teaching at the Department of Rural Village Education (*Nongcun jiaoyu ke*) of the college since 1931 and his presence there as a faculty member helped Korean anarchists to meet one another there and place their printer for the journal. Furthermore, according to Yu, Kuang Husheng, the founder of Lida College, was no doubt willing to support Korean revolutionaries in China.[55] Lida College thus became one of the main gathering places and points of communication for Korean anarchists in Shanghai.

In an article carried in June 1936 in *South China Correspondence*, titled "The Responsibility and Task of Our Youth," its author, named Ha (presumably Yi Hayu), condemned the political activities of exiled political parties aiming at gaining independence, for "the independence movement in a colonial situation should not be a political movement but a genuine revolutionary movement."[56] The reason was simple. The political movement would eventually end in vain, according to Ha, to whom anarchists were the only genuine revolutionaries, and, therefore, "the Korean revolution is an anarchist movement, if seen from historical experiences."[57] What would follow the genuine revolutionary anarchist movement was the destruction of the existing institutions by revolutionary means, which would in turn require revolutionary constructions undertaken by the whole masses, explained Ha. What the society finally accomplished would be a utopian one that would guarantee freedom, the realization of which must be the task of Korean youth, concluded Ha.[58] Here, the coalition of anarchists and the masses via the youth appeared as the key to the realization of such a utopian society. Departing from the constrained concept of the nation (*minjok*), that is, independence as a supreme goal, to apply Henry Em's analysis, the author, Ha, opened up a road to see a broad audience in the world just like Shin Chaeho did a decade ago, whose turns to anarchism from "nationalism" and to "the people" (*minjung*) from "the nation" (*minjok*) were, according to Em, an indicator of Shin's "political program that went beyond nationalism."[59] Similarly, Ha moved beyond the nation here in projecting a new society of freedom for the masses through the role and responsibility of youth.

A necessity to unite with the masses for a genuine social revolution was reemphasized in an anonymously written article, titled "Our Words," in an issue of the *South China Correspondence*, published in January 1936. This anonymous author also believed that the question of Korean independence was pertinent not only to Korea but to the world, and that the Korean revolution thus was a "unit" of all social revolutions of the world, which led the author to conclude that anarchists were real social revolutionaries. To render social revolution genuine, however, the author asserted that anarchists have to be real friends of the masses, who would be the final and perpetual victor in the revolution. In this sense, according to the author, copying other revolutions like the 1917 Russian Revolution was not desirable, for the revolutionaries had to consider particular circumstances they were surrounded and faced.[60] This author, rejecting any applicability of the universal theories or experiences to nation-based revolution, underscored the importance of accommodation to various national environments, accounting at the same time for the transnational dimensions of social revolution in the anarchist bent.

Another article in the same issue of *South China Correspondence*, titled "What Is Anarchism?" by an author with pseudonym of Baekmin, introduced the meaning of anarchism. To this author anarchism first was an idea that politically denied all kinds of domination and "compulsory power" (*ganggwon*); that economically rejected private property and communist politics of "naked power"; and finally that sought ethically to realize the principles of mutual aid and common prosperity of all peoples. Anarchism, in other words, appeared in the article as the idea not simply for a political, labor, or social movement, but for a much more complex movement that sought to destroy and uproot domination, exploitation, and "compulsory force" in society, in order to liberate the politically, economically, and ethically oppressed and fettered masses, and thus finally to realize a "free communist society" (*jayu gongsan sahoe*) where no domination and compulsory power existed.⁶¹ The author reiterated the above-mentioned goal of the LKYSC, which obviously was the construction of an ideal anarchist society by way of a social revolution, as reflected undoubtedly in the aforementioned declaration, platform, and regulations. The anarchist society the LKYSC envisioned, in short, corresponded to the one its forerunner, the LKAC, did in the 1920s.⁶² In addition to the discussions pertinent to the goal and vision for social revolution the LKYSC strove for, *South China Correspondence* carried many other articles and news regarding the question as to the formation of a national front (*minjok jeonseon*), to which I will turn later. As it will become clear, the anarchists in the LKYSC were quite interested in forming a national united front as early as mid-1936.⁶³

The LKYSC had earned its reputation as a terrorism-oriented organization which, it seems, had much to do with the various activities conducted by the League of Resisting Japan and Saving the Nation (LRJSN, Hang-il guguk yeonmaeng) and possibly its own action group, the Black Terror Party (BTP, Heuksaek gongpodan). Historian Horiuchi Minoru assumes that these organizations could have been the same one organization, that is, the LKYSC, but could have used different names occasionally to either terrify the Japanese in China, or confuse the Japanese police regarding their identity. Indeed, there is a case where a Japanese police report identified the BTP and another terrorism-oriented group called the Vigorous Blood Group (Yeolhyeol dan) as the LKYSC's "special detached forces" (*betsudō dai*).⁶⁴ Details as to how and when these groups were organized are unknown. But it seems that some of the LKYSC members, per a proposal from Chinese anarchists such as Wang Yachu and Hua Junshi,⁶⁵ could have organized jointly in October 1931 in the French Concession in Shanghai with them a separate organization, that is, the LRJSN.⁶⁶ It allegedly had seven Chinese members and seven Korean members, along with several Japanese anarchists, including Sano Ichirō (who used his Chinese name, Tian Huamin) and Yatabe Yūji (who used his Chinese name, Wu Shimin).⁶⁷ However we understand these organization's identity and activities, it is undeniable that, given the information at hand, these several organizations and their activities were conducted and led by Korean anarchists. They were terror oriented in action, but whether all could have been the same one group or separate groups, they had the shared revolutionary platform and goal bent on anarchist principles, as I demonstrate below. In other words, their actions could be called terrorist in nature but still were conducted with a vision for social revolution, not to mention for national liberation, to realize their own version of an anarchist society in Korea and in other countries. This aspect of their sharedness can be additional evidence that indicates that in the end they could possibly be one organization.

What is quite clear is that the LRJSN seemed to be an "international group" in terms of its membership. As the LSNRJ's membership was transnational, so were its goals. It aimed (1) to eradicate all the power and systems of private property in order to realize a genuine society of freedom and equality, so that Korea could become independent from Japan and subsequently build an anarchist society in the country; (2) to overthrow Japan's constitutional monarchy and abolish the system of private property; and (3) to build an anarchist society in China and other countries. Adopted in its platform was "to deny all the power in the contemporary society and construct a new society in which all the mankind in the world can newly enjoy freedom and equality in all aspects in society."[68] Something interesting about this organization was, it is said, that it expanded its organization to have three new departments to conduct activities such as the destruction of Japanese facilities in China, the assassination of important Japanese personnel, an assault on pro-Japanese Koreans, and anti-Japanese propaganda. It is impossible to confirm but Korean sources have asserted that there were the departments in the LSNRJ run by participating Russians, an American (named "Johnson"), and a Taiwanese (Lin Chengcai), respectively.[69] Besides, it had the Propaganda Department, which set up its printing place in the French Concession in Shanghai and published its journal, *Freedom* (*Jayu*) beginning in November 1931.[70]

Besides the terror-oriented group, groups like the Vigorous Blood Group (Yeolhyeol dan or Maenghyeol dan), and/or the Eradicating Traitors Group (Seogan dan) frequently appeared and were mentioned in various media in the 1930s, including anarchist newspapers. Again, all these groups could possibly be the suborganizations of the LKYSC, or the same one group but with different names used on different occasions for some reasons. The relationships among these groups as well as their identities are vague and unclear. And whether either was a subgroup of the LKYSC is still in question. The BTP obviously carried the same tasks as the LRNRJ: destroying Japanese military and administrative facilities in China, assassinations of Japanese officials/military commanders and pro-Japanese Koreans, and dissemination of anti-Japanese propaganda.[71] The BTP's various terrorism-oriented actions, it seemed, indeed raised the level of fear among the Japanese and Koreans in Shanghai who had collaborated with the Japanese. In some cases the BTP possibly called itself the Eradicating Traitors Group to conceal its identity and confuse the Japanese police, not to mention to terrify pro-Japanese Koreans. The BTP, as mentioned earlier, has been particularly known for its responsibility for the attempted assassination of Japanese consular Akira Ariyoshi in Shanghai in March 1933.

Under the Banner of the Korean National Front (Joseon minjok jeonseon yeonmaeng)

The National Government of China had been passive in dealing with the Japan's continuous military provocations, beginning in Manchuria in 1931. It had maintained the policy of "Resist on the one hand, negotiate on the other" to continue and focus on its top priority, that is, the "Anti-Bandit Military Campaign" to eradicate the communists from the Chinese soil. This policy was infamous among many Chinese who saw it as nonpatriotic and self-destructive, since it allowed the Japanese to invade and occupy Manchuria and north China by the mid-1930s without resistance. The policy had been under severe criticism by many Chinese, including the CCP, all of whom unanimously requested of the National Government united anti-Japanese resistance. Demands for a united fight against Japan finally ignited the fire of nationalism in China, leading to the Xi'an Incident in December 1936, in which Chiang Kai-shek, head of the National Government and the GMD, was house-arrested by his own generals, Zhang Xueliang and Yang Hucheng. Zhang and Yang demanded of Chiang united anti-Japanese resistance. With Chiang's agreement, China's full-scale resistance war against Japan began with the formation of the second United Front between the GMD and the CCP in 1937. The political development and subsequent decision by the National Government for China's resistance war with Japan nurtured the condition for Korean anarchists to consider their own united front with other Korean exile groups. They saw it as an opportunity that paved the way to the realization of their immediate goal of independence, and in the end of an anarchist society they envisaged, if the Chinese would win the war. The formation of the United Front in China was the most immediate, crucial factor for Korean anarchists to propose and prompt the formation of a Korean national front in China.

Besides the China factor there had been some other internal factors as well that led to the discussion and formation of the Korean national front in 1937. Korean independence activists in China, including anarchists, had been divided along various political doctrines or ideological lines as well as personal, regional, or even factional ties, and so on since the 1919 March First Movement.[72] Even inside the Provisional Government of Korea, its leaders had also been very divisive over the ultimate goal and direction of Korea's independence. Some preferred a diplomatic approach, while others insisted on armed struggle against Japan for independence, for example. Likewise, in regard to the postindependence society, some envisaged a capitalist society, while others a socialist country. The government-in-exile, crippled by the internal conflicts and divisions, had never been able to exercise its power and maintain its authority over all Koreans abroad. Korean anarchists had not been generally associated with it, not just because of their rejection of central power or the state but also because of their disappointment with its divisive leaders and their politics.[73] The national front idea was put forward by anarchists, as Yu Ja-myeong explained later in 1938, with consideration of resolving all the conflicts that had been regarded as barriers among those circles, such as factional strife, different backgrounds, and even an antipathy among the independence movement groups. They were focused on making a strong, unified entity that could lead all Korean revolutionary and independence groups toward their common national struggle for liberation.[74]

Between Japan's invasion of Manchuria in 1931 and the outbreak of the Sino-Japanese War in 1937, Korean anarchists gradually lost their physical grounds for their activities and organizations, first in Manchuria and then other major cities like Shanghai, as these area and cities were all occupied by Japan by mid-1930s. With much tightened suppression of radicalism during the years Korean anarchists in colonial Korea and Japan had to either go underground for survival or give up their belief by converting to support the colonial rule or, at least, remain silent.[75] When all went against their favor, many Korean anarchists concluded that they now had to join the Chinese anti-Japanese resistance war or arm themselves. That China in unity responded to Japan's invasion with its own all-out resistance in 1937 made Korean anarchists realize that the victory of China over Japan was indispensable for Korea's independence. In short, there existed "a demand of the time"⁷⁶ that required them to support China's resistance war. It was at this moment that they put forward the idea to form a national front and began to place their utmost priority on national struggle in unity against Japan, believing independence even as the precondition for the realization of their anarchist society in Korea.

The international situation too seemed to be favorable for Korean anarchists to propose their national front idea. As Yu Ja-myeong observed later in 1938, anarchists had witnessed the rising fascism in the world and its subsequent suppression of radicalism and democracy in the 1930s. The emergence of fascism in the world stopped the fight between socialism and democracy (i.e., capitalism) and ushered in the establishment of the united front worldwide between socialism and democracy, Yu explained.⁷⁷ To Korean anarchists, a clear example of this was the People's Front in Spain and France, as well as the United Front in China. A colony like Korea no doubt needed a unity of all the people and subsequently the establishment of its own united front to fight the colonial power. Now the priority must be given to national unity and struggle against Japan; accordingly, anarchists needed not consider the social conditions and problems in Korea at least for a while, according to Yu.⁷⁸ In short, in response to the emergence of various united front worldwide against fascism, Korean anarchists in China prioritized Korea's national unity over any internal differences such as social divisions among Korean people under capitalist domination.

The success and failure of the People's Front in Spain in 1936 particularly came as a good lesson to Korean anarchists, a lesson that revolution in a country would never be possible without response or assistance from their counterparts in the neighboring countries. Their intimate alliance with other antifascist forces in the region and the world too was of great necessity.⁷⁹ Indeed, the alliance and cooperation with other anarchists, let alone other antifascist forces (i.e., anti-Japanese forces) had always been a major concern and interest of the Korean anarchists in China since the 1920s. The national front idea was now put forward by them to propose an intense cooperation and alliance with all regional and international antifascist forces, only after making an internal unity among Korean independence groups. Also proposed by anarchists at the time, along with national front, was a movement to enlighten "the unawakened masses."⁸⁰

In short, the proposal for and establishment of the League for the Korean National Front (LKNF) in December 1937 (more on this to follow) were a direct outcome of several changes in China and the world. Above all, Korean anarchists perceived that Korean participation directly in China's anti-Japanese resistance war would contribute to China's victory, which in turn was a condition for Korea's liberation from Japanese colonialism. But first, Koreans had to be united internally without internal rift to support effectively and even join the Chinese. This was the point the LKNF emphasized most in its declaration; a national unity had to be accomplished and highlighted to overthrow Japanese imperialism and complete Korea's autonomous independence.[81]

Discussions among Korean anarchists on the possible formation of a national front among Korean independence organizations in China got underway in early 1936, or at the latest in the summer of the same year.[82] The LKYSC was the leading anarchist organization that propagated the idea of national front. If we look at the number of writings on the question of national front carried from the summer of 1936 in *South China Correspondence*, it is possible to say that the propagation of national front was an important issue as much as anarchism itself for the LKYSC in the year.[83] As mentioned above, an earlier proposal for it appeared in an article in the second issue of *South China Correspondence*, published in June 1936, written by the author named Ha (presumably Yi Hayu). Ha began his discussion with his criticism of a wrong perception among Koreans, who in his view did not understand the particular context of Korea as a colony. Many Koreans had tended to forget the colonial situation and had been politically divided before the enemy, analyzed Ha. Many left-oriented independence movement activists had particularly conducted various "formal movements" that were usually faithful to some universally applicable "theories," but they did not see the fact that Korea was a colony, Ha lamented. Historical experiences from the past, continued Ha, had also proven that Koreans needed to be aware that a Korean revolution could never be accomplished by "empty" political movements that replicated some "theoretical" and "planned" lines without considering the Korean revolution's peculiarities. This was why the liberation of an oppressed people like the Koreans could be accomplished not by political movement but rather by "a genuine revolutionary movement," which would destroy the existing institutions by recourse to revolutionary means and then proceed to a revolutionary construction on the base of all the masses, Ha asserted. The "genuine revolutionary movement" demanded Korean youth to have a new consciousness that their immediate task was to make a unanimous unity and then form a united front internally to resist the external enemy. In short, the common goal for their struggle as a colonized people had to be "national and nationwide" (*jeon minjokjeok*) in its nature and scope, Ha concluded.[84] While opposed to political movement, Ha stressed internal unity as the immediate task with which a united front was to be formed for national liberation movement.[85]

Ha was first among the anarchists who made a formal call in writing for the necessity to unite the various independence movement groups in China to set up a national front to fight Japan. The Korean youth in China, Ha believed, were assigned a mission to construct a free and ideal society in Korea, but the society was only to be made possible when the shackles of Japanese imperialism were cut off by them after making unity under their common goal for struggle. The internal unity through a national front had to be agreed and achieved unanimously, so that they could fight Japan to the end with the spirit of sacrifice.[86] There was a reason for this author to emphasize the Korean youth's responsibility for understanding the importance of internal unity before their enemy. There was a long history of internal divisions among Koreans abroad, as I mentioned above. In the November issue of *South China Correspondence*, another author named Ju (presumably Yang Yeoju)[87] went further, to express his agreement with the idea of a national front and even its expansion as necessary "at the current stage of our Korean revolutionary movement, because the national front is the only guide that opens up the way for national liberation movement."[88] In its twelfth issue, an anonymous writer also pointed out that Korean anarchists understood that without overthrowing Japanese imperialism, it would be impossible to launch any kind of a movement, whether it was for an ideal society of political, economic, and social freedom and equality and the prosperity of all mankind or for the independence of Korean people.[89]

The idea to form the LKNF received a response in the summer of 1937, when the Alliance of Korean Independence Movement Activists (Joseon dongnip undongja dongmaeng) was organized. What followed was the discussion to form the LKNF in November 1937 in Nanjing by representatives of three radical groups, including anarchist. Since the National Government of China abandoned its capital city, Nanjing, the LKNF's members had also to leave Nanjing to move to Hankou where they finally formed the LKNF a month later. These radical groups were the League of Korean Revolutionaries

(LKR, Joseon hyekmyeongja yeonmaeng), the Korean National Revolutionary Party (KNRP, Joseon minjok hyeokmyeong dang), and the Alliance for Korean National Liberation Movement (AKNLM, Joseon minjok haebang undong yeonmaeng). The LKR was an anarchist organization, reorganized and renamed in October 1937 from the LKYSC just before the establishment of the LKNF, with Yu Ja-myeong as its chairperson and twenty other anarchists as its members, such as Yu Seo, Jeong Hwaam, Na Wolhwan, Yi Hayu, Bak Giseong, and Yi Seungrae. Representing the LKR in the LKNF, Yu Ja-myeong had been meeting and discussing the possibility of setting up a national front with Kim Wonbong of the KNRP and Kim Seongsuk of the AKNLM. Kim Wonbong (1898–1958?) was the former leader of the Righteous Group in the 1920s, and had been inclined toward socialism in the 1930s.[90] Kim Seongsuk (1898–1969) was a Marxist and communist who had not been associated with the Korean Communist Party or the CCP, and never been under the guidance or sponsorship of the Comintern.[91] As explained above, the delegates from the three groups met on November 12, 1937 in Nanjing, and decided to establish the LKNF, agreeing on the LKNF's name, declaration, regulations, and platform. The LKNF was not joined by nationalist groups such as the one led by Kim Gu (Kim Koo, 1876–1949), who was then-chairman of the Provisional Government of Korea in China. In fact, Kim shortly thereafter organized a separate united front organization, mostly for Korean nationalists in China, under the banner of the Coalition of the Groups for Korea's Liberation Movement (Han-guk gwangbok undong danche yeonhaphoe).

Although a symbol of national unity, the LKNF was a loosely united organization of the three Korean radical revolutionary groups, although, according to Yu Ja-myeong, the loose collaboration among them was the LKNF's main trait.[92] It may even be possible to say that the LKNF was in fact organized along the anarchist principle, spontaneous alliance, because the participating groups in the LKNF maintained their own organizational integrity and political/ideological positions independently, not to mention platforms, and so forth. They were united only under the common, large organization and platform unanimously agreed on by all of them. After the LKNF was established in December 1937 in Hankou, Yu became in charge of its journal, *The Korean National Front* (*Joseon minjok jeonseon* or *Chaoxian minzu zhanxian* in Chinese), published in Chinese, as one of its editors with Kim Seongsuk. A year later the LKNF organized its own military organization, the Korean Volunteers Unit (KVU, *Joseon Uiyongdae*) and Kim Wonbong became its commander, while Kim Seongsuk Director of the Political Bureau. Yu led the KVU as one of its supervisors (*jido wiwon*) probably because of his proficiency in Chinese.[93]

Yu Ja-myeong, as a proponent of forming a national front, emphasized the unity of Koreans for the goal of national liberation. To him, the target of Korean struggle as of 1938 was "still Japanese imperialism," and the struggle must be conducted without internal divisions in thought and class for the sake of the common goal: "anti-Japanese independence."[94] Yu also thought that the Chinese anti-Japanese War was "a fight not only for the Chinese nation and people but for world peace, human justice, liberation of the oppressed peoples in the world,"[95] indicating its significance that transcended China's boundaries. In fact, as early as September 1932, Yi Hoeyeong discussed with Chinese anarchist Wu Zhihui and Li Shizeng the direction of Korean anarchist movement,[96] and it was possible that cooperation between China and Korea was discussed by them for the goal of united resistance against Japan's aggression in Manchuria and north China at the time. Yu's transnational understanding of the meaning of China's anti-Japanese War and its relationship to the Korean National Front were not novel but could have already been shared among Korean and Chinese anarchists, therefore.

According to the declaration of the LKNF carried in *The Korean National Front*, the only way out as of 1938 for Koreans was to overthrow Japanese imperialism and accomplish their autonomous independence after unifying all the forces within the independence camp. This meant that the Korean revolution had to be a national (*minjok*) revolution, and the Korean national front was neither expected to be a "class front" (*gyegeup jeonseon*) in character nor a "people's front" (*inmin jeonseon*), but, rather, a "national front" (*minjok jeonseon*). Furthermore, the Korean national front must also be distinguished from "the front organized by nationals or citizens" (*gungmin jeonseon*), formed in France and Spain.[97] There was a common awareness or understanding among the LKNF members as expressed in the declaration that Korea was a colony, and thus Koreans had to be united first regardless of their internal differences, political orientations, and so on, to retake independence. This common awareness displaced and deemphasized all the differences, both political and social, among Koreans and demanded of them that they unite for the national goal, no matter what.

The immediate task of the LKNF was not just its participation in China's war against Japan, as Yu Ja-myeong, using his other name Yu Sik (Liu Shi in Chinese), insisted in his article contributed to the auxiliary journal. One of its most important, eventual tasks was the "expansion of the movement to [form] a united [front] in Korea through appeals to the compatriots and parties in Korea to respond" to the formation of the LKNF in China. To Yu, the connection between the LKNF in China and those groups in Korea could never be cut off, and the LKNF must maintain its intimate relationship with the revolutionary forces within Korea.[98] What the LKNF aimed at was, as Yu reiterated, not just the unity of the independence movement groups in China but ultimately of all Koreans both at home and abroad. The national goal obviously earned its priority and for that the unity of all Koreans, no matter where they were, became the precondition for national liberation.

Apart from the unity of all Koreans, the LKNF manifested the following eventual tasks: (1) the overthrow of Japanese imperialism and the construction of a genuine democratic independent country of the Korean people; (2) absolute guarantee of the people's freedom of press, publication, assembly, association and religion; (3) confiscation of all the properties in Korea of Japanese imperialists, [Korean] traitors and pro-Japanese factions; (4) the improvement in the livelihood of the working masses; (5) providing occupational and mandatory education, using the national budget; (6) the establishment of equal political, economic, and social rights between men and women; and (7) the completion of friendly relations or alliance with the peoples and countries who are assisting or in sympathy with Korean people's liberation movement.[99] In order to accomplish these tasks, the LKNF was expected to strive for (1) the fundamental removal [in Korea] of the ruling forces of Japanese imperialism, (2) the construction of anti-Japanese united front of all the people, (3) the realization of all-out revolutionary mobilization of all the people, (4) the active deployment of military actions, (5) the participation in China's anti-Japanese war, (6) the coalition with all anti-Japanese forces in the world, and (7) the purge of the internal traitors such as pro-Japanese factions who had sided with the movement for autonomy and possessed an idea to compromise their position [with the Japanese].[100] These tasks point to the character of the LKNF—that it was a united front organization not just to fight Japan in China, but also to envision a society to be constructed.

Of particular interest in the above tasks is the LKNF's emphasis on military actions against Japanese imperialism either by having its own military forces or by participating in China's military resistance. That the LKNF stressed the military tasks meant its willingness not only to participate China's military resistance but to envisage a postindependence Korea, where its autonomy and independence could been maintained with its military power. This was an autonomous, independent Korean state that, once established, must be strong enough even in its military capacity to deal with foreign pressure and invasion. In fact, as I examined in chapter 1, Korean anarchists in China had been somewhat consistent in this regard in the sense that they had always supported the idea of establishing self-defensive forces in rural areas against any bandits or communists. Korean anarchists in the LKNF like Yu Ja-myeong didn't seem to shun this military-related issue, and were not even reluctant to help it materialize into the KVU later, as we will see below.

To understand more about Korean anarchists' rationales for the formation of the LKNF and their prioritization of the national question over the social, it is necessary to examine how and for what they justified their united front with nationalists and even communists. The LKNF's journal offers some answers. *The Korean National Front* published its first issue on April 10, 1938, which carried its inaugural address written by Yu Ja-myeong as its publisher and editor-in-chief. Given Yu's position and status in the LKNF and its journal, what he wrote in it could represent not only his personal opinion but possibly the LKNF's official position. In line with the LKNF's declaration, Yu basically saw the national question of Korea as part of the "world problem" and as deeply related to the "historical incidents" of the past forty years in both China and Korea, and to the coming future years of the two countries. In his view, in other words, if China's anti-Japanese resistance war would fail, there would remain no hope for Korea's national liberation. And, reversely, Yu predicted, China's final victory could also be determined by the support of Korean people whose prior experiences from their "twenty-year history of anti-Japanese revolution" [sic] and struggles were of paramount importance. The two countries therefore shared two common tasks to overthrow their common enemy and consolidate peace in East Asia. Simply speaking, forming a united front together against Japan was of great necessity of the time to Koreans and Chinese. But to do so, Koreans needed to be united internally first, Yu emphasized.[101] Yu then explained the meaning of the Korean revolution, which he thought also required the unity of all Korean people as a precondition for the success of it. To him, its goal was the liberation of Korean people from the double pains they had received under the political oppression and economic exploitation of Japanese imperialism. For that reason, what the Korean revolutionary camp needed to strive for was to form a unity of all Korean people without considering any class and political differences among them, just like China's anti-Japanese united front between the GMD and the CCP, which gave its priority to the national problem. Theoretically speaking, therefore, Yu believed, the Chinese united front shared much in common with the proposed Korean national front.[102] As Kashima Setsuko points out, the way the LKNF was proposed and framed as a united front organization was indeed similar to that of the Second United Front between the GMD and the CCP of the 1930s.[103] Korean anarchists put aside all the questions pertaining to their social ideals, including class issues, for the sake of the national front.[104]

Some scholars have taken the above-listed tasks of the LKNF for an indicator of the shift Korean anarchists openly made to support the idea of the state, deviating from anarchist principles. According to these scholars, the formation of the LKNF itself was even a sign that Korean anarchists simply began to deteriorate themselves from the most important anarchist principle, that is, negation of any centralized organizations, including the state.[105] Indeed, Korean anarchists participating in the LKNF were in agreement with other independence activists in China on the necessity to gain Korea's independence first and then set up an independent and autonomous Korean state. However, this need not be considered a deviation from anarchism. Independence had always been their immediate goal; the establishment of an autonomous nation-state after independence was always therefore presupposed and supported by them. What made them anarchist were their postindependence programs to build a new society based on anarchist principles and ideals. What seemed to matter was whether they were preoccupied only with independence without much consideration of or reference to how to achieve their ultimate goal of social revolution bent on anarchist principles. This matter was related to the priority they chose in their given time and space. They were willing to postpone their anarchist goal for the sake of the national goal and projected an anarchist society in the future. Maybe they wanted to spend little time on theoretical issues like the conflict between nationalism and anarchism, or they had fewer ideological attachments to them in the wake of the war in China. They were at least less important for them to consider. As John Crump suggests with regard to pre-1945 Japanese anarchism, Korean anarchists, just like their Japanese counterparts, were probably little interested in this kind of theoretical, and thus vexing, questions when their individual as well as national survivals were of most urgent concerns during the wartime years.[106] They probably thought that universal theories were not as important as the national question or didn't concretely meet the national, local, or individual reality when applied and practiced.

For the goal to unite all Korean independence organizations in China, the LKNF also sought collaboration with the Provisional Government of Korea in China under the leadership of Kim Gu. The unification between the LKNF and the Kim-led organization was on the table for discussion between them but was not realized until the "Unification Conference" was held in September 1941, when Yu Ja-myeong and Yu Rim from the LKNF finally decided to participate in the Provisional Government, representing Korean anarchist groups.[107] And they were subsequently elected in October of the same year as representatives in the Provisional Legislative Body of the government. With these two anarchists joining the Korean Provisional Government, the LKNF was finally resolved and integrated into it. Among those in the other two groups in the LKNF, many of the KNRP members had moved to Yan'an. That the two leading anarchists, two Yu's, joined the Provisional Government was indicative of how strongly and earnestly Korean anarchists wanted an actual unity among all the independence movement circles in China for their common national goal.

Korean Anarchists for Armed Struggle

Korean anarchists in the LKNF could be grouped mainly into three circles, according to a different military (or quasi-military) organization each circle established respectively. First was the group represented by Yu Ja-myeong from the LKR, which joined in organizing the KVU under the LKNF, with Kim Wonbong as its commander-in-chief. The other two circles organized respectively the Korean-Chinese Joint Guerilla Unit (KCJGU, Hanjung hapdong yugyeokdae) and the Operation Unit of Korean Youth at Warfront (OUKYW, Han-guk cheongnyeon jeonji gongjakdae). The former was led by Jeong Hwaam, and the latter by three young Korean anarchists, Na Wolhwan, Yi Hayu, and Bak Giseong, all of whom had been a former study-abroad student and converted to anarchism in Tokyo in the 1920s, but had moved to China in the early 1930s.[108] All these anarchists had been the members of the LKYSC. It seems after 1937, Korean anarchists were gradually divided and grouped into three different military units. The reason for the division is not known and, as far as I am aware, there was no sign of any serious internal ideological conflicts among them. But, in hindsight, it seems that they had conflicting views on how they would treat other socialists, particularly the communists in the course of forming the LKNF. For example, some of them like Yu Ja-myeong were certainly willing to work closely with other socialists like Kim Wonbong and Kim Seongsuk, as well as the Korean Provisional Government, under the banner of national struggle. The others like Na and Bak seemed to dislike the idea of working with other socialists, particularly communists, and rather preferred organizing a joint armed force with nationalists, including the conservative group in the Korean Provisional Government. In the case of Jeong, he seemed to keep his distance from the LKNF, and might have been in conflict with the Provisional Government.[109] This kind of slight cleavage among Korean anarchists also can be seen from their post-1945 careers as well. In post-1945 years, Bak joined the South Korean Army, fought the communists during the Korean War, and later was promoted to a general of the Korean Army. In contrast, Yu Ja-myeong, unable to return to Korea under Syngman Rhee's presidency after 1948, decided to remain in the People's Republic of China and later in the 1970s received a commendation medal from the North Korean Government. Jeong Hwaam ended his life as a political leader of many progressive political parties in South Korea, going through enormous political hardships and suppressions under the military, dictatorial regimes of South Korea.

The KVU was no doubt a direct product of the LKNF. As one KVU member frankly stated at the time, the Korean youth in China working for Korea's independence and liberation had been facing many hardships and problems before the LKNF's establishment and its participation in China's anti-Japanese resistance war. Most of them were at the age of twenty-seven and twenty-eight in the mid-1930s, and were quite determined to overthrow Japan and liberate their country. However, just like Kim Kwangju explains about his Shanghai years in the same decade, Korean youth, before China's war against Japan began, had been unable to take actions actively and openly for the national goal; they had moved from one place to another frequently, to avoid Japanese arrest and surveillance, mainly living an underground life with the consistent fear of arrest, torture, and so on.[110] China's decision to go to war with Japan allowed them to conduct their activities openly and to come out of their underground life, ironically giving them a more stable and protected life during the war, only because they were fighting the common enemy together with the Chinese. As long as they fought against Japan, their life and activity were going to be protected and, on top of that, they would be able to pursue their national goal more openly and publicly. Their anti-Japanese actions in China were justified, no matter what. The Chinese resistance war changed the whole situation somewhat to their favor, and the formation of the LKNF decisively freed them from the fear with which they had lived in China, and encouraged them to risk their lives for their national cause.

No wonder many Korean anarchists, after establishing the LKNF, expected an immediately expanded participation in the Chinese anti-Japanese war, be that combat-related or consisting of propaganda tasks. Yu Ja-myeong expressed this widely shared sentiment among Koreans in his writing carried in the second issue of *The Korean National Front*. Writing about the historical meaning of the GMD's 5th National Convention in 1938, Yu strongly expressed his desire for the GMD to help expand the international anti-Japanese movement by uniting all peoples against Japanese imperialism and then establishing an enlarged united front against Japan. For that, he made a suggestion to the GMD that Koreans be allowed not just to participate in the anti-Japanese war, but eventually to help them have their own armed force with the assistance from the high authorities in the GMD government. Koreans had had a twenty-year-long history of "anti-Japanese revolution," but, Yu admitted, they had lacked one thing, that is, their own armed force (*mujang budae*). If Koreans were given a chance to expand their abilities, in particular in the military, Yu believed that they should be able to empower themselves so as to found their own principle military force for the sake of Korean Independence, and this was beneficial to China's war efforts.[111]

Besides Yu Ja-myeong, Yi Dal, one of the most active anarchists in the KVU, also hoped just like Yu to achieve through the KVU the liberation of both Chinese and Korean people and eventually everlasting peace in East Asia, expressing his own transnational ideal beyond

Korea's independence. Yi, frequently contributing to the KVU's journal, *The Korean Volunteers Unit's Correspondence* (*Chaoxian yiyongdui tongxun*), which was to be renamed later *The Korean Volunteers Unit* (*Chaoxian yiyongdui*), expressed in his writings his belief that Korean and Chinese people had to be thoroughly united together and overthrow their common enemy, Japanese imperialism. And then Yi professed that their unity would finally lead to the establishment and consolidation of the united front among the oppressed peoples in the East (*dongbang*).[112]

Obviously, the National Government of China was not deaf to Yu's suggestion for the KVU, which was finally organized in October 1938 in Hankou under the supervision of the Political Department of its Military Affairs Committee. It was less than a year after the LKNF's inauguration in December 1937. Against Yu's hope, however, the KVU was assigned a noncombatant task, that is, propaganda-related works against the Japanese soldiers and the Koreans drafted by force to the Japanese army. The leaders and members of the KVU, including Yu, didn't lose their hope to turn it into an actual combat force and get directly involved in military warfare with the Japanese in north and/ or northeast China. But the KVU was to remain a noncombatant unit in the GMD-ruled areas, until the majority of its members decided to move to Yan'an, the revolutionary base of the CCP. The GMD's continuous passivity in resisting Japan constantly disappointed many KVU members, including the leaders of the KNRP, who finally insisted on going, and actually left soon for Yan'an, where, unlike in the GMD-controlled areas, actual military combats between the Chinese and the Japanese took place.[113] Many KVU members moved up to Yan'an in order to conduct and engage in military actions, rather than noncombatant propaganda activities in the GMD-controlled area. And once they arrived in the CCP-controlled area and north China, they reorganized themselves into the North China Branch Unit of the KVU (Joseon uiyongdae hwabuk jidae). Their decision to move to Yan'an was not made just because of their left-oriented ideological position (i.e., pro-communist stance) or the lure and conspiracy of the CCP,[114] but mainly because of their nationalist desire to fight Japan as an active combat force and eventually to become the founding military force of a future Korean state. They later reorganized themselves in Yan'an as the Korean Volunteers Army (KVA, *Joseon Uiyonggun*) with the support from the CCP.[115]

As historian Kashima Setsuko notes, the formation of the KVU signaled the first step made by Korean anarchists toward Korea's liberation through armed struggle with their own military force during China's anti-Japanese war.[116] Those who organized and participated in the KVU wanted to carry their military tasks in the combat zones where they could confront and engage in direct combats with the Japanese, but there were many limits in their status and roles in China's overall anti-Japanese war efforts. First, the KVU was under the command the National Government. This means that the KVU was not formed as a united military force with China, and thus was not treated as an equal partner to China's Nationalist Army. Therefore, second, it had many restrictions and limits in its military actions and plans as an independent force, which was exacerbated by the Korean Provisional Government's formal denunciation of it. The National Government was probably reluctant to allow and develop it to be a combat unit due to, among other things, that the KVU was not recognized by the Provisional Government of Korea that was formally assisted by the National Government. In fact, the Korean Provisional Government established its own military force called the Korean Restoration Army (Han-guk gwangbok gun) in response to the left-oriented KVU. And these could have possibly led Yu Ja-myeong and Yu Rim to their participation in the Korean Provisional Government later in 1941, probably recognizing the legitimacy of the government-in-exile.

Another major military organization in which Korean anarchists participated was the OUKYW, established in Chongqing in October 1939, together by some Korean anarchists and other nationalists associated with the Provisional Government of Korea. The leading anarchists in this military organization were Na Wolhwan, Yi Hayu, and Bak Giseong. This military unit was, similar to the KVU, placed under the command of the National Government's Military Committee in collaboration with the Korean Provisional Government. The OUKYW's commander was anarchist Na Wolhwan. Na had been a former member of the Black Friends League in Tokyo, but moved to China where he attended and graduated from the Chinese Central Military Academy under the GMD's auspices. After graduation he had been in military service for the Chinese National Government's military forces before he joined the LKNF and the OUKYW was organized. Some nationalists, associated with Kim Gu, also participated in the OUKYW, which initially had about thirty Koreans who had all "lived in different living circumstances" before joining it.[117] The OUKYW's basic goal was manifested as cooperation with the Chinese for their anti-Japanese war. But more important in their goal was to locate many Koreans in the warfront, who had been drafted forcefully to the Japanese army but deserted in China from it, in order to have the deserted Korean soldiers join the OUKYW to ensure its increased ability as a military unit. The members of the OUKYW also anticipated China's final victory in the war with Japan, which in turn would guarantee the success of a Korean revolution they envisaged.

The OUKYW too had its journal in Chinese, titled *Korean Youth* (*Hanguo qingnian*), published in June 1940, to which Korean anarchists contributed their writings and Na Wolhwan, commander of the OUKYW, was one of them. In one of his articles contributed to the journal, titled "Our Tasks" and carried in its inaugural issue, Na, sharing with the LKNF the general goal of making a united front with other Korean organizations, pointed out that Korean youth shouldered their most important task to overthrow Japanese imperialism in order to eradicate its forces from Korea and ultimately to construct a country of freedom and independence. For that, he continued, all anti-Japanese forces in China had to be united and a united Korean military unit needed to be established to lay out a foundation for Korea's liberation and independence.[118] Just like those in the LKNF and the KVU, the OUKYW members too believed that Korea's independence and China's victory in the war against Japan were certainly not two different, separate matters.[119] The OUKYW moved to Xi'an in Shaanxi Province and engaged there from spring 1940 in a noncombatant military operation to contrive to win Koreans in the Japanese army to its side. Obviously, the OUKYW too was assigned noncombatant works by the Chinese National Government. Unfortunately, Na, its commander, was murdered later by a rightist Korean, but the OUKYW continued to exist and operate until it merged in the end into the Korean Restoration Army in September 1940, and subsequently reorganized in November 1940 as the Fifth Branch Unit of the Korean Restoration Army under the command of the Korean Provisional Government. Note that the Provisional Government and its leader, Kim Ku, were known for their anticommunist stance, which may explain the possibility that OUKYW's reorganization was a reaction to the formation of the North China Branch of the KVU in Yan'an.

The anarchists in the OUKYW, just like those in the KVU, stressed the importance of having Korea's own military forces. Na

Wolhwan, for instance, explained it in his discussions on how to establish Korea's armed forces and on the reason why Korea needed its own armed forces. Dissatisfied with their task assigned from the Chinese, Na complained that active Korean military forces had been staying away from the warfront or only conducting propaganda-related works against the Japanese, neither of which had been effective in their result and been suitable as a job for the Korean youth in China. In addition, Na believed that there had been no [Korean] masses in China on whom the Korean youth could rely, and, therefore, they had no ability to expand their own military organizations in China. Having said that, Na pointed out that it was necessary for them to join the Chinese anti-Japanese resistance war in order to grow their own military ability and, at the same time, achieve a unity among all Koreans in China, despite their different political and ideological orientations. Then, Koreans and Chinese would ultimately be able to unite and consolidate the unity between two countries, defeating in the end the "Japanese fascist robbers." Na saw an opportunity to expand Korean youth's capability to build a Korean armed force, which could be founded on the Korean masses who he believed had been all scattered here and there in China, particularly, in occupied Manchuria and central China near Nanjing and Shanghai.[120] Making a unity among all those scattered Koreans was, in other words, the most urgent and important task to achieve independence as a distance goal, but also important as an immediate goal was to raise Korea's military ability in the process of achieving the unity in preparation for the coming independence. In his definition of national unity of all Koreans, the communists must have been excluded.

Compared to the above-mentioned two military units, the KCJGU was organized a little later in the fall of 1939 by Jeong Hwaam, Yu Ja-myeong, Yu Seo, and Yi Gang, around the area near Shangrao in Jiangxi Province and Jianyang in Fujian Province, also with the help from the Chinese Nationalist Army. Unlike its two counterparts, this guerrilla unit was a joint military group of Koreans and Chinese, according to Korean sources. Its main activities were centered on killing Chinese "traitors" (*hanjian*), winning Korean student-soldiers to their side who had been drafted against their will to the Japanese army, and rescuing western POW's from the Japanese army. Some Korean sources even claim that the KCJGC collaborated with a general named "Shaw," allegedly an air force commander of the Allied Powers, for the rescue operation of some western POW's in occupied

China. It was also said that two Chinese young men named Yue Guo-hua and Jin Yan, both of whom were former students of Yu Ja-myeong from Lida College in Shanghai, collaborated with the KCJGU for the assassination of some Chinese "traitors."[121] All these activities cannot be confirmed, but these anecdotes attest that this guerrilla unit was a kind of united front organization between Korean anarchists and some Chinese (possibly anarchists). It is unclear when this joint guerrilla unit stopped its military and other activities, for there is not much information available. The KCJGU could have been organized by the Korean anarchists who neither decided to move up to Yan'an nor to join the OUKYW, as Yu Ja-myeong was one of its members.

Korean anarchism of the 1920s was no less transnational than nationalist in its emphasis and ultimate pursuit, and many Korean anarchists were against nationalist movements that aimed mainly at political independence of Korea from Japan without social transformation in it. They seemed to shift this transnational position in the 1930s, not because they abandoned transnationalism or simply utilized anarchism for their national goal, but mainly because of the changes in the situation of China and the world. Japan's invasion of China since 1931, and China's all-out resistance to Japan with the formation of the second United Front between two parties, GMD and CCP, opened a door for Korean anarchists to consider their own national front, placing the national problem as their top priority. The news from Europe as to the successful People's Front in Spain in 1936 (and in France) and the worldwide movement against fascism and Japanese aggression came to them as a favorable sign for their independence movement and activities. These changes gave rise to awareness among Korean anarchists that Korea's independence was entangled with the "China problem" and, more broadly speaking, "the world problem." Thus, they came to conclude that the national problem could be solved only after joining the broader resistance against Japan and fascism. The general decline of anarchist movement in the world since the mid-1920s onward, let alone in Eastern Asia, could have possibly contributed to the shift of their focus to independence as well in hope to regenerate their movement. No doubt that the shift was also necessary for their survival during the war. More importantly, since they were without exception drawn to anarchism out of their nationalist aspiration, it was possible that many of them didn't even think that it was a shift of their focus. They could have thought that they were postponing their anarchist goal for the time being to a near future.

Implications of the future-oriented shift, however, were immense in terms of its immediate and forthcoming consequences. The LKNF placed national unity at the top of its agenda until 1945 and, for that, saw social problems and political/ideological divisions among Koreans as less important or at least not as immediate issues. Its immediate focus on struggle through military organizations resulted in its search for military organizations and actions together with Chinese against Japan. Also, Korean anarchists seemed to close their eyes to the fact that the Allied Powers were not true liberators of the colonized peoples but a different kind of colonizer or oppressor under the capitalist system, because of their attachment to their immediate goal to fight Japan together with all anti-Japanese forces of the world. As their later activities after 1945 reveal, they were not going to or unable to bring up the social issues in Korean society anymore. Many of them didn't even seem to take imperialism (and/or capitalism, therefore) seriously as their enemy anymore, as I demonstrate in the next chapter. The disappearance of class or social issues under capitalism as well as imperialism in their understanding was accompanied with the erasure of capitalism as the source of exploitation and oppression that Korean people, along with all the oppressed peoples in the world, had suffered from. In this respect I think their shift in the 1930s to '40s to national unity for independence through the national front entailed huge consequences in ensuing years in terms of the direction and character of post-1945 Korean anarchism. The shift is of greater significance if we consider that in the early 1930s many Korean anarchists in the LKYSC still identified capitalism as a target of their struggle.

Before the idea of national front was put forward, nationalism had been under severe attack by most anarchists, as exemplified in many articles carried in *Black Newspaper*. In fact, unlike their counterparts in China, Japan-based Korean anarchists seemed to be indifferent, if not opposed, to the idea of the national front. Korean anarchists in China too, it seemed, were internally divided, not over major anarchist principles or ideals but over their collaboration with other Korean socialists and communists or the Provisional Government. However we understand their internal divisions, it is still true that many Korean anarchists did not just participate in China's anti-Japanese war for its military victory over Japan, but also to lay out a new foundation for a new Korea and a new East Asia with peace in the region, just like the Japanese radicals and socialists who were more interested in the preparation for a future revolution in Japan when they joined China's anti-Japanese resistance war.[122] I don't think the active involvement or even initiative by Korean anarchists in the formation of the Korean National Front in 1930s and '40s China and their participation in the Korean Provisional Government before 1945 should be viewed as an aberration from anarchist basic principles, as some Korean historians have argued.[123] They did not lose their "anarchist voice" yet, but were only ready to accommodate anarchism to post-1945 Korea.

CHAPTER 5

Deradicalized Anarchism and the Question of National Development, 1945–1984

Against the hope that Korean anarchists had held before the end of the Pacific War, Korea was not able to gain outright independence when Japan surrendered to the Allied Powers on August 15, 1945. The Korean peninsula was divided into north and south along the 38th parallel line and occupied respectively by the United States and the U.S.S.R. The establishment of two separate regimes in north and south in 1948 followed with their respective occupier's sponsorship. In the south the United States called in pro-American and anticommunist Syngman Rhee (1875–1965), who led the establishment of the government of the Republic of Korea (South Korea) in August 1948, in the name of a United Nations' resolution. The north remained in the hands of the communists, and the Democratic People's Republic of Korea (North Korea) was established a month later, with Kim Il Sung (1912–1994) as its head. The Korean peninsula became the first and foremost warfront of the Cold War.

    The subsequent Korean War (1950–1953) consolidated the anticommunist political map of South Korea much further and deeper with Rhee's dictatorship and his suppression of communists and their progressive ideals. To make the situation worse, Bak Yeol, one of the leading anarchists who had returned to South Korea from Japan after 1945, was kidnapped to North Korea during the war,[1] and some anarchists abroad gave up their plan to return to their own homeland. Yu Ja-myeong, for example, decided to stay in communist China because of the cloudy situation in the Korean peninsula before and after the

Korean War.[2] And some Japan-based anarchists too decided to stay in Japan after 1945, making Japan their home for activities and life possibly out of their fear for potential political suppression in two Koreas. It is not clear how Korean anarchists in North Korea, if any, responded to the political environment there when North Korea was formally set up in 1948. Many of them seemed to have defected to the south but they were also constantly bewildered by the unstable political situation in the south.

To all Korean anarchists their target of struggle before 1945 had been mainly Japanese colonialism and their immediate goal was independence, albeit their distance goal was a new Korean society bent on anarchist principles. The main target was now removed, but their two goals, immediate and distant, were still untouched, due to the division of Korea by the two powers. To them the most urgent task after 1945 was therefore the construction of an autonomous, independent new Korea without which their distant goal would slip away. The goal and direction of their post-1945 activities were to be set accordingly.

The situation they faced, however, went athwart their post-1945 plan, as they saw not only incomplete national liberation with the division of their country but the growing unfavorable political environment in the south, under which they were increasingly vulnerable to new kinds of suppression, first by the new foreign occupier and ultimately by their own pro-American, antisocialist state. The anarchists in the south now faced vexing questions: Given the division of their country and incomplete national liberation, what direction did they need to take and what method they would employ to fulfill the goals of national liberation and an anarchist society in Korea? Answers to the questions rested on other related questions: Did they have to participate in the nation-building efforts in collaboration with the foreign occuper and later the anticommunist regime in the south? If they decided to do so, was it necessary to participate also in politics and organize their own political party for the goals? If they participated in politics, what kind of programs for social transformation and national development did they have to put forward for the goals? And if they did not participate in politics, what other options were available or should be acted on for the goals? These were the questions increasingly raised by many anarchists who had rushed back to their country after Japan's surrender from their exiled places. In the words of a post-1945 generation anarchist, Korean anarchists in the south faced some fundamental questions as to whether they still had to prioritize social revolution to build a new anarchist society or had to renew their struggle for national sovereignty, first in the south, despite the possibility of perpetuating the division of the peninsula.[3]

Yi Jeonggyu offered his own answers and presented two new tasks that he believed unfolded before Korean anarchists in the south after 1945: driving the communists in the north out of the peninsula and uprooting the "remnant feudal forces" in the south that had been present since the Japanese colonial period.[4] Yi's faithful disciple Lee Mun Chang notes that Korean anarchists pursued both tasks by setting "retaking freedom" as their revolutionary goal to deal with the situation. The meaning of *freedom* was defined with three broad dimensions: first, political freedom from the communist dictatorship in the north; second, freedom from foreign interventions in economy; and third, social freedom from the "feudal forces" prevalent in Korean society at the time.[5] As is clear, neither capitalism nor imperialism was considered the source that deprived Koreans of freedom. The first target of post-1945 struggle was the communists in the north, while freedom was understood mainly within the context and notion of anticommunism and equality in economy.

To realize freedom in terms of these three meanings, as I examine below, Korean anarchists decided to establish new organizations, including a political party of their own. But they met various obstacles in realizing the goal of "retaking freedom" in the south, chief among them the undemocratic dictatorial state. Not only for their survival from the suppression of the state but for the success and accomplishment of their goals, they gradually accommodated themselves to the new political climate under the dictatorships of Syngman Rhee and Park Chung Hee, both of whom placed anticommunism as the nation's founding principle. In short, Korean anarchists knew they were placed in the unease and unfavorable situation and, as a result, as I argue below, even reconceptualized anarchism to deal with the new political environment under the Cold War in the peninsula. In this sense I think it may be unfair to describe Korean anarchism after 1945 as "an aberration from original anarchism,"[6] or to say that it was wedded and reduced to nationalism, due to its support for the nation-building or silence to the dictatorship. What seemed to happen was that Korean anarchists approached and understood the postwar situation dialectically and found their answers to the post-1945 questions, emphasizing the nationalistic and anticommunist aspects of Korean anarchism. Most importantly, in doing so, they redefined themselves and gradually deradicalized their version of anarchism to envision a new society that was placed in the future. The status of anarchism was accordingly shifted from a revolutionary principle to a social movement idea. This does not mean at all that they abandoned anarchism. It rather simply explains a dialectical understanding of the relationship after 1945 between nationalism and anarchism and their subsequent application of the latter to the situation they had to cope with under the political climate they unpleasantly situated in.

Under Pressure: Searching for a New Anarchist Direction

In an effort to find an answer to the perplexing questions Korean anarchists faced after August 15, 1945, a conference was convened shortly by those who had remained inside the peninsula, along with some of those who had just returned from abroad. It was the conference of Korean anarchists in Northern and Southern Gyeongsang Provinces held in Busan from February 21 to 22, 1946. Its main organizers and participants were from the two provinces, although almost all Korean anarchists thus far had returned from abroad also attended it. Its main purpose was to find their answers to the above-mentioned questions to cope with the foreign occupation and division of Korea. The declaration adopted at it announced that Korea had just entered "the stage of national democratic revolution," where the liberation of "producers" (i.e., workers and farmers) as well as the national struggle to overcome its backwardness emerged as two essential tasks of Korean anarchists. The declaration reiterated that the sources that had exploited the producers stemmed mainly from two problems, that is, national and class problems, which were in fact interrelated because class struggle had much in common with the struggle for national economic liberation. To solve the two problems, according to the declaration, it was imperative to establish a government first under which all the production means had to be managed and operated by those who were engaged in production. And to overcome economic backwardness, Korean anarchists had to set national development as their focal task. Since national struggle was still more important than class struggle in the post-1945 period, they perceived the former in the context of economic autonomy and even saw it as a precondition for genuine national liberation. Economic autonomy of the nation was a crucial issue for them to lay out an autarkic economic system in Korea, which could make the country truly independent. In short, what was discussed and decided at this meeting was to place the accomplishment of "national democratic revolution" as their new task.[7]

A follow-up, much larger conference was soon held two months later from April 20 to 23, 1946, at Yongchu Buddhist Temple in a small town called Anui in Southern Gyeongsang Province. Titled the National Convention of Korean Anarchists (Jeon-guk anarchist daehoe) or the National Convention of Anarchist Representatives (Jeon-guk anarchist daepyoja daehoe), it was the first national convention and initiated by Yu Rim.[8] At it, ninety-seven anarchists were registered and present, and it marked a turning point in the history of Korean anarchism in terms of its direction after 1945. Attendees included almost all of those who were affiliated with two major Korean anarchist organizations at the time, the Free Society Builders Federation (FSBF, Jayu sahoe geonseolja yeonmaeng), organized in Seoul by Yi Jeonggyu and Yi Eulgyu after Japan's surrender, and the General Federation of Korean Anarchists (GFKA, Joseon mujeongbu juuija chong yeonmaeng), which probably was renamed from the Korean Anarcho-Communist Federation (KAF) that had been established in 1929 in Pyongyang during the colonial period. Yu Rim and Bak Seokhong had been the leaders of GFKA, and Yu had participated in the Korean Provisional Government in China as a representative of the GFKA. Yu had returned to Korea after 1945 with the GFKA as an independent anarchist organization. Many Korean anarchists who attended the convention were affiliated with both organizations simultaneously, mostly maintaining dual memberships. The convention was chaired by Yu Rim, Yi Jeonggyu, and Sin Jaemo, and lasted for three days. It was of cardinal significance in that Korean anarchists now formally began to identify themselves not just as anarchist but, just like Yu Rim called himself, as "one who favors an autonomous government" (*jayul jeongbu juuija*),[9] distinguishing themselves from conventional anarchists who were usually believed to negate the state. This was an identification constituted a major breakthrough to post-1945 anarchist activities.

In fact, Korean anarchists were frequently asked after 1945 about their position regarding the idea of setting up a Korea state. Since anarchists were widely believed at the time to have rejected the state, they needed to clear up any misunderstandings or prevalent suspicion that they were opposed to and thus would overthrow the state. The first reaction came from Yu Rim who, on his return to Korea, strongly denied that he was a person with "no-government principle," and emphasized that he rather was "an anarchist who rejects compulsory power." He then explained further about what it meant to be an anarchist. According to him, anarchists rejected only "heteronomous governments" (sic; *tayul jeongbu*) but not "autonomous governments" (*jayul jeongbu*). His support for the "autonomous government" was, he continued to explain, a product of the shift made after World War I by many anarchists who attested to the importance of having their own "practical organization," for which, in his case, he had participated in the Korean Provisional Government in China, which he believed was an autonomous government. After 1945 he now wanted to support a newly established Korean government, as long as it was built with the principle of autonomy.[10] To put it differently, since anarchists were only against "monopolistic naked-power" and strove for the realization of "democracy [that guarantees] equality," their eventual goal was to create a world where all mankind would labor and live freely under maximum democracy.[11]

On the first day of the convention, two reports were delivered to the attendees, one on the international situation prepared by Bak Seokhong and the other on the domestic situation by Yi Jeonggyu. In his report Bak characterized the world after 1945 as the postcolonial struggles by former colonies for their respective independence. Unfortunately, however, he lamented, Korea, unlike these former colonies, had not yet achieved independence, and the efforts to establish a unified government of Korea had not been undertaken either in a democratic way, not even autonomously by the Korean people. Worse, Bak continued, Korea seemed to be going in the opposite direction against the unification of the Korean peninsula, that is, genuine national liberation.[12] Following Bak's report, Yi Jeonggyu presented his assessment of then-domestic situation in Korea, in which he basically agreed with Bak's appraisal of the international situation and Korea's place in it, stating that all the efforts to set up a government in Korea after August 15, 1945 had been done neither autonomously nor democratically, not to mention without a united action of Korean people.[13] Both reports emphasized incomplete independence of Korea as of April 1946.

The first item on its agenda for the second day of the convention was the attitude of Korean anarchists toward the establishment of a Korean government, given the international and domestic situations the two reports analyzed. They also discussed what principles they could apply, if they favored building a central government in the south of divided Korea. These were important issues, because, just like Yu Rim, many returned anarchists to Korea from abroad after August 1945 had been continuously facing a question as to their understanding of and attitude toward the state, usually portrayed in media not as anarchists but predominantly as "believers in no-government" (*mujeongbu juuija*). To answer the question collectively, the anarchists at the convention adopted a resolution that stated they would strive for the establishment of an autonomous, democratic, and unified government in their liberated fatherland. The resolution further explained unequivocally that the goal they had pursued had been a complete liberation of Korea, which in turn was in need of one unified government. Koreans needed the unified government not just because they were a unitary people with their own rich cultural traditions but also because Korea couldn't be developed economically unless it became a unified country under the unified government. Accordingly, the role of a central government that would govern unified Korea was highly evaluated as important for the goal of national development. Here, we can see again Korean anarchists' preoccupation after 1945 with economic autonomy and development as crucial in their quest for genuine national liberation.[14]

Korea had agricultural areas in the south, but the abundant materials and sources for its industrial development were mostly concentrated in the north. Therefore, the resolution pointed out that without unification under a central government Korea could not develop itself into an industrialized country. The unified government which Korean anarchists strove to set up, however, was not simply a centralized government. It was expected to allow local autonomy as well along with autonomy in working places, and the unity of all the autonomous entities under the unified central government would be formed on the basis of the spontaneous alliance principle. Finally, it was made clear in the resolution that Korean anarchists were not "non-governmentists" (*sic*) (*mujeongbu juuija*, i.e., believers in no-government) but "non-heteronomous-governmentists" (*sic*) who were "autonomous governmentists" (*sic*), that is, "the ones who believe and favor an autonomous government" (*jayul jeongbu juuija*).[15] The newly adopted collective identification Korean anarchists enabled them to unload their anxieties and fears about anarchism being accused of a "dangerous thought," which didn't last long, though.

Another important point in the resolution was that they favored the unification of and a unified government of Korea. Making a new definition of their identity, Korean anarchists now took their first and important step toward a "Koreanization" of anarchism, in which it was redefined to serve at once the Korean situation after 1945, that is, prevention of the division of the Korean peninsula and the establishment of a unified government. In another resolution passed on the second day of the convention, Korean anarchists urged all revolutionary groups and individuals, who had shown some visible accomplishments during the national liberation struggle before 1945, to seek along with them for a chance to establish an interim, autonomous, unified government in South Korea first until the genuine unification of Korea with the north.[16]

Another immanent and important issue discussed at the convention was the question as to whether anarchists needed their own political party. It was a moot question but was raised in connection with the question about the liberation of producers, which was raised already two months earlier. The discussion revolved around how the power and voice of workers and farmers as main producers could be considered and reflected in politics to promote national development in economy. Before 1945, Korean anarchists had generally been indifferent to or had developed a cold attitude toward political movement and political parties. Likewise, they had always believed that political movement or political party's movement in a colony was meaningless, or at least bore the stigma of treason. This agenda as to an anarchist political party was brought up at the convention, due to the analysis of the domestic situation in Yi Jeonggyu's report on the first day of the convention. The post-1945 situation made Yi conclude that the most urgent task at hand was not social revolution but rather the completion of national liberation, because of the division between north and south and even the possible trusteeship in the Korean peninsula under the UN. The future of Korean society seemed to hinge on whether anarchists could successfully undertake the task of nation-building and lay out basic foundations for a new, autonomous country at its inception, no matter how political their task could be.[17]

Indeed, there was a growing consensus among anarchists that a revolutionary or independence movement itself was in a sense a political movement at a higher level, and thus that the establishment of a unified government was much needed in the postbellum situation in order to complete national liberation. What an anarchist needed to do then was: (1) to remove both powers, the United States and the Soviet Union, from the peninsula; (2) to eradicate all the forces against autonomy, democracy, unification, and nation-building; and finally (3) to participate actively in the foundational works for a new country.[18] After a long deliberation, Korean anarchists made a unanimous decision to support the idea of organizing their own political party on the basis of the necessity to accomplish the above-mentioned three tasks and also to reflect the organized power of workers and farmers in politics. It was strongly advised by the attendees, however, that the proposed anarchist party "follow the basic principles the convention has adopted." Joining the party would be up to "each individual member's spontaneous will," and those who decided not to participate in it "will support [the party] with their thought movement [*sasang undong*]."[19]

Yi Jeonggyu was one of the attendants who had an opposing view, although it was his report that generated the sense of urgency for their political involvement. In his opinion a more important task Korean anarchists faced at the time was to lay out a foundation successfully for a coming anarchist society through the efforts to raise the ability of workers and farmers, rather than to organize their own political party to represent the power and voice of workers and farmers in politics.[20] This was one of the reasons why Yi had already established the Federation for Rural Autonomy (FRA, Nongchon jachi yeonmaeng) and the Federation for Worker's Autonomy (FWA, Nodongja jachi yeonmaeng) immediately after August 1945. A major difference between Yi and other anarchists like Yu Rim who favored establishing a political party of their own, seemed to rest on the issue of how to assess the potential of Korean society in terms of its readiness for a social revolution. Yi seemed to be more forward-looking and favored delaying an anarchist revolution to the near future, while Yu was more interested in pursuing an anarchist revolution aggressively without delay, even with the help of an anarchist political party. The attending anarchists at the convention voted for Yu Rim's idea. Since they had already identified themselves as "those who favor an autonomous government," it was quite an obvious, logical decision for them to seek for a chance to establish a government of their own or at least participate in the making of national policies and programs through their political party, which was expected to implement anarchist ideals and principles in politics.

Also discussed and then passed at the convention were three basic principles Korean anarchists were expected to uphold, even when participating in politics: (1) to respect and guarantee individual freedom, (2) to safeguard peace and reject all kinds of invasive forces, and (3) to give the ownership of productive means to producers. In regard to the last principle, Korean anarchists particularly suggested that the factories and mines that once had been owned by Japanese colonizers during the colonial period be returned to and then owned by workers unconditionally. The workers were deemed to deserve the ownership, for they had all paid the Japanese with their exploited labor before 1945. For the same reason, it was also suggested that Korean farmers gain their ownership of land, which had been owned by Japanese and Korean collaborators before 1945.[21] At this point Korean anarchists could have further suggested and implemented the equal distribution of land to farmers, but they refrained from mentioning it at least for now, possibly due to the political attack from others toward them for being communists, although it would be one of the policies their party would put forward soon.

On the last day of the convention another important agenda item was placed on the discussion table: how to rearrange and reorganize the Korean anarchist camp after 1945. There had existed the KAF since 1929 in Korea as the first national organization of Korean anarchists, albeit without any actual activities under Japanese colonialism. There had been the GFKA in China which Yu Rim had represented before and after his return to Korea in 1945. The FSBF was additionally organized in Seoul in September 1945 by Yi Jeonggyu, who had stayed in Korea since he had been extradited from China to colonial Korea in December 1928 for his trial. As of April 1946, many Korean anarchists, with the exception of some leading figures, had all joined two main organizations, the FSBF and the GFKA, having dual memberships. The main issue in question at the convention, in other words, was how they could avoid any potential confusion about their membership and affiliation after 1945.[22] It seems that rather than resolving the membership issue, Korean anarchists decided to concentrate their effort and energy in the political party they were to organize together. In sum, the first national convention set the basic direction of Korean anarchist movement after 1945, a direction that was mainly a product of the post-1945 political environment surrounding the Korean peninsula. And the direction was tested first by Yu Rim with the experimental political party, and later modified by Yi Jeonggyu with his idea of rural village-based social transformation.

Anarchists in Politics: The Independence Workers and Peasants Party (Dongnip nonong dang) and the Democratic Socialist Party (Minju sahoe dang)

Following the conclusion of the first national convention, an anarchist political party was organized in July 1946, and named the Independence Workers and Peasants Party (IWPP, Dongnip nonong dang). Yu Rim, a veteran anarchist who had been a member of the Korean Provisional Government, was appointed as chairperson (*wiwonjang*) of the party's Executive Committee, which consisted of Yi Eulgyu, Yi Siu, Yang Ildong (1912–1980), Sin Jaemo, and Bang Hansang (1900–1970), in addition to Yu. The party was launched with an expectation from other anarchists that it was "to make the foundational framework [in politics and society] to build a new country from scratch."[23]

As mentioned, the decision to build a political party of anarchists was based on the consideration that their most urgent task was national liberation, when there was a widely shared sense of crisis that Koreans might be unable to build their own free, autonomous country and government, if Korea remained divided into north and south. The sense of crisis, along with the newly perceived task, didn't go unheeded, as Korean anarchists willingly postponed the goal of social revolution for the sake of complete national liberation, this time not through the united armed struggle but through an anarchist political party. Peter Zarrow notes that after the 1911 Revolution of China, Chinese anarchists like Li Shizeng, Wu Zhihui, and Cai Yuanpei might have "feared that as political revolution [i.e., the 1911 Revolution] had failed to remake China, so anarchism, which must begin as political revolution, was fated never to arrive." Neither did they want to risk another revolution and another failure, so that these Chinese anarchists "chose to pursue revolution by redefining it."[24] It is possible that Korean anarchists too thought similarly in the face of a new challenging situation after 1945, and defined the goal and ideals of anarchists much broadly so as to organize their own political party and pursue their anarchist goal through parliamentary politics.

Evident in the anarchist party's platform were the sustained emphasis on and prioritization of national liberation over social revolution. In it the IWPP's goals were explained: (1) to achieve perfect autonomy and independence of the Korean people; (2) to accomplish the utmost welfare for peasants, workers, and ordinary working people; and (3) to reject any dictatorship and collaborate with genuinely democratic domestic forces on the basis of mutually beneficial and equal principles. Sharing the general concerns other anarchists had about the situation at the time, the party, in its declaration also assessed the situation in Korea as of July 1946 as serious, because Korea's independence had not practically been achieved due to the division of it and the possible trusteeship by the United States and the Soviet Union, respectively, under a resolution of the UN. Therefore, the declaration asserted that, since the Korean people had possessed their unitary cultural tradition, they have the right to make a demand for a social system of their own to be set up in Korea. And it reiterated that for Koreans it was absolutely necessary to have such a system that could fit Korea's national condition, guarantee internal freedom and equal happiness to all individuals, and contribute to peace and progress of the mankind after taking back its autonomous independence and internationally acknowledged sovereignty.[25]

The IWPP certainly aimed at political independence of Korea but ultimately and unquestionably fostered a social revolution through anarchist principles, which they anticipated to take place in the end. This is quite evident also in the party's principle policies that were decided in correspondence with the goals reiterated in the platform and declaration. Among the policies two stood of importance. First, the equalization of land through the distribution of cultivatable land to the tillers, and, second, the establishment of an autonomous body at every factory and working place, which would be deemed responsible for managing and running them accordingly.[26] Compared to policies of other political parties of the time, these were quite radical in the sense that they were aiming at the changes in social and production relations. Because of the radical nature and direction of the policies and platform of the IWPP, a Korean anarchist later remembered that it was not so much a conventional political party as a revolutionary organization.[27] To intersperse its policies and the news and information about it the IWPP started to publish its own biweekly newspaper from August 3, 1946. In major cities and locations the party's branch organizations and offices were also subsequently set up.

The road ahead for the IWPP was, however, quite bumpy and even unpredictable. First, the anarchist party was crippled from its inception by some members who decided to participate in the national election in 1948, which was held just before the establishment of the government of the Republic of Korea in August of the year, against the party's decision to boycott it because of the party's concerns that the establishment of a separate state in the south might possibly perpetuate the division of the peninsula. In addition, the accomplishment of Korea's liberation through the anarchist party and the subsequent plan to realize the anarchist ideals through its policies were not easy tasks. The efforts by the party proved to be a failure in the end. The reason for it can be explained from many different angles. As mentioned, many anarchists ran for the National Assembly in the 1948 election against the party's decision to boycott it, which resulted in the internal division of and their subsequent expulsion from the party. What made the situation worse was that some of its core members took office in the Rhee's regime against the party's denunciation of it.[28] The anarchist party failed to gain a seat in the National Assembly after the May 30, 1950 election.

In the case of Yu Rim, he suffered from consistent political suppression of the Rhee regime, beginning first in 1951 in the wake of the Korean War and continuing throughout the 1950s. In addition, during the course of the three-year-long Korean War, many anarchists were either kidnapped or killed by North Koreans, which, to be sure, significantly lowered the level of human resources of the party and thus affected deeply its capability as a political party, let alone as a revolutionary organization, exacerbating its already waning fate. Most importantly, the general mood in South Korea increasingly marched toward antisocialism and antiradicalism, obviously due to the experiences and memories of the brutal war with North Korean communists for three years and the Rhee regime's subsequent political maneuvers to use the issue of anticommunism and turn the postwar situation in its favor. The war ended not only with the ruins and destruction of South Korean society but also with the rising state-led terrorism against anyone sympathetic to socialism, including anarchism.

In the 1950s, Korean anarchists painfully witnessed their society not only destroyed and drifting away from their ideal society but becoming unfavorable and even hostile to their belief. A new decade finally arrived but only with the tragic news of the death of Yu Rim on April 1, 1961, and his passing, it turned out, signaled the end of various new anarchist undertakings under his leadership after 1945, particularly the experimental, but unsuccessful, anarchist political party. Under the storming tide of anticommunist purges in the 1960s, anarchists reconsidered their means and ways to achieve their ultimate goal of an anarchist society, this time without their own political party and the unflinching leader, Yu. And as the new decade began, the political atmosphere was worsened with the rise of a new military dictator, Park Chung Hee, which impaired further profoundly Korean anarchists' revolutionary efforts to build an anarchist society and forced them in the end to deradicalize their anarchism further and modify their direction once again.

What Korean anarchists envisioned through the anarchist party was, according to Yi Jeonggyu's explanation, the realization of a social organization with the spontaneous alliance principle intact. Once it was realized, the organization (i.e., society) was expected to employ the system of joint production and joint consumption, and the function of politics in it would remain occupational in nature. Korean anarchists after 1945 were, Yi further explained, in agreement that democracy must not become a disguise of false freedom and equality in the modern society where colonies were liberated and capitalism was being transformed or revised; it must correspond to the genuine anarchist values of freedom and equality. Therefore, to accomplish the ideal anarchist society filled with freedom and equality, Korean anarchists in the party decided to rely on parliamentary democracy while maintaining their principles of political spontaneous alliance and decentralization of industry in their platform.[29] The efforts to realize their anarchist ideals through this anarchist political party under the leadership of Yu Rim, however, ended empty-handed. In retrospect, the Korean War altered the whole political map of South Korea into one that was about to turn out to be a nightmare for Korean anarchists.

Around the time when the IWPP gradually disappeared from the political stage, Yi Jeonggyu began to discuss and envisage the future of anarchist movement in South Korea in consideration of the hazy political aura of the 1950s. His discussion revolved around two main issues many Korean anarchists grappled with in the midst of Rhee's strengthened dictatorship and anticommunist policies after the Korean War. The first issue Yi took up was the prospect for Korean anarchist movement, in a series of his writings contributed to *Masan Daily* (*Masan Ilbo*) from May to June 1957. To no one's surprise, Yi was concerned with the question of how socialists in general had to cope with the political environment of South Korea under Rhee's dictatorship and antisocialist policies. Given the wrongdoings of the Rhee regime and their possible social consequences, Yi predicted that the sociopolitical condition of then–South Korea might allow the emergence of a Communist Party with the possible support from workers and farmers as their response to the repressive regime. Nevertheless, he firmly believed that it would be impossible to see the rise of a Communist Party in South Korea at that time, because communism would ultimately be rejected by Koreans. If that was going to be the case, an alternative party that could receive the support from both workers and farmers in place of the Communist Party was a "social democratic party" (*sahoe minju dang*), Yi assumed. The social democratic party, however, would not be able to surface either as a legitimate political party in South Korea, Yi forecasted. Rather, a Communist Party, making use of the opportunity for the social democratic party to emerge, might instead arise after camouflaging itself as a "social democratic party."[30] Among the political parties at the time, Yi indeed thought that the Progressive Party of Jo Bong-am was a pro-communist social democratic party, which to Yi was an undesirable phenomenon in South Korea.[31] What he seemed to imply was that the rise of a socialist party was inevitable in South Korea under Rhee's dictatorship. Its wrongdoings and their consequences in society would condition the rise of a socialist party which, in his belief, must be neither a communist nor a social democratic party.

Yi's next discussion was focused on the question about how anarchists could cope with then-unfavorable political climate in South Korea, and where they needed to head toward. Admitting that both the IWPP and the FSBF had all been in hibernation since the Korean War, he placed a new hope to a newly proposed political party of Korean anarchists he had just organized with others a year ago in 1956, the Democratic Socialist Party (DSP, Minju sahoe dang). According to Yi, anarchists had always maintained and advocated two principles they thought to be of essence in all aspects of human life, that is, freedom and equality. And since the anarchist notions of freedom and equality bore economic meanings, they could be combined with the principle of democracy, which he believed usually denoted political freedom and equality. The new anarchist political party, in other words, was to become one that could combine in its activity and program the economic meaning of freedom and equality anarchists had always emphasized with the general political meaning of democracy. If the combination was to take place successfully, its outcome would be what anarchists had always wished and advocated for, Yi firmly believed. Therefore, if the anarchist critique of communism could be further expanded and the interpretation and meaning of democracy could be widely shared in South Korean society at large, particularly in their respective economic implications, the DSP would emerge as a political party that could accomplish democracy completely in both political and economic senses. And if this were to happen, it in turn would mean a completion of socialism, Yi concluded. And the ideology of the party must be defined accordingly, therefore, as "democratic socialism" (*minju sahoe juui*), apparently different from "social democracy."[32]

If we consider that Yi had not been in full agreement with Yu Rim and others at the national convention of anarchists in 1946 on the issue of organizing an anarchist party, it may seem incomprehensible that Yi now was one of the driving forces and advocates of the DSP a decade later. An explanation for the change in his attitude may be found in what Edward S. Krebs explains about the Chinese anarchists' appropriation of Communist terminology in 1925, such as "mass revolution" and "workers' and peasants' revolution" in order "to counter the successes of their great rival," "which produced a change in the way in which revolution was conceived and described."[33] This was the case when Chinese anarchists were debating with the communists and had to cope with the situation where their movement waned with the rise of the CCP. Similarly, Yi could have shifted his view of an anarchist party after the consolidation of the dictatorial regimes in two Koreas, particularly after witnessing the stabilization of the communist regime in the north. This is particularly the case if we recall what he stated after 1945 that the communists in the north were one of two enemies still left after the demise of Japanese colonialism, and that he attempted (and would continue to do so) to organize workers and farmers into anarchist-led organizations to counter any possible penetration and influence of the communists into them. His shift was in a sense also a reaction to the possible ascendency of the communists in 1950s South Korea, in particular given his prediction of the rise of a Communist Party in South Korea as an inevitable consequence of the state's wrongdoings.

A question then arose: was "democratic socialism" the same as anarchism? Under the political and social environments of 1950s South Korea, Yi diagnosed, socialist movement as a "thought movement" (*sasang undong*) had no bright future, while a socialist party in the form of political movement still could have some favorable conditions. The examples from other countries had demonstrated that "thought movement" had usually preceded political movement, which had been the case in terms of both theory and reality. However, in South Korea, he unequivocally predicted, it would be the opposite in this regard because of the dominant antisocialist aura in society generated by the state. He therefore suggested that Korean anarchists consider anarchism in its Koreanized form and context, in particular, by thinking of its "democratic socialist" (*minju sahoe juui jeok*) version, which, he explained, placed its emphases on anticommunism and the political meaning of democracy combined with the anarchist notion of economic freedom and equality. This "democratic socialist" version of anarchism was supposed to be the path for anarchists to follow and realize anarchism in South Korea, Yi concluded.[34]

It must be noted that the concept of "democratic socialism" Yi coined and used was quite different from "social democracy" in many ways, and, in addition, the concept was not solely Yi's. Jeong Hwaam in his memoir also introduces the same concept along with an explanation of how he came across it and how he and Yi Jeonggyu endeavored together to form the DSP in 1956, with many progressive political figures at the time, chief among them Jo Bong-am. Jeong recalls that he became aware of the term *democratic socialism* when he was in Hong Kong before his return to Korea after 1945. According to Jeong, it was a Chinese scholar named Ding Zhou who researched and published writings on the concept of "democratic socialism" in various newspapers and magazines in Hong Kong sometime before 1950. Finding similarities with his own understanding of anarchism as he read Ding's writings, Jeong became readily interested in the concept and scrapped Ding's writings to utilize them later, thinking that he might decide later to be in politics. After returned to South Korea, Jeong found out that other anarchists like Yi Jeonggyu, Choe Haecheong, and Yi Honggeun all had also studied about and endeavored to conceptualize the same term.[35] It is not clear, though, who Ding Zhou was, and what and how he wrote about democratic socialism, because Jeong never answers these questions in his memoir. Nevertheless, what seems important to the current study is that Jeong found the affinities between his version of anarchism and Ding's concept of democratic socialism, and, given what Jeong writes in his memoir, Yi Jeonggyu's explanations of the concept mentioned above must have been similar to Jeong's understanding of anarchism, which in turn was probably the theoretical base of the new anarchist party Yi and Jeong attempted to organize together in 1956.

It is necessary here to look into the party much in detail to grasp how Yi Jeonggyu wanted to concretize in reality his "Koreanized" version of anarchism, that is, "democratic socialism," which was also Jeong Hwaam's understanding of it. On November 15, 1956, Korean anarchists, including Jeong Hwaam and his old comrades, Yi Jeonggyu, Han Hayeon, Choe Haecheong, Oh Namgi, and Kim Seongsu, proposed together the establishment of the DSP. Jeong was appointed as chairperson of the preparatory committee to organize the party. Unfortunately, however, it was never actually established, due, it seems, mainly to financial difficulties it had in the process of the formal formation of it.[36] The political pressure, either visible or invisible, from the Rhee regime could have possibly been another reason. Fortunately, Yi Jeonggyu left two writings on the party from which we can have a glimpse of how the participating anarchists wanted to concretize their version of anarchism through this party.

Yi's first writing on the party was written in October 1956, a month before the party was formally proposed by the above-mentioned committee. It could have been Yi's proposal to other anarchists to recommend setting up the preparatory committee. In this very abstract writing to explain about the party's two organizational principles, Yi emphasized first that the term *democracy* in democratic socialism must be understood as the principle in social and economic life as well as in international relations, not to mention as a political principle. In democratic socialism, therefore, democracy itself was its goal and means, which, Yi asserted, was the peculiar use of the term *democracy* and thus distinguished the party's use from those appropriations of the term in other conventional understandings and in other socialisms as well. Since "social life" had made humans continue to evolve, mutual dependency (i.e., mutual aid) was an important aspect for sociability (*sahoe seong*) of humans and was also one of the organizational principles of the party, Yi added.[37] It is quite obvious that the party was proposed to be organized with the two principles, democracy and mutual aid.

Next, Yi discussed the DSP's ideological line. He first reiterated mutual aid and mutual dependency as an element for human progress. Then he moved to a discussion of the pros and cons of both capitalism and socialism. In his understanding capitalism in general had done harm to the human society, such as the destruction of culture and economic inequality, rather than any meaningful contributions to it, although it no doubt had been extremely capable of maximizing human productivity. Socialism, on the other hand, he believed, had ensured economic freedom and equality to all humans, while it counterproduced "communist injustice," such as the enslavement of the people (*gungmin*). The mission of democratic socialism, therefore, Yi emphasized, was to place and add the socialist, rather than capitalist, economic ideas to the general meaning of democracy.[38] Of course, democracy here meant to him democratic practices both in economy and politics.

With this socialist line, according to Yi, the proposed DSP, if successfully established, would be able to materialize the "spirit" and "idea" of the Korean nation-building, both of which had been developed to embrace the "socialist idea," as well as the "democratic idea of freedom and equality." The founding "spirit" and "idea" of the Korean nation, in other words, Yi argued, had been formulated in order to establish a "democratic welfare state" on the premise that it would utilize the socialist idea. Of course, the capitalist idea of the ownership of private property too was to be allowed for the establishment of such a democratic welfare state.[39] Accordingly, having a "democratic socialist party" in Korea, Yi expounded, was of significance in that the "spirit" and "idea" of the Korea's nation-building, which were reiterated in the Korean Constitution, corresponded to those of democratic socialism, not to mention that having such a party itself had been a world trend at the time. Yi then pointed out that there was a prevailing argument that South Korea as an underdeveloped country (*hujin guk*) must go through a capitalist stage of development and must promote its own national capital (*minjok jabon*) as well, which was an anachronistic understanding of the meaning of development. That is, capitalism was a suit of "clothes" that other countries now wanted to take off, while socialism had become a new suit of "clothes" that all wanted to wear, because it fit their "bodies," as exemplified in the cases of the countries like India, Burma, Indonesia, Sweden, Norway, and so forth, Yi euphemistically explained. This new world trend, Yi believed, gave Koreans a chance to observe and reflect on the reality of the world and then to pursue a new economic and social system in Korea. Although socialist in economy, private enterprises and their various rights would be guaranteed and allowed in the new system of the new democratic welfare state. And under its new economic and social system, some key industries as well as other industries were to be either public-owned or nationalized, for they were essentially related to people's livelihood, Yi added. With the public-ownership or nationalization a planned economic system would become possible particularly in all national, public, and private economic sectors, and, as a result of this new economic system, a perfect social welfare system too could be placed in operation in the society, Yi concluded.⁴⁰

In response to many doubts raised by those who were skeptical about socialism, particularly about these two systems combined in economy and social welfare, Yi enumerated some advantages of the systems he saw. First was the strengthening of provincial (i.e., local) economy. He thought that the socialist economic system would strengthen provincial autonomy in economy, which in turn would prevent the centralization of power and, as a result, preclude any dictatorship of the regime or the consolidation of its naked power. Second, in his reply to a question that socialist policies were possibly carried out only well in a "backward country" (*hujin guk*) with no previous industrial development, Yi simply stated that the planned economy of socialism was much more needed in the economically backward countries. Yi knew that some would also claim that the capitalist idea of free competition was of more efficiency and even could promptly work for the backward countries in order for them to overcome swiftly their economic backwardness. Answering to this follow-up question, third, he recapitulated that the establishment of the socialist economic system was much needed and also had to be secured in such backward countries. Last, knowing that democratic socialism could potentially be attacked as a communism of some sort, Yi defended democratic socialism on the grounds that it was a "practical theory" (*silje iron*) that had been formulated as a result of many yearlong experiences of various kinds of socialists, who had long struggled to establish an economic order that could set and guarantee economic equality along with human rights to protect freedom and political equality. To support his claim, Yi further listed in his writing and compared the similarities and differences between communism/social democracy and democratic socialism to promote the latter.⁴¹

Since democracy was the goal and means of democratic socialism and thus must be respected as the primary principle of it, the "natural" completion of democracy meant to Yi the completion of socialism in reality. And this was why the term *democratic socialism* was chosen, Yi emphasized.⁴² Yi's understanding of the meaning of *democracy* at the time seemed to be shaped basically from its definition made at the first Congress of the Socialist International held at Frankfurt from June 30 to July 3, 1951, not to mention his adoption of the term *democratic socialism*. To him, the word "democratic" in democratic socialism denoted the realization of a socialist society through parliamentary politics of the West, which, he believed, would employ democratic means and method for political democracy. To be sure, democracy was understood by Yi, again, in two senses, both political and economic, and his understanding of democracy was formulated by a symbiosis of its meanings in both socialist economic and capitalist political democracy. Yi specifically identified five goals as something that must be fulfilled by the DSP to realize democracy in South Korea, and they were: (1) provincial autonomy under a cabinet system in politics; (2) construction of a democratic welfare nation; (3) consolidation of new social ethics in society, such as cooperation, mandatory labor for all (*gaeno*), autonomous (*jaju*), and creativity (*chang-ui*); (4) protection and promotion of national native cultures and active absorption of foreign cultures in order to contribute to the creation of a world culture based on the harmony between Eastern and Western cultures; and (5) realization of the world-as-one-family idea (*segye ilga*) as a member of the United Nations and the Socialist International.[43] As for the third point, Yi later further expressed again his own anxiety about losing the country again if such ethical values in society were to be lost among the Korean people.[44]

In order to accomplish these five goals Yi then proposed and enumerated the party's possible various policies, which intended to cover a wide range of problems and issues in South Korean society, from its cultural and economic to political and social aspects, including the accomplishment of the planned economy system and the allowance of workers' rights to participate in the management. Culturally, in particular, the DSP aimed at transforming into new social ethics such bad Korean national traits as "serving the big" (*sadae*), "blind following" (*buhwa*), "idleness" (*anil*), and "passivity" (*soguek*). Besides this cultural project, one of the party's proposed policies deserves our special attention. It was on agriculture, and undoubtedly reflected an anarchist idea regarding the combination of agriculture and industry. In the policy, the party was manifested to carry out the mechanization of agriculture and the correction of the bad effects (*pyehae*) of the cultured population's concentration in cities, in order to promote the idea of combining agriculture and industry in rural villages. At the same time, the policy also set a goal to expand cultural and welfare facilities in rural villages. The rationale behind this rural-based goal lay in the fact that farmers in rural villages occupied 70 percent of the whole South Korean population at the time, and the expansion of cultural and welfare facilities in rural villages thus were regarded as necessary for the promotion of the majority's welfare.[45]

On the other hand, Yi was now in fervent opposition to any violent revolutionary as well as dictatorial means practiced in both the Soviet Union and North Korea, although he obviously wanted to keep certain socialist ideas that embraced the general spirit of economic democracy. Speaking highly of the declaration announced at the first Socialist International in 1951, Yi briefly summarized what was affirmed at the Congress as the goal and duty of "democratic socialism": the critique of communism and the expanded and advanced interpretation of the meaning of democracy. Following the goal and duty defined for socialists at the Congress, Yi proclaimed that the enemy to the members of the proposed DSP in South Korea was not so much capitalism as communism. Yi thus suggested that they all subsequently denounce dictatorship and authority, therefore, and begin a new movement for democratic socialism that was "international" and "anti-orthodox" in its character.[46]

To be sure, Yi's proposal to Koreanize anarchism through the concept of democratic socialism was made out of consideration of the sociopolitical conditions of South Korea in the 1950s, backed by the declaration made at the first Socialist International in 1951. Internally, however, he also saw some peculiarities in the socialist movement of Korea. In regard to anarchism, Yi correctly understood that anarchism in Korea, unlike that in the developed country, had been from the onset a part of national liberation movement or, more broadly, independence movement, at least until 1945. According to his explanation, in other words, while Korean anarchists agreed with the immediate goal of Korean independence movement, that is, political liberation of Korea, they at the same time had always sought for economic liberation as well to retake the right for the economic survival of Korea.[47] This had long been a characteristic and determinant of the direction of Korean anarchism, and the liberation of Korea in two meanings had been a shared ultimate goal of Korean anarchists who had always pursued a social revolution first over a political revolution. What mattered was how to achieve the goal.

The Korean anarchist experiments with two political parties, first with the IPWP and later with the DSP, from the late 1940s to the mid-1950s, all seemed to be unsuccessful due to many reasons, chiefly the unfavorable sociopolitical environment for the realization of anarchist ideals, particularly various political barriers which they had faced since 1945. The deradicalization of anarchism by conceptualizing it as democratic socialism was not successful either, as the party using the term socialism was, it seems, neither even formally established nor participated in an election after its proposed establishment.[48] Korean anarchists seemed to make every effort to avoid any accusation of being communists and/or advocates of no-government or anarchy. They deradicalized the goal of anarchism by underscoring national development through an alternative developmental strategy that combined capitalist notions of development and democracy with socialist ideas of equality and freedom. When one of their close socialist comrades, Jo Bong-am, who participated in the discussion of rebuilding a new socialist party in 1956 with many anarchists, was baselessly accused of being a spy for North Korea, and then arrested, tried, and finally hanged in 1959 in the name of the National Security Law (*gukka boan beop*) by the Rhee regime, they seemed to simply "give up everything" "without regret" and began to concentrate on the movement to promote "cultural enlightening" and "education for the next generation," according to Lee Mun Chang.[49] And soon under the military dictatorship of Park Chung Hee who aggressively set anticommunism as the supreme national policy from the 1960s, there seemed no room and options left for anarchists to propagate their ideals and programs because of the groundless accusation and prevalent stigma of "being Commies."[50] It was no wonder that Korean anarchists either kept silent and their distance from the totalitarian politics of the Park regime in the 1960s through '70s or further accommodated and deradicalized anarchism into a more suitable idea for social movement.

Rural Problem and Industry in National Development

Korean anarchists had long been attentive to the "rural problem" (*nongchon munje*) since the 1920s. Yi Jeonggyu was one of them. He was reluctant to join the first anarchist party and moved away from politics. He instead heeded his attention to rural villagers and workers not to organize them into an anarchist party but to educate them in preparation for a coming anarchist society. In fact he had already established in 1945 the FRA and the FWA, respectively. Yi's independent move away from the IWPP to form his own anarchist organizations for social movement is also revealing in that there were internal divisions and tensions, and even possibly a rivalry, between Yi's and other anarchists led by Yu Rim, over a concrete means to realize their anarchist ideals, as well as over how to cope with the political climate in South Korea.[51] An examination of Yi's activities and thoughts after 1945 particularly reveals interesting aspects of a deradicalized version of Korean anarchism and how Yi and other anarchists endeavored to build an ideal society through the revival of rural villages in post-1945 South Korea.[52]

A month after Japan's surrender to the Allied Powers in August 1945, Yi established the FSBF and then organized in the same year the FRA and the FWA. In a detailed explanation of the FRA's platform and declaration, written in March 1946, Yi pointed to the main task he believed Korean anarchists were expected to do first after Korean's independence: "to revive (gaengsaeng) our Korea as a free and pleasant country."[53] To fulfill the first task, Yi suggested that rural villages (nongchon), which occupied most parts of Korea, be revived first. According to him, the farmers living in rural villages represented "the whole country itself," as they consisted of 90 percent of the Korean population. To Yi, farmers in rural villages obviously were the main, unique force to construct a new Korea. To revive rural villages, however, Yi continued, farmers should first broaden their knowledge, and their life must be reformed so as for them to raise their ability and qualifications to be part of the independent and free country.[54]

To materialize this idea, Yi organized the FSBF immediately after Korea's independence, with his brother, Yi Eulgyu. At its inaugural meeting on September 29, 1945 in Seoul, Yi Eulgyu announced in his opening remarks that the enemy of Korean anarchists, Japanese imperialism, had disappeared. He nevertheless admitted that the colonial conditions of dependency still lingered in Korea, because, he warned, Korea's independence was not accomplished by Koreans themselves. The colonial conditions, he suggested, therefore, not be treated lightly in the effort to build a new country of free society in Korea.[55] The FSBF embraced almost all Korean anarchists into it in order for them to partake in the task of building a new country with a hope for them to offer their "constructive roles." It particularly aimed at constructing a society in which "the tillers own land and the workers own factory." To accomplish the aim the FSBF decided to establish two more additional organizations, the FRA and the FWA, which would lay out a foundation for a coming future society they wanted to build.[56] Briefly speaking, the former was organized with a plan to raise the farmers as the owners of the new country, and the latter with a plan to remove any potential class struggle at workplace by institutionalizing the participation of workers in the management of factory.

The FSBF was the first nationwide anarchist organization in Korea that began its activity publicly and openly, with the manifested two goals its members would strive to achieve. First was to take a constructive part in building an independent Korea, and, second, to put forward a proactive and concrete plan to help construct a new country.[57] As is clear, the FSBF placed the nation-building first over social revolution as its goal and was a future-oriented anarchist organization with a forward-looking vision. Its members believed a successful nation-building after 1945 would eventually promise and guarantee their pursuit and activities for an anarchist society in Korea. Yi Jeonggyu was to deliver a similar analysis at the forthcoming national convention of Korean anarchists in 1946, in which he saw the place of social revolution secondary to the task of building a new Korea and pointed to a necessity for anarchists to participate in the national construction in order to envision their own social revolution in the near future, if not immediately. In a sense, the establishment of the FSBF was, as stated in its declaration, a sign of "unmasking" anarchists as nation-builders and "resurfacing" them from the underground they had been hiding in during the Japanese colonial rule, under which they had not been allowed to speak out openly about their own cause and doctrine as nationalists as well as anarchists.[58]

The FSBF passed at its inaugural meeting its concrete goals as follows: (1) to reject dictatorial politics and strive to build a Korea of perfect freedom, (2) to reject the collective economic system and strive to realize the principle of decentralized local autonomy (*jibang bunsan juui*) in economy, and (3) to strive for an embodiment of the ideal that sees "all mankind as one family" on the basis of mutual aid. In short, a new Korea the FSBF would build was one that was transnational in its ideal and had a system of local self-governments in its practice with the principles of spontaneous alliance among them to form their central government, and of individual freedom among its constituencies. Three major principles for the construction of such a new Korea would be "autonomy" (*jaju*), "democracy" (*minju*), and "unity" (*tong-il*). And the role of anarchists in realizing the new Korea was to collaborate with "revolutionary leftist nationalists," in order to fight their two enemies, the "native, feudal capitalist elements," which had been in collaboration with Japanese imperialism before

1945, and the "pseudo, reactionary dictatorship-worshippers" (i.e., communists).⁵⁹

The FSBF's anticommunism was not novel, given the antipathy anarchists had long held against the communists since the 1920s, but the meaning and implication of the "native, feudal capitalist elements" as their enemy were quite vague. By circumscribing the definition of "native, feudal capitalist elements" within those who had exploited their compatriots economically in service of Japanese imperialism, the FSBF's members moved away from the universal social problems under capitalism itself. Yi Jeonggyu even saw the "feudal forces" as a more serious problem than capitalism itself. In his thinking the universal values such as freedom, equality, and mutual aid had all been undermined not only by Japan's colonization but also by the Korean society's internal, native forces. Therefore, when Japanese colonialism had already been overthrown, the construction of a new society with the values in Korea after 1945 seemed to hinge only on whether or not Korean anarchists were able to eradicate the remaining "native, feudal capitalist elements" and the "pseudo, reactionary dictatorship-worshippers," together.⁶⁰

Korean anarchists in the FSBF like Yi Jeonggyu didn't necessarily oppose or want to overthrow capitalism itself after 1945, as long as it had no ties with Japanese colonialism, although they never stopped criticizing it.⁶¹ They were either deaf to the voices from the ongoing struggles against colonialism and capitalism in post-1945 years in the other parts of the world or more concerned with nationalist aspiration for a new Korean state and its economic development. While the communists in the north would remain their arch enemy, the identity of the second enemy continued to be unclear and even vague. The vagueness, as I will demonstrate, allowed Yi and his fellow anarchists to be relatively silent about the dictatorial regimes and their policies from 1948. They were even willing to treat "nationalists with genuine national conscience" as their "friendly force" (*ugun*),⁶² in addition to "revolutionary leftist nationalists," in the effort for national construction, no matter how undemocratic or silent they were about dictatorships. Avoiding the fundamental question as to inevitable social divisions in capitalist society, the FSBF under Yi's leadership defined its goal as the establishment of an equal and free society in Korea where tillers own the land and workers own the factory after removing the vague "native, feudal capitalist elements" and the communists. Of course, it rejected any compulsory power in the society that could create an environment of domination by a class over other classes and by a people over other peoples. It also denounced any invasive war and the possession of armed forces more than enough for self-defense.[63] The point here is that capitalism was not explicitly included on the list of their new enemies, when anarchists had always been attentive to and even cautious of a possibility to create a condition of domination and inequality under capitalism. This seeming passivity toward the question of capitalism, it seems, had much to do with Yi's idea of national development.

The FRA, one of the FSBF's two sister organizations, as Yi Jeong-gyu explains, was founded particularly in response to the threat of communism. After August 1945 Yi feared that the communist propaganda of "tillers owning land" could undermine the healthy development of a new Korea, if farmers listened to and favored that idea. To avoid that possibility in the situation posterior to the year 1945, Yi actually rushed to organize the FRA.[64] The idea behind the FRA about organizing and educating farmers had long been sustained, proposed, and even openly experimented by Korean anarchists, including Yi, as this study demonstrates. In the declaration of the FRA, the place of farmers and rural villages in the course of constructing a new Korea was now reconsidered more important than ever before. Rural farming villages in Korea had been the object in the past of the "feudal" extortion of heavy taxes as well as the Japanese exploitation during the colonial period. But the farmers in rural villages had been the preservers and maintainers of Korea's distinctive culture as well as tradition of "good morals and manners." Their life, however, had long been no better than that of animals, because of which it had been of no use to speak to them about Confucius, Mencius, Buddha, or the God, the FRA's declaration pointed out. To make things worse, the declaration further explained, modern achievements and technologies introduced by the West and Japan since the late nineteenth century, such as railroads, telegrams, and telephones, had only made their life "more painful and more starved." On the top of that, there was a prevailing "rural problem" that small-income farmers had only been able to make their living after borrowing a loan at high interest rate. The declaration thus indicated that this "rural problem" had become a serious and fundamental problem and immediately turned into a social problem of Korea after 1945. Since "farmers are the owners of Korea" and the revival of rural farming villages would depend on whether the life of small-income farmers could be revived, the regeneration of Korea as a new country would be determined by whether farmers and rural areas were eventually able to regain together their vitality.⁶⁵ The first step toward the revival of farmers must be taken to ensure their economic independence, for which they must be given opportunities to make extra income. If offered some extra works, in other words, farmers could make some extra income which in turn would assist them to be independent economically. The extra works not only offered them an opportunity to earn extra income to make them independent economically but could also promote the idea of "natural cooperation" among them, which, as a result, could absorb surplus labor in rural areas and allow them to work together.⁶⁶ The core of the rural problem rested on the economic hardships of small-income farmers, which could be solved by offering extra works to them for extra income.

The idea of providing farmers with extra works for extra income in rural villages as a means to solve the "rural problem" was to be further elaborated on later in the 1960s and '70s in "the Movement to Receive [Orders] and Produce [Goods]" (Susan undong) launched by Yi's other organization, the Institute for the Study of National Culture (ISNC, *Gungmin munhwa yeon-guso*). I will discuss about it below. Suffice it to say here that Korean anarchists, in particular Yi Jeonggyu and his close associates, seemed to believe that the key for their ideal anarchist society in Korea lay in rural villages and accordingly their regeneration through economic independence. Indeed Yi was deeply interested in removing poverty in rural villages, but was indifferent to the unequal social relations in rural villages. In short, empowering rural farmers in economic senses as the main constructors of a new Korea was the main task assigned to anarchists. When the task was complete, rural villages could be a part of "the civilized world" (*munmyeong segye*) and eventually could develop into "the abode world of perfect bliss" (*geungnak segye*), where "good morals are realized and rural villages are in mutual cooperation and help," Yi predicted.⁶⁷

Yi's emphasis on farmers and rural villages had much to do with his idea of nation-building. To him independence didn't mean national liberation in the socialist sense but denoted Korea's self-reliance and self-identity that could ensure that Korea become "the most civilized and wealthiest country." And self-reliance would be achieved by developing rural villages and improving farmers' livelihood, which in turn would allow Korea to be identified as "the most civilized country." Since farmers had preserved the "beautiful, pure and affectionate Korean customs," they were "the only ones to endeavor to construct a Korea," Yi believed.⁶⁸ If there would come to exist a utopia-like world in Korea, where people could find a comfortable living from generation to generation, farmers would be able to make a living as humans.⁶⁹ Of course, there was another reason for him to underscore rural villages: to combat the communists whose attempts might mobilize and organize farmers. To Yi, therefore, to organize farmers into the FRA of which he was the leader was an extended endeavor on his part, to accomplish the "Nation-Building Movement" (Geon-guk undong).⁷⁰

Despite his huge emphasis on the revival of rural villages and an economically improved life of farmers as crucial to construct a new Korea, Yi Jeonggyu fundamentally believed that the development of rural villages must be accompanied inevitably by industrial development. Ostensibly, Korea had gained political independence when the Japanese surrendered in 1945, but Yi believed that political independence might leave Korea remaining "extremely unhealthy and superficial," and without economic autonomy. To be autonomous in the economy as well as politically, therefore, Yi continued, Korea could not afford to rely only on agriculture for economic development, given the precedents and lessons from the developed countries. It was indeed unthinkable and even nonsensical for him to foster national economic development only with agriculture, because of the fact that, he claimed, during the thirty-six-year Japanese colonial rule, Korean agriculture had not been able to make any technological progress that could be utilized for national development after 1945. In order to plan on developing agriculture, it was indispensable, in his thinking, to have industrial development as well, at least for technological progress in agriculture. In other words, Yi assumed that industrial development was a decisive condition for economic independence of Korea, given the historical experiences of the developed countries and the colonial situation Korea had been placed in.⁷¹ In short, to Yi, the best developmental strategy for Korea was the combination of industrial and agricultural developments through the revival of rural villages. And, in the end, this would bring a genuine national liberation to Koreans in both political and economic senses.

Yi admitted, however, that his proposed developmental strategy would not be workable at once, since "Our country has no industrial capital and technology," not even the experiences of industrial management. Therefore, Yi continued, it was necessary for Korea first to examine carefully the traces of the developed countries in the past in order to identify the reasons for their "success" as well as any "side-effects" and "irregularities" in their developmental strategy. After examining and taking the lessons from those developed countries, Korea would be able to plan on its own path to "the nation-building through industry" (*san-eop ipguk*), Yi forecasted. If the experiences of the developed countries were taken into consideration, in other words, Yi thought that Koreans in the end would be able to preclude the influence of communism and any irregularities in economic management that might have prevented increased efficiencies and technological advance in production. Furthermore, he believed that taking lessons from the cases of the advanced countries would additionally help Koreans be better prepared for the problems that had already occurred in those countries, such as the gap between the rich and the poor, the concentration of wealth, and the labor-management disputes, all of which had been typical and conspicuous in social unrest and industrial monopoly under modern capitalism.[72]

What Yi suggested as a preemptive solution to the problems of industrialization was one that challenged the notion of development in terms of capitalist developmentalism and reflected anarchist concerns as to national autonomy and social justice in economy and national situations in the course of development. Specifically, Yi was certain that Korea, while developing its industry, had to endeavor to realize the co-ownership of factory by the state and individuals (i.e., workers). And this was of importance if workers were to have a perception that factory owners were not the target of their struggle but rather the ones with whom they needed to share a common fate. In other words, workers would endeavor to possess the status of and qualifications to be the co-owners of factory so that their representatives could participate in the management of factory along with its other owners, ultimately sharing the factory's profits.[73] Yi expected that the FWA would also be able to become a spontaneous anarchist organization that could do away various contradictions in the capitalist society and correct the problematic collectivist nature of communist society.[74]

For the realization of an anarchist society with national development, there were important conditions on the part of workers, Yi stated. First was to organize workers' unions, not according to occupations but according to industries. Second, workers must possess the qualifications and status to be able to serve as the co-owners of factory. Third, workers, representing their respective union, must be given the right to participate in the planning and management of their factory, whether owned by individuals or the state. Fourth, workers must receive dividends in every quarter from the factory.[75] In addition, workers were not just workers but also the "nationals" (*gungmin*) of Korea, a democratic country that entitled them to enjoy the right and opportunity for their free and equal individual development. They must be able to see themselves as a pillar to build a new country for which they would have a sense of mission. And they would also take responsibility for the promotion of economic autonomy of Korea and work with courage and motivation at the forefront of its industry, Yi contended.[76] In short, if the FWA's slogan of "the land to farmers, factories to workers!" was finally realized, "although it will be viewed as a capitalist country, the newly-born Korea will in fact become a country where in farming villages there are no tenant farmers or agricultural workers, at urban factories no wage-workers are employed, and [finally in society] no confrontations and struggles,"[77] Yi predicted. Simply speaking, Korea would become a uniquely alternative capitalist society where an alternative modernity on the basis of its national conditions was accomplished through his proposed alternative developmental strategy.

Notable here were growing signs of Yi's move toward a deradicalization of Korean anarchism. In the declaration of the first post-1945 anarchist organization, the FSBF, there was no mention of capitalism itself as a source of social problems or as a target of anarchist struggle to build an ideal society in Korea. As mentioned before, the declaration only accounted for the successful removal of their former enemy, Japanese imperialism, after 1945 and the emergence of two new enemies, communism and any remnant feudal forces in the post-1945 society that had collaborated with Japanese capitalists since 1910. Here Yi limited the capitalists to both Japanese and their Korean counterparts who had exploited Korean workers and farmers and still were believed to be at work after 1945, labeling them "remnant feudal forces." By doing so Yi seemed to distinguish the "feudal forces" from those whose role and responsibility as "national capitalist" were of essence for the alternative national development he envisioned. This kind of recognition came to take shape rapidly as part of the framework of Korean anarchism after 1945, due to the priority given by Yi and his followers to political unity and national autonomy of Korea. This means many Korean anarchists gradually lost their revolutionary bent, at least in terms of their emphasis placed on national liberation over social transformation. In fact, it may have been necessary and even inevitable when Korean anarchists after 1945 were all basically concerned with how to gain and maintain complete independence without any political and economic interruption or exploitation from the developed countries. Their focus, in other words, was not on how to remove the social ills under capitalism and develop Korean into a new ideal society but rather on how to develop Korea as an autonomous country with minimum social problems that had been prevalent in the capitalist countries and at the same time without communist intrusion.

In this respect, the Korean War from 1950 to 1953 was, in hindsight, a turning point in the direction of Korean anarchism after 1945. The post–Korean War years witnessed a political environment much more hostile to anarchists with the Rhee regime's anti-communist stance along with the height of the Cold War, all of which culminated in the baseless trial and execution of Jo Bong-am, leader of the Progressive Party. Personal survival once again became an issue for Korean anarchists who would conclude that it was "unthinkable," in the words of Lee Mun Chang, to speak something against the Rhee regime and its successors under their "dreadful control" and suppression of their political foes with willfully fabricated evidence and stories to arrest and torture them and any socialism-inspired intellectuals and politicians. What Korean anarchists could do was to "hold their breath" before the brutal, merciless regimes.[78]

Against the State-Led Modernization: "The Nation Thrives only if Rural Villages Thrive"

One of the main reasons why Korean anarchists turned their eyes more closely to rural villages from the 1960s and 1970s can be found in the undertakings of rapid modernization of South Korean rural villages driven by the developmental dictatorship of Park Chung Hee, often symbolized by his "New Village Movement" (Saemaeul undong). Contrary to what was propagated by his military regime, Korean anarchists believed that the state-led rural movement in fact had seriously undermined the very foundation of Korean rural villages and, as a result, pushed the rural population to migrate to cities.[79] To deal with the situation, some Korean anarchists launched various "non-compromising" and "non-resistant" movements of their own against the state-driven modernization for rural villages, which included a movement for autonomous, self-defensive rural villages and a cooperative movement that aimed at organizing urban consumers.[80]

Most of these anarchist-led movements were undertaken and/ or guided by the Institute for the Study of National Culture (ISNC, Gungmin munhwa yeon-guso) Yi Jeonggyu had established in the spring of 1947. Strictly speaking, the Institute was not an anarchist organization per se, because its members included not only anarchists but some conservative nationalists in their political orientation. Participants in and members of the Institute, who had joined the ISNC since 1947, included, among anarchists, Yi himself, some of the second-generation Korean anarchists, and the third-generation Korean anarchists who had just graduated from college in the 1960s, with growing interest in anarchism.[81] In addition, there were some "pure nationalists" (as opposed to "communist nationalists") participated as members in the ISNC, albeit the majority in its membership and activities were anarchists who welcomed "pure revolutionary leftist nationalists" in joining them as their "friendly forces" (*ugun*).[82] In many respects the ISNC was Yi Jeonggyu's own venue to embark on his own cultural and economic projects to build a new anarchist society in South Korea.[83] The Institute was an example of how seriously Korean anarchists, in this case represented by Yi Jeonggyu and his associates, took Korean traditions, national culture, and farming villages after 1945 in realizing their anarchist vision in South Korea, as well as in thinking of national development. This is evident in the mission of the Institute, which stated its goal as uncovering the "national essence" (*bonjil*) of Korea and the "capability" (*yeongnyang*) of Koreans by way of conducting researches on Korean culture.

After its establishment in 1947, the ISNC, however, had not been active, but in the years after the end of the Korean War in 1953, it became a little active again with the shift of its main focus to the recovery of the destroyed national economy of South Korea after the war, with an aim to help stabilize people's devastated livelihood in the postwar situation. In the postwar years both economic recovery and stabilization were deemed to be the keys to solve all the cultural and social problems prevalent after the war in then–South Korea. Therefore, the ISNC increasingly shifted its focus to research and works that could make contributions to the much-needed immediate economic reconstruction of South Korea from the ashes of the war, for which it particularly paid attention to farmers and thus initiated a movement in the ensuing years to support them in dire situation, as I examine below. Simply speaking, the two main issues the ISNC was manifested to tackle in its postwar activities were rural culture (i.e., "national essence") and how it could be promoted and developed (i.e., rural culture's "capability"). To put it differently, the ISNC's ultimate task was to achieve South Korea's viability as an independent, autonomous country, by identifying "broadly-defined overall cultural capability of Koreans" and utilizing their own unique rural culture.[84]

To fulfill the task, the ISNC was involved in various activities and projects that reflected its name, Institute for the Study of National Culture. Due to its unequivocal emphasis on the nation (*minjok*) and/or nationals (*gungmin*) in its quest for an ideal anarchist society in Korea, which no doubt sounds quite contradictory if we consider the universal messages and goals of anarchism and the transnational character of Korean anarchism I have argued for, the ISNC's name itself often brought to mind images that seemed unlikely for an anarchist institute. The choice of the Institute's name, the Study of National Culture, was probably based on a certain awareness among anarchists that Korea's national liberation was not accomplished yet, which invited a new prioritization of complete national liberation over social revolution in a universal sense, as their continuous task even after 1945, as Lee Mun Chang explains.[85] What I think important was their willingness to respond proactively to the national environment in the process of realizing their ultimate anarchist ideals. Another possible reason for adopting and using such a name was to avoid any misunderstanding and/or political accusations as to the identity and underlying ideology of the ISNC and its activities.

The main subject of the ISNC's research activities was "the promotion of the Korean nation's subjectivity (*jucheseong*) and the establishment of an autonomous and cooperative [cultural] structure for the people's life,"[86] while its two major goals that served as its principles to build a new society were, first, the completion of autonomy and independence of Korea, through which Korea's unification could be finally realized, and, second, the realization of a "free community" (*jayu gongdongche*) in society through spontaneous cooperation among its members. The institute's immanent role then was to place "foundational layers" (*gicheung*) in society to build a free society of which the masses were the subject (*juche*). And the foundation for such a new society would only be laid out by an autonomous, self-regulating communitarian life of the masses.[87] To put it differently, in the words of Lee Mun Chang, the immediate task the nation faced was the realization of national liberation, not only in the sense of political independence but in the sense of having a "free society" composed of "communities of autonomous cooperation through direct democracy" by the people who were "the real owners of the land."[88]

What Yi Jeonggyu found most bothersome in the late 1960s and early 1970s when South Korea was in its early phase of modernization, was the loss of the subjectivity among his fellow Koreans. To him, South Koreans at that time seemed to have become oblivious of who they were and what they had lost and forgotten from the past. Criticizing the path South Korea had taken thus far for modernization and how Koreans had lost themselves during the modernization process, Yi rewrote the ISNC's mission statement around that time, which further underlined the importance of "seeking ourselves" through the investigation and research of "our culture," which he identified with "the living culture of general, common people" (*ilban seo-min cheung ui saenghwal munhwa*). This "living culture" had to be developed and promoted in order for Koreans to have a clear understanding of their raison d'être, so that they could inherit the cultural traditions from their ancestors and finally could also receive and digest foreign cultures with which they could form and develop a new "culture of mine," both individually and nationally. Making such a new Korean culture out of the symbiosis of traditional Korean rural culture and foreign cultures became the ISNC's new mission by the early 1970s. And the newly made culture was supposed to be antielitist and antiurban in its character.[89]

What was taken into account in the propagation for the new synthetic culture was a Korean traditional social practice of production and consumption. Determinant in the formation of the new culture, in other words, was social relations in Korean society that had been shaped from the prevailing culture of production and consumption in society. Hence, what the ISNC suggested was the control of consumption with reference to production in terms of the latter's efficiency and artistic aspect. Underlying importance was placed on the control in society of consumption so that a culture of ethical production and consumption could be urgently formulated along with the formation of an autonomous and cooperative lifestyle among Koreans, in order to consolidate "our tradition of people's culture."[90] This synthetic culture was to empower Koreans "to embody a spontaneous, cooperative free community and a free society, both of which would strive for complete, autonomous and independent unification of the nation."[91] And the "commoners" (*baekseong*) who were "the owners of the land" would enable the realization of "a direct democratic, autonomous and cooperative community."[92] In order to achieve such a free society of the commoners, as Lee Mun Chang explains, the ISNC endeavored to lay out "a basic layer of the free society" of which the masses (*minjung*) were the main body. The anarchists in the ISNC expected to found such a society on the basis of an autonomous and self-regulating communal life and understood their immediate task in the national liberation movement of gaining complete and autonomous independence of Korea.[93]

What we can see here is the emphasis Yi Jeonggyu and his fellow anarchists like Lee placed on the importance of a cultural transformation of individuals in the process of building an anarchist society in Korea, in this case, farmers themselves who were viewed as the preservers of native culture and genuine "owners" of Korea.[94] Means to be used for the transformation were tradition (or national culture) and education, as Yi Jeonggyu underlined the importance of tradition in search for a new culture and national development and the role of education in the creation of such new individuals for a new society. And Yi explained that traditions, good or bad, could all be constructively succeeded, if they were able to be turned into something positive; the tradition of struggle, resistance, and overthrow from the past could be rendered into more constructive, cooperative elements in society. Such Korean traditions as understanding, yielding, cooperation, forbearance, mutual aid, and so on could be inherited for the constructive succession of tradition in the modern society.[95] It is notable here that Yi's suggested means for a new society was tradition, but his goal was not the restoration of a traditional society but the construction of a modern society that could combine certain positive aspects of both traditional and modern societies.

Yi also set the goal of education not as its revival of traditions but as its availability and utility for humanity. More specifically, education was to serve the construction of a democratic society in Korea, which could in turn contribute to the construction of common welfare for the whole mankind: the ultimate goal of higher education in Korea was to breed "individuals who can devote themselves to the welfare of mankind" (*hongik ingan*).[96] These individuals, after successfully finishing their higher education, would possess a consciousness as a "free person" (*jayu in*) and, at the same time, as a responsible member not only of the Korean society but of the whole human society. And as a faithful citizen of the world as well as of Korea, these individuals would promote native Korean culture and would play a role simultaneously as a bridge for the cultural exchanges between the East and the West. By doing so they would begin to improve the quality of Korean life in both material and emotional aspects, and consequently scheme to integrate all the nations of the world into "one world," both materially and emotionally.[97] Two principles, freedom and equality, were to be upheld in the course of constructing "one world" where common welfare would be realized for the all mankind.[98]

For all the above tasks and goals, the main target of the ISNC's activities was rural farming villages, which subsequently gave rise to the focal question as to how to balance development between rural and urban areas, as mentioned above. Korean anarchists in the late 1960s and early 1970s widely shared the anxieties and concerns about the unbalanced development led by the state. As of the early 1970s, they even deeply believed that there had been a crisis in Korean society. Yi Jeonggyu, then-director of the ISNC, expressed the concerns and anxieties in his keynote speech delivered on November 17, 1971, at a seminar for rural leaders, held at and by YMCA in Seoul. In the speech, titled "Issues in Making Rural Villages Autonomous," Yi made it clear that he had perceived a serious crisis in politics and economy in South Korea at the time. He in fact called for special attention to the "rural problem" which, according to him, fundamentally stemmed from the gap in development in then–South Korea between rural and urban areas. Modernization through industrialization had been pushed hard by then–South Korean military regime and, as a result, factories had been built and cities had been expanded for economic development under the state's policy with the influx of rural population into cities as workers. All these phenomena, Yi analyzed, had entailed and impaired the impoverished conditions of the rural population in farming villages.[99] What made him more concerned and caused him to lament were the obvious polarizations, first, into differences in wealth between rural villages and cities and, second, subsequent cultural differences that were described as "civilization" versus "barbarism." Development in cities should have never been pursued at the expense of rural villages, but the impoverishment in rural villages unfortunately had been prevalent, an outcome of which was the ostensible modernization achieved in the cities of South Korea, Yi noted. A healthy society, however, he believed, could only exist with a balanced development between cities and rural villages.[100] In short, South Korean rural villages as of the early 1970s were, in Yi's view, so "empty" and the reason for that lay in modernization and urbanization pushed by the state.[101] This was deemed a national crisis, and to overcome it, Yi believed, Koreans needed to understand an important fact, that "the nation thrives only if the rural villages thrive."[102] The future of the nation would be determined decisively by the prosperity in rural villages, and Yi wanted all Koreans to grasp it, if they were to overcome the national crisis of the 1970s.[103]

In his criticism of the impoverishment of South Korean rural villages, however, Yi didn't raise any questions regarding the responsibility and accountability of the then–South Korean military government. Neither did he criticize the government and its policies directly. Rather, Yi posited that in South Korea some economic issues surely could be prioritized and of importance as well to avoid any economic setbacks, but, without internal political stability and national unity, the country in the end would be unable to deal with the rural problem and cope with the ever-changing international situation. His emphasis on political stability and national unity may explain, in part, why Yi was silent about the military dictatorship that usually brought political unity within, albeit under coercion and thus usually fragile. Yi nevertheless believed there would be no stability whatsoever, both internally and externally, without "making rural villages autonomous" (*nongchon jajuhwa*), especially in economy. Neither were "democratic autonomous forces" able to grow in South Korea. Hence, Yi proposed that the leaders of the rural movement use the slogan that read "The nation thrives only if rural villages thrive."[104]

While criticizing the state's urban-based policies, Yi often maintained harsh attitudes toward rural farmers themselves for not possessing a sense of responsibility as "the owners of the land." More important than the state were, according to him, rural leaders who needed to realize "the rural problem" and understand farmers, whose willingness to live a better life was crucial. In particular, rural villagers should have trained themselves to be democratic citizens, but they had rather been passive in attitude and often relied on the authorities for the training. Farmers themselves, as well as rural leaders, thus were just as responsible for the "rural problem" as the political leaders and government were, Yi contended. Farmers might have made insufficient efforts, but now they had to be determined and make efforts to have "mental readiness" with a strong will to live well and endure "today's hardships," Yi noted.[105]

The training of farmers and, as a result, their increased knowledge wouldn't solve the rural problem. Their self-criticism was also much needed for them to become "democratic citizens." And their self-criticism could begin with the effort to overcome a tendency among them to rely on the government officials in solving the rural problem. If there were "weaknesses" and "loopholes" in rural villages, these had to be corrected autonomously and made up for by farmers themselves, Yi insisted. As the state-led modernization had proceeded, rural villages would increasingly face various challenges they had to deal with. The first challenge was to place "modern functions in the rural structure," which Yi believed could ensure the seamless workings of democratic, autonomous functions of the modern in rural areas. The second one was the spread of "the urban consumption trend" that could cause various difficulties in the rural life. The third challenge was "urbanization" that accompanied "civilizational pollution" in rural villages, which must be avoided at all costs in order to prevent the same side-effects as seen in the city from happening in rural villages. And the final challenge was related to "the question as to how to guide the youth" in rural villages, who could have been swayed by modernization in the city but nevertheless needed to be raised as a backbone of rural construction.[106]

Anarchist Solutions: The Movement to Receive and Produce (Susan undong) and the Council of the National Leaders for Rural Movement (Jeon-guk nongchon jidoja hyeopuihoe)

As mentioned earlier, Yi Jeonggyu believed that the solution to the rural problem exclusively hinged on how to revive the life of low-income rural farmers who were able to make their living only after gaining a loan of high interest. Attempts had been made to resolve the dire situation of the low-income rural farmers, such as expansion of cultivatable lands, commercialization of farming lands, and collectivization of farming villages. However, all seemed to have failed to take care of the "rural problem." The keys to solve it, in fact, Yi hinted, were elsewhere, and they would be made available if two questions were answered. The first question was whether farmers in general could be offered additional sources of income, and the second one was whether surplus labor the farmers might be able to offer could be used and incorporated into the "natural cooperative works" in rural villages. The point, in other words, was whether farmers, especially low-income farmers, could be offered opportunities to make some extra earnings with which they could make their living better. The opportunities could be made available, Yi claimed, by gearing up "the natural cooperation" among farmers and absorbing any surplus labor forces in rural farming villages into it.[107] With this basic idea the ISNC launched "the Movement to Receive [Orders] and Produce [Goods]" (Susan undong), which intended to provide rural villagers on the basis of the spirits of self-reliance and cooperation with some extra work during the time when they couldn't till the land, to start their own small-scale domestic industry to improve their living standards and eradicate poverty by their own effort with additionally earned income.[108]

Here again, the "rural problem" was perceived as basically economic in its nature, rather than as a product of complex social and political problems associated with the conventional vertical, exploitive socioeconomic relations that had existed in rural villages, for example, between tenant farmers and landowners or farmers and the state. Neither were they seen as a product of class divisions in capitalist society or of modernization. Anyway, the movement, without any analysis of the origins of the rural problem, simply viewed poverty and starvation as two main sources of the "chronic rural problem"[109] in South Korean society, which had only resulted from the lack of or insufficient income farmers could make. Simply speaking, the movement was intended to give as many jobs as possible to farmers (and fishermen in fishing villages) through promoting a small-scale domestic industry in every rural village, which did not require any huge capital investment from the state and any specialized skills on the part of farmers.[110] The basic underlying principle of the movement was that "those who work shall gain income and the profit shall belong to all" (*noja yugeup iik gwijeon*). And this principle, according to Lee Mun Chang, was framed after Kropotkin's idea of "fields, factories and workshops."[111] In short, if an appropriate domestic home industry could offer some additional jobs and works to low-income farmers, it was expected to solve the "rural problem" from the bottom up and, as a result, to promote and develop an "appropriate home industry" in all rural villages. The idea was first materialized and experimented in a small town called Jin-geon in Gyeonggi Province, a province surrounding the capital city, Seoul. The first successful home industry factory was open there in 1965, where farmers were trained gradually as labor-intensive skilled workers and then were provided with some extra jobs during the slack season (particularly winter), mainly to boost their income. The factory was called "the Jin-geon Center for Receipt and Production," where sweaters, children's wear, handcraft articles, and other such products were made by farmers and shipped out for sale.[112]

A close look at the movement reveals that it was also launched with a vision of alternative national development and social stabilization in Korean society. In the words of the initial drafter of it, Dr. Son Useong, the movement was expected from its inception to "serve as a means to shorten the national itinerary for economic autonomy as well as to improve practically the overall livelihood of Koreans."[113] Hence, its two ultimate goals were to distribute national income equally to all Koreans in order to improve their livelihood and subsequently to help national economy continue to grow at a high rate. To achieve successfully the goal of national economic growth, low-income families in rural villages were particularly urged to voluntarily participate in and join the movement. That way, the movement could aim at utilizing the unemployed human resources to promote labor-intensive local/regional small-scale industries, such as domestic home industry and at the same time to develop rapidly national productivity and supplying-power for export. With the increased income of Koreans, particularly rural villagers, the movement was expected to contribute to the growth of national economy and the founding of social stabilization.[114] In short, while having the long-term goal to contribute to national economy and social stability, the movement tackled immediately the issue of dispelling poverty or at least alleviating the level of it in farming and fishing villages by providing villagers with extra jobs available from the domestic home industry.[115]

Besides the economic and social aspects, the movement was also expected to entail broad cultural impacts in South Korea, which eventually would nurture and grow the national culture of "mutual support" (*sangho jiji*) and "mutual cooperation" (*sangho hyeopdong*) in life through the actual practice of forming a cooperative body voluntarily inside the domestic home industry factories in farming and fishing villages. The Movement to Receive and Produce would even be able to correct the dominant social ethos like mutual distrust that was a trait of the contemporary capitalist society.[116] The cultural aspect was apparent in the program introduced at the Jin-geon Center, which envisioned through training the youth in the area a new future when everyone would grow to become central and independent figures for the restoration of their native place, as well as for the "purification" of local society. Besides the youth in the area, another important object of the movement in this regard was college students who came down annually to rural villages during their summer vacations to give a hand to the farmers. These college students from cities were expected to go through a training that could help them study about the masses in rural villages and develop practical attitudes and understanding that were deemed required for future national leaders.[117]

Yi Jeonggyu's own assessment of the movement also attested to this cultural intention. To Yi, the movement no doubt was a venue for both farming and fishing villagers to participate voluntarily in the "nation-building through industry" project by helping the nation to consolidate its autonomous economy. What seemed to be of greater importance was that by doing so they would go through a phase of "life training," in which the villagers would come to realize how much more beneficial a life with mutual cooperation and mutual aid could be to them. Their realization then would become of significance as an acquired habit for their life and ultimately as an immeasurable benefit for the future of the nation. And there was an additional cultural benefit; the final products of the domestic home industry in rural villages would all be branded with Korean national characters and "spirits," enhancing the prestige of Korean national culture. In short, unlike those produced by mass production of the machine industry, the goods from the domestic home industry under the Movement to Receive and Produce would bring in far more important, various cultural outcomes to individual Koreans and their nation, Yi concluded.[118]

With all the anticipated visible, meaningful outcomes from the movement, the ISNC under Yi's directorship planned on soliciting support for its cause from a wide range of social and political stratum in South Korea. In doing so it strongly disclosed its nationalist intention in the movement. For example, it held an invitational gathering on July 2, 1968, where Yi reiterated to the participants the various meanings of the movement clearly. As he made it clear, the movement had no intention to seek passively to promote extra earnings for farming families or attempt to decentralize the manufacturing industry; its ultimate plan rather was to pave the way to "modernization in rural farming villages" for the sake of "the nation's one-hundred-year grand plan."[119] His call for support seemed successful at least for the time being, since many centers in the name of the movement were built in various locations to function as a main venue for farming villagers in their respective rural location to manufacture their home-crafted products for export. They were also slated to serve as a "vanguard organization for the modernization of rural villages" and as an "autonomous [*jayul jeok*] and communal [*gongdong sahoe jeok*] cooperative body" in rural villages.[120]

To sum up, the Movement to Receive and Produce clearly took aim at assisting the idea and project of the "nation-building with industry," while offering extra jobs readily to rural villagers for their economic need. In this sense, the ideal behind the movement could be labeled as "modernist anarchism" that saw industrial development as inevitable and even indispensable for national liberation in economy. Seen from a different angle, however, it disclosed the elements of "antimodernist anarchism." The ultimate direction of the movement was toward the revival of rural population and their life against the state-led and urban-based modernization. Also, its main agenda was its search for alternative development, and its principles were undoubtedly mutual aid and mutual cooperation, an explicit sign of anarchist ideals, particularly of Kropotkin. These principles were used as a response to the competition-based ones of the modern society and the state-driven modernization project that placed its emphasis on cities.

Likewise, the society the movement intended to build in the end was surprisingly similar to the one the prewar Japanese "pure anarchists" strove to construct. John Crump notes in his study of Hatta Shūzō and Japanese pure anarchism that Japanese pure anarchists before 1945 envisioned building "a decentralized society of largely self-supporting communes engaged in both agriculture and small-scale industry."[121] Yi Jeonggyu's emphases on rural villages and on farmers as the owners of the country, it seems, also shared much in common with the Japanese pure anarchists like Hatta, who saw and understood "the sheer size of the agricultural population" that "account[s] for a majority of the [whole] population and occup[ies] a vast area of land"[122] in Japan. Korean anarchists like Yi in his emphasis on the importance of farmers and farming rural villages had openly criticized since 1945 that they had suffered from the "double exploitations" by cities and "feudal forces," and their Japanese counterparts in the 1930s seemed to have already echoed in advance this later observation by their Korean comrades.[123] There is no evidence that shows any direct links and ties between the Movement to Receive and Produce and the prewar Japanese anarchist ideas. But it is safe to say that there were some conspicuous transnational linkages between Japanese prewar anarchism and postwar Korean anarchism in thinking of an alternative development trajectory based on rural villages against the urban-based development of the modern society.

The Movement to Receive and Produce seemed to be successful for a while, as it bore its fruit not only with the completion of the Jin-geon Center but also with the construction of the Institute for Skill Training to Receive and Produce at the town of Geumgok (Geumgok susan gisul hullyeonwon) at which rural youth and women were trained as skilled workers and produced sweaters as well for export.[124] It is unclear, though, when and how the movement ended, since there is no explanation about its fate even in the volume published by the ISNC for its own history.[125] It is nevertheless possible to say that the strengthened dictatorship of Park Chung Hee and his state-led modernization drive in the 1970s could have prevented the movement from further developing and growing.[126] The abrupt and unknown end of the movement, however, didn't stop Yi Jeonggyu and his fellow anarchists at the ISNC from experimenting other undertakings to organize and train rural farming villagers during the decade.

An undertaking was launched by the ISNC in the early 1970s to form an organization of rural village leaders and college students. Yi Jeonggyu was at the center of it, who initiated a meeting on November 10, 1971 of representatives of some college student groups as well as some "rural movement" (*nongchon undong*) leaders from various rural villages. All attendants agreed to accept the basic idea underlining the slogan it adopted as the guiding principle for the revival of rural villages, "The nation thrives only if rural villages thrive." As a follow-up decision, the next meeting was accordingly scheduled to discuss the possibility of organizing the Council of the National Leaders for Rural Movement (Jeon-guk nongchon jidoja hyeopuihoe). And subsequently the mission of the Council was penned at a preliminary meeting held later to organize the Council: to revive the cooperative "potential energy" (*jeo-ryeok*) rural villages naturally possessed and to promote the autonomous functions of communal life in rural villages, so that a balanced development between urban and rural areas and a stable foundation for people's social structure could be accomplished in South Korea. Also decided at this preliminary meeting was that the Council would consist of those who had worried about economic collapse and cultural degeneration in rural villages.[127] The point of departure for this Council was, just like the Movement to Receive and Produce, the revival of rural villages as a precondition for national development.

Yi Jeonggyu continued to play a special role in the establishment of the Council as its main sponsor, because he disagreed profoundly with the state-led modernization and urbanization that had been processed and was unhappy with the negative consequences they had entailed in rural villages, which he believed had an important but undesirable effect on the plan for national economic development. His disagreement, however, again was not necessarily lifted to a critique of then–South Korean military regime and its overall modernization policies or developmental strategy. On the contrary, Yi wanted to make the Council as a practical backbone or an assisting body for the success of the New Village Movement, although many rural leaders in the Council, including him, were deeply concerned with the top-down structure of the state-led movement that was managed and dominated by the governmental administration,[128] as well as with certain social and cultural negative consequences it had left in South Korean society.

The formal formation of the Council was initially scheduled in December 1972, a year after its first meeting, but had to be postponed because of Park Chung Hee's bloodless coup in October 1972 to introduce a new constitution that allowed his lifetime presidency, for which the martial law was proclaimed in October 1972 and all the political and other activities were prohibited. Next year the Council was finally organized at its inaugural general assembly held from March 25 to 26 at Ehwa Women's University in Seoul. Bak Seung-han, who had been affiliated with the ISNC and was one of the second-generation anarchists,[129] was appointed as Chair of the Council. It was allowed to be held and organized under the martial law. At the inaugural meeting the Council openly identified itself as an organization of farmers and also announced that the "symptoms of capitalism" had appeared in South Korea as a consequence of modernization. Visible among the symptoms the Council identified were the growing passive speculation and commercialized production in rural villages, a higher rent for tenancy, the increased number of absentee landowners, and finally an emergence of possible two new classes in society like "agricultural workers" (*nong-eop nodongja*) and "enterprise owners" (*gieop-ga*). And Bak pointed out that these symptoms had caused many subsequent problems: absorption of rural economy into urban economy, stagnation in rural villages, migration of farmers to cities, and, as a result of all these, rapidly growing population in cities. The state-led New Village Movement, however, could not take care of these symptoms, Bak contended. In his view the state-led movement had been concentrating mainly on "material increase in income" of rural villagers, rather than promoting autonomy, self-support (*jarip*), and cooperation in rural villages.[130] This concern as to the material-based modernization was shared with Yi Jeonggyu, who gave an address at the meeting to congratulate the launching of the Council, when he pointed out that the "rural problem" was to be taken care of by farmers themselves and not by those who had nothing to do with them or rural life.[131]

The Council seemed to be involved in many social movements in rural villages, such as the rural autonomy movement, the consumers' cooperation society movement, and so forth.[132] The Council, however, seemed to be unable to develop those movements further and rather would remain passive, eventually being dissolved in the early 1980s under the Chun Doo Hwan military regime.[133] The emphases placed on agriculture and farmers/rural villages by the ISNC from 1946 had evidently survived until the 1970s. This time, its main activities were led by some of the second-generation anarchists who had diverse backgrounds but had no prior experiences in the pre-1945 national struggles. The Council obviously pointed to the emergence of capitalist ills in South Korea as a result of the state-led modernization but still didn't attack capitalism itself, yet worried only about the negative consequences of it.

A Forgotten Path: The Federation Anarchist Korea (Han-guk jaju in yeonmaeng)

Around the time when the discussion of the formation of the Council of the National Leaders for Rural Movement was on its way, a group of Korean anarchists, numbered about one hundred, gathered at Jin-gwan Buddhist Temple in Seoul on June 22, 1972, to embark on a new nationwide anarchist organization,[134] possibly with an aim to revive their movement collectively. Established at the meeting was the Federation Anarchist Korea (FAK, Han-guk jaju in yeonmaeng). Unlike its original English translation, its Korean name literally means "the Korean Federation of Autonomous Persons." The organization's name in Korean didn't include the word *anarchism,* probably to avoid any unnecessary impression about it as a violent or an antigovernmental socialist organization under Park's military regime and its anticommunist policies. Of course, the term *autonomous person (jaju in)* had long been adopted after 1945 to describe the identity of Korean anarchists not as those who negated the state but as those who favored an autonomous government and upheld the principle of spontaneous will of individuals, not to mention freedom and equality. Participants in the FAK included veteran and senior anarchists such as Yi Jeonggyu, Yi Eulgyu, Jeong Hwaam, and Choe Gapryong, in terms of their careers and experiences from the colonial period. Choe was appointed as executive secretary of the FAK, along with four other secretaries. The FAK was initially organized with hope to succeed the IWPP that had been forced to be resolved in May 1962 in the wake of the military coup led by General Park Chung Hee. If the ISNC had been Yi Jeonggyu's individual "think-tank" for the realization of his version of anarchism, the FAK was basically formed as a renewed national organization of Korean anarchists, with an expectation to succeed and inherit mainly the anarchist ideals of the IWPP, particularly its leader, Yu Rim, who died in April 1, 1961, chief among his ideals being anarchist participation in politics through the formation of a political party and the importance of mass movement and education.[135]

At the inaugural meeting the FAK's goal was defined "to strive for the concrete realization of the Federation's platform and the construction of an anarchist ideal world in order for all mankind to have a peaceful and autonomous life."[136] To realize the goal the FAK also passed its platform on its inauguration day, which demonstrated its transnational ideals as well as many anarchist principles it had inherited from the pre-1945 anarchist movement. The platform first described the FAK's members as "autonomous persons" who strove to construct a spontaneous society as an outcome of their unity formed with spontaneity. Second, it defined equality as something "uninterruptable" and then rejected any political appropriation of it as a concept that might divide humans into the ruler and the ruled. The FAK seemed to be concerned more with equal social relations. Third, it denied that any kind of action that could end up taking away someone else's works without one's own labor. Fourth, "the principle of economic life" was adopted in the platform to ensure an anarchist principle that everyone would work according to ability and consume according to needs. Fifth, the FAK envisaged that a society that would be realized after applying the above-mentioned principles must be open to a possibility to have various patterns of life according to various regional and occupational peculiarities. Obviously, the FAK made sure of local differences and diversities in the practice of anarchist principles in building a new society. Last, the FAK would respect and value the traditional culture each nation had historically inherited and strive for world peace under which various cultures of the nations could remain in harmony.[137]

After the inaugural meeting in 1972, however, the FAK became inactive and even in hibernation for a long time. Four months after the FAK's inauguration, the Yushin Constitution was announced by Park Chung Hee, which enabled him to be lifetime president of South Korea and possibly prevented the FAK from beginning its various planned projects and activities. The brutal suppression of any communism-inspired or antigovernmental organizations throughout the 1970s continued in the 1980s under a new military dictatorship, which must have also hindered the FAK from rejuvenating its activities. The FAK was able to awake from its long winter hibernation and hold its convention again on August 21, 1987, fifteen years after its inauguration, in the wake of the 1987 June Democratization Movement that swept the country, at the auditorium of Keimyung University in Daegu, with attendance of fifty anarchists. On the second day of the renewed convention, their venue was moved to the auditorium of Anui High School in the town of Anui to continue their convention. Called "the holly place [*seongji*] of anarchism," Anui had hosted the first national convention of Korean anarchists in 1946, and was the hometown of many second-generation anarchists, where schools were established after 1945 by some of them to realize their educational ideals.[138] The FAK has been inactive again since 1987 for unknown reasons.[139]

Post-1945 Korean Anarchism

The activities and ideas of Korean anarchists after 1945 shifted from accomplishing a social revolution through anticapitalism and anticolonialism to educating/organizing farmers and workers in order for them to be qualified and prepared to be the leading forces in the construction of a new Korean nation-state, as well as to accomplishing a rural area-based national development by combining industry and agriculture for the nation-building with industry. They even organized political parties of their own, but ended up realizing the wall standing between them and politics. The shift finally was accompanied by a sign of deradicalization of anarchism. As Lee Mun Chang notes, Korean anarchists after 1945 gave up their goal of revolution and have mainly focused on "extremely ordinary" works such as "educating the next generation" and advocating "cultural enlightenment." Unlike pre-1945 Korean anarchism, which had the transnational linkages with regional anarchism in search of a social revolution that was both national and transnational in its goal and scope, post-1945 Korean anarchism can be characterized with its nationalist concerns and deradicalized practice in terms of the decreased concerns with the social, in favor of the national goal of an alternative development on the basis of national unity and political stability.

The shift was not a sudden one but was a continuation of the emphasis placed on the national problem since the national front was proposed and formed by Korean anarchists in 1930s China, as I demonstrated in chapter 4. The shift may indicate Korean anarchists' retreat from their radical advocacy of the 1920s and '30s, when the task of "constructing an anarchist communist society" in Korea was propagated and deeply shared among them and with other anarchists. But it occurred in the process of a Koreanization of anarchism after 1945, to meet the concrete conditions in South Korea under which Korean anarchists pursued economic development with emphasis on rural villages and national culture in an attempt to realize their anarchist ideals in South Korea.[140] This is quite obvious if we consider that after 1945 they didn't want to or at least were reluctant to mention or take up the questions of imperialism, colonialism, or capitalism critically and seriously, making them targets in their postwar struggle and movement for the completion of national liberation. In fact, rather than struggles against capitalists or imperialists, cooperation and responsibilities of farmers and workers in the course of "constructing a new Korea" with national capitalists were usually more preferred and even underscored by Korean anarchists. The reason they refrained from mentioning capitalism as their target of struggle was probably due to their primary goal to achieve national development through industrialization, an idea that can be called a kind of "modernist anarchism," in the sense that it saw industrialization as indispensable and even essential for the realization of anarchist ideals in terms of economic autonomy. They also gradually began to shift their attention away from workers who were now no less under control of the state-backed union than independent workers' unions.[141]

To Korean anarchists national development became the most important task when Korea's independence didn't seem to be complete. To them national development was the only way to make Korea an autonomous modern nation-state and ensure its economic independence in the world of capitalism, and it couldn't be done without reconstructing rural villages, increasing farmer's living standards, and rediscovering national culture. Awakening and encouraging farmers and workers in order to make them self-reliant were therefore regarded as the first step toward the goal of national liberation and development,[142] which could be achieved through a development strategy that stressed national voices. To many Korean anarchists Korea's economic independence was an important element that would in turn guarantee its political independence in the international arena under capitalism.

But economic independence couldn't be pursued simply by following the already known developmental trajectory of the advanced countries. It needed to avoid the mistakes the developed countries had committed and further required the reconstruction of rural villages, especially through an increase in farmer's living standards and rediscovering national culture that could make up for the shortcomings of the urban-focused modernization of the advanced countries. National development with combination of industry and agriculture would ensure Korea would avoid all the problems of the capitalist industrialization. In a word, a "balanced development of industry and agriculture"[143] was the best developmental strategy for South Korea, as Yi Jeonggyu believed.

When the state-led modernization seemed to be going in a wrong direction, destroying rural villages and thus impoverishing rural population in the 1960s and 1970s under the "developmental dictatorship" of Park Chung Hee, Yi Jeonggyu and his associates attempted to remind Koreans of the importance of preserving and learning from Korea's own past, including native culture and tradition, mostly of rural villages. They envisioned a society in post-1945 Korea, which can be described as a "genuinely ideal society" built through the revival of rural villages that could be realized by the "Free Community Movement" (*jayu gongdongche undong*), a movement that aimed at constructing "spontaneous free communities" in society and strove for "the completion of autonomous independence and unification of the [Korean] nation[*minjok*]."[144] Awakening, encouraging, and educating farmers and workers in order to have them possess the senses of the "owners of the land" and of self-reliance were regarded as an important step toward genuine autonomy and development in both political and economic senses.[145]

In the years before and after the Korean War, the political and military tensions from the Cold War were at their peak and clouded the Korean peninsula. What followed was the strengthening of dictatorship in both Koreas, which reached its peak in the 1950s through '70s and, as a result, impaired the already worsening political situation of divided Korea. As Yi Jeonggyu stated after the Korean War, there seemed for him no other way after the war but to ask for foreign aid, because of all the material and spiritual losses caused by the "Communist Bandits' Rebellion." Proposing a new life movement to overcome the losses in the postwar years, Yi thus suggested that Koreans think more about their place than themselves and also more about the whole country than their own place. In other words, the nation's survival and stability had increasingly become much more important to Yi after the Korean War, because, he thought, there was no way to save the devastated Korean nation if there was no unity of all Koreans. The emphasis here was placed on the national reconstruction with unity and stability. Much needed for the nation were cooperation among individuals without internal conflicts and their cultural transformation to form new habits, values, and attitudes, as well as their anticommunism.[146]

Korean anarchists seemed to fear that their anarchist ideals would be fated to fail under the situation where anarchism was considered "without any good reason"[147] "a cousin of communism."[148] "Sandwiched" between two different political systems in two Koreas, both hostile to their belief, they could do nothing but "hold their breath" for survival to avoid possible arrest and potential torture, albeit the condition in general has gotten better in South Korea since the 1990s.[149] As Yi Jeonggyu states, due to the political climate after 1945, Korean anarchists decided "to cooperate with those who were on the side of freedom and democracy in order to suppress the Communist rebels,"[150] and to make every effort to foster Korea's complete independence. Accordingly, many anarchists complied with the political aura of South Korea under the Cold War and dictatorship. In short, they practiced and deradicalized anarchism after reflecting the sociopolitical conditions of post-1945 South Korea.

The passing of Yi Jeonggyu in December 1984 drew the end of a long era in the history of anarchism in Korea, which began in foreign soils in the early 1920s for the cause of national liberation and social revolution, and thus marked the end of a revolutionary anarchist movement that aimed at radical social transformation for a new society with anarchist principles that had been deeply shared with many other anarchists in the region. In terms of political democracy and national development, it is possible, though, for Yi and his associates to think that there have been some measurable successes in South Korea, given the political changes toward democracy since 1987 and the economic prosperity since the 1990s, although these were hardly the outcome of their activities.

Conclusion

This study calls into question the conventional use and notion of "Korean anarchism," if it is understood, first, within the context of the geographical and historical boundaries of Korea and, second, as an ideological principle that has been practiced in unity and with uniformity among all Korean anarchists. As I have demonstrated in this study, anarchism in Korea can best be understood, above all, as a product of the interactions, both direct and indirect, between Korean anarchists and their Chinese and Japanese counterparts, among others, in such cities as Beijing, Shanghai, Quanzhou, Tokyo, and Osaka. Their interactions were quite intense and substantial and entailed mutual influence and inspiration among themselves, which in many cases led to their common discourse/language and joint activities, either organizational or publication, for the universal goal of anarchism as well as their respective national goal. What is important here is the transnational character and regional elements embedded in Korean anarchism as a result of such interactions that accompanied a movement of Korean anarchists and their ideas from one to other locations in the region, followed by a production of various place-based practices. The spatial movement and, as a result, transnationality in Korean anarchism can't be understood and confined within the physical and historical contexts of Korea that we conventionally know, and, therefore, I argue, must not be underestimated in the study of "Korean anarchism."

Scholars have always constructed the history of Korean anarchism within the national context that it served the goal of independence against Japanese colonialism. The nationalist line of interpretation is misleading, however, because of the transnational and regional linkages in Korean anarchism this study demonstrates, which culminated in the idea of social revolution that was widely shared with other anarchists from its origins in the 1920s and in its subsequent development in the later decades. Although most Korean anarchists readily saw the question of independence as their immediate goal, their ultimate goal was social revolution bent on anarchist principles. They usually remained in conflict with nationalists and against their movement, which they thought would aim only at political independence of Korea without solving social problems prevalent in capitalist society. They believed that there would be no genuine national liberation without social revolution. Anarchism's transnational messages such as freedom and equality on the basis of mutual aid and spontaneous alliance were to be crucial in the Korean acceptance and subsequent practice of it.

Simply speaking, the study of Korean anarchism must consider its origins in foreign soils, that is, China and Japan. And I think the emphasis needs to be given to the fact that East Asian anarchists, including Korean, were closely connected to one another through their readings of various anarchist texts, their common discourse and concerns shared with one another, the understanding of and the solution to the national and world problems, and, in many cases, their joint actions and organizations to deal with the problems they faced and identified. The process of their sharing often forged common radical culture and language among themselves and formulated their shared vision and joint actions. And I argue that we need to consider this process of interactions and sharing in our understanding of Korean anarchism that was a product of much broader transnational discourse and activities of regional anarchists. This is what nationalist historiography has missed.

This study demonstrates the existence of some kind of transnational radical networks of discourse and practice that connected regional anarchists and radicals. And the transnationalism in Korean anarchism was a product of the networks in which such locations as Tokyo and Shanghai served as their nodes. To put it differently, Korean anarchists before 1945 were constantly on the move within the "ecumene" where the intense and sustained interactions among East Asian anarchists occurred in those metropolitan cities of Eastern Asia. And as a result, Korean anarchism emerged as a part of regional anarchism, more broadly regional radicalism, and the history of Korean anarchism, therefore, needs to be understood and constructed within the history of regional anarchism and vice versa. Although Korean anarchists developed their own different versions of anarchism from those of their regional counterparts who nevertheless shared much in common in terms of their solutions to the problems of their contemporary society and world.

The transnational and regional character of Korean anarchism I argue for, however, doesn't necessarily deny or even minimize the role of nationalism in its history and development. This book, rather, suggests a dialectical and nuanced understanding of the relationship between nationalism and anarchism and underlines the process that Korean anarchists read anarchism with *their* understanding of immediate national goal and, conversely, articulated that goal with *their* understanding of anarchism in particular settings. The transnational character underscores the close relationship (and often tensions) between national consciousness as a motive to fight foreign colonialism and anarchism as a longing to resist national boundaries and pursue universal goals. A Eurocentric understanding of anarchism as an idea that rejects any form of government misses this kind of tension or ambiguity in the relationship in colonies and semicolonies. Anarchism in Korea had its both nationalist and transnational dimensions, which were not necessarily viewed as contradictory by Korean anarchists. This was the vagueness that explains why they fought for national liberation and joined the Provisional Government, despite their poignant criticism of various nationalist movements before 1945. They were even doubtful many times of such terms as "the state," "fatherland," and "patriotism," and usually found and identified themselves as part of the "oppressed peoples" of the world under capitalism. They had to grapple with the tension and maintain the ambiguous attitude between the ideals of freedom and equality and the national goal. To them, anarchism appeared as a promise not only for freedom and equality in a new society but for national survival and autonomy, both politically and economically. The ambiguous relationship and tension between nationalism and anarchism were to be crucial in Korean anarchism. And unlike many South Korean scholars, I have moved away throughout this study from separating anarchism from nationalism.

Next is the question about the understanding of "Korean anarchism" as a principle practiced in unity among all Korean anarchists. Throughout this study, I have used the term *Korean anarchism*, but refrained from describing it as a principle Korean anarchists have practiced with uniformity, no matter where they were and no matter when they did. In fact, as I have demonstrated, there were many different practices of anarchism among themselves, according to their location and environment. Anarchism was generally accepted by Koreans with reference to their common national aspiration but, in applying it to their activities and programs, they considered local conditions and demands, as well as the national and transnational goals. This exactly was the main reason for the diverse directions and methods they have taken in experimenting and implementing anarchist ideals and principles at different locations and times.

To be sure, place was important in the practice of anarchism among Korean anarchists in two major locations, China and Japan. Korean anarchist organizations in Japan were products of study-abroad students, mostly "poor work-study students," in search of higher education, while their counterparts in China were organized by exiled Koreans there, working for independence. The Japan-based Korean anarchists were, in general, more interested in the social aspects, due to their intense interactions with Japanese "pure anarchists," and had more chances to publish their own journals and newspapers, albeit they were short-lived and/or under strict censorship. And their activities were often part of the latter's movement. Given the wide range and depth of the interactions between Korean and Japanese anarchists, it is safe to say that Korean anarchists in Japan were equipped more with theoretical understanding of anarchism and their movements were guided more by its social revolutionary principles. Important to their understanding of it were the works of Ōsugi Sakae, as much as those of Kropotkin.

Even among Korean anarchists in Japan, there were visible signs of different practices of anarchism, according to location. While Tokyo as a concentration place of regional radicals nurtured various anarchist movements and became a node of regional anarchist networks, Osaka appeared as a location where Korean anarchists had to deal with the prevailing labor issues among Korean workers there with a local-based application of anarchism. The Osaka-based Korean anarchists obviously were more mindful of the labor and "life-related" issues in the industrializing city, such as the improvement of working conditions at factory, and usually refrained from using the word *black*, the color that was associated with anarchism. As Go Sunheum's case demonstrates, the activities of Korean anarchists in Osaka had something to do with supporting the livelihood of them and their compatriots, who were often from the same province, most notably Jeju Island, utilizing a kind of "place-based networks" in the Korean community there. Also, they seemed to have less conflicts and tensions with both nationalists and other socialists and, for their movement, made use of national consciousness as much as social consciousness among Koreans there. On the contrary, Korean anarchists in Tokyo, receiving consistent and strong support and sponsorship from their Japanese comrades, continued to propagate anarchism and put the word *black* in the name of their organizations and publications, as if they were not afraid of the Japanese police surveillance, even during the 1930s, as exemplified in the publication of *Black Newspaper*. As a result, the Tokyo-based Korean anarchist movement was overall in close relationship with Japanese anarchist movement. Targeting liberation, both national and social, the Korean anarchist movement in the two cities, nonetheless, was basically a social revolutionary movement, rather than just a political or mass movement for national liberation.

Korean anarchists in colonial Korea were more attentive to the social problems of their colonized compatriots under the direct colonial condition, deprioritizing the political question of independence, which would only bring in further suppression and subsequent hardships on them and their families. They even utilized in their activities a new term *the destitute and humble class* Yi Hyang coined in consideration of the colonial situation of Korea, rather than *property-less class* or proletariat, and focused on the "livelihood struggle" in industrializing northern Korea. They had to directly face and deal with the colonial rule and responded accordingly to it with consideration of the demands and necessities of their compatriots in different locations. Accommodations followed. Evidence indicates that the rise and development of anarchist movement in colonial Korea was largely a product of and even dependent on those who had returned from Japan to the peninsula throughout the 1920s. But there certainly was an independent and unique practice of anarchism in colonial Korea, as exemplified in the invention of the term. And many Korean anarchists in colonial Korea also maintained their contacts with those in China as well, including those in Manchuria. There were some visible internal divisions as well among those in colonial Korea over the focus of activities.

Similarly, Korean anarchists in Manchuria too adopted a place-based approach and were more concerned with the livelihood of Korean migrants there. Their priority was given to the issue of economic survival of the migrants in the treacherously harsh land, which denoted no strong attachment to the question of national liberation in their movement, at least temporarily. And moreover, anarchists in Manchuria seemed to be in line with those within colonial Korea in terms of avoiding words like *independence* or *black* in their activities, at least for their own survival, as well as the pressing issues they had to deal with.

The national front idea proposed by Korean anarchists when Japan invaded China in the 1930s was a reflection of their situation in wartime China, where they confronted the question of both individual and national survival. Enjoying relative freedom of activity with the support of Chinese anarchists and the National Government of China, they were willing to be flexible in their attitude toward nationalists and even communists, and accordingly prioritized the national goal over their anarchist goal, which marked a turning point in the Korean anarchist movement in China. The national front idea and the subsequent proposal for armed struggle against Japan in league with the Chinese were, to be sure, a logical outcome under the wartime situation in China, but also a reflection of the long-held idea to make alliance with the Chinese for their shared transnational goal. Korean anarchists in 1930s Japan, unlike their counterparts in China of the same decade, were not able to involve in any kind of armed struggle for independence, but rather had to go underground or were forced to remain silent with their Japanese comrades until 1945, unless they gave up their anarchist faith and converted to worship the Japanese emperor. An exception was *Black Newspaper*, which carried its own resilient struggle against Japanese imperialism by delivering to its readers the issues related to colonial Korea and the information and news about Korean anarchists in the region, with no sign of fear of suppression by Japanese police.

Among the China-based Korean anarchists, there was a seeming consensus that their efforts to build an anarchist society in Korea would be meaningless if Korea did not even exist. This was the main rationale for them in proposing the national front idea and shifting their emphasis to national unity and independence. In fact, they might not have even thought that it was a shift in their movement, if we consider the role of national aspiration in their acceptance of anarchism. Japan's invasion of China since 1931 had them rethink their priority gradually, and formulate their plan for both national and transnational goals. Their national front idea was backed by those who had moved to China during the "combat period" from colonial Korea, Japan, and Manchuria to avoid the Japanese police arrest and harsh torture. The relative freedom available in China enticed many Korean anarchists to migrate to China from the late 1920s throughout the 1930s.

It is possible that the China-based Korean anarchists might have been influenced by the GMD anarchists like Li Shizeng and Wu Zhihui, in their anarchist thinking and activities, especially with regard to the national front idea. This might also explain the reason why the post-1945 anarchist movement in South Korea under the leadership of Yu Rim and then Yi Jeonggyu, both of whom had maintained their relationship with the Chinese counterparts in China, moved toward the question of national liberation and national development. Under their leadership, Korean anarchists since 1945 didn't seem to be interested in answering the question of radical transformation of Korean society, and endeavored to experiment their anarchist ideals through anarchist political parties and social movements. Anarchism in Korea after 1945 was deradicalized under their leadership. Anarchists even defined themselves as "autonomous persons" and "believers in an autonomous government," not as social revolutionaries. By mid-1950s they used a new name for anarchism, "democratic socialism." The new definition and name were coined by former China-based anarchists, most notably Yi Jeonggyu and Yu Rim. The latter, who had already attempted to implement "Koreanized [*han-guk jeok*] anarchism" by participating in the Provisional Government of Korea in China,[1] emphasized the goal of establishing an autonomous Korean state, and hoped to realize the anarchist ideals of freedom and equality through an anarchist party as well as an autonomous government with mobilized workers and peasants. He tested their realization with the IWPP. This "Yu Rim Line" defended unflinchingly the ideals against the undemocratic, dictatorial state.[2] As Yu's undertaking with the IWPP was foiled under the Rhee regime's suppression, many anarchists under the leadership of Yi Jeonggyu and his associates increasingly turned their eyes to the question of national development through reviving rural villages. They began various social movements for modest social and cultural changes.[3] This "Yi Jeonggyu Line," which seemed to assign the major role of solving social problems under capitalism to the state, didn't receive the dictatorial regime's suppression and, it seems, was well received from many Korean anarchists in the 1960s and '70s, when they were forced to "give up" their radical ideals unwillingly. What happened after 1945 in the anarchist camp symbolizes the retreat from its original plan to build an anarchist communist society with freedom and equality guaranteed in society, which was no doubt stated in the declaration of the KAF in 1928 and in the platform of the LKYSC in the 1930s.

Yi Jeonggyu's national development strategy was deemed more suitable in the postbellum situation of Korea, which stressed training and educating farmers in rural villages after accommodating the political climate of South Korea. If Yu Rim was more focused on the realization of freedom and equality in society against the Rhee's dictatorship through anarchist participation in politics, Yi seemed to understand it within the national context in which national survival in unity through national development and economic autonomy was underscored more than the social. To Yi, of course, the economic backwardness of South Korea hindered it from developing into an autonomous country without economically driven social problems. With his deradicalized anarchism, anarchists might have been able to assist the realization of national autonomy in politics and economy but certainly had to witness the idea of freedom and equality slipping away and placed in the far distant future. However we evaluate the two different lines, they at least vindicate that Korean anarchists after 1945 were not in unity either and rather had diverse visions for and approaches to the realization of an anarchist society in Korea.

After 1945, anarchism as a social revolutionary idea and vision for a radical and fundamental transformation of society lost its vitality and acceptability in South Korea, whether by force or voluntarily. When the state-led modernization through industrialization in the 1960s and '70s turned out to be disastrous to rural villages, Korean anarchists like Yi Jeonggyu, rather than leading a challenge to the state, passively reminded Koreans of the importance of protecting rural villages and learning from Korea's own past, culture, and traditions in the course of "constructing a new Korea." And they emphasized cooperation and responsibility of farmers and workers in national development, while decoupling anarchism with any radical struggle against capitalism of which social problems in then–South Korea were evidently a product. What followed was their pursuit of an alternative national development with the slogan of "the nation thrives only if rural villages thrive" to avoid the shortcomings of capitalist industrialization, which were conspicuous in the advanced countries. And they launched the Movement to Receive and Produce to solve the rural problem and lay out a foundation for Korea's economic autonomy in the world of capitalism. It was perceived by many anarchists as essential to achieve the goal of Korea's genuine national liberation. In doing so, Korean anarchists believed that they had to fight the communists in the north and the "feudal forces" that had survived in the south from the colonial period, to realize genuine national liberation in the sense of both political and economic autonomy. Overthrowing capitalism was not considered by them, therefore. In short, they set their post-1945 goal as "nation-building through industry," with special emphasis on rural villages and their role in the cultural changes in the future.

An examination of the Korean anarchist movement since the 1920s reveals that social revolution was its common answer to the problems in colonies like Korea and in post-1945 Korean society, which was no doubt shared with their Asian counterparts. The anarchist ideas of freedom and equality were most attractive to them. Mutual aid was, not surprisingly, a widely accepted principle for both the progress of mankind and a social revolution in Korea, not to mention for Korea's independence, possibly due to the affinity of it to such an existing idea practiced in Korean rural villages as mutual cooperation. Their shared idea and vision of social revolution were to help Korean anarchists transcend their national boundaries and share the transnational concerns and solutions in their struggle for independence and liberation of Korea after 1945. The shift made after 1945 to the idea of national development didn't necessarily entail the loss of their transnational longing for a cosmopolitan world but was indicative of their search for an alternative development with the anarchist principles intact. In any case, Korean anarchists always seemed to be unwilling to be in unity and conformity in their thinking and practice of anarchism, possibly due to their deep faith in such anarchist principles as spontaneity and individual freedom, no matter where they were.

Many Korean anarchists must have been delighted with the recent economic development of South Korea, since it has been at least a sign of accomplishment of the goal of national development they have endeavored. And yet, they must have realized that it has been achieved only at the expense of political freedom and economic equality. To many Koreans anarchism still means and represents an idea of freedom.[4] And it has provided others with "an anarchist sensibility" that underlines its egalitarianism in their fight against the neoliberal globalization.[5] Now, the task to realize the two ideals has been handed over to the new generation of Korean anarchists who, facing the deepening and widening inequality between haves and have nots and witnessing the violations of individual rights and freedom, have to arm themselves with a new practice of anarchism, in alliance with the like-minded others.

This task is quite evidently recognized by some Korean anarchists who are keen to the importance of the emerging issues of social alienation and inequality under globalization. They plan on dealing with them as South Korea becomes a "multicentered society" (*da jungsim sahoe*) and make sure of creating an environment where the participation of "various social elements" (i.e., the masses) in politics is guaranteed. They are particularly attentive to the fate of the self-employed and the alienated labor forces, such as irregular and part-time workers in South Korea, including non-Korean migrant workers, under the regime of globalization. Some of these anarchists are weighing in on the revival of an anarchists party, this time based on and in collaboration with the newly defined masses and the civil societies working for them.[6] On the other hand, some other anarchists seems to think that their main task lies in bringing the pre-1945 activities of Korean anarchists back to the memory of Koreans and honoring them properly, before any other new anarchist projects for the future can be planned and launched. Their concern and target seems to be the trend in Korean politics toward conservatism. These anarchists focus on mobilizing and educating Korean youths for the changes projected in the future.[7] As is clear, there are still slight divisions and disagreements among Korean anarchists over the question of what to do in this new century to inherit and concretize their previous generation's endeavors.

Despite such differences, Korean anarchists need to revive the ideals from the earlier years and regroup themselves to resist together the current state's disastrous policies under neoliberalism, which have destroyed rural villages once again and taken away the two long-cherished anarchist ideals, freedom and equality. Their initial goal of independence has been slipped away, and the chance to achieve genuine national liberation with political and economic autonomy has thus become slimmer under the neoliberal globalization. In this situation, the precious ideals and vision for an ideal society that Korean anarchists used to uphold before 1945 have been washed out and their nationalistic experiences and sacrifices for independence are only highlighted and honored by the current state. It may be a time for Korean anarchists today to look for a new kind of struggle and solidarity with their domestic, regional, and global comrades and come up with a new place-based approach to overcome the forces, both national and global, that have deepened the pains and sorrows of the weak, and finally to get closer to the realization of their cherished ideals and vision. At least, it seems that, just like before, they all still share the same fate and issues with their comrades in the region and the world.

Notes

The following abbreviations are used for notes. All other abbreviations are indicated in the notes.

CMUK   *Chōsen minzoku undōshi kenkyū* [Studies on the History of Korean National Movement]

CMZ   *Choaxian minzu zhanxian* [The Korean National Front]

CYD   *Chaoxian yiyongdui* [The Korean Volunteers Unit]

HMUY   *Han-guk minjok undongsa yeon-gu* [Studies on the History of Korean National Movement]

HNJ   *Huainianji* [Collection of Cherishing Memories]

HQ   *Hanguo qingnian* [Korean Youth]

HS   *Heuksaek sinmun* [Black Newspaper]

JRS   *Jiyū rengō shimbun* [Spontaneous Alliance Newspaper]

NT   *Namhwa tongsin* [South China Correspondence]

QLXX   *Quanzhou liming xueyuan xinxi* [News on Quanzhou Liming College]

TS   *Tongsin* [Correspondence]

YWH   *Yeoksa wa hyeonsil* [History and Reality]

Introduction

1. See Lee Key-baik ed., *Han-guksa simin gangjwa* [The Citizens' Forum on Korean History], special issue on "20 segi han-guk eul umjigin 10 dae sasang" [The Ten Thoughts that Moved Korea in the Twentieth Century] 25 (August 1999): iii–v for Lee Key-Baik's assessment. In addition to anarchism the issue includes to the "ten thoughts" nationalism, social Darwinism, liberal democracy, communism, social democracy, modernization theory,

"self-strengthening" idea, the *minjung* (the masses) cultural movement idea, and Kim Il-Sung's *juche* (self-reliance) idea.

2. Since the 1990s, the number of scholarly works on Korean anarchism in the form of both book and article have increased unprecedentedly, which culminated in the publication of a book on the centennial history of Korean anarchism by scholars from various disciplines, with the funding from the Korea Research Foundation. Gu Seunghoe et al., *Han-guk anarchism 100 nyeon* [One Hundred Years of Korean Anarchism] (Seoul: Ihaksa, 2004) [hereafter *HAB*].

3. See, for example, *HAB*, Introduction and passim.

4. An earliest case of it can be found in Kim Changsun and Kim Junyeop, *Han-guk gongsan juui undongsa* [A History of the Korean Communist Movement], 5 vols. (Seoul: Cheonggye yeon-guso, 1986, new edition).

5. Yi Horyong, *Han-guk ui anarchism—sasang pyeon* [Anarchism in Korea—Its Ideas] (Seoul: Jisik san-eop sa, 2001) [hereafter *HASP*], 137–166; Bak Hwan, *Sikminji sidae hanin anarchism undongsa* [A History of Korean Anarchist Movement during the Colonial Period] (Seoul: Seonin, 2005) [hereafter *SSAU*]; Oh Jang-Whan, *Han-guk anarchism undongsa yeon-gu* [A Study on the History of Korean Anarchist Movement] (Seoul: Gukak jaryowon, 1998) [hereafter *HAUY*]; and *HAB*.

6. Horiuchi Minoru, "Nanka kanjin seinen renmei to kokushoku kyōhudan" [The League of Korean Youth in South China and the Black Terror Party], *CMUK* 8 (April 1992): 9.

7. *HASP*; *SSAU*; and *HAUY*.

8. John Crump, "Anarchism and Nationalism in East Asia," *Anarchist Studies* 4-1 (March 1996): 46, 47, and 49.

9. Song Seha, "Chōsenjin ni yoru anakizumu undō no kako to genzai" [The Past and Present of Anarchist Movements by Koreans], *Anakizumu* [Anarchism] 3 (May 1974): 16.

10. See Guksa pyeonchan wiwonhoe ed., *Han-guk dongnip undongsa* [A History of Korean Independence Movement], 5 vols. (Seoul: Guksa pyeonchan wiwonhoe, 1969); *HASP*, 294–314; Kang Man-gil ed., *Shin Chaeho* (Seoul: Goryeo daehakgyo chulpanbu, 1990); and Shin Yongha, "Shin Chaeho ui mujeongbu juui dongnip sasang" [Shin Chaeho's Anarchist Ideas of Independence], in Kang, *Shin Chaeho*, 78–147.

11. The relationship between the rise of radicalism in China in terms of its "internationalist utopianism" and national consciousness is extensively discussed in Arif Dirlik, *Anarchism in the Chinese Revolution* (Berkeley: University of California Press, 1991): chapter 2, and Rebecca E. Karl, *Staging the World: Chinese Nationalism at the Turn of the Twentieth Century* (Durham, NC: Duke University Press, 2002).

12. To see anarchism not as a social revolutionary idea but as an adopted nationalist idea for the goal of independence is a general trend in South Korean scholarship on Korean anarchism. See *HASP*; *SSAU*; and Kim Myeongseop,

"Jaeil hanin anarchism undong yeon-gu" [A Study on the Korean Anarchist Movement in Japan] (PhD diss., Dan-gook University, 2001).

13. For Jeong's life as an anarchist, see his memoirs in two different editions. Jeong Hwaam, *Jeong Hwaam hoego rok: Eo-neu anarchist ui momeuro sseun geundaesa* [Memoir of Jeong Hwaam—A Modern History Written by an Anarchist with His Body] (Seoul: Jayu mun-go, 1992) [hereafter *JHH*] and Jeong Hwaam, *I joguk eodiro gal geosin ga: na ui hoego rok* [Where Will This Country Head? My Memoirs] (Seoul: Jayu mun-go, 1982) [hereafter *IJEG*]. The former is a revised and expanded version of the latter.

14. Quoted in Kim Hakjun ed., *Hyeokmyeongga deul ui hang-il hoesang: Kim Seongsuk, Jang Geonsang, Jeong Hwaam, Yi Ganghun ui dongnip tujaeng* [Revolutionaries' Recollections of Anti-Japanese Struggles: Struggles for the Independence by Kim Seongsuk, Jang Geonsang, Jeong Hwaam, and Yi Ganghun], interviewed by Lee Chong-sik (Seoul: Mineumsa,1988) [hereafter *HHH*], 281.

15. Yi Jeonggyu, "Udang Yi Hoeyeong seonsaeng yakjeon" [A Brief Biography of Mr. Yi Hoeyeong], in *Ugwan munjon* [Collected Works of Yi Jeonggyu] by Yi Jeonggyu (Seoul: Samhwa insoe, 1974) [this volume is abbreviated hereafter as *UM*], 56.

16. Sim Yongcheol, "Naui hoego" [My Memoir], in *20 segi jungguk joseon jok yeoksa jaryojip* [Historical Materials on the Koreans in China in the Twentieth Century] by Sim Yonghae and Sim Yongcheol (Seoul: Jungguk joseon minjok munhwa yesul chulpansa, 2002), 300 and 511. Sim also used to use his pen name, Sim Geukchu in Korean or Shen Keqiu in Chinese.

17. Henry Em, "Nationalism, Post-Nationalism, and Shin Ch'ae-ho," *Korea Journal* 39-2 (summer 1999): 313.

18. Yi Jeonggyu, "Jaseo" [Preface] (May 7, 1974), in *UM*, 11.

19. Xiaoqun Xu, "Cosmopolitanism, Nationalism, and Transnational Networks: The *Chenbao Fujuan*, 1921–1928," *The China Review* 4-1 (Spring 2004): 145–173.

20. Dirlik, *Anarchism*.

21. See, for example, Yu Ja-myeong, *Yu Ja-myeong sugi: han hyeokmyeong ja ui hoeeok rok* [Yu Ja-myeong's Memoirs: A Revolutionary's Memoirs] (Cheon-an: Dongnip gi-nyeomgwan han-guk dongnip undongsa yeon-guso, 1999) [hereafter *YJS*], 59–60, 71, 74. Yu named his memoirs after Peter Kropotkin's book, *A Revolutionary's Recollection*. See *YJS*, 74–75.

22. See Dongyoun Hwang, "Korean Anarchism before 1945: A Regional and Transnational Approach," in *Anarchism and Syndicalism in the Colonial and Postcolonial World, 1870–1940: The Praxis of National Liberation, Internationalism, and Social Revolution*, eds. Steven Hirsch and Lucien van der Walt (Leiden: Brill, 2010), 95–130.

23. Alifu Delike [Arif Dirlik], "Dongyade xiandaixing yu geming: quyu shiye zhongde zhongguo shehui zhuyi" [Eastern Asian Modernity and Revolution: Chinese Socialism in Regional Perspective], *Makesi zhuyi yu xianshi* [Marxism and Reality] 3 (2005): 8–16.

24. The current scholarship on Korean anarchism recognizes the interactions between Korean and other Asian anarchists in China and Japan but only describes their joint activities and alliances without explaining the historical implications of them to both Korean and regional anarchism.

25. See, for example, *HAUS*.

26. Delike, "Dongyade xiandaixing," 8–16; Arif Dirlik, "Socialism in China: A Historical Overview," in *The Cambridge Companion to Modern Chinese Culture*, ed. Kam Louie (New York: Cambridge University Press, 2008), 155–172; and Arif Dirlik, "Anarchism in Early Twentieth Century China: A Contemporary Perspective" *Journal of Modern Chinese History* 6–2 (December 2012): 131–146.

27. Karl, *Staging the World*.

28. Christopher E. Goscha, *Thailand and the Southeast Asian Networks of the Vietnamese Revolution, 1885–1954* (London: Curzon Publishers, 1999).

29. See Dongyoun Hwang, "Beyond Independence: The Korean Anarchist Press in China and Japan in the 1920s–1930s," *Asian Studies Review* 31-1 (2007): 3–23 for the publication activities of Korean anarchists in China and Japan, and also Hwang, "Korean Anarchism," 95–130.

30. For the question of place in anarchist practice, see Arif Dirlik, "Anarchism and the Question of Place: Thoughts from the Chinese Experience," in *Anarchism and Syndicalism*, eds. Hirsch and van der Walt (Leiden: Brill, 2010), 131–146. Quotes are from 132–133.

31. See Robert Wuthnow, *Communities of Discourse: Ideology, and Social Structure in the Reformation, the Enlightenment, and European Socialism* (Cambridge, MA: Harvard University Press, 1989), 9, 15.

32. I'd like to thank one of the anonymous reviewers for the SUNY Press for suggesting the use of the term *networks of practice*, which I modified to *networks of discourse and practice*.

33. The definition is John and Jean Comaroff's and is introduced by Arif Dirlik for his argument of regional perspective," in Delike, "Dongyade xiandaixing," 15 and 16n11.

34. See Dongyoun Hwang, "Geupjin juuija deul ui Tokyo roui idong gwa jipjung—1900–1920 nyeondae dongbu asia geupjin juui ui daedu, hwaksan, geurigo geu uimi [The Movement and Concentration of Radicals to Tokyo: The Rise, Development, and Implications of Radicalism in Eastern Asia from the 1900s to 1920s], in Dongyoun Hwang's *Saeroun gwageo mandeulgi: gweonyeok sigak gwa dongbu asia yeoksa jaeguseong* [Making a New Past: A Reconstruction of Eastern Asian History from Regional Perspective], (Seoul: Hyean, 2013), 178–208.

35. I have already suggested this possibility elsewhere. Hwang, "Geupjin juuija deul," 178–208.

36. Nym Wales and Kim San, *Song of Ariran: A Korean Communist in the Chinese Revolution* (San Francisco: Ramparts Press, 1941) [hereafter *SOA*].

37. *SOA*, 89, 107, and 118.

38. Dirlik, *Anarchism*, esp. chapter 3.

39. John Crump, *Hatta Shūzō and Pure Anarchism in Interwar Japan* (New York: St. Martin's Press, 1993), 21–43. Ōsugi's extreme commitment to individual liberation, I suspect, led him to his antipathy even against anarchism, when he said, "For some reason, I hate anarchism a bit." Quoted in Peter Duus and Irwin Schneider, "Socialism, Liberalism, and Marxism, 1901–1931," in *The Cambridge History of Japan*, vol. 6, ed. Peter Duus (Cambridge and New York: Cambridge University Press, 1999), 693. Also see Ōsugi Sakae, *The Autobiography of Ōsugi Sakae*, trans. and intro. Byron K. Marshall (Berkeley: University of California Press, 1992).

40. At his trial Bak also showed some antipathy against anarchism by stating that he was not an anarchist but rather a nihilist. Kim Sam-ung, *Bak Yeol pyeongjeon* [A Commentary Biography of Bak Yeol] (Seoul: Garam gihoek, 1996), 89–90, 99, and 102.

41. *SOA*, 139.

42. *SOA*, 140.

43. Arif Dirlik, "Anarchism in East Asia," *Encyclopaedia Britannica*, accessed August 21, 2015, http://www.britannica.com/topic/anarchism#toc224793.

44. *HHH*, 276. This is how Jeong Hwaam described the Koreans' general understanding of anarchism.

45. For the rise of a regional identity among radicals as "Asians," see Dongyoun Hwang, "20segicho dongbu asia geupjin juui wa 'asia' gae-nyeom" [Radicalism and the Idea of 'Asia' in Early Twentieth Century East Asia], *Daedong munhwa yeon-gu* [The Journal of Eastern Studies] 50 (June 2005): 121–165.

46. I want to note here that sources for the study of Korean anarchism are very fragmentary and limited, as the activities of Korean anarchists had mostly been conducted in secret. Even the prominent anarchist Yi Jeonggyu lamented after 1945 that he was not able to locate information and materials on his own anarchist life and activities. See Yi Jeonggyu, "Jaseo," 12. The discussion below, therefore, relies on the limited, fragmented sources available, both primary and secondary.

Chapter 1. Beyond Independence: The Dawn of Korean Anarchism in China

1. *HASP*, 82–95 and passim.

2. Dirlik, *Anarchism*, 82.

3. Peter Zarrow, *Anarchism and Chinese Political Culture* (New York: Columbia University Press, 1990), 209.

4. See, for example, Jo Sehyeon, "1920 nyeondae jeonban-gi jae jungguk hanin anarchism undong—hanjung anarchist ui gyoryu reul jungsim euro" [The Korean Anarchist Movement in the Early 1920s—Focusing on the Interactions between Korean and Chinese Anarchists], *Han-guk geunhyeondaesa*

yeon-gu [Studies on Korean Modern and Contemporary History] 25 (Summer 2003): 338–373.

5. Zhonggong zhongyang makesi engesi leining sidalin zhezuo fanyiju yanjiushi ed., *Wusi shiqi qikan jieshao* [Introduction to Periodicals during the May Fourth Period] 3, part 1 (Shenyang: Sanlian shudian, 1979), 186.

6. Yungong, "Guangming yundong de qiantu" [The Future of the Light Movement], *Guangming* [The Light] 1 (December 1, 1921): 10. Quoted in *HASP*, 157.

7. Chushen, "Zhonghan de guangming yundong" [The Light Movement in China and Korea], *Guangming* [The Light] 1 (December 1, 1921): 17. Quoted in *HASP*, 157.

8. *HASP*, 145, 151–153.

9. Nammyeong, "Kropotkin ui jugeum e daehan gamsang" [Reflections on Kropotkin's Death], *Cheon-go* [Heavenly Drum] 2 (February 1921), in *Danjae Shin Chaeho ui Cheon-go* [Shin Chaeho's *Cheon-go* journal], ed. and annotated. Choe Gwangsik (Seoul: Asia Research Center, Korea University, 2004), 173–178.

10. For Shifu, see Edward S. Krebs, *Shifu: Soul of Chinese Anarchism* (Lanham, MD: Rowman & Littlefield, 1998). Shifu himself worked with Japanese anarchist Yamaga Taiji (1892–1970), who briefly assisted Shifu in Guangzhou in the publication of *Minsheng* (Voice of People). See Tamagawa Nobuaki, *Chūgoku anakizumu no kage* [Shades of Chinese Anarchism] (Tokyo: Sanichi Shohō, 1974) [hereafter *CANK*], 88–94 and Krebs, *Shifu*, 126.

11. Mujeongbu juui undongsa pyeonchan wiwonhoe ed., *Han-guk anarchism undongsa* [A History of Korean Anarchist Movement] (Seoul: Hyeongseol chulpansa, 1989) [hereafter *HAUS*], 141–142, and Ha Girak, "Danjae ui anarchism [Shin Chaeho's Anarchism], in *Danjae Shin Chaeho seonsaeng tansin 100 ju-nyeon gi-nyeom nonjip* [Collected Articles on Mr. Shin Chaeho's 100th Birthday], ed. Danjae Shin Chaeho seonsaeng gi-nyeom sa-eophoe (Seoul: Hyeongseol chulpansa, 1980), 352–353.

12. *HAUS*, 141–142, 315.

13. Hankyoreh sinmunsa ed., *Balgul: Han-guk hyeondae sa inmul* [Excavations: Persons in Modern Korean History] (Seoul: Hankyoreh simunsa, 1992), 42.

14. For a commentary biography of Yi with emphasis on his relationship with other Korean anarchists, see Yi Deok-il, *Anarchist Yi Hoeyeong gwa jeolmeun geudeul* [Yi Hoeyeong and Those Who Were Young] (Seoul: Ungjin datkeom, 2001).

15. Ibid.

16. *YJS*, 12.

17. Mizuno Naoki, "Tōhō hiappaku minzoku regōkai (1925–1927) ni tsuite" [On the United Society of the Eastern Oppressed Peoples (1925–1927)], in *Chūgoku kokumin kakumei no kenkyū* [A Study of the National Revolution in China], ed. Hazama Naoki (Kyōto: Kyōto daigakko jinbun kagaku kenkyūjo, 1992), 309–350.

18. Dongyoun Hwang, "Raising the Anarchist Banner of National Struggle: Yu Ja-myeong (1894–1985) and the League for the Korean National Front, 1937–1941" (unpublished paper).

19. For the Righteous Group, see Kim Yeongbeom, *Han-guk geundae minjok undong gwa Uiyeoldan* [Modern Korean National Movement and the Righteous Group] (Seoul: Changjak gwa bipyeongsa, 1997).

20. Shin Chaeho, "Declaration of the Korean Revolution (1923)," trans. Dongyoun Hwang, in *Anarchism: A Documentary History of Libertarian Ideas: From Anarchy to Anarchism (300 CE to 1939)*, vol. 1, ed. Robert Graham (Montreal: Black Rose Books, 2005), 373–376. Also see Ha, "Danjae ui anarchism," 353.

21. See a short chronology of Yu's life in Danju Yu Rim seonsaeng gi-nyeom sa-eophoe ed., *Danju Yu Rim jaryojip* [Collected Materials on Mr. Yu Rim] vol. 1 (Seoul: Danju Yu Rim seonsaeng gi-nyeom sa-eophoe, 1991) [hereafter *DYRJ*], 262–264.

22. Personal communication with Mr. Kim Young-Chun, Mr. Sin Nage, and Ms. Park Jeong-Hee on June 17, 2015.

23. Lee Mun Chang, *Haebang gonggan ui anarchist* [Korean Anarchists in the Space after Liberation] (Seoul: Ihaksa, 2008) [hereafter *HGA*], 56.

24. *HGA*, 56.

25. Yi Jeonggyu, "Silcheon ha-neun saram doera" [Become a Man of Words] (April 1956), in *UM*, 356.

26. Quoted in Bak Hwan, *Manju hanin minjok undongsa yeon-gu* [A Study of the History of Korean National Movement in Manchuria] (Seoul: Iljogak, 1991) [hereafter *MHMU*], 284.

27. Nihon anakizumu undō jinmei jiten hensan iinkai ed., *Nihon anakizumu undō jinmei jiten* [Biographical Dictionary of Japanese Anarchist Movement] (Tokyo: Poru shuppan, 2004) [hereafter *NAUJJ*], 703 and *HAUY*, 136.

28. Edward S. Krebs notes that some Chinese anarchists used the term *dang* (political party) to refer to their movement during this time probably in response to the rise of the Chinese Communist Party. Edward S. Krebs, "The Chinese Anarchist Critique of Bolshevism during the 1920s," in *Roads Not Taken: The Struggle of Opposition Parties in Twentieth-Century China*, ed. Roger B. Jeans (Boulder, CO: Westview Press, 1992), 205.

29. Zhongguo dier lishi dang'an guan ed., *Zhongguo wuzhengfu zhuyi he zhongguo shehuidang* [Chinese Anarchism and the Chinese Socialist Party] (n.p.: Jiangsu renmin chubanshe, 1981), 160–161.

30. Yi Horyong, "Yi Hoeyeong ui anarchist hwaldong" [The Anarchist Activities of Yi Hoeyeong], *Han-guk dongnip undonngsa yeon-gu* [Studies on the History of Korean Independence Movement] 33 (2009): 208n87.

31. Oh Jang-Whan, "Yi Jeonggyu ui mujeongbu juui undong" [Yi Jeonggyu's Anarchist Movement], *Sahak yeon-gu* [Historical Studies] 49 (1995): 187–188.

32. For more on Fan's life and activities, see *NAUJJ*, 525 and *HAUS*, 308 and 312. For a very brief description of the journal, see *NAUJJ*, 752. Lin's

name appears in an English article, "Information of Korean Anarchist Activities" carried on the last page of the first issue (June 1, 1928) of *Talhwan* [The Conquest], a Korean anarchist journal published in China.

33. For Eroshenko's activities in China, see Xu Xiaoqun, "Cosmopolitanism, Nationalism," 154–161.

34. Oh Jang-Whan, "Yi Jeonggyu," 182–185.

35. *HHH*, 292.

36. *HAUS*, 137.

37. Yi Horyong, "Yi Hoeyeong ui anarchist," 204.

38. Bak Hwan, "Yi Hoeyeong gwa geu ui minjok undong" [Yi Hoeyeong and His National Movement], in *MHMU*, 283–285.

39. Yi Jeonggyu, "Udang Yi Hoeyeong seonsaeng yakjeon" [A Brief Biography of Mr. Yi Hoeyeong], in *UM*, 50.

40. Jeong certainly was an important Korean anarchist in China, but Yi Gyuchang, a son of Yi Hoeyeong, recalls that Jeong had some personal issues that often displeased his comrades in China. See Yi's testimony in Gukka bohuncheo ed., *Dongnip yugongja jeung-eon jaryojip* [A Collection of the Testimonies of the Men of Merit for Independence], vol. 1 (Seoul: Gukka bohuncheo, 2002) [hereafter *DYJJ*], 160.

41. *HAUS*,137 and *HHH*, 277.

42. *HHH*, 267; Choe Gapryong, *Hwang-ya ui geom-eun gitbal* [A Black Flag in the Wilderness] (Seoul: Imun chulpansa, 1996) [hereafter *HYGG*], 81.

43. *HHH*, 50, 371–372.

44. *HASP*, 125.

45. *NAUJJ*, 712; Horiuchi Minoru, "Yu Giseok," *CMUK* 8 (April 1992): 121, and Jo Sehyun, "1920 nyeondae jeonban-gi jae jungguk" 367.

46. *HAUS*, 296–297 and *NAUJJ*, 712, 772.

47. Shen Keqiu, "Fuchen zai xiaoyan miman de shidai langchaozhong—Ji Liu Shuren de yisheng" [Drifting Along in the Tidal Wave of the Times When Smoke of Gunpowder Filled the Air—Remembering Liu Shuren's Life], *HNJ* 5 (February 1990): 30. Yu is known in China as Liu Xu. It seemed that Yu never forgot that he was Korean. See Shen Keqiu, "Huainian Liu Xu xiong" [Cherishing the Memory of Yu Seo], *HNJ* 2 (July 1987): 55. I am grateful to Professor Sakai Hirobumi for sharing these materials with me.

48. *HAUS*, 296–297 and *NAUJJ*, 712, 772; and Shen Keqiu, "Fuchen zai," 37. According to some Chinese sources and Jeong Hwaam's recall, Wang was not so much an anarchist as head of a terror-minded "gangster" or, to use Jeong's word, a "bandit (*yumin*), who used to involve in politics." Wang, however, is described as a "patriotic killer" (*aiguo shashou*) by Shen Keqiu, "Fuchen zai," 37. It is true that Wang worked closely with many Korean anarchists in the 1920s and '30s and used to be in charge of the "military force section" (*junshibu*) of the Chinese Anarchists Alliance in Shanghai, when it was secretly formed at Huaguang Hospital in 1922. See Zheng Peigang, "Wuzhengfu zhuyi zaizhongguo de ruogan shishi" [Some Facts about Anarchist Movement in

China], in *Wuzhengfu zhuyi sixiang ziliao xuan* [Collected Materials on Anarchist Ideas], 2 vols., eds. Ge Maochun, Jiang Jun, and Li Xingzhi (Beijing: Beijing daxue chubanshe, 1984) [this volume is abbreviated hereafter as *WZSX*], 965–966; Guo Zhao, "Shenmi de Wang Yachu" [Mysterious Wang Yachu], *Wenshi ziliao xuanji* [Collected Materials on Literature and History] 19 (May 1989): 114–130; Shen Meijuan, "'Ansha dawang' Wang Yachu" [Wang Yachu, The Great Master of Assassination], *Zhuanji wenxue* [Biographical Literature] 56-4 (April 1990): 120–132; Guan Dexin, "Guan yu 'Ansha dawang Wang Yachu' buzheng" [Supplementary Additions to 'Wang Yachu, The Great Master of Assassination'], *Zhaunji wenxue* [Biographical Literature] 56-4 (April 1990): 119; and *HHH*, 319.

49. Sim Yongcheol, "Naui hoego," 93.
50. *WZSX*, 1063.
51. *NAUJJ*, 335.
52. Shen Keqiu, "Huainian Liu Xu," 57.
53. *YJS*, 286–287. Sim Yongcheol, "Naui hoego," 133 and 202–203, and Shen Rongche [Sim Yonghcheol], "Ershiliuge chunqiu—Ji Shen Ruqiu de duanzan yisheng" [Twenty-Six Years—Remembering Shen Ruqiu's Short Life], *HNJ* 5 (February 1990): 63.
54. Sim Yongcheol, "Naui hoego," 133, 202–203.
55. See Yi Horyong, "Yi Hoeyeong," 209 for a different explanation by a Japanese police report about the journal that it was originally published by a group of other Koreans but was probably used by Yi as the Federation's publication.
56. *HAUS*, 289.
57. *HAUS*, 139.
58. Ibid.
59. Bak Hwan, "Yi Hoeyeong," 288.
60. *HAUS*, 133, 142, 289.
61. Dirlik, *Anarchism*, 87–100 and Dirlik, "Anarchism and the Question of Place," 142.
62. Dirlik, *Anarchism*, 66.
63. For example, Jeong Hwaam and Yi Hayu were able to establish the Institute for Korean Studies (Chaoxianxue dianguan) in China after Japan's surrender in August 1945, and, under it, the Shin Chaeho School (Shen Caihao xueshe) with support from Chinese anarchist Li Shizeng, Wu Zhihui, Yang Jialuo, and Zhu Xi. In the same year, Yu Rim, Jeong Hwaam, Heo Yeolchu, and Yu Ja-myeong in collaboration with Chinese anarchist Ba Jin, Zhu Xi, and Bi Xiushao hold a Conference of Korean and Chinese Anarchists (*Hanzhong wuzhengfu zhuyizhe dahui*) together in Shanghai. See *HAUS*, 393.
64. Paula Harrell, *Sowing the Seeds of Change: Chinese Students, Japanese Teachers, 1895–1905* (Stanford: Stanford University Press, 1992), 145 and Wang Shaoqiu, *Jindai zhongri wenhua jiaoliushi* [A Modern History of Sino-Japanese Cultural Exchanges] (Beijing: Zhonghua shuju, 1992), 348, 365.

65. Joshua Fogel "The Other Japanese Community: Leftwing Japanese Activities in Wartime Shanghai," in *Wartime Shanghai*, ed. Wen-hsin Yeh (New York: Routledge, 1998), 45–46.

66. Fogel, "The Other Japanese Community," 46.

67. Yi Honggeun, "Yeoksa jeok jingun e ui dongcham" [Joining the Historical March Forward], *Gungmin munhwa hoebo* [The Bulletin of National Culture] 11 (April 1983): 9–10.

68. Sano might have also used a different Chinese name, Lin Zhaoxiong. See *NAUJJ*, 304. According to Yu Ja-myeong, Sano used to teach Japanese to Chinese children and youth at an orphanage-like institute in Nanjing, which was organized with an aim to educate those whose parents had been sacrificed during the 1911 Revolution. See *YJS*, 194–195.

69. *YJS*, 209, 291–292.

70. Olga Lang, *Pa Chin and His Writings: Chinese Youth between the Two Revolutions* (Cambridge, MA: Harvard University Press, 1967), 153. Yu Ja-myeong claims, in his memoir, that the story was about him, since he had gray hair relatively early in his life, and thus was nicknamed "a young man with gray hairs," of which Ba Jin was probably aware. See *YJS*, 288.

71. Kim Myeongseop, "Han-il anarchist deul ui sasang gyoryu wa banje yeondae tujaeng" [Interactions in Thought and Anti-Imperialist Struggles in Alliance by Korean and Japanese Anarchists], *HMUY* 49 (December 2006): 53.

72. Han Sangdo, *Jungguk hyeokmyeong sok ui han-guk dongnip undong* [A History of Korean Independence Movement in the History of the Chinese Revolution] (Paju: Jipmundang, 2004), 115.

73. *HHH*, 295, 296; *YJS*, 208, 291–292; *NAUJJ*, 5, 333; and *HAUS*, 309. Huaguang Hospital's Deng was the first person Yamaga Taiji contacted when he arrived in Shanghai with a mission to get a passport for Ōsugi Sakae, who was planning on taking a trip to Europe to attend a conference of anarchists. Also, Ōsugi was able to find and rent a room in the French Concession in Shanghai only with Deng's help. See *CANK*, 98.

74. *HAUS*, 309.

75. *SOA*, 111–121.

76. Jo Sehyun, "1920 nyeondae jeonban-gi," 369–370 and Wakabayashi Masahiro, *Taiwan kōnichi undōshi kenkyū* [A Study of Taiwan's Anti-Japanese Movement History] (Tokyo: Kenbun shuppan, 1983/2010 rev. and extended ed., 2nd printing), 259. Wakabayashi mistook Luo Hua for a communist.

77. See the chronology in *UM*, 4.

78. Jiang Kang, "Kuang Husheng yu lida xueyuan" [Kuang Husheng and Lida College], *QLXX* 3 (1982): 13. I am grateful to Professor Sakai Hirobumi for sharing the issues of this journal with me.

79. Ming K. Chan and Arif Dirlik, *Schools into Fields and Factories: Anarchists, the Guomindang, and the National Labor University in Shanghai, 1927–1932* (Durham, NC: Duke University Press, 1991), 42, 43.

80. *YJS*, 198. For Yu's impression of Kuang, see Liu Ziming [Yu Jamyeong], "Kuang Husheng xiansheng yinxiangji" [On My Impression of Mr. Kuang Husheng], *QLXX* 3 (1982): 10–11.
81. *YJS*, 205–208.
82. *CANK*, 104.
83. *DYJJ*, 150, 154–155, 157.
84. *HHH*, 350–351.
85. Chan and Dirlik, *Schools into Fields*, 3–4.
86. Yi Jeonggyu, "Jungguk bokgeonseong nongmin jawi undong gwa han-guk dongjideul ui hwalyak" [The Self-Defensive Movement of the Peasants in China's Fujian Province and the Activities of Korean Comrades], in *UM*, 128–130, 132.
87. Chan and Dirlik, *Schools into Fields*, 4.
88. Yi Jeonggyu, "Jungguk bokgeonseong," 30–137.
89. *HHH*, 295.
90. Yi Jeonggyu, "Jungguk bokgeonseong," 130.
91. For Ishikawa's activities at Laoda, see Ishikawa Sanshirō, *Jijōden—ichijiyūjin no tabi* [An Autobiography: The Travel of a Free Person] vol. 2 (Tokyo: Rironsha, 1956), 124–128.
92. *CANK*, 100–102 and *HYGG*, 42–43. For Yamaga's activities in China, see Sakai Hirobumi, "Yamaga Taiji to Chūgoku—'Tasogare nikki' ni miru nitchū anakisuto no kōryū" [Yamaga Taiji and China: The Interactions between Japanese and Chinese Anarchists that Are Described in *A Diary at the Dusk*], *Mao to win: gindai chūgoku no shisō to bungaku* [Cat Head Hawk: Thoughts and Literature of Modern China] 2 (December 1983): 30–49 and Mukai Kō, *Yamaga Taiji, hito to sono shōkai* [Yamaga Taiji: The Person and His Life] (Tokyo: Aokahō, 1974), esp. 36–49, 70–90.
93. Yi Jeonggyu, "Jungguk bokgeonseong," 128.
94. *HAUS*, 298.
95. Various sources present a different date of its establishment. *HAUS* states its founding date differently as May or July 14, 1928 (*HAUS*, 131, 308), while *JRS* 32 (February 1, 1929) as June 14, 1928. Yi Horyong notes that the meeting was held in Shanghai on June14, 1929. See *HASP*, 200.
96. See "Taiheiyō engan no rōdōsha ni yoru tōhō museifu shugisha renmei" [The Eastern Anarchist League by the Workers on the Rims of the Pacific], *Jiyū rengō* [Spontaneous Alliance] 32 (February 1, 1929): 3.
97. According to *HAUS*, Shin might have attended a different meeting of the Eastern anarchists, possibly held in Tianjin. See *HAUS*, 308.
98. "Taiheiyō engan," 3.
99. *NAUJJ*, 773.
100. *HAUS*, 131.
101. *HHH*, 278–281; *HAUS*, 312–319; and Shakai mondai shiryo kenkyūkai ed., *Shakai mondai shiryo sōsho* [Collected Materials on Social Problems], vol. 1 (Tokyo: Tōyō bunkasha, 1977), 26.

102. *HHH*, 275.

103. *HS* 23 (November 31, 1933): 2.

104. For an English translation of it, see "What We Advocate," *Talhwan* [The Conquest] 1 (June 1, 1928), in *Anarchism: A Documentary History of Libertarian Ideas: From Anarchy to Anarchism (300 CE to 1939)*, vol. 1, ed. Robert Graham (Montreal: Black Rose Books, 2005), 381–383.

105. See *Talhwan* 1 (June 1, 1928), 2–8. Nos. 1 and 2 of it were reprinted by Gungmin munhwa yeon-guso gojeon ganhaeng hoe (Publication Committee of the Institute for the Study of National Culture) in Seoul in 1984.

106. "Hyeokmyeong wolli wa talhwan" [The Principles of Revolution and Retaking], *Talhwan* [The Conquest] supplementary to no. 1 (June 15, 1928): 3–4.

107. Ugwan [Yi Jeonggyu], "Talhwan ui je ilseong" [The First Voice of *The Conquest*), *Talhwan* supplementary to no. 1 (June 15, 1928): 2.

108. *HAUY*, 158–161.

109. Pasarov (?), "Mujeongbu juui ja ga bon han-guk dongnip undong" [Korean Independence Movement in the eyes of an Anarchist], *Talhwan* [The Conquest] supplementary to no. 1 (June 15, 1928): 5–7. I have not been able to identify who this possibly Russian anarchist was.

110. *HASP*, 158–159 and Jo Sehyun, "1920 nyeondae jeonban-gi," 358–359.

111. Jo Sehyun, "1920 nyeondae jeonban-gi," 370.

112. Kim and Kim, *Han-guk gongsan juui*, 124.

113. Dirlik, *Anarchism*, 270–271.

114. *DYRJ*, 75.

115. Yi Jeonggyu, "Jungguk bokgeonseong," 128.

116. Qin Wangshan, "Annaqi zhuyi zhe zai fujian de yixie huodong" [Various Activities of Anarchists in Fujian], *Fujian wenshi ziliao* [Literary and Historical Materials of Fujian] 24 (1990): 181 and Qin Wangshan, "Chaoxian he riben annaqi zhuyi zhe zai quan binan yinqi de shijian" [An Incident Caused by Korean and Japanese Anarchists Who Took Refuge in Quanzhou], *Fujian wenshi ziliao* [Literary and Historical Materials of Fujian] 24 (1990): 203.

117. Jiang Kang, "Quanzhou mujeongbu juui e daehan chobojeok yeon-gu" [A Preliminary Examination of the Anarchist Movement in Quanzhou], in Han-guk minjok undong sa yeon-guhoe ed., *Han-guk dongnip undong gwa jungguk—1930 nyeondae reul jungsim euro* [Korean Independence Movement and China: The 1930s] (Seoul: Gukak jaryowon, 1997), 312.

118. Yi Jeonggyu, "Jungguk bokgeonseong," 134.

119. Yi Jeonggyu, "Jungguk bokgeonseong," 133–135.

120. *CANK*, 106.

121. Dirlik, *Anarchism*, 95.

122. *HHH*, 279.

123. Ibid.
124. Yi Jeonggyu, "Jungguk bokgeonseong," 133–136.
125. Yi Jeonggyu, "Jungguk bokgeonseong," 146–148.
126. In addition, the GMD seemed to utilize the Quanzhou Movement as an opportunity to strengthen its influence in the area, with which anarchists were in conflict. See Yi Jeonggyu, "Jungguk bokgeonseong," 140.
127. Qin Wangshan, "Chaoxian he riben," 203.
128. Jiang Kang, "Quanzhou mujeongbu," 317–318.
129. Liu Xu [Yu Seo], "Zhuzhang zuzhi dongya wuzhengfu zhuyizhe datongmeng (jielu)" [Proposing to Organize the Greater Alliance of East Asian Anarchists (excerpts)], *Minzhong* [People's Tocsin] 16 (December 15, 1926), in *WZSX*, 716–720.
130. Ibid.
131. *YJS*, 199.
132. Xie Zhen, "Shenqie huainian Liu Ziming xiansheng" [Deeply Cherishing the Memory of Mr. Yu Ja-myeong], in *HNJ* 1 (?), ed. Jiang Kang (Quanzhou: Quanzhou pingmin zhongxue, minsheng nongjiao jioayouhui, 1986), 57; Shen Keqiu [Sim Yongcheol], "Huainian Liu Xu xiansheng" [Chering the Memory of Mr. Yu Seo], *HNJ* 2 (July 1987): 55; Yu Fuzuo, "Ji pingmin zhongxue" [Remembering Common People's Middle School], *HNJ* 4 (October 1988): 42–44; and *YJS*, 200.
133. See the sections on selected letters in *QLXX* 1 (1982): 16 and in *Minyou xinxi* [News on the Alumni of People's Livelihood Agricultural School] 7 (March 1990): 12.
134. Jiang Kang, "Quanzhou mujeongbu," 324–325; *YJS*, 198–201; and *NAUJJ*, 336. Yu Fuzuo recalls that he met a Japanese teacher at Common People's Middle School, who he remembers used Chinese name, Wu Siming. This Japanese was probably Yatabe who used to use his Chinese name, Wu Shimin, but Yu probably remembered or pronounced by mistake as Wu Siming. Yu Fuzuo, "Ji pingmin zhongxue," 42.
135. See Gu Yeping, "Quanzhou minzhong yundong zhongde liming gazhong yu pingmin zhongxue" [Dawn Advanced Middle School and Common People's Middle School in the Mass Movement in Quanzhou], *Quanzhou shifan xueyuan xuebao* [Journal of Quanzhou Normal University , Social Science] 24-5 (September 2006): 32–48. For the "Fujian Incident," see Lloyd E. Eastman, *The Abortive Revolution: China under Nationalist Rule, 1927–1937* (Cambridge, MA: Harvard University Press, 1974), 85–139.
136. Ki-baik Lee, *A New History of Korea*, trans. Edward W. Wagner with Edward J. Shultz (Cambridge, MA: Harvard University Press, 1984), 365.
137. *SSAU*, 238.
138. Yi Eulgyu, *Siya Kim Jongjin seonsaeng jeon* [A Biography of Mr. Kim Jongjin] (Seoul: Eulyu munhwasa, 1963).
139. *HAUS*, 323–324.

140. *SSAU*, 241–243.
141. *HAUS*, 325–328 and *SSAU*, 246–262.
142. *HAUS*, 326–327.
143. *HAUS*, 325.

Chapter 2. The Wind of Anarchism in Japan

1. Bruce Cumings, *Korea's Place in the Sun* (New York: W. W. Norton & Company, 1st ed., 1997), 121.

2. Mikiso Hane, "Introduction," in *The Prison Memoirs of a Japanese Woman*, Kaneko Fumiko. trans. Jean Inglis (New York: M. E. Sharpe, 1991), xiii. This book is an English translation of Kaneko Fumiko, *Nani ga watashi o kō sasetaka* [What Has Made Me Run Like This?] (Tokyo: Kokushoku senzensha, 1971).

3. Robert A. Scalapino, *The Japanese Communist Movement, 1920–1966* (Berkeley: University of California Press, 1967), 11.

4. Chen Jian and Liang Weilin, "Huiyi 30 niandai zhonggong dongjingzhibu de chengzhang licheng" [Recollection of the Developing Process of the Chinese Communist Party's Tokyo Branch in the 1930s], *Zhonggong dangshi ziliao* [Materials on the History of the Chinese Communist Party] 10 (Internal publication) (October 1984): 169.

5. An early example of it can be found in the Asian Solidarity Society (*Yazhou heqinhui*), formed in Tokyo in 1907 by like-minded Asian radicals from Japan, China, Vietnam, India, and so on under the banner of anti-imperialism. See Rebecca E. Karl, "Creating Asia: China in the World at the Beginning of the Twentieth Century," *American Historical Review* 103-4 (October 1998): 1096–1118.

6. Selçuk Esenbel, "Japan's Global Claim to Asia and the World of Islam: Transnational Nationalism and World Power, 1900–1945," *American Historical Review* 109-4 (October 2004): 1148.

7. The case of *Discussion on Asia* (*Ajia Kōron*), a journal published by Yu Tae-gyeong in 1917 in Tokyo, demonstrates a perceived racial unity without a Japanese expansionist version of Asianism and an early joint effort by Korean and Taiwanese radicals in Tokyo. Besides Korean and Taiwanese radicals, Chinese and Japanese, including Abe Isō at Waseda University, also contributed their writings to the journal, because of which it was particularly utilized by the Taiwanese to inform the Japanese of the colonial situation and discriminatory policies by the Japanese colonial government in Taiwan. See Chi Hsu-feng, "Zasshi *Ajia Kōron* ni miru taishōki higashi ajia chishikijin renkei—zaikyō taiwanjin to chōsenjin no kōryū o chūshin ni" [The Alliance of East Asian Intellectuals during the Taishō Period, seen in the *Ajia kōron* Magazine], *Asia munhwa yeon-gu* [Asian Cultural Studies] 17 (November 2009): 67–77.

8. Ju Taedo, "Hakji gwang ui yeoksajeok samyeong" [A Historical Role of the Light of Learning], *Hakji gwang* [The Light of Learning] 29 (April, 1930): 52–53.

9. Quoted in Park Chan Seung, "Sikminji sigi doil yuhaksaeng gwa geundae jisik ui suyong" [Study-Abroad Students in Japan and Their Reception of Modern Knowledge during the Colonial Period], in *Jisik byeondong ui sahoe sa* [A Social History of Knowledge Transformation], ed. Han-guk sahakhoe (Seoul: Munhak gwa jiseongsa, 2003), 152.

10. Robert A. Scalapino, "Prelude to Marxism: the Chinese Student Movement in Japan, 1900–1910," in *Approaches to Modern Chinese History*, eds. Albert Feuerwerker, Rhodes Murphy and Mary C. Wright (Berkeley, CA: University of California Press, 1967), 192–193 and Wang Shaoqiu, *Jindai zhongri wenhua*, 344–347.

11. *SOA*, 89.

12. Rekishigaku kenkyūkai ed., *Ajia gendaishi 1: teikokushugi no jidai* [A Modern History of Asia 1: The Period of Imperialism] (Tokyo: Aoi shōten, 1983), 287.

13. Kim Myeonggu, "1910 nyeondae doil yuhaksaeng ui sahoe sasang" [Social Thought of the Study-Abroad Students in Japan in the 1910s], *Sahak yeon-gu* [Historical Studies] 64 (2001): 91–125. The quote is from 125.

14. For a general discussion of socialism in Japan, see Duus, "Socialism, Liberalism, and Marxism," 654–710, and for Japanese anarchism before and after the "winter period," see Crump, *Hatta Shūzō*, 21–43.

15. For Chinese students on study abroad in Japan, see Paula Harrell, *Sowing the Seeds of Change: Chinese Students, Japanese Teachers, 1895–1905* (Stanford: Stanford University Press, 1992) and Douglas R. Raynolds, *China, 1898–1912: The Xinzheng Revolution and Japan* (Cambridge, MA: Council on East Asian Studies, Harvard University, 1993).

16. For the Chinese Tokyo anarchists, see Dirlik, *Anarchism*, 100–109 and Zarrow, *Anarchism and Chinese*, 31–58. For the Chinese Communists, see Hwang, *Saeroun yeoksa*, 178–208.

17. *HGA*, 56.

18. Park Chan Seung, "Sikminji sigi doil yuhak gwa yuhaksaeng ui minjok undong" [Study Abroad to Japan and the National Movement of the Study-Abroad Students during the Colonial Period], in *Asia ui geundaehwa wa daehak ui yeokhal* [Modernization in Asia and the Role of University], ed. Hallym daehakgyo Asia munhwa yeon-guso (Chuncheon: Hallym daehakgyo chulpansa, 2000), 162.

19. Im Kyeongseok, *Han-guk sahoe juui ui giwon* [The Origins of Socialism in Korea] (Seoul: Yeoksa bipyeongsa, 2003), 32–40.

20. Yang Sanggi, "Shinsaiki igo no zainichi chōsenjin anakizumu undō no henrin" [A Glimpse of Anarchist Movement by Koreans in Japan after the Kantō Earthquake], *Anakizumu* [Anarchism] 25 (June 1984): 23–24.

21. Park Chan Seung, "Sikminji sigi doil," 177 and Kim Gwang-yeol, "Taishō gi ilbon ui sahoe sasang gwa jaeil hanin" [The Socialist Thoughts during Taishō Japan and Koreans in Japan], *Ilbon hakbo* [The Korean Journal of Japan Studies] 42 (June 1999): 335–351. There were three groups of Korean students in Japan: (1) who came to Japan because their parents were wealthy; (2) who came with the government's scholarship or religious organizations' sponsorship; and (3) work-study students from poor families.

22. *HAUY*, 124.

23. Quoted in Oh Jang-Whan, "1920 nyeondae," 167.

24. Chōsen Gang Chang, "Warera no gaihō wa anakizumu da" [Our Liberation Is Anarchism], *JRS* 47 (May 1, 1930): 4. It is unclear who the author of it was, but it must be Korean.

25. *Hak ji gwang* [The Light of Learning], special issue (January 1920: 13–19 and no. 20 (July 1920): 7–15 (reprinted by Doseo chulpan Yeoknak, 2004). Also see *HASP*, 112.

26. "Rekishi kyōkasho zainichi korian no rekishi," sakusei iinkai, ed.,*Rekishi kyōkasho zainichi korian no rekishi* [History Textbook, A History of Koreans in Japan] (Tokyo: Meishi shōten, 2013) [hereafter *RKZK*], 23.

27. Kim Myeongseop, "Hanil anarchist deul," 44. The year Na converted to anarchism could be 1914. See *NAUJJ*, 699.

28. Chujeong Im Bongsun seonsaeng pyeonchan wiwonhoe, *Chujeong Im Bongsun seonsaeng sojeon* [A Short Biography of Mr. Im Bongsun] (Seoul: Chujeong Im Bongsun seonsaeng sojeon pyeonchan wiwonhoe, 1969), 30.

29. Gwon Daebok ed., *Jinbodang: Dang ui hwaldong gwa sageon gwangye jaryojip* [The Progressive Party: Materials on the Party's Activities and Incidents] (Seoul: Jiyangsa, 1985), 358–359.

30. Ibid.

31. Yi Gyeongmin, "Jo Bong-am no shisō to kōdō" [Thoughts and Actions of Jo Bong-am], *CMUK* 1 (April 1991): 93–94.

32. For a detailed study of Choe's life and anarchist activities, see *SSAU*, 265–340.

33. *SSAU*, 290.

34. *NAUJJ*, 706.

35. Yi Honggeun, "Yeoksa jeok jin-gun," 9.

36. *HS* 23 (November 31, 1933): 2 and Gungmin munhwa yeon-guso ed., *Hang-il hyeokmyeongga gupa Baek Jeonggi* [Baek Jeonggi: A Man of Righteous Deed and Revolutionary who Resisted Japan] (Seoul: Gungmin munhwa yeon-guso chulpanbu, 2004), 182.

37. For more on Dongheung Korean Labor League, see Horiuchi Minoru, "Zainichi chōsenjin anakizumu rōdō undō (gaihō zen)" [Anarchist Labor Movement of Koreans in Japan, prior to Liberation], *Zainichi chōsenjinshi kenkyū* [Studies on the History of Koreans in Japan] 16 (October 1986): 38–58.

38. *HAUS*, 378, 380.

39. Thomas A. Stanley, *Ōsugi Sakae, Anarchist in Taisho Japan: The Creativity of the Ego* (Cambridge, MA: Council on East Asian Studies, Harvard University, 1982), ix.

40. Kim Myeongseop, "Hanil anarchist deul," 46.

41. Kim Sam-ung, *Bak Yeol pyeongjeon*, 55.

42. Choe Gapryong, *Eoneu hyeokmyeongga ui ilsaeng, ujin Choe Gapryong jaseojeon* (A Revolutionary's Life: Memoirs of Ujin Choe Gapryong) (Seoul: Imun chulpnasa, 1995) [hereafter *EHGI*], 19–20, 22–23, 157–158.

43. Bak Giseong, *Nawa joguk: hoego rok* [I and My Country: A Memoir] (Seoul: Sion, 1984): 50, 63.

44. Bak, *Nawa Joguk*, 55.

45. Chujeong Im Bongsun seonsaeng pyeonchan wiwonhoe, *Chujeong Im Bongsun*, 30.

46. The Japanese police usually listed many Koreans in Japan, colonial Korea and China, as "persons of most interest under surveillance."

47. For a list of its members as of 1922, see Kim Myeongseop, "1920 nyeondae chogi jaeil joseonin ui sasang danche" [The Thought Groups of Koreans in Japan in the Early 1920s], *Hanil minjok munje yeon-gu* [Studies on the Korean-Japanese National Questions], Inaugural Issue (March 2001): 21.

48. *HASP*, 126; *HAUY*, 94; Kim Myeongseop, "Hanil anarchist deul," 46, and Yi Horyong, "Bak Yeol ui mujeongbu juui sasang gwa dongnip gukka geonseol gusang" [Bak Yeol's Anarchism and His Vision of an Independent Country], *Han-guk hakbo* [Journal of Korean Studies] 87 (Summer 1997): 156, 160.

49. *NAUJJ*, 574 and Kim Sam-ung, *Bak Yeol pyeongjeon*, 34.

50. Stanley, *Ōsugi Sakae*, 168.

51. *HAUS*, 284–285.

52. Bak Yeol, "Han bullyeong seonin eurobuteo ilbon ui gwollyeokja gyegeup ege jeonhanda" [A Message Delivering to the Class in Power of Japan from a Rebellious Korean], reprinted in Korean translation in Kim Sam-ung, *Bak Yeo pyeongjeon*, 228.

53. See Kim Myeongseop, "Bak Yeol, Kaneko Fumiko ui ban cheon-hwangje tujaeng gwa anarchism insik" [Bak Yeol and Kaneko Fumiko, and Their Struggle against Emperorship and Understanding of Anarchism], *Hanil minjok munje yeon-gu* [Studies on the Korean and Japanese National Questions] 4 (June 2006): 126–140; Oh Jang-Whan, "1920 nyeondae," 183–190; and Yi Horyong, "Bak Yeol," 153–165.

54. Yi Horyong, "Bak Yeol," 156, 160n31.

55. John Crump, *Hatta Shūzō*, 82 and Suzuki Yasuyuki, *Nihon museifushugi undōshi* [A History of Japanese Anarchist Movement] (Tokyo: Kokushoku sensensha, 1932, reprinted 1990), 51–54.

56. "Sōkanni saishite" [On the Occasion of Launching the Journal], *Kokutō* [Black Wave] 1 (1923), 1, reprinted in Kaneko, *Nani ga watashi*, 533.

57. In her prison memoirs Kaneko expressed her "boundless sympathy" "for all the oppressed, maltreated, exploited Koreans," which was "the flame that ignited" her antagonism against the authorities and so forth "in the struggle for this wretched class of mine." Kaneko, *Prison Memoirs*, 217.

58. "Sengen" [Declaration], *Kokutō* [Black Wave]1 (1923): 1, reprinted in Kaneko, *Nani ga watashi*, 533.

59. Oh Jang-Whan, "1920 nyeondae," 160–162, 165.

60. Yi Gangha, "Warera no sakebi" [Our Outcries], *Kokutō* [Black Wave] 1 (1923): 1, reprinted in Kaneko, *Nani ga watashi*, 533. Also see *HAUY*, 98 and *HASP*, 131.

61. Retsusei [Bak Yeol], "Chokusetsu kotō no hyōhon" [An Example of Direct Actions], *Kokutō* [Black Wave] 1 (1923): 1, reprinted in Kaneko, *Nani ga watashi*, 533. Also see *HAUY*, 101.

62. The journal's publishers seemed to use *hutoi* that means "thick," "fat," "bold," or "impudent" as a euphemism for *hutei* that means "recalcitrant" or "rebellious," because of the similarity of the two words in pronunciation. They used *hutoi senjin* as the journal's official title on the first page of its two issues, but also used *hutei* in katakana in place of *hutoi* in its title at the top of every page of the two issues, which was probably the reason for Japanese police to ban it. I translate the Japanese word *hutoi* as *recalcitrant*, because of the katakana part (*hutei*) of the title, while underlining the possible intention of innuendo or insinuation in the use of *hutoi* as *fat* or *bold* for the journal's name. For the meanings of *hutoi* in Eanglish translation, see F. J. Daniels, *Eibun o kaku tame no jishō* [Basic English Writers' Japanese-English Wordbook] (Tokyo: The Hokuseido Press, 1970, 9th ed., 1973), 540, and Bunkachō, *Gaikokujin no tameno kanji jiten* [Dictionary of Chinese Characters for Foreigners] (Tokyo: Daizōshō insatsu kyoku, 1967, 2nd ed., 1982), 549.

63. "Hutoi senjin katkan ni saishite" [On Publishing *Recalcitrant Koreans*], *Hutoi senjin* [Recalcitrant Koreans]: 1, reprinted in Kaneko, *Nani ga watashi*, 541.

64. Bak Yeol, "Ajia monrō shugi ni tsuite" [About Asian Monroe-ism]," *Hutoi senjin* [Recalcitrant Koreans] 2 (1923): 1, reprinted in Kaneko, *Nani ga watashi*, 545.

65. I argued elsewhere that East Asian radicals and anarchists developed a different definition and understanding of Asia, which was "liberating" in its meanings and implications and was not limited to and confined to a geographical construction of Asia. See Hwang, "20 segi cho dong asia," 121–165.

66. Kim Myeongseop, "1920 nyeondae," 25, 28.

67. John Crump, *The Anarchist Movement in Japan* (pamphlet), (n.p.: n.d.), 16–17 and Kim Myeongseop, "Hanil anarchist deul," 50. A contemporary Japanese anarchist, Suzuki Yasuyuki (1903–1970), called Kokuren's anarchism "militant (*sentōteki*) anarchism." Suzuki, *Nihon museifu shugi*, 43–46.

68. Quoted in Oh Jang-Whan, "1920 nyeondae," 169.

69. Kim Myeongseop, "1920 nyeondae," 118–122,
70. Yi Honggeun's recollection. Quoted in *HAUY*, 100.
71. Quoted in *HAUY*, 110–111.
72. Yuk Honggeun, "Iwayuru dasū no shōtai" [The Identity of the so-called Majority], *Gen shakai* [Contemporary Society] 4. Quoted in Oh Jang-Whan, "1920 nyeondae," 177–179.
73. Komatsu Ryuji, *Nihon anakizumu undōshi* [A History of Japanese Anarchist Movement] (Tokyo: Aoki shōten, 1972) [hereafter *NAUS*], 196–226.
74. Kim Sam-ung, *Bak Yeol pyeongjeon*, 89, 102.
75. *NAUS*, 113–139 and *HAUY*, 110.
76. *NAUJJ*, 194.
77. *HAUY*, 114–115.
78. Quoted in *HAUY*, 105. "Hatta Shūzō gun yuku" [Mr. Hatta Shūzō Passes Away], *JRS* 89 (February 10, 1934): 3.
79. *NAUJJ*, 775, 777.
80. Yi Honggeun, "Yeoksa jeok jin-gun," 12 and *NAUS*, 198.
81. Andrew Gordon, *The Evolution of Labor Relations in Japan: Heavy Industry, 1853–1955* (Cambridge, MA: Council on East Asian Studies, Harvard University, 1985), 421.
82. Oh Jang-Whan, "1920 nyeondae," 173.
83. *RKZK*, 11, 14, 33–34.
84. *HASP*, 114–116.
85. Jeong Hyegyeong, *Ilje sidae jaeil joseonin minjok undong yeon-gu* [A Study on the National Movements by Koreans in Japan during the Japanese Colonial Period] (Seoul: Gukak jaryowon, 2001) [hereafter *ISJMU*], chapter 1.
86. *RKZK*, 33.
87. *ISJMU*, 269–270.
88. *ISJMU*, 274.
89. Quoted in *HAB*, 167.
90. *NAUJJ*, 247; Oh Jang-Whan, "1920 nyeondae," 173–174n47; and *ISJMU*, 272, 279.
91. *NAUJJ*, 278; *HAUS*, 284; and Kim Taeyeop, *Tujaeng gwa jeung-eon* [Struggle and Testimony] (Seoul: Pulbit, 1981) [hereafter *TGJ*], 83–84.
92. *NAUJJ*, 218–219.
93. *TGJ*, 45–47.
94. *TGJ*, 53.
95. See *TGJ*, 77–100 for the description of his labor union-related activity as "The Beginning of Struggle."
96. *TGJ*, 84.
97. *TGJ*, 85–86, 93.
98. *TGJ*, 78, 84–85.
99. Bak Yeol, "Kyōsha no sengen" [The Declaration of the Strong], *Chigasei* [The Voice of Self] Inaugural Issue (March 20, 1926:) 1, reprinted in

Zainichi chōsenjin undō kankei kikanshi (Kahozen) [Publications Associated with the Movements of Koreans in Japan (Pre-Liberation)], Chōsen mondai shiryo sōsho [Series on the Materials on Korean Problems] vol. 5, ed. Bak Kyeongsik (Tokyo: Ajia mondai kenkyūjo, 1983) [hereafter *CMSS*], 201.

100. [Yi] Chunsik, "Sengen" [Declaration], *Chigasei* [Voice of Self] Inaugural Issue (March 20, 1926): 1, reprinted in *CMSS*, 201.

101. Toppa [Kim Taeyeop], "Chōsen no undō" [The Movement in Korea], *Chigasei* Inaugural issue (March 20, 1926): 2, 4, reprinted in *CMSS*, 202, 204.

102. Sikchun [Yi Chunsik], "Seizon o kakuritsu seyo!" [Let's Establish the Existence!], *Chigasei* May Issue (April 20, 1926): 1, reprinted in *CMSS*, 205.

103. Toppa, "Chōsen no undō," 2.

104. *EHGI*, 110.

105. Sikchun, "Seizon o kakuritsuseyo!," 1. Because of the Japanese censorship, there were many deletions in the writing, which prevents the author from fully translating what Yi wrote.

106. Bak Yeongseon, "Jiyū!" [Freedom!], *Chigasei* Inaugural issue (March 20, 1926): 1, reprinted in *CMSS*, 210.

107. Toppa [Kim Taeyeop], "Gūzō yori ningen e" [From Idol to Humanity], *Chigasei* May issue (April 20, 1926): 1–2, reprinted in *CMSS*, 205–206.

108. *ISJMU*, 273, 277–278.

109. *ISJMU*, 276n450.

110. *HAUS*, 283, 285.

111. *ISJMU*, 280–281.

112. Ibid.

113. See chapter 3 of *TGJ*.

114. *TGJ*, 151–153.

115. *TGJ*, 84.

116. Kim Sanghyeon, *Jaeil han-guk in: gyopo 80nyeonsa* [Korean in Japan: An Eighty-Year History of the Compatriots] (Seoul: Eo-mun gak, 1969), 28, 36–39.

117. *HAUY*, 124.

118. *SOA*, 139.

119. Iwasa's house was once raided by Japanese police when he was teaching Esperanto to Korean students. See Oh Jang-Whan, "1920 nyeondae," 158n8.

120. Crump, *Hatta Shūzō*, 82.

121. See, for example, Kim Myeongseop, "Jaeil joseonin anarchist deul ui nodong undong" [The Labor Movement of Korean Anarchists in Japan], *Han-guk dongnip undongsa yeon-gu* [Studies on the History of Korean Independence Movement] 21 (2003): 187–214.

122. Yang Sanggi, "Shinsaiki igo," 25. For the conflicts between Japanese pure anarchists and anarcho-syndicalists, see Crump, *Hatta Shūzō*.

123. *HASP*, 233–246.

Chapter 3. Pushing the Limits in Colonial Korea

1. After reading of the biographies of Korean anarchists who were arrested by Japanese police, I am convinced that it was impossible for them to be released alive from their Japanese prison, unless they either were sick enough to die soon due to malnutrition and/or torture or gave up their anarchist faith.
2. Michael Edson Robinson, *Cultural Nationalism in Colonial Korea, 1920–1925* (Seattle: University of Washington Press, 1988), 6.
3. Sun Zhongshan, "Jianguo fanglue" [A General Plan for Nation-Building], *Sun Zhongshan xuanji* [Selected Works of Sun Zhongshan] (Hong Kong: Zhonghua shuju xianggang fenju, 1956), 175.
4. *HAUS*, 216–217.
5. Horiuchi Minoru, "Nitteika chōsen hokubu chihōni okeru anakizumu undō" [Anarchist Movements in the Northern Part of Korea during the Japanese Colonial Period], *CMUK* 5 (December 1988): 81.
6. Ibid.
7. Horiuchi, "Nitteika chōsen," 61.
8. *YJS*, 59–60.
9. *YJS*, 71. For a short description of "the Morito Incident," see the entry to Morito in *NAUJJ*, 649.
10. *HHH*, 40–41, 46, 49.
11. *HHH*, 40–41.
12. Quoted in Yi Gyeongmin, "Jo Bong-am no shisō," 94.
13. Quoted in *HASP*, 166.
14. *HAUS*, 217–219.
15. Lee Chong-Ha, "Esperanto, Anarchism," in *Esperanto wa na* [Esperanto and Me] vol. 1, ed. Han-guk Esperanto hyeophoe pyeonjipbu (Seoul: Han-guk Esperanto hyeophoe, 2011), 202–203.
16. *HAUS*, 296–297; "Fangwen Fan Tianjun xiansheng de jilu" [Records of a Visit to Mr. Fang Tianjun], in *WZSX*, 1043, 1066, and *NAUJJ*, 712, 772.
17. Shin Chaeho, "Nanggaek ui sinnyeon manpil" [A Miscellaneous Writing of a Man of Nonsense and Emptiness on the Occasion of a New Year]," in *Shin Chaeho*, ed. An Byeongjik (Seoul: Han-gilsa, 1979), 180.
18. Horiuchi, "Nitteika chōsen," 61 and Yi Horyong, "Ilje gangjeom gi gungnae anarchist deul ui gongsan juui e daehan bipanjeok hwaldong" [The Activities of Criticisms against Communists by Anarchists in Korea during the Japanese Occupation Period], *YWH* 59 (March 2006): 257–287.
19. Song Seha, "Chōsenjin ni yoru anakizumu," 14. Song (1907–1973) was a member of Tokō Labor Alliance in Tokyo. This article was carried in the journal as part of its special issue on "Korean Anarchist Movement," published by the Center for the Study of Japanese Anarchism.
20. *HAB*, 169.

21. *HAB*, 161–185.
22. *HAB*, 187–188.
23. Horiuchi, "Nitteika chōsen," 63. Also quoted in Kim Myeongseop, "1920 nyeondae," 24.
24. *Chigasei* [The Voice of Self] Inaugural issue (March 20, 1926): 4.
25. Horiuchi, "Nitteika chōsen," 63 and *HAB*, 188–189.
26. Quoted in *HAB*, 188–189.
27. *NAUJJ*, 512.
28. *HAUS*, 223–224 and *NAUJJ*, 217–218.
29. Quoted in Horiuchi, "Nitteika chōsen," 63.
30. Quoted in *HAB*, 189.
31. *HAUS*, 219–230.
32. Kim Hyeong-yun, *Masan yahwa* [Anecdotes on Masan] (Busan: Taehwa chulpansa, 1973), 231–233; Mizuno Naoki, "Bengonin Fuse Tatsuji to chōsen" [Lawyer Fuse Tatsuji and Korea], *Kikan sanjenri* [Quarterly Three Thousand Ri] 34 (Summer 1983): 28–36.
33. *HAUS*, 232–234.
34. *HAUS*, 234–235.
35. This is an assessment made by Korean anarchists who compiled *HAUS*. See *HAUS*, 237–238.
36. *HAUS*, 196–197 and *HAB*, 189–192.
37. *HAB*, 194.
38. For Yi's anarchist literary theory, see Kim Taekho, "Anarchist Yi Hyang ui munhak ron yeon-gu" [A Study on the Literary Theory of Anarchist Yi Hyang], *Hanjung inmunhak yeon-gu* [Studies on Humanities in Korea and China] 26 (2009): 99–120.
39. *HAUS*, 247–248.
40. Kim Taekho, "Anarchist Yi Hyang," 112–117.
41. *HAUS*, 245–246.
42. Quoted in Yi Horyong, "Ilje gangjeom gi gungnae," 277 and *HAB*, 199.
43. Quoted in *SSAU*, 300.
44. *HAUS*, 256–257.
45. *HAB*, 197.
46. *HAUS*, 257, 265; Horiuchi, "Nitteika chōsen," 64–65, 90; *SSAU*, 307, 298–315.
47. Horiuchi, "Nitteika chōsen," 90 and *HAB*, 197.
48. *HAUS*, 257 and Horiuchi, "Nitteika chōsen," 64–65.
49. *HAUS*, 253–254.
50. *HAUS*, 258–259 and Horiuchi, "Nitteika chōsen," 72. The Japanese anarchist newspaper *JRS* carried news on this convention, the formation of the Korean Anarcho-Communist Alliance, the arrest of Yi Honggeun and Choe Gapryong later in *JRS* 79 (April 10, 1932): 3.
51. *HAB*, 199.

52. *HAB*, 201 and *DYRJ*, 40.

53. For a critique of national movement by one of the KAF's founding members around the same time as the KAF was established, see Yi Honggeun, "Kaihō undō to minzoku undō" [Liberation Movement and National Movement], *JRS* 40 (October 1, 1929): 4.

54. See *HAUS*, 260–266 and *SSAU*, 326.

55. *EHGI*, 29–30. Also quoted in Yi Horyong, "Ilje gangjeom gi gungnae," 274–275, 283.

56. *HAUS*, 196–198.

57. *HAUS*, 339–429.

58. This is Kim Seongsuk's description. See *HHH*, 51.

59. *HAB*, 202.

60. Horiuchi, "Nitteika chōsen," 62.

61. Evidence of the existence of this kind of a network can be best found in the journals and newspapers published by Korea anarchists themselves, in which various information and news about the activities of their comrades in other places in the region were detailed. See the articles and news carried here and there in the Korean anarchist journals and newspapers I listed in the bibliography.

62. Personal communication with Mr. Kim Young-Chun on March 31, 2014, and on June 17, 2015. Mr. Kim, one of the third-generation Korean anarchists, told me some renowned Korean anarchists had converted and joined, probably under coercion and pressure, the Concordia Association (*Kyōwa kai*) in the late 1930s and early '40s in support of Japanese pan-Asian ideas and colonial rule of Korea, which, according to him, was the very reason why some Korean anarchists were quite passive in "cleaning out" pro-Japanese Korean collaborators immediately after 1945. Their conversion was probably a product of many factors under the Japanese colonial rule, including political coercion and economic hardships, which, therefore, I think, deserves scholarly attention rather than political and moral attack.

63. Horiuchi, "Nitteika chōsen," 61.

64. Horiuchi, "Nitteika chōsen," 70.

65. Crump, *Hatta Shūzō*, 28–29.

Chapter 4. Korean Anarchists in Wartime China and Japan

1. The decline of anarchism in China after the 1920s is even described as "the bankruptcy of anarchism" (*wuzhengfu zhuyi de pochan*). Xu Shanguang and Liu Jianping, *Zhongguo wuzhengfu zhuyi shi* [A History of Anarchism in China] (n.p.: Hubei renmin chubanshe, 1989), 257–295. Similarly, anarchism in Japan in the 1930s is depicted as "the end of anarchism" (*anakizumu no shuen*). See *NAUS*, 238–245.

2. *SOA*, 310, 312.

3. *JHH*, 126, and *HAUS*, 339–429.
4. *NAUJJ*, 771, 775, 776.
5. *NAUJJ*, 781, 792. *Jiyū rengōshugi* can be also translated into "Libertarian Federalism," given that the Japanese anarchist newspaper *Jiyū rengō* (Free Alliance) was formally called *Libera Federacio*.
6. *NAUS*, 217.
7. *HAUY*, 202 and *HAUS*, 423.
8. *HAUY*, 202 and *NAUS*, 218.
9. Crump, *Hatta Shūzō*, 178.
10. *HAUS*, 401.
11. Horiuchi, "Zainichi chōsenjin anakizumu," 52. According to *NAUJJ*, its first issue came out on July 22. See *NAUJJ*, 782.
12. See its 49th issue (July 1, 1930) that reported on its first page the inauguration of the new Korean anarchist newspaper, and see also many others issues of it for the advertisement on *Black Newspaper*.
13. *HAUS*, 401.
14. Horiuchi, "Zainichi chōsenjin anakizumu," 52.
15. See, for example, "Kokushin no dōshi hippararu" [The Comrades from *Black Newspaper* were Detained], *JRS* 91 (June 5, 1934): 3.
16. *HAUS*, 401.
17. *HAUS*, 404.
18. "Heuksaek undong e jeokgeuk jeok hyeopryeok eul yomang handa" [We Expect Active Support for the Black Movement], *HS* 35 (February 1, 1935): 1.
19. "Fuatsho ka kanken chōsen kyōdai e banko" [The Fascist Authorities Committed an Act of Brutality to Korean Brothers], *JRS* 82 (July 10, 1933): 3.
20. "Aikoku undō o sute mattaki gaihō undō e" [Discarding Patriotic Movement and Moving toward the Completion of Liberation Movement], *Jiyū rengō* [Spontaneous Alliance] 39 (September 1, 1929): 1.
21. Yi Honggeun, "Gaihō undō to minzoku undō," 4.
22. "Minjok undong ui oryu" [Fallacies in the National Movement], *HS* 26 (February 28, 1934): 2.
23. "Aeguk undong ui jeongche" [The True Identity of Patriotic Movement], *HS* 34 (December 28, 1934), 2.
24. Ibid.
25. Ibid.
26. Gwang, "Jayu pyeongdeung ui sinsahoe reul geonseol haja" [Let's Construct a New Society of Freedom and Equality], *Haebang undong* [Liberation Movement] Renewed Issue (May 1929). Quoted in Kim Myeongseop, "Jaeil hanin anarchism undong yeon-gu," 140.
27. "Mujeongbu undong ui hyeonsil seong eul gangjo ham" [To Emphasize the Practical-ness of Anarchist Movement], *HS* 31 (August 29, 1934): 2.
28. Geumwol, "Inganjeok yokgu wa jidowolli ui bulpilyo" [Human Desires and No Need for a Leading Principle], *HS* 33 (October 24, 1934): 2.

29. Ibid.
30. See *HS* 27 (April 18, 1934): 2.
31. *HHH*, 272–273.
32. *HAUY*, 200.
33. See *HAUS*, 343–348.
34. See *HS* 27 (April 17, 1934): 2.
35. *NAUJJ*, 139.
36. Gungmin munhwa yeon-guso ed., *Hang-il hyeokmyeongga gupa Baek Jeonggi uisa*, 180–183.
37. *NAUJJ*, 705. For more on Yi's activities, see Yi Ganghun, *Yi Ganghun yeoksa jeung-eon rok* [Historical Records of Yi Ganghun's Testimony] (Seoul: Inmul yeon-guso, 1994).
38. "Go!" [Notice!], *HS* 30 (July 31, 1934): 2.
39. Crump, *Anarchist Movement*, 24–25.
40. Song Seha, "Chōsenjin ni yoru anakizumu," 15.
41. Kim Gwangju, "Sanghae sijeol hoesang gi" [Recollection of My Days in Shanghai], Part I, *Sedae* [Generation] 3-11 (December 1965): 266–267, and Kim Gwangju, "Sanghae sijeol hoesang gi" [Recollection of My Days in Shanghai] Part II, *Sedae* [Generation] 4-1 (January 1966): 351, 357.
42. Horiuchi Minoru, "Nanka kanjin seinen renmei to kokushoku kyōhudan" [The League of Korean Youth in South China and the Black Terror Party], *CMUK* 8 (April 1992): 23–24, 29.
43. As for its establishment date, different sources have suggested different dates such as 1929, April 1930, April 1931, September 1931, or after 1931. See Horiuchi, "Nanka kanjin seinen," 10–12 and *SSAU*, 119–121.
44. For a full list of its members and their pseudo- or pen names, see Yi Horyong, "Ilje gangjeom gi jae jungguk han-guk in anarchist deul ui minjok haebang undong—terror hwaldong eul jungsim euro" [The National Liberation Movement by Korean Anarchists in China during the Japanese Colonial Period: Their Terrorist Activities], *HMUY* 35 (June 2003): 271; *SSAU*, 122–124; and Horiuchi, "Nanka kanjin seinen," 20.
45. Yi Honggeun, "Yeoksa jeok jin-gun," 11.
46. See *HHH*, 449.
47. The Alliance's platform, goals and regulations, and declaration can all be found, in Korean, online at "Namhwa hanin cheongnyeon yeonmaeng" [The League of Korean Youth in South China], Woodang [Yi Hoeyeong] Memorial Hall, accessed February 7, 2006, http://www.woodang.or.kr/life/youth.htm. The LKYSC's platform was also reported in a Japanese anarchist newspaper. See "Nanshi saijū no senjin seinen renmei, senkoku to kōryō hatbyō" [The League of Korean Youth in South China Announced Its Declaration and Platform], *JRS* 47 (May 1, 1930): 1.
48. For the Chinese anarchist's idea, see Chan and Dirlik, *Schools into Fields*.
49. "Namhwa hanin cheongnyeon yeonmaeng."

50. See Crump, *Hatta Shūzō*, 63, 137–138, and "Nanshi saijū no senjin," 1.

51. "Namhwa hanin cheongnyeon yeonmaeng."

52. "Our Words" [*Warera no go*], *NT* 1. Quoted in Horiuchi, "Nanka kanjin seinen," 28. The *NT* has not survived and thus not available in original text but some parts, albeit abbreviated, are available in Japanese translation in Japanese police report.

53. Krebs, "Chinese Anarchist Critique," 217.

54. One of its young members was Yi Gyuchang, who testifies that the journal was printed at Lida College. See his interview in *DYJJ*, 155. A list of articles and their authors carried in the journal, composed from the Japanese police report, can be found in *SSAU*, 147 and some of them are translated in Korean in *SSAU*, 161–186.

55. Liu Ziming, "Kuang Husheng xiansheng," 10.

56. Ha, "Waseinen no sekinin to sono shimei" [The Responsibilities and Mission of Our Youth], *NT* 2 (June 1936), which is abbreviated, translated in Japanese, and reprinted in *Shakai mondai shiryo sōsho* [Collected Materials on Social Problems], vol. 1, ed. Shakai mondai shiryo kenkyūkai (Tokyo: Tōyō bunkasha, 1977) [hereafter *SMSS*], 68–69. Also quoted in *HAUY*, 218. It is unclear what language *South China Correspondence* used in publication.

57. Quoted in *HHH*, 145.

58. Ha, "Waseinen no sekinin," 68–69.

59. Em, "Nationalism, Post-Nationalism," 313.

60. Quoted in *HAUY*, 220.

61. Ibid and *SSAU*, 133.

62. *SSAU*, 131.

63. *HASP*, 282–283.

64. *SMSS*, 25–27.

65. For Wang, see n. 48 in chapter 1. I have not been able to locate information on Hua Junshi, who seemed to be Wang's associate.

66. The Federation was also called the Black Terror Party (BTP), according to Jeong Hwaam. See *JHH*, 127 and *HS*, passim.

67. *HAUS*, 339–341. The LSNRJ might have been responsible for the attempted assassination in 1934 of Wang Jingwei, then President of the Administrative Yuan of the National Government of China, according to some Korean anarchists' recollection. See *JHH*, 127 and *HHH*, 320–321.

68. *SSAU*, 138. In a Korean anarchist newspaper of the 1930s, the BTP's ultimate aim was explained to be almost the same as that of the LSNRJ: "the denunciation of all powers of the contemporary society and the establishment of a new society in which all mankind can enjoy freedom and equality in all aspects of life in a new world." See Horiuchi, "Nanka kanjin seinen," 21–23. Quote is from 23. Its two main proposed actions stated in its platform were "destruction" and "direct action." See *HS* 23 (November 31, 1933): 2. It is not clear, again, whether *HS*'s editor was confused with the identity of the BTP, or the LSNRJ and the BTP were in fact the same group.

69. *SSAU*, 138; Yi Horyong, "Yi Hoeyeong," 217–218; and *HS* 23 (November 31, 1933): 2.

70. Yi Horyong, "Ilje gangjeom gi jae jungguk," 292.

71. *JHH*, 127.

72. "Chaoxian minzu zhanxian lianmeng chuangli xuanyan" [Declaration of the Establishment of the League for the Korean National Front), *CMZ* Inaugural issue (April 10, 1938): 15.

73. As Yi Jeonggyu later states, many Koreans were disappointed with political cleavages and conflicts among independence activists particularly in the Provisional Government of Korea, which in turn came to them as evidence of impurity of politics and thus made them hate and enraged with politics. This disappointment, Yi Jeonggyu posits, explains why the righteous Korean youth were inclined toward anarchism that denounced politics and government. See Yi Jeonggyu, "Han-guk sahoe juui undong ui jeonmang" [A Prospect for Korean Socialist Movement], in *UM*, 265.

74. Ziming [Yu Ja-myeong], "Chaoxian minzu zhanxian lianmeng jiecheng jingguo" [On the Process of Establishing the League for the Korean National Front], *CMZ* Inaugural issue (April 10, 1938): 3.

75. This too was the case to Japanese anarchists in the 1930s. Crump, *Hatta Shūzō*, 185–186.

76. Kashima Setsuko, "Chōsen minzoku sensen renmei ni tsuite" [About the League for the Korean National Front], *CMUK* 7 (April 1991): 14, 16.

77. Ziming, "Chaoxian minzu zhanxian," 3.

78. Ibid.

79. *HS* 26 (February 28, 1934), 1.

80. Also see Ziming [Yu Ja-myeong], "Zhongguo guomindang dahui de lishi de yiyi" [The Historical Meaning of the Guomindang's Convention], *CMZ* 2 (April 25, 1938): 3.

81. "Chaoxian minzu zhanxian lianmeng," 14.

82. Ziming, "Chaoxian minzu zhanxian," 3; Kashima, "Chōsen minzoku sensen," 15; and Yi Horyong, "Ryu Ja-myeong ui anarchist hwanldong" [The Anarchist Activities of Yu Ja-myeong], *YWH* 53 (2004): 241.

83. See *SSAU*, 147 and Yi Horyong, "Ilje gangjeom gi jae jungguk," 282–283.

84. Ha, "Waseinen no sekininto," 68–69.

85. Ibid.

86. Ibid.

87. Yang Yeoju was a pseudonym of Oh Myeonjik (1892–1937). See Yi Gyuchang's testimony in *DYJJ*, 145 and *NAUJJ*, 242.

88. Ju, "Minjok jeonseon ui ga-neung seong" [The Possibility of the National Front], *NT* 1–10 (November 1936). Quoted in *HASP*, 310.

89. "Minjok jeonseon ui gyeolseong eul chokgu handa" [Urging the Formation of the National Front], *NT* 12 (December 1936). Quoted in *HASP*, 301.

90. After 1945 Kim was active in South Korea in promoting the talk and unification between two Koreas. He joined the communist-led united front movement and later went to North Korea in April 1948, as a member of the group to negotiate the unification issue with North Korean leader Kim Il-Sung. Probably out of a fear of being arrested by and threats to his life from the Syngman Rhee regime, he decided to remain in North Korea and assisted Kim in the establishment of the Democratic People's Republic of Korea. He took high offices in North Korea, but later in 1958, disappeared from the political scene as he was allegedly executed along with the "Yan'an faction" in North Korea.

91. Kim Seongsuk is described by Kim San as Kim Chung-ch'ang who "taught" him "Marxist theory" and "deeply influenced" his life. See *SOA*, 119. Kim Seongsuk described himself later in the 1960s as a "nationalist (*minjokjeok*) communist." See *HHH*, 65, 100.

92. Ziming, "Chaoxian minzu zhanxian," 5.

93. Yu's ability in Chinese is well-known to Chinese. Xie Zhen, "Shenqie huainian Liu Ziming xiansheng" [Dearly Cherishing the Memory of Mr. Yu Ja-myeong], *HNJ* (1986), 57.

94. Ziming, "Zhongguo guomindang dahui," 3.

95. Ziming [Yu Ja-myeong], "Huanying shijie xuelian daibiaotuan" [Welcoming the Representatives of the World Students Union], *CMZ* 4 (May 25, 1938): 2.

96. Yi Horyong, "Yi Hoeyeong," 218.

97. "Chaoxian minzu zhanxian lianmeng," 14.

98. Liu Shi [Yu Ja-myeong], "Weichaoxian geming liliang tongyi er douzheng" [The Unification of Ability and the Struggle for the Korean Revolution], *CMZ* 4 (May 25, 1938): 4.

99. "Choaxian minzu zhanxian lianmeng jiben gangling" [Basic Platform of the Korean National Front], *CMZ* Inaugural issue (April 10, 1938): 16.

100. "Choaxian minzu zhanxian lianmeng douzeng gangling" [Platform for the Struggle of the Korean National Front], *CMZ* Inaugural issue (April 10, 1938): 16.

101. Ziming [Yu Ja-myeong], "Chuangkanci" [Inaugural Editorial], *CMZ* Inaugural issue (April 10, 1938): 1.

102. Ibid.

103. Kashima, "Chōsen minzoku sensen," 20.

104. Kashima Setsuko, "Chōsen giyūtai no seiritsu to katsudō" [The Establishment and Activities of the Korean Volunteers Unit], *CMUK* 4 (November 1987): 52.

105. *HASP*, 246.

106. Crump, *Hatta Shūzō*, 100.

107. Yu Rim must have considered collaborating with the Chinese/Korean communists before he decided to join the Korean Provisional Government. According to a Korean source, Yu traveled to Yan'an to meet with

the CCP's leader Mao Zedong between 1938 and 1941. Yu obviously was impressed by the CCP's revolutionary strategy that emphasized rural villages, but in the end decided to work with the nationalists in Chongqing. See Kim Young-Chun, "Jeonseol ui anarchist, Danju Yu Rim ui bulkkot insaeng" [Legendary Anarchist Yu Rim and His Sparking Life], *Sindong-a* [New East Asia] 50-8 (August 2007): 569–570.

108. *JHH*, 214.

109. *JHH*, 177.

110. Dongming, "Zhuanzhan ebei de yizhi guojiduiwu" [An International Troop Fighting around Northern Hebei], *CYD* 34 (May 15, 1940): 15. *CYD* and *Chaoxian yiyongdui tongxun* [The Korean Volunteers Unit Correspondence] are reprinted in Gukka bohuncheo ed., *Hae-oe ui han-guk dongnip undong jaryo* [Materials on Korean Independence Movement Abroad], vol. 8 (Jungguk pyeon [China] No. 4) (Seoul, Gukka bohuncheo, 1993).

111. Ziming, "Zhongguo guomindang dahui," 1.

112. Li Da [Yi Dal], "Jiaqiang zhonghan liangminzu de tuanjie—xiang chongqing gejie jinyiyan" [Enhancing the Unity between Chinese and Korean Peoples—A Suggestion to All Circles in Chongqing], *CYD* 34 (May 15, 1940): 1.

113. For the passivity of the Nationalist Army during the anti-Japanese resistance war, see Lloyd E. Eastman *Seeds of Destruction: Nationalist China in War and Revolution, 1937–1949* (Stanford: Stanford University Press, 1984) and Ch'i Hsi-sheng. *Nationalist China at War: Military Defeats and Political Collapse, 1937–45* (Ann Arbor: The University of Michigan Press, 1982).

114. See Lee Chong-sik, "Korean Communists and Yenan," *The China Quarterly* 9 (January–March 1962): 182–192.

115. In Yan'an the Korean Independence Alliance in North China (*Hwabuk joseon dongnip dongmaeng*) was to be finally organized as the first revolutionary organization formed by Koreans inside the CCP-controlled Anti-Japanese Bases in north China. Han Sangdo, "Hwabuk joseon dongnip dongmaeng gwa jungguk gongsandang" [The Korean Independence Alliance in North China and the Chinese Communist Party], *Yeoksa hakbo* [Journal of Historical Studies] 174 (June 2002): 115.

116. Kashima, "Chōsen giyūtai," 47.

117. Dam, "Seongrip yurae wa guemhu ui gongjak bangchim" [The Backgrounds of Its Establishment and the Plan Afterwards], *HQ* [Korean Youth] 1-2 (July 15, 1940), reprinted in Korean translation in *SSAU*, 226. Also see Chu Heonsu ed., *Jaryo han-guk dongnip undong* [Materials on Korean Independence Movement], vol. 3 (Seoul: Yonsei daehakgyo chulpanbu, 1973) [hereafter *JHDU*], 113–116. Some issues of *HQ* are reprinted in *JHDU*, 113–164.

118. Luo Yuehuan [Na Wolhwan], "Women de renwu" [Our Tasks], *HQ* 1-1 (July 15, 1940), reprinted in *JHDU*, 116–117.

119. Bak Hwan, "Jung-il jeonjaeng ihu jungguk jiyeok hanin mujeongbu juui gyeyeol ui hyangbae—han-guk cheongnyeon jeonji gongjakdae reul

jungsim euro" [The Trends of Korean Anarchists in China after the Outbreak of the Sino-Japanese War: On the Operation Unit of the Korean Youth at Warfront], *HMUY* 16 (1997), 128–130.

120. Na Wolhwan, "Urideuleun eoteoke han-guk mujangbudaereul geollip halgesinga?" [How Do We Build Korean Armed Forces?], *HQ* 1-2. Quoted in *SSAU*, 203–205.

121. *HAUS*, 388.

122. Margaret (Peggy) B. Denning, "Chinese Communist Mobilization of Japanese POWs in Yan'an, 1939–1945," in *Resisting Japan: Mobilizing for War in Modern China, 1935–1945*, ed. David Pong (Norwalk, CT: Eastbridge, 2008), 127–174.

123. See, for example, Yi Horyong, "Yu Ja-myeong," 221–253 and Han Sangdo, "Yu Ja-myeong ui anarchism ihae wa hanjung yeondaeron" [Yu Ja-myeong's Understanding of Anarchism and His Idea of Korean-Chinese Alliance], *Dongyang jeongchi sasangsa* [History of Political Thoughts in the East] 7-1 (2008): 153.

Chapter 5. Deradicalized Anarchism and the Question of National Development, 1945–1984

1. In 1948 Bak published a book on his plan for a new Korean revolution, in which he emphasized "the nation-building through a thought" (*shisō rikkoku*) and the role of youth in nation-building. I don't analyze this book in this study but it certainly deserves scholarly attention. Bak Yeol, *Shin chōsen kakumei ron* [On a New Korean Revolution] (Tokyo: Chūgai shuppan kabushiki geisha, 1948).

2. *YJS*, 363–372.

3. *HGA*, 6.

4. Yi Jeonggyu, "Jaseo," 12.

5. Ibid.

6. *HASP*.

7. Ha Girak, *Talhwan—baekseong ui jagi haebang uiji* [Retaking: The Will of Common People to Liberate Themselves] (Seoul: Hyeongseol chulpansa, 1994) [hereafter *THBJ*], 219–221.

8. Kim Young-Chun, "Danju Yu Rim ui anarchism gwa dongnip undong" [Yu Rim's Anarchism and Independence Movement], unpublished paper, 6. I am grateful to Mr. Kim for sharing this paper with me.

9. Personal communication with Mr. Kim Young-Chun on March 5 and 31, 2014.

10. This was what Yu Rim said to a reporter from *Chosun Daily* (*Joseon ilbo*) on December 5, 1945. See *DYRJ*, 75.

11. *DYRJ*, 73. 75.

12. *THBJ*, 223–226.

13. *THBJ*, 228–229.
14. *THBJ*, 229–231.
15. *THBJ*, 231.
16. *THBJ*, 231–232.
17. *DYRJ*, 87.
18. *DYRJ*, 87.
19. *THBJ*, 234.
20. *THBJ*, 223–234.
21. *THBJ*, 231–232.
22. *DYRJ*, 87.
23. Ibid.
24. Zarrow, *Anarchism*, 207–208.
25. *THBJ*, 236–237.
26. *THBJ*, 235.
27. *THBJ*, 236.
28. Personal communications with Mr. Kim Young-Chun on March 5 and 31, 2014. According to Mr. Kim, Yi Eulgyu's decision in 1948 to take a relatively high position as a member of the Audit and Inspection Committee (*gamchal wiwonhoe*) in the Rhee's administration, had resulted in the party's decision (possibly led by Yu Rim) to expel him from it, when Yi was one of its core members. This could have resulted in personal antipathy among some leading anarchists, and possibly impared the party's waning fate, which may have been a reason for the internal division and conflict among anarchists, that still linger in the anarchist camp of today's South Korea.
29. Yi Jeonggyu, "Han-guk sahoe juui," 267–268.
30. Yi Jeonggyu, "Han-guk sahoe juui," 268.
31. Yi Jeonggyu, "Han-guk sahoe juui," 270.
32. Yi Jeonggyu, "Han-guk sahoe juui," 269–270.
33. Krebs, "Chinese Anarchist Critique," 217.
34. Yi Jeonggyu, "Han-guk sahoe juui," 270–271.
35. *IJEG*, 309.
36. See *IJEG*, 315 and his later version of it, *JHH*, 310.
37. Yi Joenggyu, "Minju sahoe dang ui jojik wolli" [The Organizational Principles of the Democratic Socialist Party], in *UM*, 226–229.
38. Yi Joenggyu, "Minju sahoe dang ui noseon" [The Ideological Line of the Democratic Socialist Party), in *UM*, 231–235.
39. Yi Joenggyu, "Minju sahoe dang ui noseon," 236–238.
40. Yi Joenggyu, "Minju sahoe dang ui noseon," 238–239.
41. Yi Joenggyu, "Minju sahoe dang ui noseon," 240–245.
42. Yi Joenggyu, "Minju sahoe dang ui noseon," 246.
43. Yi Joenggyu, "Minju sahoe dang ui noseon," 248–249.
44. Yi Jeonggyu, "Minjok jeok banseong" [National Self-Reflections], in *UM*, 260.
45. Yi Joenggyu, "Minju sahoe dang ui noseon," 250–252.

46. Yi Joenggyu, "Minju sahoe dang ui noseon," 245–246.

47. Yi Jeonggyu, "Han-guk sahoe juui," 263–264.

48. I was not able to locate the party's name from the list of political parties that participated in the fourth general election on March 31, 1958 in South Korea and earned any seat in the National Assembly. The DSP was probably a paper party that was registered but did not gain any seat in election. See "Yeokdae sen-geo jeongbo" [Information on the Results of Previous Elections], Jung-ang seon-geo gwalli wiwonhoe [the Central Election Management Committee (of South Korea)], accessed December 10, 2014, http://info.nec.go.kr/electioninfo/electionInfo_report.xhtml?electionId=0000000000&requestURI=%2Felectioninfo%2F0000000000%2Fcp%2Fcpri06.jsp&topMenuId=CP&secondMenuId=CPRI06&menuId=&statementId=CPRI06_%2391&oldElectionType=0&electionType=2&electionName=19580502&searchType=1&electionCode=2&cityCode=0&maxMinCode=-1&genderCode=0&x=22&y=6.

49. *HGA*, 7.

50. Even academics and journalists were easily accused of being pro-communist or commies so that any reference to communism or socialism has become a taboo to them since the 1960s. See, for example, Chung Moon Sang, "Munhwa dae hyeokmyeong eul bo-neun han-guk sahoe ui han siseon—Lee Young Hee sarye" [A Perspective on the Chinese Cultural Revolution in South Korea Society: A Case of Lee Young Hee], *Yeoksa bipyeong* [Critical Review of History] 77 (Winter 2006), 212–241.

51. There seemed to be a tension and conflict between Yi and Yu, and Yi seemed to be the target of criticism from other anarchists for some reasons. Yi were aware of the criticism and responded to it by saying that there had been "no conversion in [his] thinking" (*sasang ui jeonhwan*) or "no changes in the degree of [his] thinking and revolutionary vigor." See Yi Jeonggyu, "Jaseo," 13.

52. Oh Jang-Whan, "Yi Jeonggyu ui mujeongbu juui undong" [Yi Jeonggyu's Anarchist Movement], *Sahak yeon-gu* [Historical Studies] 49 (1995): 178–179 and Dongyoun Hwang, "Yi Jeonggyu, cho gukkajeok han-guk anarchism ui silhyeon eul wihayeo" [Yi Jeonggyu, towards a Realization of Transnational Korean Anarchism], *Yeoksa bipyeong* [Critical Review of History] 93 (winter 2010): 198–230.

53. Yi Jeonggyu, "Joseon nongchon jachi yeonmaeng seoneon gangnyeong haeseol" [An Explanation of the Platform and Declaration of the Federation for Rural Autonomy], in *UM*, 176.

54. Yi Jeonggyu, "Joseon nongchon jachi," 176, 183–185.

55. *THBJ*, 197.

56. *THBJ*, 194–199.

57. Yi Jeonggyu, "Jayu geonseolja yeonmaeng seoneon mit gangnyeong" [The Declaration and Platform of the Free Society Builders Federation], in *UM*, 173.

58. Yi Jeonggyu, "Jayu geonseolja yeonmaeng," 174.
59. Yi Jeonggyu, "Jayu geonseolja yeonmaeng," 174–175 and *JHBU*, 265.
60. Yi Jeonggyu, "Jayu geonseolja yeonmaeng," 174–175.
61. *JHBU*, 266.
62. Yi Jeonggyu, "Han-guk sahoe juui," 266.
63. *JHBU*, 266.
64. Yi Jeonggyu, "Han-guk nodongja jachi yeonmaeng hoego" [Recollection of the Federation for Workers Autonomy], in *UM*, 214.
65. Yi Jeonggyu, "Joseon nongchon jachi," 178, 180.
66. Yi Jeonggyu, "Nongchon buheung gwa yeongse nong munje" [The Revival of Rural Villages and the Problem of Small-Income Farmers], in *UM*, 368–369.
67. Yi Jeonggyu, "Joseon nongchon jachi," 187.
68. Yi Jeonggyu, "Joseon nongchon jachi," 183–184.
69. Yi Jeonggyu, "Joseon nongchon jachi," 187–188.
70. Oh Jang-Whan, "Yi Jonggyu," 209.
71. Yi Jeonggyu, "Han-guk nodongja jachi," 215.
72. Ibid.
73. Yi Jeonggyu, "Han-guk nodongja jachi," 217.
74. Yi Jeonggyu, "Han-guk nodongja jachi," 215.
75. Yi Jeonggyu, "Han-guk nodongja jachi," 216–217.
76. Yi Jeonggyu, "Han-guk nodongja jachi," 218.
77. Ibid.
78. *HGA*, 8–9.
79. *HGA*, 14.
80. *HGA*, 14–15.
81. Personal communication with Mr. Lee Mun Chang on December 10, 2012. Mr. Lee told me that those who had participated in the revolutionary activities before 1945, such as Yi Jeonggyu, were the second-generation Korean anarchists, most of whom he believed had disappeared after the Korean War, 1950–1953. The third-generation Korean anarchists were, according to him, those who became interested in anarchism as students, mostly college, after the April 19th Revolution of 1960. According to his definition, such seniors as Shin Chaeho and Yi Hoeyeong belong to the first generation.
82. *HGA*, 3, 6–7.
83. It seems that two different versions of English translation of the Institute's name have been used. They are National Culture Research Institute and People[']s Anarchist Culture Research Institute, freely used by individual members of the Institute on various occasions. I basically follow the former, with some changes, the Institute for the Study of National Culture (ISNC), to stick more closely to the original meaning of the name in Korean, but at the same time to indicate and emphasize the shift of focus in its activities since the 1950s to national culture and development.

84. Yi Jeonggyu, "Hoego wa jeonmang" [Retrospect and Prospect], in *UM*, 364–365, and Yi Jeonggyu, "Gaehoesa" [Opening Remarks] (October 1960), in *UM*, 359.

85. *HGA*, 7.

86. Lee Mun Chang, "Jayu gongdongche undong ui eoje wa oneul—'gungmin munhwa yeon-guso' 50 nyeonsa reul jungsim euro" [Today and Yesterday of the Free Community Movement—Focused on the Fifty-Year History of 'The Institute for the Study of National Culture'], in *Gungmin munhwa yeon-guso 50nyeonsa—jayu gongdongche undong ui baljachwi* [A Fifty-Year History of the Institute for the Study of National Culture: The Footsteps of the Free Community Movement], ed. Gungmin munhwa yeon-guso 50 nyeonsa ganhaeng wiwonhoe. (Seoul: Gungmin munhwa yeon-guso, 1998) [hereafter *GMY*], 3.

87. *HGA*, 6 and Lee Mun Chang, "Jayu gongdongche," 3.

88. *HGA*, 7.

89. Yi Jeonggyu, "Sadan beop-in gungmin munhwa yeon-guso seollip chwiji seo" [The Mission Statement of the Institute for the Study of National Culture], in *UM*, 378.

90. Yi Jeonggyu, "Sadan beop-in gungmin," 379.

91. Lee Mun Chang, "Jayu gondongche," 3.

92. Lee Mun Chang, "Jayu gondongche," 7.

93. Lee Mun Chang, "Jayu gondongche," 6–7.

94. In his unpublished manuscript Yi Jeonggyu described anarchism as "social aesthetic" (*sahoe mihak*), seeing it as a form of natural beauty and taste that other kinds of socialism did not possess. Yi underlined the importance of understanding anarchism as "social aesthetic," if anarchists want to pursue a "cultural struggle" (*munhwa tujaeng*), not "social struggle" (*sahoe tujaeng*). See Yi Jeonggyu, *Sahoe mihak euro seoui mujeongbu juui* [Anarchism as Social Aesthetic], unpublished manuscript. I am grateful to Mr. Song Heonjo and the Institute for the Study of National Culture for sharing this invaluable material with me.

95. Yi Jeonggyu, "Jeokgeuk jeok geungjeong jeok in myeon euro jeontong eul gyeseung baljeon sikija—je 11 hoe haksaeng ui nal gi-nyeomsa" [Let's Inherit and Develop Traditions into Active and Positive Ones—A Congratulatory Address on the Occasion of the 11th Anniversary of Students Day], in *UM*, 302.

96. Yi Jeonggyu, "Daehak gyoyuk gwa geu sa-myeong" [College Education and Its Mission], in *UM*, 307, and Yi Jeonggyu, "Sungkyunkwan daehakgyo chongjang chwiimsa" [Inaugural Address as Sungkyunkwan University's President], in *UM*, 295–296.

97. Yi Jeonggyu, "Daehak gyoyuk," 308.

98. Yi Jeonggyu, "Daehak gyoyuk," 306.

99. Yi Jeonggyu, "Nongchon jajuhwa ui munjejeom" [Issues in Making Rural Villages Autonomous] (November 17, 1971), in *UM*, 382.

100. Ibid.
101. Yi Jeonggyu, "Nongchon undong jidoja gandamhoe gyehoek insa malsseum" [A Greeting Address and the Plan for the Preliminary Meeting of the Rural Movement Leaders], *TS* 1 (October 1971): 3. This is Yi's opening remarks at a preliminary meeting with rural movement leaders in October 1971.
102. Yi Jeonggyu, "Nongchon jajuhwa," 385.
103. Ibid.
104. Yi Jeonggyu, "Nongchon undong," 3–4.
105. Yi Jeonggyu, "Nongchon buheung," 367.
106. Yi Jeonggyu, "Nongchon jajuhwa," 382–384.
107. Yi Jeonggyu, "Nongchon buheung," 368.
108. Yi Jeonggyu, "Gungmin susan undong chujin e gwanhan gaehwang" [An Outline of the Movement to Receive and Produce], in *UM*, 374, and Yun Inhoe, "'Gungmin munhwa yeon-guso' wa nongchon undong" [The Institute for the Study of National Culture and the Rural Movement], in *GMY*, 446. Yun was a board member of the ISNC.
109. *HGA*, 12.
110. Son Useong, "Gungmin susan undong ui uiui" [The Meanings of the National Movement to Receive and Produce], *Gungmin munhwa hoebo* [Bulletin of National Culture] 1 (May 1966), reprinted in *GMY*, 88.
111. *HGA*, 7.
112. Yi Jeonggyu, "Gungmin susan undong chujin," 374–375.
113. Son Useong, "Gungmin susan undong ui uiui," 89.
114. "Gungmin susan undong yogang" [The Outline of the National Movement to Receive and Produce], in *GMY*, 101.
115. "Susan undong chujin ui jeonmang" [A Prospect for the National Movement to Receive and Produce] (July 1968)," in *GMY*, 109.
116. "Susan undong chujin ui jeonmang," 110.
117. "Burak danwi cheongso-nyeon gyoyuk gyehoek" [A Plan to Educate the Youth in Villages] and "Haksaeng hwaldong jido" [Guiding Students' Activities], in *GMY*, 123, 136–160.
118. Yi Jeonggyu, "Gungmin susan undong chujin," 376.
119. This is what Yi stated in his invitation letter to various leading figures in South Korean government and society. Yi Jeonggyu, "Chocheong ui malsseum" [Inviting Words] (July 2, 1968), in *GMY*, 110.
120. Yi Jeonggyu, "Gungmin susan undong chujin," 376.
121. Crump, *Hatta Shūzō*, 63.
122. Crump, *Hatta Shūzō*, 122.
123. Crump, *Hatta Shūzō*, 92 and passim.
124. See *GMY*, 161–180.
125. There is no mention of how the movement ended in the volume (*GMY*) compiled and edited by the ISNC.
126. Personal communication with Mr. Song Heonjo on December 11, 2011. Mr. Song was one of Yi Jeonggyu's students.

127. The outcome of the preliminary meeting was carried in *TS* 2 (1973): 4.

128. Yi Jeonggyu, "Insa ui malsseum" [Welcoming Words] (March 1972), *TS* 2 (1973): 1, 7.

129. Personal communication with Mr. Lee Mun Chang on December 10, 2011.

130. Bak Seunghan, "Insa malsseum" [Welcoming Words], *TS* 4(1973): 4.

131. Yi Jeonggyu, "Gyeokryeo sa' [Words of Encouragement], *TS* 4(1973): 5.

132. See *GMY*, 230–310.

133. Personal communication with Mr. Song Heonjo on December 11, 2012. Mr. Song was involved in the Council in the 1970s.

134. Ha Girak describes this meeting as the third convention of the FAK without explaining when and where it was first organized. See *JHBU*, 354. On the contrary, the FAK's homepage explains the meeting in 1972 as the inaugural convention of the FAK. See "Han-guk jaju in yeonmaeng yeonhyeok" [History of the Federation Anarchist Korea], Han-guk jaju in yeonmaeng [The Federation Anarchist Korea], accessed May 6, 2014, http://www.jajuin.org/korea_01_03.htm. I follow the explanation on the FAK's homepage.

135. Personal communication with Mr. Kim Young-Chun, Mr. Sin Nage, and Ms. Park Jeong-Hee on June 17, 2015.

136. "Han-guk jajuin yeonmaeng jeonggwan" [Platform of the Federation Anarchist Korea], Han-guk jajuin yeonmaeng [The Federation Anarchist Korea], accessed May 10, 2014, http://www.jajuin.org/korea_01_04.htm.

137. Ibid.

138. Yi Dongwon, "Anarchism ui seongji Anui!" [Anui: A Holly Place of Anarchism!], *Hamyang sinmun* [Hamyang County Newspaper] (April 6, 2015), accessed June 24, 2015, http://hy.newsk.net/?doc=news/print_news.htm&ns_id=5383.

139. The FAK still exists but without visible activities. In an effort to revive it, the Society to Commemorate Yu Rim (Yu Rim gi-nyeom sa-eop hoe) was formed by an anarchist group from the FAK, composed of the former members of the IWPP. This society has been much more active under the leadership of Mr. Kim Young-Chun, a third-generation anarchist. Personal communication with Mr. Kim Young-Chun on March 5 and 31, 2014.

140. Hwang, "Korean Anarchism," 198–230.

141. According to Mr. Lee Mun Chang, Korean anarchists have become passive and/or inactive in organizing and educating workers, compared to their many attempts to organize and educate rural villagers, which still continues, because most Korean workers participated in the Federation of Korean Trade Unions (FKTU, Han-guk nochong) under the dictatorial regimes. The FKTU is believed to be friendly to the South Korean government and used to be under its "control." Personal communication with Mr. Lee Mun Chang on December 10, 2012. Mr. Kim Young-Chun, on the other hand, told me that

the former members of the IWPP were a leading force in initially organizing the FKTU. Personal communication with Mr. Kim Young-Chun, Mr. Sin Nage, and Ms. Park Jeong-Hee on June 17, 2015.

142. *HGA*, 7, 18.

143. Yi Jeonggyu, "Joseon nongchon jachi," 190 and Yi Jeonggyu, "Hoego wa jeonmang," 366.

144. *HGA*, 1, 3.

145. *HGA*, 7, 18.

146. Yi Jeonggyu, "Pyehae jaegeon gwa sinsaenghwal undong" [The Reconstruction from the Ruins and the New Life Movement], in *UM*, 279–284.

147. Yi Jeonggyu, "Jaseo," 11.

148. *HHH*, 276.

149. *HGA*, 8–9.

150. Yi Jeonggyu, "Jaseo," 13.

Conclusion

1. Kim Seongguk, "Danju Yu Rim gwa han-guk anarchism ui dokjaseong [Yu Rim and the Peculiarities of Korean Anarchism], *Sahoe josa yeon-gu* [Studies on Social Investigation] 16 (2001), 59.

2. Yu's followers seem to remember and praise Yu as an anarchist who, throughout his life, never compromised his anarchist belief and principles with the dictatorial Rhee regime. Personal communication with Mr. Kim Young-Chun, Mr. Shin Nage, and Ms. Park Jeong-Hee on June 17, 2015.

3. Unlike the anarchists directly associated with Yi Jeonggyu's ISNC, Jeong Hwaam and Yang Ildong, for example, continued to participate in politics by joining various progressive/opposition parties after the failed attempt to establish the DSP in 1956.

4. *Hankyoreh 21* [Koreans 21], a special issue on "Anarchism, 21 segi ui jayu" [Anarchism, Freedom for the 21st Century] 307 (May 11, 2000): 42.

5. Barbara Epstein, "Anarchism and the Anti-Globalization Movement," *Mionthly Review* 53, no. 4 (September 2001), accessed September 12, 2001, http://www.monthlyreview.org/0901epstein.htm.

6. Personal communication with Mr. Kim Young-Chun, Ms. Park Jeong-Hee, and Mr. Shin Nage on June 17, 2015. They are all associated with the Society to Commemorate Mr. Yu Rim.

7. This was the impression I got from a personal communication with Mr. Lee Mun Chang on December 10, 2012, and also from the audience at my talk for the ISNC members and aftertalk conversations with them on June 19, 2015.

Bibliography

"Aeguk undong ui jeongche" [The True Identity of Patriotic Movement]. *Heuksaek sinmun* [Black Newspaper] 34 (December 28, 1934).
"Aikoku undō o sute mattaki gaihō undō e" [Discarding Patriotic Movement and Moving toward the Completion of Liberation Movement]. *Jiyū rengō* [Spontaneous Alliance] 39 (September 1, 1929).
An, Byeongjik, ed. *Shin Chaeho*. Seoul: Han-gilsa, 1979.
Bak, Giseong. *Nawa joguk: hoego rok* [I and My Country: A Memoir]. Seoul: Sion, 1984.
Bak, Hwan. "Jung-il jeonjaeng ihu jungguk jiyeok hanin mujeongbu juui gyeyeol ui hyangbae—Han-guk cheongnyeon jeonji gongjakdae reul jungsim euro" [The Trends of Korean Anarchists in China after the Outbreak of the Sino-Japanese War: On the Operation Unit of Korean Youth at Warfront]. *Han-guk minjok undongsa yeon-gu* [Studies on the History of Korean National Movement] 16 (1997): 113–154.
———. *Sikminji sidae hanin anarchism undongsa* [A History of Korean Anarchist Movement during the Colonial Period]. Seoul: Seon-in, 2005.
———. *Manju hanin minjok undongsa yeon-gu* [A Study of the Korean National Movement in Manchuria]. Seoul: Iljogak, 1991.
———. "Yi Hoeyeong gwa geu ui minjok undong" [Yi Hoeyeong and His National Movement]. In *Manju hanin minjok undong sa yeon-gu* [A Study of the Korean National Movement in Manchuria], Bak Hwan, 272–295. Seoul: Iljogak, 1991.
Bak, Kyeongsik, ed. *Zainichi chōsenjin undō kankei kikanshi (Kaihōzen)* [Publications Associated with the Movements of Koreans in Japan, the Pre-Liberation Period], *Chōsen mondai shiryō sōsho* [Series on the Materials on Korean Problems], 5. Tokyo: Ajia mondai kenkyūjo, 1983.
Bak, Seok-yun. "'Jagi' ui gaejo" [Transformation of the Self]. *Hak ji gwang* [The Light of Learning] 20 (1920) (rev. 2nd ed.): 7–15.
Bak, Seunghan. "Insa malsseum" [Welcoming Words]. *Tongsin* [Correspondence] 4 (1973): 3–4.
Bak, Yeol. "Han bullyeong seonin eurobuteo ilbon ui gwollyeokja gyegeup ege jeonhanda" [A Message Delivering to the Class in Power in Japan

from a Rebellious Korean]. In *Bak Yeol pyeongjeon* [A Commentary Biography of Bak Yeol], Kim Samung, 223–230. Seoul: Garam Gihoek, 1996.
———. *Shin chōsen kakumei ron* [On a New Korean Revolution]. Tokyo: Chūgai shuppan kabushiki gaisha, 1948.
———. "Ajia monrō shugi ni tsuite" [About Asian Monroe-ism]. *Hutoi senjin* [Recalcitrant Koreans] 2 (1923): 1. Reprinted in *Nani ga watashi o kō saseta ka* [What Made Me the Way I Am?], Kaneko Fumiko, 545. Tokyo: Kokushoku sensensha, 1971.
———. "Kyōsha no sengen" [The Declaration of the Strong]. *Chigasei* [The Voice of Self], Inaugural Issue (March 20, 1926): 1.
Bak, Yeongseon. "Jiyū!" [Freedom!]. *Chigasei* [The Voice of Self] Inaugural issue (March 20, 1926). Reprinted in *Zainichi chōsenjin undō kankei kikanshi (Kahozen)* [Publications Associated with the Movements of Koreans in Japan (Pre-Liberation)], Chōsen mondai shiryo shosyo [Series on the Materials on Korean Problems], vol. 5, edited by Bak Kyeongsik, 201. Tokyo: Ajia mondai kenkyūjo, 1983.
Bi, Xiushao. "Wo xinyang wuzhengfu zhuyi de qianqian houhou" [Before and After I Had Faith in Anarchism]. In *Wuzhengfu zhuyi sixiang ziliao xuan* [Collected Materials on Anarchist Ideas), 2 vols., edited by Ge Maochun, Jiang Jun, and Li Xingzhi, 1022–1039. Beijing: Beijing daxue chubanshe, 1984.
Bunkachō. *Gaikokujin no tame no kanji jiten* [Dictionary of Chinese Characters for Foreigners]. Tokyo: Daizōshō insatsu kyoku, 1967, 2nd ed., 1982.
"Burak danwi cheongsonyeon gyoyuk gyehoek" (A Plan to Educate the Youth in Villages) (November 1965). Reprinted in *Gungmin munhwa yeon-guso osipnyeon sa* [A Fifty-Year History of the Research Institute for National Culture], edited by Gungmin munhwa yeon-guso osipnyeon sa pyeonchan wiwonhoe, 123–125. Seoul: Gungmin munhwa yeon-guso, 1998.
Chan, Ming K. and Arif Dirlik. *Schools into Fields and Factories: Anarchists, the Guomindang, and the National Labour University in Shanghai, 1927–1932*. Durham: Duke University Press, 1991.
Chaoxian minzu zhanxian [The Korean National Front] Inaugural Issue (April 10, 1938), 2 (April 25, 1938), and 4 (May 25, 1938). Reprinted in *Jingwang, Chaoxian mizu zhanxian, Chaoxian yiyongdui (tongxun)*, edied by Dongnip gi-nyeomgwan han-guk dongnip undongsa yeon-guso. Hanguk dongnip undongsa jaryo chongseo, vol. 2, 149–240. Chungnam Cheonwon gun: Dongnip gi-nyeomgwan han-guk dongnip undongsa yeon-guso, 1988.
"Chaoxian minzu zhanxian lianmeng chuangli xuanyan" [Declaration of the Establishment of the League for the Korean National Front). *Choaxian minzu zhanxian* [The Korean National Front], Inaugural issue (April 10, 1938): 14–15.
"Choaxian minzu zhanxian lianmeng douzeng gangling" [Platform for the Struggle of the Korean National Front]. *Choaxian minzu zhanxian* [The Korean National Front], Inaugural issue (April 10, 1938): 16.

"Choaxian minzu zhanxian lianmeng jiben gangling" [Basic Platform of the Korean National Front]. *Choaxian minzu zhanxian* [The Korean National Front], Inaugural issue (April 10, 1938): 16.

Chaoxian yiyongdui [Korean Volunteers Unit] 34 (May 15, 1940). Reprinted in *Hae-oe ui han-guk dongnip undong jaryo* [Materials on Korean Independence Movement Abroad], vol. 8 (Jungguk pyeon [China], no. 4), edited by Gukka bohuncheo, 372–390. Seoul, Gukka bohuncheo, 1993.

Chen, Jian and Liang Weilin. "Huiyi 30 niandai zhonggong dongjingzhibu de chengzhang licheng" [Recollection of the Developing Process of the Chinese Communist Party's Tokyo Branch in the 1930s]. *Zhonggong dangshi ziliao* [Materials on the History of the Chinese Communist Party] 10 (Internal publication) (October 1984): 169–180.

Ch'i, Hsi-sheng. *Nationalist China at War: Military Defeats and Political Collapse, 1937–45*. Ann Arbor, MI: University of Michigan Press, 1982.

Chi, Hsu-feng. "Zasshi *Ajia kōron* ni miru taishōki higashi ajia chishikijin renkei—zaikyō taiwanjin to chōsenjin no kōryū o chūshin ni" [The Alliance of East Asian Intellectuals during the Taishō Period, seen in the *Ajia kōron* Magazine]. *Asia munhwa yeon-gu* [Asian Cultural Studies] 17 (November 2009): 67–99.

Chigasei [sic, The Voice of Self]. Inaugural issue (March 20, 1926), May Issue (April 20, 1926). Reprinted in *Zainichi chōsenjin undō kankei kikanshi (Kaihōzen)* [Publications Associated with the Movements of Koreans in Japan, the Pre-Liberation Period], *Chōsen mondai shiryō sōsho* [Series on the Materials on Korean Problems] 5, edited by Bak, Kyeongsik, 201–208. Tokyo: Ajia mondai kenkyūjo, 1983.

Choe, Bongchun. "Yu Ja-myeonge ui hang-il yeokjeong gwa joseon hyeokmyeong undong – geuui hoegorok eul jungsim euro" [The Traces of Yu Ja-myeong's Anti-Japanese Resistance and the Korean Revolutionary Movement]. *Inmun gwahak nonchong* [Studies of Humanities Science] 43 (2005): 179–223.

Choe, Gapryong. *Hwang-ya ui geom-eun gitbal* [A Black Flag in the Wilderness]. Seoul: Imun chulpansa, 1996.

———. *Eoneu hyeokmyeong ga ui ilsaeng, ujin Choe Ggapryong jaseojeon* [A Revolutionary's Life: Memoirs of ujin Choe Gapryong]. Seoul: Imun chulpansa, 1995.

Choe, Seungman. "Sangjo ron" [On Mutual Aid]. *Hak ji gwang* [The Light of Learning] 19 (1920): 13–19.

Chōsen Gang, Chang. "Warera no gaihō wa anakizumu da" [Our Liberation is through Anarchism]. *Jiyū rengō shimbun* [Spontaneous Alliance Newspaper] 47, May 1, 1930.

Chu, Heonsu, ed. *Jaryo han-guk dongnip undong* [Materials on Korean Independence Movement], vol. 3. Seoul: Yonsei daehakgyo chulpanbu, 1973.

Chujeong Im Bongsun seonsaeng pyeonchan wiwonhoe. *Chujeong Im Bongsun seonsaeng sojeon* [A Short Biography of Mr. Im Bongsun]. Seoul: Chujeong Im Bongsun seonsaeng sojeon pyeonchan wiwonhoe, 1969.

Chung, Mun Sang. "Munhwa daehyeokmyeong eul bo-neun han-guk sahoe ui han siseon—Lee Young Hee sarye" [A Perspective on the Chinese Cultural Revolution in South Korean Society: A Case of Lee Young Hee]. *Yeoksa bi-pyeong* [Critical Review of History] 77 (Winter 2006): 212–241.

Chunsik [Yi Chunsik]. "Seonen" [Declaration]. *Chigasei* [The Voice of Self], Inaugural issue (March 20, 1926). Reprinted in *Zainichi chōsenjin undō kankei kikanshi (Kahozen)* [Publications Associated with the Movements of Koreans in Japan (Pre-Liberation)], Chōsen mondai shiryo shosyo [Series on the Materials on Korean Problems], vol. 5, edited by Bak Kyeongsik, 201. Tokyo: Ajia mondai kenkyūjo, 1983.

Chushen. "Zhonghan de guangming yundong" [The Light Movement in China and Korea]. *Guangming* [The Light] 1 (December 1, 1921).

Crump, John. *Hatta Shūzō and Pure Anarchism in Interwar Japan*. New York: St. Martin's Press, 1993.

———. "Anarchism and Nationalism in East Asia." *Anarchist Studies* 4-1 (March 1996): 45–63.

———. *The Anarchist Movement in Japan* (pamphlet). n.p.: n.d.

Cumings, Bruce. *Korea's Place in the Sun*. New York: W. W. Norton & Company, 1997.

Dam. "Seongrip yurae wa guemhu ui gongjak bangchim" [The Backgrounds of Its Establishment and the Plan Afterwards]. *Hanguo qingnian* [Korean Youth] 1, no. 2 (July 15, 1940). Reprinted in Korean translation in *Sikminji sidae hanin anarchism undong sa* [A History of Korean Anarchism during the Colonial Period], Bak Hwan, 226–230. Seoul: Seon-in, 2005.

Daniels, F. J. *Eibun o kaku tame no jishō* [Basic English Writers' Japanese-English Wordbook]. Tokyo: The Hokuseido Press, 1970, 9th ed., 1973.

Danjae Shin Chaeho seonsaeng ginyeom sa-eophoe, ed. *Danjae Shin Chaeho seonsaeng tansin 100 ju-nyeon ginyeom nonjip* [Collected Articles on Mr. Shin Chaeho on His 100th Birthday]. Seoul: Hyeongseol chulpansa, 1980.

Danju Yu Rim seonsaeng gi-nyeom sa-eophoe, ed. *Danju Yu Rim jaryojip* [Collected Materials on Mr. Yu Rim], vol. 1. Seoul: Danju Yu Rim seonsaeng gi-nyeom sa-eophoe, 1991.

Delike, Alifu [Arif Dirlik]. "Dongyade xiandaixing yu geming: quyu shiye zhongde zhongguo shehui zhuyi" [Eastern Asian Modernity and Revolution: Chinese Socialism in Regional Perspective]. *Makesi zhuyi yu xianshi* [Marxism and Reality] 3 (2005): 8–16.

Denning, Margaret (Peggy) B. "Chinese Communist Mobilization of Japanese POWs in Yan'an, 1939–1945." In *Resisting Japan: Mobilizing for War in Modern China, 1935–1945*, edited by David Pong, 127–174. Norwalk, CT: Eastbridge, 2008.

Dongming. "Zhuanzhan ebei de yizhi guojiduiwu" [An International Troop Fighting around Northern Hebei]. *Chaoxian yiyongdui* [The Korean Volunteers Unit] 34 (May 15, 1940).

Dongnip gi-nyeomgwan han-guk dongnip undongsa yeon-guso, ed. *Jingwang, Chaoxian mizu zhanxian, Chaoxian yiyongdui (tongxun)*. Han-guk dongnip undongsa jaryo chongseo, vol. 2. Chungnam Cheonwon gun: Dongnip gi-nyeomgwan han-guk dongnip undongsa yeon-guso, 1988.

Dirlik, Arif. "Anarchism in Early Twentieth Century China: A Contemporary Perspective." *Journal of Modern Chinese History* 6, no. 2 (December 2012): 131–146.

———. "Anarchism and the Question of Place: Thoughts from the Chinese Experience." In *Anarchism and Syndicalism in the Colonial and Postcolonial World, 1870–1940: The Praxis of National Liberation, Internationalism, and Social Revolution*, edited by Steven Hirsch and Lucien van der Walt, 131–146. Leiden: Brill, 2010.

———. "Socialism in China: A Historical Overview." In *The Cambridge Companion to Modern Chinese Culture*, edited by Kam Louie, 155–172. New York: Cambridge University Press, 2008.

———. "Anarchism in East Asia." Encyclopaedia Britannica. Accessed August 21, 2015. http://www.britannica.com/topic/anarchism#toc224793.

———. *Anarchism in the Chinese Revolution*. Berkeley: University of California Press, 1991.

Duus, Peter and Irwin Schneider. "Socialism, Liberalism, and Marxism, 1901–1931." In *The Cambridge History of Japan*, vol. 6, edited by Peter Duus, 654–710. Cambridge, MA: Cambridge University Press, 1999.

Eastman, Lloyd E. *The Abortive Revolution: China under Nationalist Rule, 1927–1937*. Cambridge, MA: Harvard University Press, 1974.

———. *Seeds of Destruction: Nationalist China in War and Revolution, 1937–1949*. Stanford: Stanford University Press, 1984.

Em, Henry. "Nationalism, Post-Nationalism, and Shin Ch'ae-ho." *Korea Journal* 39, no. 2 (summer 1999): 283–317.

Epstein, Barbara. "Anarchism and the Anti-Globalization Movement." *Mionthly Review* 53, no. 4 (September 2001). Accessed September 12, 2001. http://www.monthlyreview.org/0901epstein.htm.

Esenbel, Selçuk. "Japan's Global Claim to Asia and the World of Islam: Transnational Nationalism and World Power, 1900–1945." *American Historical Review* 109, no. 4 (October 2004): 1140–1170.

"Fangwen Fan Tianjun xiansheng de jilu" [Records of a Visit to Mr. Fan Tianjun]. In *Wuzhengfu zhuyi sixiang ziliao xuan* (Collected Materials on the Ideas of Anarchism), 2 vols., edited by Ge Maochun, Jiang Jun and Li Xingzhi, 1039–1048. Beijing: Beijing daxue chubanshe, 1984.

Fogel, Joshua. "The Other Japanese Community: Leftwing Japanese Activities in Wartime Shanghai." In *Wartime Shanghai*, edited by Wen-hsin Yeh, 42–61. New York: Routledge, 1998.

"Fuatsho ka kanken chōsen kyōdai e banko" [The Fascist Authorities Committed an Act of Brutality to Korean Brothers]. *Jiyū rengō simbun* [Spontaneous Alliance Newspaper] 82 (July 10, 1933).

Ge, Maochun, Jiang Jun, and Li Xingzhi, eds. *Wuzhengfu zhuyi sixiang ziliao xuan* [Collected Materials on the Ideas of Anarchism], 2 vols. Beijing: Beijing daxue chubanshe, 1984.

Geumwol. "Inganjeok yokgu wa jidowolli ui bulpilyo" [Human Desires and No Need for a Leading Principle]. *Heuksaek sinmun* [Black Newspaper] 33 (October 24, 1934).

"Go!" [Notice!]. *Heuksaek sinmun* [Black Newspaper] 30 (July 31, 1934).

Gordon, Andrew. *The Evolution of Labor Relations in Japan: Heavy Industry, 1853–1955*. Cambridge, MA: Council on East Asian Studies, Harvard University, 1985.

Goscha, Christopher E. *Thailand and the Southeast Asian Networks of the Vietnamese Revolution, 1885–1954*. London: Curzon Publishers, 1999.

Graham, Robert, ed., *Anarchism: A Documentary History of Libertarian Ideas*, vol. 1 (From Anarchy to Anarchism, 300 CE to 1939). Montreal: Black Rose Books, 2005.

Gu, Seunghoe, Kim Kyeongbok, Kim Myeongseop, Bak Cheolhong, Bak Hwan, Song Jae-u, Oh Duyeong, Oh Jang-Whan, Yi deok-il, and Yi Horyong. *Han-guk anarchism 100 nyeon* [One Hundred Years of Korean Anarchism]. Seoul: Ihaksa, 2004.

Gu, Yeping. "Quanzhou minzhong yundong zhongde liming gazhong yu pingmin zhongxue" [Dawn Advanced Middle School and Common People's Middle School in the Mass Movement in Quanzhou]. *Quanzhou shifan xueyuan xuebao* [Journal of Quanzhou Normal College, Social Science] 24, no. 5 (September 2006): 32–48.

Guan, Dexin. "Guanyu 'Ansha dawang Wang Yachu' buzheng" [Supplementary Additions to 'Wang Yachu, The Great Master of Assassination']. *Zhaunji wenxue* [Biographical Literature] 56, no. 4 (April 1990): 119.

Guangming. [The Light] 1 (December 1, 1921).

Gukka bohuncheo, ed. *Dongnip yugongja jeung-eon jaryojip* [A Collection of the Testimonies of the Men of Merit for Independence], vol. 1. Seoul: Gukka bohuncheo, 2002.

———, ed. *Hae-oe ui han-guk dongnip undong jaryo* [Materials on Korean Independence Movement Abroad], vol. 8 (Jungguk pyeon [China], no. 4). Seoul, Gukka bohuncheo, 1993.

Guksa pyeonchan wiwonhoe, ed. *Han-guk dongnip undongsa* [A History of Korean Independence Movement]. 5 vols. Seoul: Guksa pyeonchan wiwonhoe, 1969.

Gungmin munhwa hoebo [The Bulletin of National Culture] 1 (May 1966) and 11 (April 1983).

Gungmin munhwa yeon-guso, ed. *Hang-il hyeokmyeongga gupa Baek Jeonggi uisa* [BaekJeonggi, A Man of Righteous Deed and Revolutionary who Resisted Japan]. Seoul: Gungmin munhwa yeon-guso chulpanbu, 2004.

Gungmin munhwa yeon-guso osipnyeonsa pyeonchan wiwonhoe, ed. *Gungmin munhwa yeon-guso osipnyeon sa* [A Fifty-Year History of the Institute for the Study of National Culture]. Seoul: Gungmin munhwa yeon-guso, 1998.

"Gungmin susan undong yogang" [The Outline of the National Movement to Receive and Produce], in *Gungmin munhwa yeon-guso 50 nyeon sa* [A Fifty-Year History of the Institute for the Study of National Culture], edited by Gungmin munhwa yeon-guso, 90–103. Seoul: Gungmin munhwa yeon-guso, 1998.

Guo, Zhao. "Shenmi de Wang Yachu" [Mysterious Wang Yachu]. *Wenshi ziliao xuanji* [Collected Materials on Literature and History] 19 (May 1989): 114–130.

Gwang. "Jayu pyeongdeung ui sinsahoe reul geonsel haja" [Let's Construct a New Society of Freedom and Equality]. *Haebang undong* [Liberation Movement], Renewed Issue (May 1929).

Gwon, Daebok, ed. *Jinbodang: Dang ui hwaldong gwa sageon gwan-gye jaryojip* [The Progressive Party: Materials on the Party's Activities and Incidents]. Seoul: Jiyangsa, 1985.

Ha [Yi Hayu]. "Waseinen no sekinin to sono shimei" [The Responsibilities and Mission of Our Youth], *Namhwa Tongsin* [South China Correspondence] 2 (June 1936). Abbreviated, translated in Japanese, and reprinted in *Shakai mondai shiryo sōsho* [Collected Materials on Social Problems], vol. 1, edited by Shakai mondai shiryo kenkyūkai, 68–59. Tokyo: Tōyō bunkasha, 1977.

Ha, Girak. "Danjae ui anarchism" [Shin Chaeho's Anarchism]. In *Danjae Shin Chaeho seonsaeng tansin 100 ju-nyeon gi-nyeom nonjip* [Collected Article on Mr. Shin Chaeho in Commemoration of His 100th Birthday], edited by Danjae Shin Chaeho seonsaeng gi-nyeom sa-eophoe, 351–405. Seoul: Hyeongseol chulpansa, 1980.

———. *Talhwan—baekseong ui jagi haebang uiji* [Retaking: The Will of Common People to Liberate Themselves]. Seoul: Hyeongseol chulpansa, 1994.

———. *Jagi reul haebang haryeo neun baekseongdeul ui uiji* [The Will of Common People to Liberate Themselves]. Busan: Doseo chulpan sinmyeong, 1993.

Hak ji gwang [The Light of Learning], 2 vols. Reprinted. Seoul: Doseo chulpan yeoknak, 2004.

"Haksaeng hwaldong jido" [Guiding Students' Activities]. In *Gungmin munhwa yeon-guso osipnyeon sa* [A Fifty-Year History of the Institute for the Study of National Culture], edited by Gungmin munhwa yeon-guso osipnyeon sa pyeonchan wiwonhoe, 136–160. Seoul: Gungmin munhwa yeon-guso, 1998.

Hallym daehakgyo Asia munhwa yeon-guso, ed. *Asia ui geundaehwa wa daehak ui yeokhal* [Modernization in Asia and the Role of University]. Chuncheon: Hallym daehakgyo chulpansa, 2000.

Han-guk jajuin yeonmaeng [The Federation Anarchist Korea]. "Han-guk jajuin yeonmaeng jeonggwan" [Platform of the Federation Anarchist Korea]. Accessed May 10, 2014. http://www.jajuin.org/korea_01_04.htm.

Han-guk jajuin yeonmaeng [The Federation Anarchist Korea]. "Han-guk jajuin yeonmaeng yeonhyeok" [History of the Federation Anarchist Korea]. Accessed May 6, 2014. http://www.jajuin.org/korea_01_03.htm.

Han, Sangdo. "Yu Ja-myeong ui anarchism ihae wa han-jung yeondae ron" [Yu Ja-myeong's Understanding of Anarchism and His Idea of Korean-Chinese Alliance]. *Dongyang jeongchi sasangsa* [History of Political Thoughts in the East] 7, no. 1 (2008): 139–160.

———. *Jungguk hyeokmyeong sok ui han-guk dongnip undong* [A History of Korean Independence Movement in the History of the Chinese Revolution]. Paju: Jipmundang, 2004.

———. "Hwabuk joseon dongnip dongmaeng gwa jungguk gongsandang" [The Korean Independence Alliance in North China and the Chinese Communist Party]. *Yeoksa hakbo* [Journal of Historical Studies] 174 (June 2002): 113–139.

Hane, Mikiso. "Iintroduction." In *The Prison Memoirs of a Japanese Woman*, Kaneko Fumiko, translated by Jean Inglis. New York: M. E. Sharpe, 1991.

Hanguo qingnian [Korean Youth] 1, no. 2 (July 15, 1940).

Hankyoreh 21 [The Korean 21] 307 (May 11, 2000).

Hankyoreh sinmunsa, ed. *Balgul: Han-guk hyeondae sa inmul* [Excavations: Persons in Modern Korean History]. Seoul: Hamkyoreh sinmunsa, 1992.

Harrell, Paula. *Sowing the Seeds of Change: Chinese Students, Japanese Teachers, 1895–1905*. Stanford: Stanford University Press, 1992.

"Hatta Shūzō gun yuku" [Mr. Hatta Shūzō Passes Away]. *Jiyū rengō shimbun* 89 (February 10, 1934).

Heuksaek sinmun [Black Newspaper] 23, 26–37 (December 31, 1933, February 28 1934–April 22, 1935).

"Heuksaek undong e jeokgeuk jeok hyeopryeok eul yomang handa" [We Expect Active Support for the Black Movement]. *Heuksaek sinmun* 35 (February 1, 1935).

Hirsch, Steven and Lucien van der Walt, eds. *Anarchism and Syndicalism in the Colonial and Postcolonial World, 1870–1940: The Praxis of National Liberation, Internationalism, and Social Revolution*. Leiden: Brill, 2010.

Horiuchi, Minoru. "Nanka kanjin seinen renmei to kokushoku kyōhudan" [The League of Korean Youth in South China and the Black Terror Party]. *Chōsen minzoku undōshi kenkyū* [Studies on the History of Korean National Movements] 8 (April 1992): 7–34.

———. "Yu Giseok" [Yu Seo]. *Chōsen minzoku undōshi kenkyū* [Studies on the History of Korean National Movement] 8 (April 1992): 120–123.

———. "Nitteika chōsen hokubu chihōni okeru anakizumu undō" [Anarchist Movements in the Northern Part of Korea during the Japanese Colonial Period]. *Chōsen minzoku undōshi kenkyū* [Studies on Korean National Movements] 5 (December 1988): 59–86.

———. "Zainichi chōsenjin anakizumu rōdō undō (gaihō zen)" [Anarchist Labor Movement of Koreans in Japan, prior to Liberation], *Zainichi chō-*

senjinshi kenkyū [Studies on the History of Koreans in Japan] 16 (October 1986): 38–58.

Huainianji [Collection of Cherishing Memories] 2 (July 1987), 4 (October 1988), and 5 (February 1990).

"Hutoi senjin katkan ni saishite" [On Publishing *Recalcitrant Koreans*]. *Futoi senjin* [Recalcitrant Koreans]: 1. Reprinted in *Nani ga watashi o kō saseta ka* [What Made Me the Way I Am?], Kaneko Fumiko, 541. Tokyo: Kokushoku sensensha, 1971.

Hwang, Dongyoun. *Saeroun yeoksa mandeulgi: gwonyeok sigak gwa dongbu asia yeoksa jaeguseong* [Making of a New Past: Regional Perspective and a Reconstruction of the History of Eastern Asia]. Seoul: Hyean, 2013.

———. "Geupjin juuija deul ui Tokyo roui idong gwa jipjung—1900–1920 nyeondae dongbu asia geupjin juui ui daedu, hwaksan, geurigo geu uimi" [The Movement and Concentration of Radicals to Tokyo: The Rise, Development, and Implications of the Radicalism in Eastern Asia from the 1900s to 1920s]. In *Saeroun yeoksa mandeulgi: gwonyeok sigak gwa dongbu asia yeoksa jaeguseong* [Making of a New Past: Regional Perspective and a Reconstruction of the History of Eastern Asia], by Dongyoun Hwang, 178–208. Seoul: Hyean, 2013.

———. "Korean Anarchism before 1945: A Regional and Transnational Approach." In *Anarchism and Syndicalism in the Colonial and Postcolonial World, 1870–1940: The Praxis of National Liberation, Internationalism, and Social Revolution*, edited by Steven Hirsch and Lucien van der Walt, 95–130. Leiden: Brill, 2010.

———. "Yi Jeonggyu, chogukka jeok anarchism ui silhyeon eul wihayeo" [Yi Jeonggyu, towards a Realization of Transnational Korean Anarchism]. *Yeoksa bipyeong* [Critical Review of History] 93 (2010): 198–230.

———. "Beyond Independence: The Korean Anarchist Press in China and Japan in the 1920s–1930s." *Asian Studies Review* 31, no. 1 (2007): 3–23.

———. "20 segicho dong asia geupjin juui wa 'Asia' gae-nyeom" [Radicalism and the Idea of 'Asia' in Early 20th Century East Asia]. *Daedong munhwa yeon-gu* [The Journal of Eastern Studies] 50 (June 2005): 121–165.

"Hyeokmyeong wolli wa talhwan" [The Principles of Revolution and Retaking]. *Talhwan* [The Conquest] supplementary to no. 1 (June 15, 1928): 3–4.

Im, Kyeongseok. *Han-guk sahoe juui ui giwon* [The Origins of Socialism in Korea]. Seoul: Yeoksa bipyeong sa, 2003.

Ishikawa, Sanshirō. *Jijōden—Ichi jiyūjin no tabi* [An Autobiography: the Travel of a Free Person], vol. 2. Tokyo: Rironsha, 1956.

Jeong, Hyegyeong. *Ilje sidae jaeil joseonin minjok undong yeon-gu* [A Study on the National Movements by Koreans in Japan during the Japanese Colonial Period]. Seoul: Gukak jaryowon, 2001.

Jeong, Hwaam. *Jeong Hwaam hoego rok—Eo-neu anarchist ui momeuro sseun geundaesa* [Memoir of Jeong Hwaam—A Modern History Written by an Anarchist with His Body]. Seoul: Jayu mun-go, 1992.

———. *I joguk eodiro gal geosin ga: naui hoego rok* [Where Will This Country Head? My Memoirs]. Seoul: Jayu mun-go, 1982.

Jiang, Kang. "Quanzhou mujeongbu juui e daehan chobojeok yeon-gu" [A Preliminary Examination of the Anarchist Movement in Quanzhou]. In *Han-guk dongnip undong gwa jungguk—1930 nyeondae reul jungsim euro* [Korean Independence Movement and China: The 1930s], edited by Han-guk minjok undongsa yeon-guhoe, 311–338. Seoul: Gukak jaryo-won, 1998.

———. "Kuang Husheng yu lida xueyuan" [Kuang Husheng and Lida College]. *Quanzhou liming xueyuan xinxi* [News on Quanzhou Liming College] 3 (1982): 13.

Jiyū rengō [Spontaneous Alliance], 32.

Jiyū rengō shimbun [Spontaneous Alliance Newspaper], 32, 40, 47, 79, 82, 89, and 91.

Jo, Sehyeon. "1930 nyeondae hanjung anarchist ban fascism tujaeng gwa gukje yeondae—Bajin gwa Yu Ja-myeong eul jungsim euro" [Anti-Fascist Struggles of Korean and Chinese Anarchists and International Collaboration in the 1930s—with Emphasis on Bajin and Yu Ja-myeong]. *Dongbuk a munhwa yeaon-gu* [Cultural Studies on Northeast Asia] 17 (2008): 327–355.

———. "1920 nyeondae jeonban-gi jae jungguk hanin anarchism undong—hanjunganarchist ui gyoryu reul jungsim euro" [The Korean Anarchist Movement in the Early 1920s—Focusing on the Interactions between Korean and Chinese Anarchists]. *Han-guk geunhyeondae sa yeon-gu* [Studies on Korean Modern and Contemporary History] 25 (Summer 2003): 338–373.

Ju. "Minjok jeonseon ui ga-neung seong" [The Possibility of the National Front]. *Namhwa Tongsin* [South China Correspondence] 1–10 (November 1936).

Ju, Taedo. "Hakji gwang ui yeoksajeok samyeong" [A Historical Role of the Light of Learning]. *Hakji gwang* [The Light of Learning] 29 (April, 1930): 52–53.

Jung-ang seon-geo gwalli wiwonhoe [Central Election Management Committee]. "Yeokdae sen-geo jeongbo" [Information on the Results of Previous Elections]. Accessed December 10. 2014. http://info.nec.go.kr/electioninfo/electionInfo_report.xhtml?electionId=0000000000&requestURI=%2Felectioninfo%2F0000000000%2Fcp%2Fcpri06.jsp&topMenuId=CP&secondMenuId=CPRI06&menuId=&statementId=CPRI06_%2391&oldElectionType=0&electionType=2&electionName=19580502&searchType=1&electionCode=2&cityCode=0&maxMinCode=-1&genderCode=0&x=22&y=6.

Kaneko, Fumiko. *Nani ga watashi o kō saseta ka* [What Made Me the Way I Am?]. Tokyo: Kokushoku sensensha, 1971.

———. *The Prison Memoirs of a Japanese Woman*. Translated by Jean Inglis. New York: M. E. Sharpe, 1991.

Kang, Man-gil, ed. *Shin Chaeho*. Seoul: Goryeo daehakgyo chulpanbu, 1990.

Karl, Rebecca E. "Creating Asia: China in the World at the Beginning of the Twentieth Century." *American Historical Review* 103, no. 4 (October 1998): 1096–1118.

———. *Staging the World: Chinese Nationalism at the Turn of the Twentieth Century*. Durham, NC: Duke University Press, 2002.

Kashima, Setsuko. "Chōsen giyūtai no seiritsu to katsudō" [The Establishment and Activities of the Korean Volunteers Unit]. *Chōsen mizoku undōshi kenkyū* [Studies of Korean National Movement] 4 (November 1987): 45–68.

———. "Chōsen minzoku sensen renmei ni tsuite" [About the League for the Korean National Front]. *Chōsen minzoku undōshi kenkyū* [Studies on the History of Korean National Movements] 7 (April 1991): 7–36.

Kim, Changsun and Kim Junyeop. *Han-guk gongsan juui undongsa* [A History of the Korean Communist Movement], 5 vols. Seoul: Cheonggye yeonguso, 1986, new ed.

Kim, Gwangju. "Sanghae sijeol hoesang gi" [Recollection of My Days in Shanghai], Part I. *Sedae* [Generation] 3, no. 11 (December 1965): 244–273.

———. "Sanghae sijeol hoesang gi" [Recollection of My Days in Shanghai], Part II. *Sedae* [Generation] 4, no. 1 (January 1966): 345–357.

Kim, Gwangyeol. "Taishō gi ilbon ui sahoe sasang gwa jaeil hanin" [The Socialist Thoughts during Taishō Japan and Koreans in Japan]. *Ilbon hakbo* [The Korean Journal of Japanology] 42 (June 1999): 335–352.

Kim, Hakjun, ed. *Hyeokmyeong gadeul ui hang-il hoesang: Kim Seongsuk, Jang Geonsang, Jeong Hwaam, Yi Ganghun ui dongnip tujaeng* [Revolutionaries' Recollections of Anti-Japanese Struggles: Struggles for the Independence by Kim Seongsuk, Jang Geonsang, Jeong Hwaam, and Yi Ganghun]. Interviewed by Lee Chong-sik. Seoul: Mineumsa, 1988.

Kim, Hyeongyun. *Masan yahwa* [Anecdotes on Masan]. Busan: Taehwa chulpansa, 1973.

Kim, Myeonggu. "1910 nyeondae doil yuhaksaeng ui sahoe sasang" [Social Thought of the Study-Abroad Students in Japan in the 1910s]. *Sahak yeon-gu* [Historical Studies] 64 (2001): 91–125.

Kim, Myeongseop. "Han-il anarchist deul ui sasang gyoryu wa banje yeondae tujaeng" [Interactions in Thought and Anti-Imperialist Struggles in Alliance by Korean and Japanese Anarchists]. *Han-guk minjok undongsa yeon-gu* [Studies on the History of Korean National Movements] 49 (December 2006): 41–68.

———. "Jaeil joseonin anarchist deul ui nodong undong" [The Labor Movement of Korean Anarchists in Japan]. *Han-guk dongnip undongsa yeon-gu* [Studies on Korean Independence Movements] 21 (2003): 187–214.

———. "Bak Yeol, Kaneko Fumiko ui ban cheonhwangje tujaeng gwa anarchism insik" [Bak Yeol and Kaneko Fumiko, and Their Struggle against Emperorship and Understanding of Anarchism]. *Hanil minjok munje yeon-gu* [Studies on the Korean-Japanese National Questions] 4 (June 2003): 105–145.

———. "1920 nyeondae chogi jaeil joseonin ui sasang danche" [The Thought Groups of Koreans in Japan in the Early 1920s]. *Han-il minjok munje yeon-gu* [Studies on the Korean-Japanese National Questions], Inaugural issue (March 2001): 7–32.

———. "Jaeil hanin anarchism undong yeon-gu" [A Study on the Korean Anarchist Movement in Japan]. Doctoral diss., Dan-gook University, 2001.

Kim, Sam-ung. *Bak Yeol pyeongjeon* [A Commentary Biography of Bak Yeol]. Seoul: Garam gihoek, 1996.

Kim, Sanghyeon. *Jaeil han-guk in: gyopo 80 nyeon sa* [Korean in Japan: An Eighty-Year History of the Compatriots]. Seoul: Eo-mun gak, 1969.

Kim, Seongguk. "Danju Yu Rim gwa han-guk anarchism ui dokjaseong" [Yu Rim and the Peculiarities of Korean Anarchism]. *Sahoe josa yeon-gu* [Studies on Social Investigation] 16 (2001): 57–88.

———. "Yu Ja-myeong gwa han-guk anarchism ui hyeongseong" [Yu Ja-myeong and the Formation of Korean Anarchism]." In *Han-guk sahoe sasangsa yeon-gu* [Studies on the History of Social Thoughts in Korea], edited by Kim Gyeong-il, 289–315. Seoul: Nanam chulpan, 2003.

Kim, Taekho. "Anarchist Yi Hyang ui munhak ron yeon-gu" [A Study on the Literary Theory of Anarchist Yi Hyang]. *Hanjung Inmunhak yeon-gu* [Studies on Humanities in Korea and China] 26 (2009): 99–120.

Kim, Taeyeop. *Tujaeng gwa jeung-eon* [Struggle and Testimony]. Seoul: Pulbit, 1981.

Kim, Yeongbeom. *Han-guk geundae minjok undong gwa Uiyeoldan* [Modern Korean National Movement and the Righteous Group]. Seoul: Changjak gwa bipyeong sa, 1997.

Kim, Young-Chun. "Jeonseol ui anarchist Danju Yu Rim ui bulkkot insaeng" [Legendary Anarchist Yu Rim and His Sparking Life]. *Sindong-a* [New East Asia] 50, no. 8 (August 2007): 562–573.

———. "Danju Yu Rim ui anarchism gwa dongnip undong" [Yu Rim's Anarchism and Independence Movement]. Unpublished paper.

"Kokushin no dōshi hippararu" [The Comrades from *Black Newspaper* were Detained]. *Jiyū rengō shimbun* [Spontaneous Alliance Newspaper] 91 (June 5, 1934).

Komatsu, Ryūji. *Nihon anakizumu undōshi* [A History of Japanese Anarchist Movement]. Tokyo: Aoki shōten, 1972.

Kondō, Kenji. *Ichi museifu shugisha no kaisō* [Memoirs of an Anarchist]. Tokyo: Heibonsha, 1966.

Krebs, Edward S. *Shifu: Soul of Chinese Anarchism*. Lanham, MD: Rowman & Littlefield, 1998.

———. "The Chinese Anarchist Critique of Bolshevism during the 1920s." In *Roads Not Taken: The Struggle of Opposition Parties in Twentieth-Century China*, edited by Roger B. Jeans, 203–223. Boulder, CO: Westview Press, 1992.

Lang, Olga. *Pa Chin and His Writings: Chinese Youth between the Two Revolutions*. Cambridge, MA: Harvard University Press, 1967.

Lee, Chong-Ha. "Esperanto, Anarchism." In *Esperanto wa na* [Esperanto and Me], vol. 1, edited by Han-guk Esperanto hyeophoe pyeonjipbu, 202–204. Seoul: Han-guk Esperanto hyeophoe, 2011.

Lee, Chong-sik. "Korean Communists and Yenan." *The China Quarterly* 9 (January–March 1962): 182–192.

Lee, Ki-baik. *A New History of Korea*, translated by Edward W. Wagner with Edward J. Shultz. Cambridge, MA: Harvard University Press, 1984.

———, ed. *Han-guksa simin gangjwa* [The Citizens' Forum on Korean History]. special issue on *20 segi han-guk eul umjigin 10 dae sasang* [The Ten Thoughts that Moved Korea in the Twentieth Century] 25 (August 1999).

Lee, Mun Chang. *Haebang gonggan ui anarchist* [Korean Anarchists in the Space after Liberation]. Seoul: Ihaksa, 2008.

———. "Jayu gongdongche undong ui eoje wa oneul—'gungmin munhwa yeon-guso' 50 nyeonsa reul jungsim euro" [Today and Yesterday of the Free Community Movement—Focused on the Fifty Year History of 'the Institute for the Study of National Culture']. In *Gungmin munhwa yeon-guso 50 nyeonsa—jayu gongdongche undong ui baljachwi* [A Fifty-Year History of the Institute for the Study of National Culture: The Footsteps of the Free Community Movement], edited by Gungmin munhwa yeon-guso 50 nyeonsa ganhaeng wiwonhoe, 3–18. Seoul: Gungmin munhwa yeon-guso, 1998.

Li, Da [Yi Dal]. "Jiaqiang zhonghan liangminzu de tuanjie—xiang chongqing gejie jinyiyan" [Enhancing the Unity between Chinese and Korean Peoples—A Suggestion to All Circles in Chongqing]. *Chaoxian yiyongdui* [The Korean Volunteers Unit] 34 (May 15, 1940): 1.

Liu, Shi [Yu Ja-myeong]. "Weichaoxian geming liliang tongyi er douzheng" [The Unification of Ability and the Struggle for the Korean Revolution]." *Chaoxian mizu zhanxian* 4 (May 25, 1938): 14.

Liu Xu [Yu Seo]. "Zhuzhang zuzhi dongya wuzhengfu zhuyizhe datongmeng (jielu)" [Proposing to Organize the Greater Alliance of East Asian Anarchists, (excerpts)]. *Minzhong* [People's Tocsin] 16 (December 15, 1926). Reprinted in *Wuzhengfu zhuyi sixiang ziliao xuan* [Collected Materials on Anarchist Ideas], 2 vols., edited by Ge Maochun, Jiang Jun, and Li Xingzhi, 716–720. Beijing: Beijing daxue chubanshe, 1984.

Liu, Ziming [Yu Ja-meyong]. "Kuang Husheng xiansheng yinxiangji" [On My Impression of Mr. Kuang Husheng]. *Quanzhou Liming xueyuan xinxi* [News on Quanzhou Liming College] 3 (1982): 10–11.
Luo Yuehuan [Na Wolhwan]. "Women de renwu" [Our Tasks]. *Hanguo qingnian* [Korean Youth] 1, no. 1 (July 15, 1940). Reprinted in *Jaryo han-guk dongnip undong* [Materials on Korean Independence Movement], vol. 3, edited by Chu Heonsu, 116–117. Seoul: Yonsei daehakgyo chulpanbu, 1973.
"Minjok jeonseon ui gyeolseong eul chokgu handa" [Urging the Formation of the National Front]. *Namhwa Tongsin* [South China Correspondence] 12 (December 1936).
"Minjok undong ui oryu" [Fallacies in the National Movement]. *Heuksaek sinmun* [Black Newspaper] 26 (February 28, 1934).
Minyou xinxi [News on the Alumni of People's Livelihood Agricultural School] 7 (March 1990).
Mizuno, Naoki. "Tōhō hiappaku minzoku regōkai (1925–1927) ni tsuite" [On the United Society of the Eastern Oppressed Peoples, 1925–1927]. In *Chūkoku kokumin kakumei no kenkyū* [A Study of the National Revolution in China], edited by Hazama Naoki, 309–350. Kyōto: Kyōto daigakko jinbun kagaku kenkyūjo, 1992.
———. "Bengonin Fuse Tatsuji to chōsen" [Lawyer Fuse Tatsuji and Korea]. *Kikan anjenri* [Quarterly Three Thousand *Ri*] 34 (Summer 1983): 28–36.
Mujeongbu juui undongsa pyeonchan wiwonhoe, ed. *Han-guk anarchism undongsa* [A History of Korean Anarchist Movement]. Seoul: Hyeongseol chulpansa, 1989.
"Mujeongbu undong ui hyeonsil seong eul gangjo ham" [To Emphasize the Practical-ness of Anarchist Movement]. *Heuksaek sinmun* [Black Newspaper] 31 (August 29, 1934).
Mukai, Kō. *Yamaga Taiji, hito to sono shōkai* [Yamaga Taiji: The Person and His Life]. Tokyo: Aokahō, 1974.
Na, Wolhwan. "Urideuleun eoteoke han-guk mujangbudaereul geollip halgesinga?" [How Do We Build Korean Armed Forces?]. *Hanguo qingnian* [Korean Youth] 1-2.
"Namhwa hanin cheongnyeon yeonmaeng" [The League of Korean Youth in South China]. Accessed February 7, 2006. http://www.woodang.or.kr/life/youth.htm.
Nammyeong [Shin Chaeho]. "Kropotkin ui jugeum e daehan gamsang" [Reflections on Kropotkin's Death]. *Cheon-go* [Heavenly Drum] 2 (February 1921). Reprinted in *Danjae Shin Chaeho ui Cheon-go* [Shin Chaeho's *Cheon-go* journal], edited and annotated by Choe Gwangsik, 173–178. Seoul: Asia Research Center, Korea University, 2004.
"Nanshi saijū no senjin seinen renmei, senkoku to kōryō hatbyō" [The League of Korean Youth in South China Announced Its Declaration and Platform]. *Jiyū rengō shimbun* [Spontaneous Alliance Newspaper] 47 (May 1, 1930): 1.

Nihon anakizumu undō jinmei jiten hensan iinkai, ed. *Nihon anakizumu undō jinmei jiten* [Biographical Dictionary of Japanese Anarchist Movement]. Tokyo: Poru shuppan, 2004.

Oh, Jang-Whan. *Han-guk anarchism undongsa yeon-gu* [A Study on the History of Korean Anarchist Movement]. Seoul: Gukak jaryowon, 1998.

———. "1920 nyeondae jaeil hanin anarchism undong sogo" [A Brief Study of Korean Anarchist Movement in Japan in the 1920s]. In *Ilje ui joseon chimryak gwa minjok undong* [Imperial Japan's Invasion of Korea and National Movement], edited by Han-guk minjok undongsa yeon-gu hoe, 153–191. Seoul: Gukhak jaryowon, 1998.

———. "Yi Jeonggyu ui mujeongbu juui undong" [Yi Jeonggyu's Anarchist Movement]. *Sahak yeon-gu* [Historical Studies] 49 (1995): 177–220.

Ōsugi, Sakae. *The Autobiography of Ōsugi Sakae*, translated and introduction by Byron K. Marshall. Berkeley: University of California Press, 1992.

"Our Words" [*Warera no go*]. *Namhwa Tongsin* [South China Correspondence] 1 (1936?).

Park, Chan Seung. "Sikminji sigi doil yuhak gwa yuhaksaeng ui minjok undong" [Study-Abroad to Japan and the National Movement of the Study-Abroad Students during the Colonial Period]. In *Asia ui geundaehwa wa daehak ui yeokhal* [Modernization in Asia and the Role of University], edited by Hallym daehakgyo Asia munhwa yeon-guso, 161–212. Chuncheon: Hallym daehakgyo chulpansa, 2000.

———. "Sikminji sigi doil yuhaksaeng gwa geundae jisik ui suyong" [Study-Abroad Students in Japan and Their Reception of Modern Knowledge during the Colonial Period]. In *Jisik byeondong ui sahoesa* [A Social History of Knowledge Transformation], edited by Han-guk sahoe sahak-hoe, 151–187. Seoul: Munhak gwa jiseongsa, 2003.

Pasarov (?). "Mujeongbu juui ja ga bon han-guk dongnip undong" [Korean Independence Movement in the eyes of an Anarchist]. *Talhwan* [The Conquest], supplementary to no. 1 (June 15, 1928).

Personal communication with Mr. Kim Young-Chun on March 5 and 31, 2014.

Personal communication with Mr. Kim Young-Chan, Mr. Sin Nage, and Ms. Park Jeong-Hee on June 17, 2015.

Personal communication with Mr. Lee Mun Chang on December 10, 2012.

Personal communication with Mr. Song Heonjo on December 11, 2011.

Qin, Wangshan. "Annaqi zhuyizhe zai fujian de yixie huodong" [Various Activities of Anarchists in Fujian]. *Fujian wenshi ziliao* [Literary and Historical Materials of Fujian] 24 (1990): 180–202.

———. "Chaoxian he riben annaqi zhuyizhe zai quan binan yinqi de shijian" [An Incident Caused by Korean and Japanese Anarchists Who Took Refuge in Quanzhou]. *Fujian wenshi ziliao* [Literary and Historical Materials of Fujian] 24 (1990): 203–208.

Quanzhou liming xueyuan xinxi [News on Quanzhou Liming College] 1 (1982) and 3 (1982).

Raynolds, Douglas R. *China, 1898–1912: The Xinzheng Revolution and Japan.* Cambridge, MA: Council on East Asian Studies, Harvard University, 1993.

Rekishigaku kenkyūkai, ed. *Ajia gendaishi 1: teikokushugi no jidai* [A Modern History of Asia 1: The Period of Imperialism]. Tokyo: Aoi shōten, 1983.

"Rekishi kyōkasho zainichi korian no rekishi" sakusei iinkai, ed. *Rekishi kyōkasho zainichi korian no rekishi* [History Textbook, A History of Koreans in Japan]. Tokyo: Meishi shōten, 2013.

Retsusei [Bak Yeol]. "Chokusetsu kotō no hyōhon" [An Example of Direct Actions]. *Kokutō* [Black Wave] 1 (1923). Reprinted in *Nani ga watashi o kō sasetaka* [What Has Made Me Run Like This?], Kaneko Fumiko, 533. Tokyo: Kokushoku senzensha, 1971.

Robinson, Michael Edson. *Cultural Nationalism in Colonial Korea, 1920–1925.* Seattle: University of Washington Press, 1988.

Sakai, Hirobumi. "Yamaga Taiji to chūgoku—'Tasogare nikki' ni miru nitchū anakisuto no kōryū" [Yamaga Taiji and China: The Interactions between Japanese and Chinese Anarchists that Are Described in *A Diary at the Dusk*]. *Mao to win: gindai chūgoku no shisō to bungaku* [Cat Head Hawk: Thoughts and Literature of Modern China] 2 (December 1983): 30–49.

Scalapino, Robert A. *The Japanese Communist Movement, 1920–1966.* Berkeley: University of California Press, 1967.

———. "Prelude to Marxism: The Chinese Student Movement in Japan, 1900–1910." In *Approaches to Modern Chinese History*, edited by Albert Feuerwerker, Rhodes Murphy and Mary C. Wright, 190–215. Berkeley, CA: University of California Press, 1967.

"Sengen" [Declaration]. *Kokutō* [Black Wave] 1 (1923). Reprinted in *Nani ga watashi o kō saseta ka* [What Has Made Me Run Like This?], Kaneko Fumiko, 533. Tokyo: Kokushoku senzensha, 1971.

Shakai mondai shiryo kenkyūkai, ed. *Shakai mondai shiryo sōsho* [Collected Materials on Social Problems], vol. 1. Tokyo: Tōyō bunkasha, 1977.

Shen, Keqiu. "Fuchen zai xiaoyan miman de shidai langchaozhong—Ji Liu Shuren de yisheng" [Drifting Along in the Tidal Wave of the Times When Smoke of Gunpowder Filled the Air—Remembering Liu Shuren's Life]. *Huainianji* [Collection of Cherishing Memories] 5 (February 1990): 30–41.

———. "Huainian Liu Xu xiong" [Cherishing the Memory of Yu Seo]. *Huainianji* [Collection of Cherishing Memories] 2 (July 1987): 55–57.

Shen, Meijuan. "'Ansha dawang' Wang Yachu" [Wang Yachu, The Great Master of Assassination]. *Zhuanji wenxue* [Biographical Literature] 56, no. 4 (April 1990): 120–132.

Shen, Rongche [Shen Keqiu]. "Ershi liuge chunqiu—Ji Shen Ruqiu de duanzan yisheng" [Twenty-Six Years—Remembering Shen Ruqiu's Short Life]. *Huainianji* [Collection of Cherishing Memories] 5 (February 1990): 60–68.

Shin, Chaeho. "Nanggaek ui sinnyeon manpil" [A Miscellaneous Writing of a Man of Nonsense and Emptiness on the Occasion of a New Year]. In *Shin Chaeho*, edited by An Byeongjik, 175–184. Seoul: Han-gilsa, 1979.

Shin, Yongha. "Shin Chaeho ui mujeongbu juui dongnip sasang" [Shin Chaeho's Anarchist Ideas of Independence)." In *Shin Chaeho*, edited by Kang Man-gil, 78–147. Seoul: Goryeo daehakgyo chulpanbu, 1972.

Sikchun [Yi Chunsik]. "Seizon wu kakuritsuseyo!" [Establish the Existence!] *Chigasei* [The Voice of Self] May Issue (April 20, 1926): 1. Reprinted in *Zainichi chōsenjin undō kankei kikanshi (Kahozen)* [Publications Associated with the Movements of Koreans in Japan (Pre-Liberation)], Chōsen mondai shiryo sōsho [Series on the Materials on Korean Problems], vol. 5, edited by Bak Kyeongsik, 205. Tokyo: Ajia mondai kenkyūjo, 1983.

Sim, Yongcheol [Shen Keqiu]. "Na ui hoego" [My Memoir]. In *20 segi jungguk joseon jok yeoksa jaryojip* [Historical Materials on the Koreans in China in the Twentieth Century], Sim Yonghae and Sim Yongcheol, 77–301 (in Korean), 375–511 (in Chinese). Seoul: Jungguk joseon minjok munhwa yesul chulpansa, 2002.

Sim, Yonghae and Sim Yongcheol. *20 segi jungguk joseon jok yeoksa jaryojip* [Historical Materials on the Koreans in China in the Twentieth Century]. Seoul: Jungguk joseon minjok munhwa yesul chulpansa, 2002.

"Sōkanni saishite" [On the Occasion of Launching the Journal]. *Kokutō* [Black Wave] 1 (1923). Reprinted in *Nani ga watashi o kō saseta ka* [What Has Made Me Run Like This?], Kaneko Fumiko, 533. Tokyo: Kokushoku senzensha, 1971.

Son, Useong. "Gungmin susan undong ui uiui" [The Meanings of the National Movement to Receive and Produce]. *Gungmin munhwa hoebo* [The Bulletin of National Culture] 1 (May 1966). Reprinted in *Gungmin munhwa yeon-guso osipnyeon sa* [A Fifty-Year History of the Institute for the Study of National Culture], edited by Gungmin munhwa yeon-guso osipnyeon sa pyeonchan wiwonhoe, 88–90. Seoul: Gungmin munhwa yeon-guso, 1998.

Song, Seha. "Chōsenjin ni yoru anakizumu undō no kako to genzai" [The Past and Present of Anarchist Movements by Koreans]. *Anakizumu* [Anarchism] 3 (May 1974): 14–16.

Stanley, Thomas A. *Ōsugi Sakae, Anarchist in Taisho Japan: The Creativity of the Ego*. Cambridge, MA: Council on East Asian Studies, Harvard University, 1982.

Sun, Zhongshan. "Jianguo fanglue" [A General Plan for Nation-Building]." In *Sun Zhongshan xuanji* [Selected Works of Sun Zhongshan], 104–419. Hong Kong: Zhonghua shuju xianggang fenju, 1956.

"Susan undong chujin ui jeonmang" [A Prospect for the National Movement to Receive and Produce] (July 1968)." In *Gungmin munhwa yeon-guso osipnyeon sa* [A Fifty-Year History of the Research Institute for National Culture], edited by Gungmin munhwa yeon-guso osipnyeon sa pyeonchan wiwonhoe, 109–110. Seoul: Gungmin munhwa yeon-guso, 1998.

Suzuki, Yasuyuki. *Nihon museifushugi undōshi* [A History of Japanese Anarchist Movement]. Tokyo: Kokushoku sensensha, 1932, reprinted 1990.

"Taiheiyō engan no rōdōsha ni yoru tōhō museifu shugisha renmei" [The Eastern Anarchist League by the Workers on the Rims of the Pacific]. *Jiyū rengō* [Spontaneous Alliance] 32 (February 1, 1929): 3.

Talhwan [The Conquest] 1 and supplement issues (June 1 and 15, 1928). Reprinted by Gungmin munhwa yeon-guso gojeon ganhaeng hoe [Committee of the Institute for the Study of National Culture to Publish Classical Works]. Seoul: Gungmin munhwa yeon-guso gojeon ganhaeng hoe, 1984.

Tamagawa, Nobuaki. *Chūgoku anakizumu no kage* [Shades of Chinese Anarchism]. Tokyo: Sanichi shohō, 1974.

Tongsin [Correspondence] 2 (1973) and 4 (1973).

Toppa [Kim Taeyeop]. "Chōsen no undō" [The Movement in Korea]. *Chigasei* [The Voice of Self] Inaugural issue (March 20, 1926): 2, 4. Reprinted in *Zainichi chōsenjin undō kankei kikanshi (Kahozen)* [Publications Associated with the Movements of Koreans in Japan (Pre-Liberation)], Chōsen mondai shiryo sōsho [Series on the Materials on Korean Problems] vol. 5, edited by Bak Kyeongsik, 202, 204. Tokyo: Ajia mondai kenkyūjo, 1983.

———. "Gūzō yori ningen e" [From Idol to Humanity]. *Chigasei* [The Voice of Self] May Issue (April 20, 1926): 1–2. Reprinted in *Zainichi chōsenjin undō kankei kikanshi (Kahozen)* [Publications Associated with the Movements of Koreans in Japan (Pre-Liberation)], Chōsen mondai shiryo sōsho [Series on the Materials on Korean Problems] vol. 5, edited by Bak Kyeongsik, 205–206. Tokyo: Ajia mondai kenkyūjo, 1983.

Ugwan [Yi Jeonggyu]. "Talhwan ui je ilseong" [The First Voice of *The Conquest*). *Talhwan* [The Conquest] supplementary to no. 1 (June 15, 1928).

Wakabayashi, Masahiro. *Taiwan kōnichi undōshi kenkyū* [A Study of Taiwan's Anti-Japanese Movement History]. Tokyo: Kenbun shuppan, 1983, 2010 rev. and extended ed., 2nd printing.

Wang, Shaoqiu. *Jindai zhongri wenhua jiaoliushi* [A Modern History of Sino-Japanese Cultural Exchanges]. Beijing: Zhonghua shuju, 1992.

Wayles, Nym and Kim San. *Song of Ariran: A Korean Communist in the Chinese Revolution*. San Francisco: Ramparts Press, 1941.

Woodang [Yi Hoeyeong] Memorial Hall, "Namhwa hanin cheongnyeon yeonmaeng" [The League of Korean Youth in South China]. Accessed February 7, 2006. http://www.woodang.or.kr/life/youth.htm.

Wuthnow, Robert. *Communities of Discourse: Ideology, and Social Structure in the Reformation, the Enlightenment, and European Socialism*. Cambridge, MA: Harvard University Press, 1989.

Xie, Zhen. "Shenqie huainian Liu Zuiming xiansheng" [Deeply Cherishing the Memory of Mr.Yu Ja-myeong]. *Huainianji* [Collection of Cherishing Memories], edited by Jiang Kang, n.p., 1986: 57–62.

Xu, Shanguang and Liu Jianping. *Zhongguo wuzhengfu zhuyi shi* [A History of Anarchism in China], n.p.: Hubei renmin chubanshe, 1989.

Xu, Xiaoqun. "Cosmopolitanism, Nationalism, and Transnational Networks: The *Chenbao Fujuan*, 1921–1928." *The China Review* 4, no. 1 (Spring 2004): 145–173.

Yang, Bichuan. *Riju shidai Taiwan fankang shi* [A History of Taiwanese Resistance against Japanese Occupation]. Taipei: Daoxiang chubanshe, 1988.

Yang, Sanggi. "Shinsaiki igo no zainichi chōsenjin anakizumu undō no henrin" [A Glimpse of Anarchist Movement by Koreans in Japan after the Kantō Earthquake]. *Anakizumu* [Anarchism] 25 (June 1984): 20–27.Yi, Deok-il. *Anarchist Yi Hoeyeong gwa jeolmeun geudeul* [Yi Hoeyeong and Those Who Were Young]. Seoul: Ungjin datkeom, 2001.

Yi, Dongwon. "Anarchism ui seongji Anui!" [Anui: A Holly Place of Anarchism!], *Hamyang sinmun* [Hamyang County Newspaper] (April 6, 2015). Accessed June 24, 2015. http://hy.newsk.net/?doc=news/print_news.htm&ns_id=5383.

Yi, Eulgyu. *Siya Kim Jongjin seonsaeng jeon* [A Biography of Mr. Kim Jongjin]. Seoul: Eulyu munhwasa, 1963.

Yi Gangha. "Warera no sakebi" [Our Outcries]. *Kokutō* [Black Wave] 1 (1923). Reprinted in *Nani ga watashi o kō sasetaka* [What Has Made Me Run Like This?], Kaneko Fumiko, 533. Tokyo: Kokushoku senzensha, 1971.

Yi, Gyeongmin. "Jo Bong-am no shisō to kōdō" [Thoughts and Actions of Jo Bong-am]. *Chōsen minzoku undōshi kenkyū* [Studies on the History of Korean National Movement] 1 (April 1991): 89–118.

Yi, Honggeun. "Gaihō undō to minzoku undō" [Liberation Movement and National Movement]. *Jiyū rengō shimbun* [Spontaneous Alliance Newspaper] 40 (October 1, 1929).

———. "Yeoksa jeok jin-gun e ui dongcham" [Joining the Historical March Forward]. *Gungmin munhwa hoebo* [The Bulletin of National Culture] 11 (April 1983): 9–13.

Yi, Horyong. "Bak Yeol ui mujeongbu juui sasang gwa dongnip gukka geonseol gusang" [Bak Yeol's Anarchism and His Vision of an Independent Country]. *Han-guk hakbo* [Journal of Korean Studies] 87 (Summer 1997): 153–181.

———. *Han-guk ui anarchism–sasang pyeon* [Anarchism in Korea–Its Ideas]. Seoul: Jisik san-eop sa, 2001.

———. "Yi Hoeyeong ui anarchist hwaldong" [The Anarchist Activities of Yi Hoeyeong]. *Han-guk dongnip undonngsa yeon-gu* [Studies on the History of Korean Independence Movement] 33 (2009): 185–225.

———. "Ryu Ja-myeong ui anarchist hwaldong" [Anarchist Activities of Yu Ja-myeong]. *Yeoksa wa hyeonsil* [History and Reality] 53 (September 2004): 221–253.

———. "Ilje gangjeom gi gungnae anarchist deul ui gongsan juui e daehan bipanjeok hwaldong" [The Activities of Criticisms against Communists by Anarchists in Korea during the Japanese Occupation Period]. *Yeoksa wa hyeonsil* [History and Reality] 59 (March 2006): 257–287.

———. "Iljae gangjeom gi jae jungguk han-guk in anarchist deul ui minjok haebang undong terror hwanldong eul jungsim euro" [The National Liberation Movement by Korean Anarchists in China during the Japanese Colonial Period: Their Terrorist Activities]. *Han-guk minjok undongsa yeon-gu* [Studies on Korean National Movements] 35 (June 2003): 282–283.

Yi, Ganghun. *Yi Ganghun yeoksa jeung-eon rok* [Historical Records of Yi Ganghun's Testimony]. Seoul: Inmul yeon-guso, 1994.

Yi, Jeonggyu. *Sahoe mihak euro seoui mujeongbu juui* [Anarchism as Social Aesthetic]. Unpublished manuscript.

———. *Ugwan munjon* [Collected Works of Yi Jeonggyu]. Seoul: Samhwa insoe, 1974. [Abbreviated below as *UM*].

———. "Jaseo" [Preface] (May 7, 1974). In *UM*, 11–15.

———. "Udang Yi Hoeyeong seonsaeng yakjeon" [A Brief Biography of Mr. Yi Hoeyeong]. In *UM*, 23–74.

———. "Jungguk bokgeon seong nongmin jawi undong gwa han-guk dongjideul ui hwalyak [The Self-Defensive Movement of the Peasants in China's Fujian Province and the Activities of Korean Comrades]. In *UM*, 128–154.

———. "Gungmin susan undong chujin e gwanhan gaehwang" [An Outline of the National Movement to Receive and Produce]. In *UM*, 374–377.

———. "Nongchon buheung gwa yeongse nong munje" [The Revival of Rural Villages and the Problems of Small-Income Farmers]. In *UM*, 367–370.

———. "Nongchon jajuhwa ui munjejeom" [Problems in Making Rural Villages Autonomous] (November 17, 1971). In *UM*, 380–385.

———. "Minju sahoe dang ui jojik wolli" [The Organizational Principles of the Democratic Socialist Party]. In *UM*, 226–230.

———. "Minju sahoe dang ui noseon" [The Ideological Line of the Democratic Socialist Party]. In *UM*, 231–254.

———. "Sadan beobin gungmin munhwa yeon-guso seollip chwiji seo" [The Mission Statement of the Institute for the Study of National Culture]. In *UM*, 378–379.

———. "Jayu geonseolja yeonmaeng seoneon mit gangnyeong" [The Declaration and Platform of the Free Society Builders Federation]. In *UM*, 173–175.

———. "Daehak gyoyuk gwa geu sa-myeong" [College Education and Its Mission]." In *UM*, 306–308.

———. "Sungkyunkwan daehakgyo chongjang chwiimsa" [Inaugural Address as the Sungkyunkwan University's President]. In *UM*, 295–296.

———. "Joseon nongchon jachi yeonmaeng seoneon gangnyong haeseol" [An Explanation of the Platform and Declaration of the Federation for Rural Autonomy]. In *UM*, 176–213.

———. "Silcheon haneun saram doera" [Become a Man of Words] (April 1956), In *UM*, 354–358.

———. "Minjok jeok banseong" [National Reflections]. In *UM*, 259–262.

———. "Hoego wa jeonmang" [Retrospect and Prospect). In *UM*, 364–366.

———. "Gaehoesa" [Opening Remarks] (October 1960). In *UM*, 359–360.

———. "Han-guk sahoe juui undong ui jeonmang" [A Prospect for Korean Socialist Movement]. In *UM*, 263–271.

———. "Han-guk nodongja jachi yeonmaeng hoego" [Recollection of the Federation for Workers Autonomy]. In *UM*, 214–221.

———. "Pyehae jaegeon gwa sinsaenghwal undong" [The Reconstruction from the Ruins and the New Life Movement]. In *UM*, 279–286.

———. "Jeokgeuk jeok geungjeongjeok in myeon euro jeontong eul gyeseung baljeon sikija—je 11 hoe haksaeng ui nal gi-nyeomsa" [Let's Inherit and Develop Traditions into an Active and Positive One—A Congratulatory Address on the Occasion of the 11th Anniversary of the Students' Day]. In *UM*, 301–302.

———. "Nongchon undong jidoja gandamhoe gyehoek insa malsseum" [A Greeting Address and the Plan for the Preliminary Meeting of the Rural Movement Leaders]. *Tongsin* [Correspondence] 1 (October 1971): 3–4.

———. "Insa ui malsseum" [Welcoming Words] (March 1972). *Tongsin* [Correspondence] 2 (1973): 1.

———. "Gyeokryeo sa [Words of Encouragement]. *Tongsin* [Correspondence] 4 (1973): 5–7.

———. "Chocheong ui malsseum" [Inviting Words] (July 2, 1968). In *Gungmin munhwa yeon-guso osipnyeon sa* [A Fifty-Year History of the Research Institute for National Culture]. Gungmin munhwa yeon-guso osipnyeon sa pyeonchan wiwonhoe, 110–112. Seoul: Gungmin munhwa yeon-guso, 1998.

Yu, Fuzuo. "Ji pingmin zhongxue" [Remembering Common People's Middle School]. *Huainianji* [Collection of Cherishing Memories] 4 (October 1988): 42–44.

Yu, Ja-myeong. *Yu Ja-myeong sugi: han hyeokmyeong ja ui hoeeok rok* [Yu Ja-myeong's Memoirs: A Revolutionary's Memoirs]. Cheon-an: Dongnip gi-nyeom gwan han-guk dongnip undongsa yeon-guso, 1999.

Yuk Honggeun. "Iwayuru dasū no shōtai" [The Identity of the so-called Majority]. *Gen shakai* [Contemporary Society] 4.

Yun, Inhoe. "'Gungmin munhwa yeon-guso' wa nongchon undong" [The Institute for the Study of National Culture and the Rural Movement]. In *Gungmin munhwa yeon-guso osipnyeon sa* [A Fifty-Year History of the Research Institute for National Culture], edited by Gungmin munhwa yeon-guso osipnyeon sa pyeonchan wiwonhoe, 446–448. Seoul: Gungmin munhwa yeon-guso, 1998.

Yungong. "Guangming yundong de qiantu" [The Future of the Light Movement]. *Guangming* [The Light] 1 (December 1, 1921).

Zhang, Yunhou, Yin Xuyi, Hong Qingxiang, and Wang Yunkai, eds. *Wusi shiqi de shetuan* [Societies of the May Fourth Period] 4. Beijing: Sanlian shudian, 1979.

Zarrow, Peter. *Anarchism and Chinese Political Culture*. New York: Columbia University Press, 1990.

Zheng, Peigang. "Wuzhengfu zhuyi zaizhongguo de ruogan shishi" [Some Facts about the Anarchist Movement in China]. In *Wuzhengfu zhuyi sixiang ziliao xuan* [Collected Materials on Anarchist Ideas], 2 vols., edited by Ge Maochun, Jiang Jun, and Li Xingzhi, 939–971. Beijing: Beijing daxue chubanshe, 1984.

Zhongguo dier lishi dang'anguan, ed. *Zhongguo wuzhengfu zhuyi he zhongguo shehuidang* [Chinese Anarchism and the Chinese Socialist Party], n.p.: Jiangsu renmin chubanshe, 1981.

Zhonggong zhongyang makesi engesi leining sidalin zhezuo fanyiju yanjiushi, ed. *Wusi shiqi qikan jieshao* [Introduction to Periodicals during the May Fourth Period] 3, part 1. Shenyang: Sanlian shudian, 1979.

Ziming [Yu Ja-myeong]. "Chaoxian mizu zhanxian lianmeng jiecheng jingguo" [On the Establishment of the League for the Korean National Front]. *Chaoxian minzu zhanxian* [The Korean National Front] Inaugural issue (April 10, 1938): 3–5.

———. "Chuangkanci" [Inaugural Editorial]. *Chaoxian minzu zhanxian* [The Korean National Front] Inaugural issue (April 10, 1938): 1.

———. "Zhongguo guomindang dahui de lishi de yiyi" [The Historical Meaning of the Guomindang's Convention]. *Chaoxian minzu zhanxian* [The Korean National Front] 2 (April 25, 1938): 3.

———. "Huanying shijie xuelian daibiaotuan" [Welcoming the Representatives of the World Students Union]. *Chaoxian minzu zhanxian* [The Korean National Front] 4 (May 25, 1938): 2.

Index

Akagawa Haruki, 35, 45
Alliance of the Societies of Korean Propertyless People (Chōsen muchansha shakai dōmei, ASKPP), 76, 79, 83
An Bong-yeon, 107
An Gonggeun, 130
An Jaehong, 58
An Usaeng, 34
An Yeonggeun, 107
Anarchism: and Bolshevism, 31, 32; and globalization, 217–18; decline of, 112; Eurocentric understanding of, 2–3, 211; individualist, 68, 70; -oriented organizations, 75, 82, 83, 89, 96, 102, 103; -oriented journals, 20–21, 35, 62; tension with nationalism, 4–6. *See also* Korean anarchism; Korean anarchists; Kropotkin, Peter; Mutual aid; Nihilism
Anarchist Communist Party (Japan), 128
Anarcho-syndicalism, 13, 20, 41, 73, 87–88, 115
Anju heuk-u hoe (Anju Black Friends Society), 107
Ariyoshi Akira, 72, 126
Asianism, 57–59, 71, 234n7. *See also* Bak Yeol; Korean anarchists

Ba Jin, 29–31, 229n63; and "A Story of Hair," 34; and Yu Ja-myeong, 230n70
Baek Jeonggi, 31, 65, 126; and *Labor Newspaper*, 127
Bak Giseong, 55, 64, 142, 148, 151; and League (or Federation) of Free Youth, 66
Bak Seokhong, 81, 161–62
Bak Seungbyeong, 27
Bak Seung-han, 201
Bak Yeol, 13, 63, 67–72 *passim*, 79, 157; and Bloody Righteous Group and Iron Righteous Group and Righteous Deed Group, 68; and Japanese anarchists, 67–68; and nihilism, 68, 225n40; criticized Bolshevism, 72–73; *On a New Korean Revolution*, 250n1; on Asianism, 71; "treason incident" and influence in colonial Korea, 97–99, 104, 112. *See also* Kaneko Fumiko
Bakunin, 36
Bang Hansang, 98, 167
Black Flag League (Heiqi lianmeng). *See* Heukgi yeonmaeng
Black Friends Society (Kokutomo kai). *See* Heuk-u hoe
Black Labor Society (Kokurō kai). *See* Heungno hoe

Black Movement Society (Heuksaek undongsa; Kokushoku undōsha), 73–74; and *Black Friends*, 73, 74; and *Free Society*, 74
Black Wave Society (Kokutō kai). See Heukdo hoe
Black Youth Free Alliance, 119; and *Free Alliance-ism*, 119
Black Youth League (*Kokuren*), 72, 74, 238n67
Bonneung-a yeonmaeng (League of the Men of Instincts), 102–3
Bu Namhui, 75
Bukseong hoe (North Star Society; Hoksei kai), 68, 100

Cai Xiaoqian, 48
Cai Yuanpei, 22, 24, 29, 53, 167
Chen Fanyu, 48
Chen Guangguo, 35
Chen Kongshan, 25
Chen Mingshu, 48
Chen Weiqi (Chen Weiguang), 25, 46
Cheolsan Heuk-u hoe (Cheolsan Black Friends Society), 107
Chiang Kai-shek, 30, 44, 48, 49, 117, 128, 137
Chinese Communist Party (CCP), 12, 34, 45, 54, 85, 118, 137, 142, 146, 150, 154, 172, 227n28, 248n107, 249n115. See also Communism
Choe Gapryong, 64–65, 81, 101, 104–5, 109, 203, 242n50; and anarchist syndicalism, 113; and Convention of All Korea Black Movement Activists, 107–8; and "destitute and humble class," 106
Choe Gyujong, 72–73
Choe Haecheong, 173–74
Choe Jungheon, 65
Choe Seokyeong, 130
Choe Seonmyeong, 76–77, 79

Choe Seungman, 62
Common People's Middle School (Pingmin zhongxue), 44, 47–48, 233n134
Communism, 23, 28, 32, 42, 46, 51, 186, 221n1, 252n50; anarchism as a "cousin" of, 16, 207; anarchist critique and rejection of, 72, 159, 169, 171, 173, 178–79, 182–83, 207; as anarchist new enemy, 187; compared with democratic socialism, 176; in China, 12; Korean, 1; Soviet style and Leninist, 26; Vietnamese, 8
Communist International (Comintern), 34, 142
Compulsory power, 41, 43, 123, 125, 134, 162, 182

Dancheon heuk-u hoe (Black Friends Society in Dancheon), 103
Dawn Advanced Middle School (Liming gaoji zhongxue), 23, 44, 47–48, 233n135
Democratic socialism. See *Minju sahoe juui*
Democratic Socialist Party (DSP). *See* Minju sahoe dang
Deng Mengxian, 34; and Huaguang Hospital, 38, 228n48, 230n73
"destitute (poor) and humble class," 103, 112, 116, 213. See also Yi Hyang
Direct action, 96, 246n68; Bak Yeol and against communism and capitalism, 70, 72–73; and the masses, 43, 62, 68, 102, 119; terrorism and, 3, 22
Dirlik, Arif, 8, 9, 20, 224n32
Dong-a Ilbo (*East Asia Daily*), 95
Dongheung (Tōkō) Korean Labor League (or Labor Alliance [of Koreans] or Labor Union), 65, 108, 120, 88, 241n19

Dongnip nonong dang, 170–71, 203, 257n141; and the Federation Anarchist Korea, 179, 256n139; and "Yu Rim Line," 215; goals and platform of, 167–68. *See also* Yu Rim

Eastern Anarchist Federation (EAF), 34, 38–40, 47, 54, 101; and *The East*, 39
Em, Henry, 5, 134, 223n17
Eom Hyeongsun, 50
Equality Society (Pingshe), 35; and *Equality*, 35–36
Eroshenko, Vasilij, 26–27 *passim*, 33, 53, 228n33
Esperanto, 30, 38, 48, 87, 91, 240n119; *A Shortcut to Esperanto*, 95; Association for the Study of World Language (China), 25; Beijing Special School for, 25; Korean Association of, 95; *Lectures on Proletarian Esperanto*, 95

Fabianism, 79, 90
Fan Benliang, 26, 27, 31, 33, 227n32
Federation of Black Friends and Free Youth (Kokutomo jiyū seinen renmei), 120
Federation of Free Youth (Jiyū seinen renmei), 119; and *Free Youth*, 74, 119
Fraternal Society of Koreans in Osaka (Ōsaka chōsenjin shinbokkai), 75
Fraternal Society of Korean Students in Tokyo, Japan (Zai nihon tōkyō chōsen ryūgaksei gakuyū kai), 62; and *Hak ji gwang*, 62
Free Commune Society (Jiyū komyūn shakai), 119; and *Free Commune*, 119
Free People's Federation (Jiyūjin renmei), 61

Fuse Tatsuji, 100, 242n32

General Federation of Korean Anarchists (GFKA). *See* Joseon mujeongbu juuija chong yeonmaeng
Go Sunheum, 79, 97; and different practice of anarchism, 86; and Jeju Island and women, 76; and livelihood struggle, 212; and organizations for workers, 77
Goscha, Christopher E., 8
Great unity (*datong*; *daedong*), 4, 30
Gungmin munhwa yeon-guso (Institute for the Study of National Culture, ISNC), 184, 189–93 *passim*; and nationalist intention, 198; and Susan undong and rural movement, 196, 200–2. *See also* Lee Mun Chang; Yi Jeonggyu
Guomindang (GMD), 34, 36, 37, 40, 44, 45–46 *passim*, 48–49, 53–54, 137, 146, 154; anarchists in, 22, 39, 45, 53, 215, 233n126; and Korean anarchists, 149–51, 154, 225; Laoda and, 38
Gwanseo Heuk-u hoe (Gwanseo Black Friends Society), 64, 105, 107–8; and its first name, 105. *See also* Joseon gongsan mujeongbu juuija yeonmaeng

Hamheung jayu so-nyeon hoe (Free Youth Society in Hamheung), 103
Hamheung jeongjin cheongnyeon hoe (Hamheung Society of the Youth Moving Forward), 103
Han Gukdong, 128
Han Hayeon, 119, 174
Han Hyeonsang, 72, 73
Han Won-yeol, 64
Han Yeongbok, 27

Han-guk cheongnyeon jeonji gongjakdae (Operation Unit of Korean Youth at Warfront OUKYW), 66, 147, 151–52 passim, 154, 250n119; and *Korean Youth*, 152

Han-guk gwangbok gun (Korean Restoration Army), 151–52

Han-guk jaju in yeonmaeng (Federation Anarchist Korea, FAK), 202–4

Han-guk nochong (Federation of Korean Trade Union), 256n141

Hang-il guguk yeonmaeng (League of Resisting Japan and Saving the Nation), 65, 135–36; and *Jayu*, 136

Hanjok chong yeonhaphoe (United Society of All Korean People, USAKP,), 23, 50

Hanjung hapdong yugyeokdae (Korean-Chinese Joint Guerilla Unit, KCJGU), 147, 153–54

Hasegawa Ichimatsu, 75

Hatta Shūzō, 71–72, 74, 88, 132, 199

Heo Yeolchu, 48, 229n63

Heukdo hoe, 63, 68–69, 73, 97, 100; and *Kokutō*, 67, 69–71. See also Bak Yeol; Kaneko Fumiko

Heukgi yeonmaeng: and *Eastern Miscellaneous*, 29; in Beijing, 29; in Seoul and Chungju, 97–99

Heuksaek cheongnyeon dongmaeng (Beijing Branch of the Black Youth Alliance), 29

Heuksaek gongpodan (Black Terror Party, BTP), 65, 124, 126, 135, 246n66. See also Hang-il guguk yeonmaeng; Seogan dan; Namhwa hanin cheongnyeon yeonmaeng

Heuksaek jeonseon sa (Black Front Society), 105

Heuksaek sinmun (Black Newspaper), 118, 120–25, 127–28, 155, 213–14, 244n12

Heuk-u hoe, 64, 99; and *Mass Movement*, 71; and *Recalcitrant Koreans*, 69, 71 passim, 238n62; and *The Contemporary Society*, 69, 72–73. See also Bak Yeol

Heungno hoe: in Seoul, 70, 97; in Tokyo, 68, 71

Hirano Shōken, 72

Ho Chih Minh, 31

Hong Hyeong-ui, 119

Hong Jin-u, 97

Hong Jin-yu, 72

Hong Yeong-u, 66; and *Free Youth*, 74; and League (or Federation) of Free Youth, 119

Horiuchi Minoru, 1, 84, 92, 106, 115, 130, 135

Hua Lin, 30

Icheon jayuhoe (Icheon Free Society), 102

Im Bongsun, 66

Im Kyeongseok, 59

Independence Workers and Peasants Party (IWPP). See Dongnip nonong dang

Irie Ichirō, 119

Ishikawa Sanshirō, 38, 88, 231n91

Iwasa Sakutarō: and "Greater Alliance of East Asian Anarchists," 46–47; and Korean anarchists, 67–68, 71–72, 74, 87, 240n119; and Laoda 38; in Quanzhou, 45–47

Jae jungguk joseon mujeongbu juuija yeonmaeng, 31–33

Jae jungguk mujeongbu gongsan juuija yeonmaeng, 40 passim, 123; and *Talhwan*, 40–43 passim, 54, 228n32

Jaeman joseon mujeongbu juuija yeonmaeng, 49–52
Jang Dosin, 130
Jang Sangjung, 73; and *Debate on Freedom*, 119; and *Movement for Mutual Aid*, 119
Jang Sumin, 48
Jayu sahoe geonseolja yeonmaeng (Free Society Builders Federation, FSBF). *See* Yi Jeonggyu
Jeong Chanjin, 66
Jeong Cheol, 107
Jeong Haeri, 130
Jeong Hwaam, 31, 35, 46, 126, 130, 142, 148, 203, 223n13, 229n63, 246n66, 257n3; about Wang Yachu, 228n48; and armed struggle, 147, 153; and Eroshenko, 26; and Korean understanding of anarchism, 225n44; and Lida College, 37–38; on capitalism and independence, 4, 29; on converting to anarchism, 28–29; on democratic socialism, 173–74
Jeong Hyegyeong, 83
Jeong Taeseong, 79
Jeong Taesin, 62, 75
Jeong-ui gongbo (*Justice Newspaper*), 31–32, 40. *See also* Yi Hoeyeong
Jeon-guk anarchist daehoe (National Convention of Korean Anarchists), 161–66
Jeon-guk nongchon jidoja hyeopuihoe (Council of the National Leaders for Rural Movement), 195, 200, 202. *See also* Rural problem; Yi Jeonggyu
Jin Yan, 154
Jing Meijiu, 30
Jin-geon Center for Receipt and Production, 197, 200. *See also* Susan undong; Yi Jeonggyu
Jin-u yeonmaeng (True Friends League), 98–100

Jo Bong-am, 94, 171, 173, 188; radicalized in Tokyo, 63; and Democratic Socialist Party, 179
Jo Jungbok, 100, 111
Jo Sehyun, 43
Joseon gongsan mujeongbu juuija yeonmaeng, 107, 109–10 *passim*, 161, 166, 216, 242n50, 243n53
Joseon hyeokmyeongja yeonmaeng (League of Korean Revolutionaries, LKR), 141–42, 147
Joseon minjok haebang undong yeonmaeng (Alliance for Korean National Liberation Movement), 142
Joseon minjok hyeokmyeong dang (Korean National Revolutionary Party, KNRP), 142, 147, 150
Joseon minjok jeonseon yeonmaeng, 139–52 *passim*, 155; and Alliance of Korean Independence Movement Activists, 141; and *The Korean National Front*, 142, 143, 145, 149. *See also* National Front; Na Wolhwan; Yi Hayu; Yu Ja-myeong
Joseon mujeongbu juuija chong yeonmaeng, 161
Joseon nodong gongje hoe (Association for Labor and Mutual Relief in Korea), 76, 96; and *Mutual Relief*, 97
Joseon Uiyongdae, 143, 145, 147–52 *passim*; and *Korean Volunteers Unit*, 150; and *Korean Volunteers Unit's Correspondence*, 150; North China Branch Unit in Yan'an, 150, 152
Joseon Uiyonggun (Korean Volunteers Army, KVA), 150

Kaneko Fumiko, 67, 69, 72, 79, 98, 104, 238n57; and nihilism, 71. *See also* Bak Yeol

Karl, Rebecca E., 8
Kim Gu (Kim Koo), 142, 147, 151
Kim Gwangju, 34, 129
Kim Gyuseon, 48
Kim Hansu, 107
Kim Hyeong-yun, 100, 111
Kim Il Sung, 157, 122n1, 248n90
Kim Jeonggeun, 98, 99
Kim Jongjin, 23, 32, 49–51
Kim Junghan, 72, 97
Kim Jwajin, 52; and Sinminbu, 51
Kim Myeongseop, 34, 38
Kim Myeongsu, 34
Kim Saguk, 63
Kim San (Jang Jirak), 12–14, 35, 58, 87, 248n91; and Helen Foster and *Song of Ariran*, 12
Kim San (student at Jinling University), 100–1; and Rural Village Society, 34
Kim Seongsu, 174
Kim Seongsuk, 94, 130, 142, 143, 148, 248n91
Kim Suhyeon, 79
Kim Taeyeop, 76, 79–80 *passim*, 84; and labor issues, 77–78, criticized nationalists, 81; met Liu Shaoqi in Shanghai, 85; on "people," 80–81; on self, 82
Kim Wonbong, 23, 142–43, 147–48. *See also* Uiyeoldan; Joseon minjok jeonseon yeonmaeng
Kim Yabong, 50
Kim Yaksu, 63
Kim Yongchan, 101
Kim Yongho, 107
Kitahara Tatsuo, 100
Kondo Kenji, 71–72
Korean anarchism: and local economic survival, 51–53, 213; and "place-based networks," 60, 212; and regional anarchism, 7–17, 54–55, 90, 205, 209–13; as anti-modernist, 199; as militant, 118, 127; as modernist, 199, 205; as part of nationalism, 1–3; deradicalized and Koreanized, 14–16, 160, 170, 179–80, 187–88, 205–7, 215–16; place-based, diverse practice of, 6, 9, 16–17, 52–53, 60, 70, 96, 103, 219; transnationality of, 7, 9, 14, 17, 54, 81, 106, 109, 121, 132, 134, 200, 205, 209–12, 214, *passim*; *see also* Korean anarchists; *Minju sahoe juui*; National development; National Front
Korean Anarchist Federation in China (KAFC). *See* Jae jungguk mujeongbu gongsan juuija yeonmaeng
Korean Anarchist League in China (KALC). *See* Jae jungguk joseon mujeongbu juuija yeonmaeng
Korean anarchists: and Asian solidarity, 16, 47; and Japanese journals, 65; and livelihood struggle, 114, 116, 213; and personal survival, 28, 42, 96, 129, 207, 215, *passim*; and social Darwinism, 15; and social revolution, 2–3, 5–7, 43, *passim*; and transnational, regional networks, 11–14, 16, 34, 39, 60, 67, 74, 85, 105, 113–14, 128, 210–12; defined, 15, 43, 161–63; *see also* Communism; Go Sunheum; Korean anarchism, Minju sahoe dang; Yi Jeonggyu; Yu Rim
Korean Anarcho-Communist Federation (KAF). *See* Joseon gongsan mujeongbu juuija yeonmaeng
Korean Volunteers Unit (KVU). *See* Joseon Uiyongdae
Kōtoku Shūsui, 22, 59, 65; *Modern Anarchists*, 65; *On the Obliteration of Christ*, 22
Kropotkin, Peter: and Yu Ja-myeong's memoirs, 223n21; mutual aid and influences on

Korean anarchists, 15, 22, 40, 62, 65, 67, 76, 81, 94, 95, 97, 111–12, 196, 212; Shin Chaeho and, 22, 95; study of, 23; translated works of, 36, 41, 64, 65, 95, 121. *See also* Mutual aid
Kuang Husheng, 36, 133. *See also* Lida College
Kurihara Kazuo, 72

Labor (night) school, 36, 77, 105; Korean, 79
Lang, Olga, 34, 230n70
League for the Korean National Front (LKNF). *See* Joseon minjok jeonseon yeonmaeng
League of Korean Anarchists in Manchuria (LKAM). *See* Jaeman joseon mujeongbu juuija yeonmaeng
League of Korean Youth in South China (LKYSC). *See* Namhwa hanin cheongnyeon yeonmaeng
Lee Chong-ha, 95
Lee Mun Chang, 159, 179, 188, 190–92, 196, 205, 253n81, 256n141, 257n7
Lenin, 26
Li Shizeng, 22, 24, 29, 32, 36, 43, 45, 53, 143, 167, 215, 229n63
Liang Longguang, 45
Lida College, 23, 36–37, 44–45, 48, 132–33, 154, 246n64
Lin Bingwen, 31, 39, 40
Lin Chengcai, 136
Lin Yaokun, 35
Liu Sifu (Shifu), 22, 226n10
Lu Jianbo, 30, 34–35, 38
Lu Xun, 26–27, 30
Luo Hua, 35, 230n76

Malatesta, 36
Mao Yipo, 30, 34, 36, 38, 40
March First Movement of 1919, 1, 19–20, 22, 24, 61, 80, 93, 138
Marxism, 13, 57, 63

Max Stirnir, 70
minjok (the nation), 5, 14, 78, 134–35, 137, 142–43, 175, 190, 207
Minju sahoe dang, 171–78 *passim*
Minju sahoe juui, 15, 172, 215; and anarchism, 172–73; and Jeong Hwaam, 173; compared with social democracy, 173; explained by Yi Jeonggyu, 173–79. *See also* Minju sahoe dang
minjung (people; masses), 5, 81, 134, 192, 222n1
Mochizuki Katsura (Kei), 68, 71–72, 74
Modernization, 200, 201, 206, 221n1; anarchist critique of state-led and rural problem, 15, 188–202, 216; and alternative national development, 197–99; urban-based, 206
Morito Tatsuo, 93; and "Morito Incident," 241n9
Movement for Self-Defensive Rural Communities in Quanzhou (Quanzhou Movement), 37, 38, 46, 54, 117, 233n125; and anarchist alliance, 39, 46–47; and anarchist education, 47–48; and Iwasa Sakutarō, 46–47; and Korean anarchists, 46, 48; and Laoda and Guomindang, 44–45; and people's militia, 45–46; the goal of, 45
Mukumoto Unyū, 72
Mutual aid, 15, 16, 21–22 *passim*, 35, 50, 62, 64, 65, 70, 76, 81–82, 84, 97, 134, 182, 213; and alternative development, 199; as Korean tradition, 192, 198, 210; as mutual dependency, 174; as universal, transnational idea 174, 181; democracy and, 174; in journal's name, 119; writing on, 62. *See also* Korean anarchists

Na Gyeongseok, 62

Na Wolhwan, 66, 142, 148, 151–53
Naked power, 134, 176; monopolistic, 162; "naked power-ism," 105; no-, 51
Namheung Dawn Society (Nagyo reimei kai), 76–77
Namhwa hanin cheongnyeon yeonmaeng, 37, 65, 66, 127, 129–33, 135–36, 140, 142, 148, 155, 216, 245n47; and Yeolhyeol dan, Maenghyeol dan, Vigorous Blood Group, 135–36; and *Namhwa tongsin*, 133–35, 140–41
National development, 15, 158, 160, 163, 164, 185, 186, 189, 206, 208, 217; alternative, 139, 187, 192, 206, 216; and national autonomy, 14; and national liberation, 215; and rural village, 15, 201, 204, 215; capitalism and, 183; national struggle over class struggle for, 160; with industrialization, 186, 205
National Front: anarchist discussion and formation of, 14–15, 118, 132, 214, 138–42; anarchist divided over and consequences of, 155–56, 215; and fascism, 15, 139, 154; and military force, 145, 149; and the Chinese united front and anarchists, 146, 155; as united front for national struggle, 20, 23, 53, 128, 135, 138–39, 154, 205; in Manchuria, 43; for national liberation and unity 138–39, 143–45. *See also* Joseon minjok jeonseon yeonmaeng; Yi Hayu; Yu Ja-myeong
Natives Society (Dominsha), 119; and *Natives* and Society of the Youth in Farming Villages, 119
New Advance Society (Shinshin kai), 79, 82–83. *See also* Kim Taeyeop; Yi Chunsik

New Taiwanese Anarchist Society (Xin taiwan ansha), 26; and *New Taiwan*, 26
New Village Movement (Saemaeul undong), 188, 201–2
Nihilism, 63, 73. *See also* Bak Yeol; Kanoko Fumiko; Yu Uyeol
Niiyama Hatsuyo, 72
Nodongja jachi yeonmaeng (Federation for Worker's Autonomy, FWA), 165, 179–81, 187
Noguchi Shinaji, 72
Nongchon jachi yeonmaeng (Federation for Rural Autonomy, FRA), 165, 179–81, 183, 185

Oh Chiseop, 119; and *Movement for Mutual Aid*, 119
Oh Jang-Whan, 42, 70, 110–11
Oh Namgi, 174
Osaka Free Workers Federation (Ōsaka jiyū rōdōsha renmei), 83
Osaka Korean Study-Abroad Students' Fraternal Society (Ōsaka chōsen ryūgakusei gakuyū kai), 76
Ōsugi Sakae, 13, 38, 47, 62, 64–65 *passim*, 67–68, 73, 87, 111, 212, 225n39, 230n73; *A Heart Seeking Justice*, 64; *The Philosophy of Labor Movement*, 65

Paris Chinese Anarchist, 13, 22, 32, 33, 45, 53, 131. *See also* Li Shizeng; Wu Zhihui
Park Chan Seung, 59
Park Chung Hee, 159, 170, 179, 188, 200–1, 203–4, 206. *See also* Modernization
Peace Preservation Law, 117
Peng Huaying, 35
People's Front, 15, 139, 143, 154. *See also* National Front; Yi Hayu; Yu Ja-myeong

Provisional Government of Korea, 12, 19–20, 31, 35, 65, 138, 142, 147, 151–52 *passim*, 247n73; anarchist critique of, 19, 31, 148; anarchist divided over, 155; anarchist participation, support of, 2, 14, 23, 24, 43, 147–48, 151, 156, 161–62, 167, 211, 249n107; and Koreanization of anarchism, 215

Qin Wangshan, 45–47 *passim*

Radical networks of discourse and practice, 11–12, 16; and ecumene, 21, 210. See also Korean anarchism; Korean anarchists
Rebellious Society (Futeisha), 72, 98
Recalcitrant Koreans (Hutoi senjin). See Heuk-u hoe
Reclus, Elisée, 36
Regional perspective, 7–9. See also Korean anarchism
Robinson, Michael, 90
Rural problem, 108, 179, 183–84, 193–95, 202, 216; anarchist solutions to, 195–96. See also Modernization; Susan undong; Yi Jeonggyu

Sakai Hirobumi, 228n47, 230n78
Sakai Toshihiko, 67, 94
Sang-ae hoe (Mutual Love Society), 60
Sano Ichirō (Tian Huamin), 30, 34, 136, 230n68
Sea of Learning Society (Xuehuishe), 30; and *Sea of Learning*, 30
Seo Dongseong, 98
Seo Sanggyeong, 97
Seogan dan (Eradicating Traitors Group), 136–37
Seon-gu dokseo hoe (Pioneer Society for Reading Books), 111

Shanghai National Labor University (Laoda), 36, 37–40 *passim*, 44–45, 48, 54, 117, 231n91; and Korean anarchists, 37–38, 54, 132
Shen Zhongjiu, 31, 37
Shin Chaeho, 21, 27, 29, 31, 39–40, 81, 95, 102; and *Heavenly Drum*, 21, 27; and Kropotkin, 85; and *New Greater Korea*, 21; and the Declaration of the Korean Revolution, 23, 41, 102; as a first generation anarchist, 253n81; on *minjung* and *minjok*, 5, 134; School, 229n63
Shiroyama Hideo, 35
Sim Yongcheol (Sim Geukchu; Shen Keqiu), 4, 29–31 *passim*, 48
Sim Yonghae (Sim Yeochu; Shen Ruiqiu), 29; and *Korean Youth*, 30; worked at *National Customs Daily*, 30
Sin Gichang, 97
Sin Hyeonsang, 130
Sin Jaemo, 99, 161, 167
Sin saenghwal (New Life), 97
Sin Taegyun, 75
Sin Yeong-u, 97
Sin-ganhoe (New Branch Society), 58
Sinheung hakgyo (Newly Burgeoning School), 49
Sinminbu. See Kim Jwajin
Social Democracy, 63, 90, 172–73, 176, 221n1; Social Democratic Party, 171 *passim*
Social justice, 4, 61, 136
Social revolution. See Korean anarchists
Socialism, 1, 57, 61, 62–64, 90, 139, 142; and anarchism, 12, 19, 21, 37, 38, 91; and Korean anarchists, 23–24, 28, 59, 68, 81, 84, 91–97 *passim*, 127, 169; anti, 169; European, 4; in China, 8; in

Socialism *(continued)*
  Korea, 3; Japanese, 59. *See also*
  Communism; Korean anarchism;
  Marxism
Society for Korean Labor Alliance
  in Japan (Zainichi chōsen rōdō
  dōmei kai), 79
Society for Korean Labor Alliance in
  Osaka (Ōsaka chōsen rōdō dōmei
  kai), 76
Society of Korean Students in
  Tokyo, Japan (Zai nihon tōkyō
  chōsen ryūgaksei gakuyū kai), 62
Society of Like-Minded Korean Poor
  Work Study Students (Chōsen
  kugaksei dōyūkai), 68
Society of Like-Minded Work-
  Study Students in Tokyo (Tōkyō
  kugaksei dōyūkai), 61
Society of Taiwanese and Korean
  Comrades (Taihan tongzhi hui),
  35
Society of the Masses
  (Minzhongshe), 29; and *The
  Masses*, 31
Society to Protect Korean Woman
  Workers (Chōsen jokō hogo kai),
  76. *See also* Go Sunheum
Son Useong, 197. *See also* Susan
  undong
Song Heonjo, 254n94
Song Jiha, 66
South China Correspondence (*Namhwa
  tongsin*). *See* Namhwa hanin
  cheongnyeon yeonmaeng
Spontaneous Alliance (or Free
  Alliance), 16, 32, 41–42, 50, 104–6,
  131, 142, 163, 170, 181, 210
Spontaneous Alliance (or *Free
  Alliance*), 121, 244n5
Spontaneous Alliance Newspaper
  (or *Free Alliance Newspaper*), 91,
  120–21
Stanley, Thomas A., 65

Sun Yat-sen, 37, 91
Susan undong (Movement to
  Receive and Produce), 196–200,
  201, 216. *See also* Modernization;
  National development; Rural
  problem; Son Useong; Yi
  Jeonggyu
Syngman Rhee, 148, 157, 159;
  regime, 248n90

Tak Mucho, 35
Takatsu Seido, 67
Take Riyōji, 35, 72
Talhwan (*The Conquest*). *See* Jae
  jungguk mujeongbu gongsan
  juuija yeonmaeng
Terrorism, 3, 96, 112, 128–30 *passim*,
  169; -oriented, 96, 101, 130, 135,
  137
Tokyo Chinese Anarchists, 13
Transnationalism, 8, 16, 154, 210. *See
  also* Korean anarchism; Korean
  anarchists
Tubo (*News on Struggles*), 43

Uchiyama Kanzō, 34
Uiyeoldan (Righteous Group), 23,
  102, 142, 227n19
Union of Free Korean Workers in
  Sakai (Chōsen sakai jiyū rōdōsha
  kumiai), 83
Union of Korean Free Labor
  (Chōsen jiyū rōdō kumiai), 64
United Front. *See* National Front
United Society of the Eastern
  Oppressed Peoples, 23
Uri gye (Our Mutual Loan Club), 76

The Voice of Self Society (Jigasei
  sha), 79, 81–83; and *The Voice of
  Self*, 79, 81–82, 84
Voitinsky, George, 34

Wang Shuren, 40

Wang Yachu, 30, 135, 229n48
Wei Huilin, 31
Won Simchang, 64, 73, 126–27, 130; and *Movement for Mutual Aid*, 119
Wong Zesheng, 36
Wonsan cheongnyeon hoe (Wonsan Youth Society), 103
Wonsan ilban nodong johap (Wonsan General Labor Union), 64
Wonsan jayu nodongja yeonmaeng (League of Free Workers in Wonsan), 103
Work-study (*gohak*), 60–68 *passim*, 78, 105; student, 59, 61, 67, 71, 112, 127, 212, 236n21
Wu Kegang, 37, 45
Wu Zhihui, 29, 32, 36, 43, 45, 53, 143, 167, 215, 229n63
Wuthnow, Robert, 11

Xiang Peiliang, 29
Xu Zhuoran, 45

Yamaga Taiji, 38, 226n10, 230n73, 231n92
Yamakawa Hitoshi, 68; *The Apparatus of Capitalism*, 94
Yang Ildong, 167, 257n3
Yang Jachu, 126
Yang Sanggi, 60, 88
Yang Yeoju (Oh Myeonjik), 141, 247n87
Yatabe Yūji (Wu Shimin), 48, 135
Yeo Unhyeong, 35, 65
Yi Chunsik, 79; on people, 81; on freedom, 81–82
Yi Dal, 50, 125, 126, 130, 149
Yi Dongsun, 128
Yi Eulgyu, 25; after 1945, 28, 38 *passim*, 100, 119, 161, 180, 203; and anarchist party, 167, 251n28; and Manchuria, 23, 50, 52; as "Korea's Kropotkin," 24; in Quanzhou, 45–46; on post-1945 situation, 180

Yi Gang, 153
Yi Gangha, 70, 97
Yi Ganghun, 50, 126–27
Yi Gihwan, 45–46
Yi Gyeongson, 34
Yi Gyuchang, 37, 228n40, 246n54, 247n87
Yi Hayu, 81, 126, 142; 148, 229n63; and armed struggle, 151; on national front, 140–41; on political revolution, 133–34
Yi Hoeyeong, 22, 31, 37, 39; and vision of post-independence society, 32; as a first generation anarchist, 253n83; converting to anarchism, 27–28; in Manchuria, 49, 143; transnational understanding of anarchism, 28
Yi Honggeun, 34, 64, 73, 101, 104–8 *passim*, 242n50; and democratic socialism, 173; and Japanese anarchist journals, 74; on national struggle and liberation, 121–22
Yi Horyong, 43, 231n95
Yi Hyang, 102–3, 106–7. *See also* "destitute and humble class"
Yi Hyeok, 91, 107, 111
Yi Jeonggyu (in Japan), 119; and *Liberation Movement*, 119, 124
Yi Jeonggyu (one of Yi brothers), 24, 27, 28, 31, 36, 38, 35, 59, 100–1, 113; against anarchist party, 165; against class struggle, 181; against social democracy, 170–71; and customer's cooperative association, 111; and Dawn Middle School, 25; and Eastern Anarchist Federation, 39–41; and Free Society Builders' Federation, 161, 166, 171, 180–83, 187; and "great unity," 4; and Laoda, 37–38; and rural problem and national development, 25–26, 27, 169, 170, 179–88, 189–95,

Yi Jeonggyu *(continued)*
198–203, 206–8, 215–16, 225n46, 247n73, 253n81, 255n126, 257n3; and tension between nationalism and anarchism, 5–6; at anarchist national convention, 161–62, 164; criticized communism, 46; deradicalized and Koreanized anarchism, 16, 178–207; in Quanzhou, 44–47; on anarchist new tasks after 1945, 159; on democratic socialism and Democratic Socialist Party, 171–76; on future of anarchism, 170; on "retaking," 41–42; tension with Yu Rim, 180; understanding of democracy, 176–77; "Yi Jeonggyu Line," 215

Yi Jihwal, 66
Yi Seokgyu, 101
Yi Seungrae, 142
Yi Siu, 167
Yi Sunchang, 107
Yi Suyong, 128
Yi Yongjun, 65
Yi Yunhi, 97, 119
Yokota Shōjirō, 62, 75
Yu Hyeontae, 108
Yu Ja-myeong, 3, 22, 24, 27–28, 31, 130, 145, 148, 157, 229n63; and Korean Provisional Government, 43, 151; and Lida College, 36–37, 133, 154; as Yu Sik or Liu Shi, 144; in Quanzhou, 48; on anarchist military force, 145, 149, 153–54; on influence of Japanese publication, 93; on national front, 138–39, 142–44, 147–48; on Sano Ichirō, 230n68; rejected communism and class struggle, 23

Yu Jicheong, 46
Yu Rim, 23, 43, 50, 108–9, 166, 169, 170, 227n21, 229n63, 256n139, 257n6; and anarchist national convention, 161–63 *passim*; and anarchist networks, 113; and anarchist party, 166–67, 170, 172, 203, 251n28; and Korean Provisional Government, 147, 151; and Yan'an, 248n107; defined anarchist, 43, 161–63, 250n10; tension with Yi Jeonggyu, 180; "Yu Rim Line," 215–16

Yu Seo (Yu Giseok), 29, 31, 130, 142; and armed struggle; 153; and Chinese anarchist journals, 30, 47; in Quanzhou, 45–48; on "Greater Alliance of East Asian Anarchists," 47

Yu Uyeol, 101–2
Yuan Xingguo, 31
Yue Guohua, 154
Yuk Honggeun, 73
Yuk Hongpyo, 72
Yun Jahyeong, 35

Zarrow, Peter, 20, 167
Zhang Ji, 29
Zheng Yingbai, 48
Zhou Zuoren, 26
Zhuang Hongshu, 36

Printed in Poland
by Amazon Fulfillment
Poland Sp. z o.o., Wrocław